THE HEART OF THE PATH

The Heart of the Path

SEEING THE GURU AS BUDDHA

Lama Zopa Rinpoche

Edited by Ailsa Cameron

LAMA YESHE WISDOM ARCHIVE • BOSTON

www.LamaYeshe.com

A non-profit charitable organization for the benefit of all
sentient beings and an affiliate of the Foundation for
the Preservation of the Mahayana Tradition
www.fpmt.org

First published 2009

LAMA YESHE WISDOM ARCHIVE
PO Box 356
WESTON
MA 02493, USA

Library of Congress Cataloging-in-Publication Data

Thubten Zopa, Rinpoche, 1945-
The heart of the path : seeing the guru as Buddha / Thubten Zopa Rinpoche ;
edited by Ailsa Cameron ; foreword by H.H. Sakya Trizin.
p. cm.
Includes bibliographical references and index.
Summary: "Guru devotion is a greatly misunderstood but extremely important
topic in the practice of Tibetan Buddhism. In this exhaustive treatment
of the subject the author explains clearly what it is, what it is not,
and how to practice it"—Provided by publisher.
ISBN 978-1-891868-21-4
1. Teacher-student relationships—Religious aspects—Buddhism. 2. Guru worship
(Rite)—China—Tibet. 3. Spiritual life—Buddhism. I. Cameron, Ailsa. II. Title.
BQ7758.C62T538 2009
294.3'61—dc22
2008052190

10 9 8 7 6 5 4 3 2 1

Cover photograph by Nicholas Ribush, Chenrezig Institute, Australia, 1975
Designed by Gopa & Ted2 Inc.

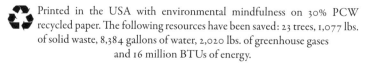

Printed in the USA with environmental mindfulness on 30% PCW
recycled paper. The following resources have been saved: 23 trees, 1,077 lbs.
of solid waste, 8,384 gallons of water, 2,020 lbs. of greenhouse gases
and 16 million BTUs of energy.

Please contact the Lama Yeshe Wisdom Archive
for more copies of this and our free books

Contents

Publisher's Dedication

Henry Lau and Lama Zopa Rinpoche, Malaysia, 2002

WE DEDICATE THIS BOOK to the memory of our dear friend, the faithful Henry Lau Hwee Tiang (1947–2008), who was a devoted disciple of Lama Zopa Rinpoche and a great supporter of the FPMT and many of its projects, such as the Lama Yeshe Wisdom Archive, Wisdom Publications, the Jade Buddha Project and Sera-je Monastery's Drati Khangtsen Project.

Publisher's Acknowledgments

W E ARE extremely grateful to our friends and supporters who have made it possible for the LAMA YESHE WISDOM ARCHIVE to both exist and function: to Lama Yeshe and Lama Zopa Rinpoche, whose kindness is impossible to repay; to Peter and Nicole Kedge and Venerable Ailsa Cameron for their initial work on the ARCHIVE; to Venerable Roger Kunsang, Lama Zopa's tireless assistant, for his kindness and consideration; and to our sustaining supporters: Barry and Connie Hershey, Joan Halsall, Roger and Claire Ash-Wheeler, Claire Atkins, Thubten Yeshe, Tony Steele, Richard Gere, Doren & Mary Harper, Tom & Suzanne Castles, Lily Chang Wu and Hawk Furman.

This book would not have become a reality were it not for the Herculean efforts of its editor, Ven. Ailsa Cameron, who worked on it for eight years, going through hundreds of transcripts of Lama Zopa Rinpoche's teachings stretching back to the early 1970s, extracting the relevant sections and then editing them into this beautiful and coherent document, by far the best book on guru devotion published in the West and certainly the best book I have ever read. Ven. Ailsa details what she did in her preface, but we all owe her a deep debt of gratitude.

We are also extremely grateful to all those who have become members of the ARCHIVE over the past few years. Details of our membership program may be found at the back of this book, and if you are not a member, please do consider joining up. Due to the kindness of those who have, we now have several editors working on our vast collection of teachings for the benefit of all. We have posted our list of individual and corporate members on our Web site, www.LamaYeshe.com.

In particular, we thank our major benefactors to this project: Dominic & Catherine Ang, Christine Arlington, Marcel Bertels, Tiffany Ch'ng Jia Li, Drolkar Chan & Ng Lee Hwang, Chandrakirti Tibetan Buddhist Meditation Centre, Maline Chua, Sharlyn Chua Bee Keng, Adrian Dec, Kirra Givanni, Goh Pik Pin, Elaine Ho , Wendy Hobbs, Ginger Hsu and Henry Wang, H. Jayabalan, Ven. Sangye Khadro, Kiew Zan Li, Catherine Lau (in memory of Henry Lau), Elizabeth Lee, Lee Tin Yan, Alfred Leyens, Lim Chip Keong & Family, Lim Hong Jie, Joey Lim Zuo Yi, Bernard & Charlotte Loo & Family, Low Mee Wah, Tara Melwani, Ong Siew Nga, Poon King, Nicholas Redmond (in memory of Dermot Redmond), Sim Hong Boon, Ven. Sophia Su, Toh Sze Gee, Cecilia Tsong, Tsong Tse Yang (in memory of Chong Un Lai), Oanh Vovan, Charmaine Wai, Ven. Yangchen, Bobby Yap, Serina Yap and Bernard Chung, Yeo Puay Huei, Chan Yew Mun, Daniel Yong Yeoh and Ven. Geshe Tenzin Zopa. All contributors to this book are listed on our Web site and we are extremely grateful to them without exception. Thank you so much.

Furthermore, we would like to express our appreciation for the kindness and compassion of all those other generous benefactors who have contributed funds to our work since we began publishing free books. Thankfully, you are too numerous to mention individually in this book, but we value highly each and every donation made to spreading the Dharma for the sake of the kind mother sentient beings and now pay tribute to you all on our Web site.

Finally, I would like to thank the many other kind people who have asked that their donations be kept anonymous; my wife, Wendy Cook, for her constant help and support and for copy-editing this book; our dedicated office staff, Jennifer Barlow and Ven. Tenzin Desal; Ven. Thubten Labdron (Trisha Donnelly) for her help with archiving and editing; Ven. Bob Alcorn for his incredible work on our Lama Yeshe DVDs; David Zinn for his digital imaging expertise; Veronica Kaczmarowski, Evelyn Williames, FPMT Australia and Mandala Books (Brisbane) for much appreciated assistance with our distribution in Australia; Dennis Heslop, Philip Bradley, Mike Gilmore and our other friends at Wisdom Books (London) for their great help with our distribution in Europe; our volunteer transcribers; and Jonathan Steyn in London for his help with our audio work.

If you, dear reader, would like to join this noble group of open-hearted altruists by contributing to the production of more books by Lama Yeshe or Lama Zopa Rinpoche or to any other aspect of the Lama Yeshe Wisdom Archive's work, please contact us to find out how.

—*Dr. Nicholas Ribush*

*Through the merit of having contributed to the spread of the Buddha's
teachings for the sake of all sentient beings, may our benefactors
and their families and friends have long and healthy lives,
all happiness, and may all their Dharma
wishes be instantly fulfilled.*

Lama Zopa Rinpoche and H.H. Sakya Trizin, Dehra Dun, India, 2008

Foreword

IN ALL BUDDHIST traditions guru devotion is very important. It is the spiritual master who introduces you to the Triple Gem and leads you to the path to liberation and enlightenment.

The significance of steadfast trust and dedication toward the guru, I feel, stands on three grounds. Foremost, there are innumerable quotations from the sutras as well as *shastras* stating that a qualified guru is the source of all the qualities and benefits required to be liberated from the cycle of samsaric suffering.

Secondly, examining through logical reasoning, we ourselves can recognize the truth underlying guru devotion. For example, the sun brightly shines all the time in all the directions but without necessary instruments we cannot utilize its tremendous energy. Likewise, the Buddha's blessings are showering down on all sentient beings all the time but we cannot receive them without the presence of a guru because our defilements and karmic propensities prevent us from seeing the Buddha. Thus we do not have the fortune of hearing instructions and receiving blessings directly. It is only through the guru—who is ordinary form like us and we can see and hear—that we can receive the Buddha's teachings and therefore receive the holy blessings.

Lastly, the pith instructions found in the biographies of all the ancient masters tell us that all those who followed the guru's advice with unshakable faith have attained realizations and those who failed to do so did not.

In the Vajrayana path the importance of the guru increases many fold as it is the qualified master who, through bestowing the unbroken lineage of empowerments, which can be traced back to the Buddha himself, opens the gateway to the path of the enlightened ones and helps us to realize the actual nature of the mind.

I hope that Lama Zopa Rinpoche's book entitled *The Heart of the Path* will be of great benefit to the followers of Buddhist philosophy.

With blessings,
The Sakya Trizin
18 November 2008

Editor's Preface

LAMA ZOPA RINPOCHE, spiritual director of the Foundation for the Preservation of the Mahayana Tradition (FPMT), is an inspiring example of guru devotion practice, of devoting to the guru with thought and with action. Rinpoche is the disciple of many renowned Tibetan lamas, including His Holiness Trijang Rinpoche, his root guru; His Holiness Ling Rinpoche; His Holiness the Fourteenth Dalai Lama; His Holiness Song Rinpoche; His Holiness Serkong Tsenshab Rinpoche; Serkong Dorje Chang; Khunu Lama Tenzin Gyaltsen; His Eminence Chogye Trichen Rinpoche; His Holiness Sakya Trizin; and His Eminence Trulshik Rinpoche. Rinpoche's guru devotion is impeccable, and his many gurus would agree with His Holiness the Dalai Lama's comment, "Rinpoche is someone who follows my guidance sincerely, very expansively, and with one hundred percent trust. He possesses unwavering faith and pure *samaya*; not only has he pure samaya and faith but whatever I instruct, Zopa Rinpoche has the capability to accomplish it."[1]

Yangsi Rinpoche[2] has also said, "Usually, when we talk of perfect examples of demonstrating pure guru devotion, we talk of Milarepa, Marpa, Tilopa and Naropa. But in our generation, the quality of Lama Zopa Rinpoche's guru devotion is a perfect example. When we reflect on the kindness of spiritual teachers, in addition to reflecting upon the historical teachers and

---

[1] A comment made during a long-life puja offered to His Holiness by FPMT in December 2006 in Sarnath, India.
[2] Yangsi Rinpoche, the incarnation of Geshe Ngawang Gendun, one of Lama Yeshe's gurus, is the director of Maitripa College in Portland, Oregon.

their great activities, we can also think of the great teachers of today, whose lives are totally dedicated to the service of the Dharma."[3]

Rinpoche himself, of course, denies any accomplishment of guru devotion: "Even though I cannot find any guru devotion anywhere within my body, from my head down to my feet, I will just imitate what Pabongka Dechen Nyingpo and other lamas say in the *lam-rim* when they talk about how they practiced the root of the path to enlightenment."[4] During the fifty years that Rinpoche has been teaching Dharma to Westerners, he has taught extensively on the subject of guru devotion. Most of these teachings have been transcribed and more than fifty of them, given between 1979 and 2005, are the source material for *The Heart of the Path*.

Rinpoche himself recommended as important to be included in this book the teachings on guru devotion he gave during a commentary on *Lama Tsongkhapa Guru Yoga* at Jinsiu Farlin, the FPMT center in Taipei, Taiwan, in June 1996. While these teachings are the nucleus of the book, in addition, other major sources for this book were commentaries on *Lama Tsongkhapa Guru Yoga* given at Tushita Retreat Centre, India, in 1986; at Vajrapani Institute, California, in 1988; at Chenrezig Institute, Australia, and Cham Tse Ling, Hong Kong, in 1989; in Sydney, Australia, in 1990; and at Istituto Lama Tzong Khapa, Italy, in 2004. Also included is material from mahamudra commentaries given at Chenrezig Institute in 1980; at Vajrapani Institute and Vajrayogini Institute, France, in 1981; and in Adelaide in 2004. Other major sources are a *Lama Chöpa* [Skt: *Guru Puja*] commentary at Mahamudra Centre, New Zealand, in 1985; a *Six-Session Guru Yoga* commentary at Katoomba, Australia, in 1991; a Vajrayogini commentary at Mahamudra Centre in 1994; a Most Secret Hayagriva initiation in Sydney in 2000; Kadampa teachings at Root Institute, India, in 2003; and general teachings at Dorje Chang Institute, New Zealand, in 2004. Valuable material was also used from Rinpoche's translation of and commentary to *The Essence of Nectar* at Kopan Monastery, Nepal, in 1982–83.[5] In addition, material was drawn from the transcripts of more than thirty minor teachings.[6]

---

[3] *Practicing the Path*, p. 65.

[4] From a talk on guru devotion given at Vajrapani Institute, California, on October 24, 1986. (Lama Yeshe Wisdom Archive number 624.)

[5] The relevant LYWA transcripts are, respectively, #1047, 266, 305, 788, 322, 721, 1478, 360, 127, 325, 1443, 176, 851, 741, 1223, 1404, 1481, 1383 and 1384.

[6] Material was used from the following LYWA transcripts: #17, 60, 68, 197, 350, 425, 441,

Rinpoche's teachings on guru devotion were largely based on Pabongka Dechen Nyingpo's commentaries on guru devotion, not only in *Liberation in the Palm of Your Hand* but also in a separate text, an elaborate explanation of guru devotion, included in Pabongka Rinpoche's collected works.[7] In addition, Rinpoche taught on the subject of guru devotion from Lama Tsongkhapa's *The Great Treatise on the Stages of the Path to Enlightenment* and other lam-rim and tantric texts.

Since Rinpoche has praised *Liberation in the Palm of Your Hand* as an experiential commentary that presents the teachings in a simple and clear way, the structure of *The Heart of the Path* closely follows that of *Liberation*. Chapter 1, *Why Do We Need a Guru?*, explains why guru devotion is the root of the path to enlightenment. Chapter 2, *The Power of the Guru*, while given only a passing mention by Pabongka Rinpoche in the first of the eight benefits of correct devotion, is featured as a separate chapter here as it was emphasized by Rinpoche in his teachings and explains the potential for incredible benefit and danger in relation to the guru. Chapter 3, *Checking the Guru*, again unlike in *Liberation*, is a separate chapter because of the crucial importance of being careful in choosing the person who is to become the most powerful and important in our life. In *Liberation*, the qualities of a guru and a disciple, chapters 4 and 5, are discussed between *the disadvantages of incorrect devotion to a guru* and *devoting with thought*; here these topics follow the chapter on checking the guru. In chapter 6, *Who to Regard as Guru*, Rinpoche tells stories from his own childhood to illustrate this issue and goes on to answer many questions commonly asked on this topic.

With chapter 7, *The Benefits of Correct Devotion to a Guru*, Rinpoche begins discussion of the four major guru devotion outlines (see appendix 1). The second major outline is covered in chapter 8, *The Disadvantages of Incorrect Devotion to a Guru*.

The third, and most important, guru devotion outline, *how to devote to a guru with thought*, which means seeing the guru as a buddha, is covered in depth in the following six chapters. Chapter 9 emphasizes the importance of faith. In chapter 10, *Why We Should Look at the Guru as a Buddha*, the

---

442, 469, 477, 509, 513, 514, 515, 558, 560, 561, 585, 624, 677, 715, 826, 831, 886, 944, 1022, 1064, 1078, 1087, 1255, 1329, 1405 and 1543.
[7] The work is *Abbreviated Notes from Explanatory Discourses Given on* [*the First Panchen Lama's*] Six-Session Guru Yoga, [*Chandragomin's*] Twenty [*Stanzas on the Bodhisattva*] Vows, [*Ashvaghosha's*] Fifty Stanzas on the Guru, *and the Root and Secondary Tantric Vows*.

point is made simply and clearly that we practice guru devotion for our own benefit, or profit, not for that of the guru. Chapter 11 explains that it is possible for us to see the guru as a buddha, just as it is possible to see ourselves in a positive way, and also explains how to use any faults we see to enhance our devotion. In chapter 12, with many quotations and lines of reasoning, Rinpoche details various techniques and meditations we can use to train our mind to see the guru as a buddha. The techniques are summarized in chapter 13 in the form of a debate with the superstitious mind that refuses to see the guru as a buddha. Finally, in chapter 14, the guru's kindness is discussed.

The fourth major outline is explained in chapter 15, *Devoting to the Guru with Action*. In chapters 16 through 18, Rinpoche discusses whether it is necessary to do absolutely everything that the guru tells us to do, and then describes the exceptional cases of Tilopa and Naropa and Milarepa and Marpa.

In chapter 19, Rinpoche describes in more detail the tantric practice of guru yoga, in which the guru is seen as a buddha not only in essence but even in aspect, and illustrates the practice in relation to *Six-Session Guru Yoga* and Pabongka Dechen Nyingpo's own powerful prayer *Calling the Lama from Afar*.

In chapter 22, Rinpoche gives some general advice in relation to teaching and studying guru devotion.

In chapter 23, Rinpoche gives guidelines on how to go about achieving the realization of guru devotion and how to know when we have achieved it.

The book concludes, in chapter 24, with some dedications related to the practice of guru devotion that Rinpoche commonly uses to dedicate merits.

As with Pabongka Rinpoche's style in *Liberation in the Palm of Your Hand*, the general style in this book is informal, with many stories. While there are also a lot of quotations, they should be regarded more as paraphrases than word-for-word translations, especially as many were done from memory rather than directly from a text.[8]

This book has come about only through the dedicated efforts of many people. For their help with transcribing, I would like to thank Jennifer

---

[8] For the precise sourcing of the quotations from Pabongka Rinpoche's *Liberation*, see *Liberation in Our Hands, Part Two*.

Abbott, Ven. Paloma Alba, Lea Bridge, Frank Brock, Merry Colony, Martin Daellenbach, Carol Davies, Krissie Foulkes, Katarina Hallonblad, Brian Hart, Su Hung, Peter Lance, Alfred Leyens, Ven. Carolyn Lawler, Maureen O'Malley, Allan Marsh, Carolyn Murdoch, Ven. Ingrid Nordzin, Elea Redel, Trish Roberts, Gareth Robinson, Segen Speer-Senner, Ven. Tenzin Tsapel, Ven. Tenzin Tsomo, Ven. Sarah Thresher, Ven. Thubten Gyatso, Ven. Thubten Munsel, Ven. Thubten Labdron, Ven. Yeshe Chodron and Ven. Yeshe Khadro. For their help with checking some of the transcripts, I would like to thank Karyn Ellis, Nick Ribush and Sandra Tideman, and for his help with the bibliography, Gareth Sparham. For keying in handwritten and printed hard copies of some transcripts, thanks to Lea Bridge, CAS of Nepal, Jackie Freeman, Katarina Hallonblad, Brian Hart, Ven. Kaye Miner, Susan Stabile and Kathy Vichta. I would especially like to thank Nick Ribush and Kyogan O'Neil for the material they prepared on Rinpoche's commentary to *The Essence of Nectar*. Sincere thanks also to Geshe Lobsang Jamyang and Yaki Platt for helping to answer some final questions.

I would also like to thank all the many people involved in the recording, archiving and preserving of Rinpoche's teachings, including all the people working in FPMT centers who arranged and recorded these teachings and especially Nick Ribush and everyone else involved in the Lama Yeshe Wisdom Archive.

Heartfelt thanks also to Claire Atkins and Ven. Lhagsam for generously providing me with the material conditions conducive to editing this book.

Finally, from my heart, I would like to thank Lama Zopa Rinpoche for his infinite generosity, compassion, patience and wisdom in tirelessly and constantly teaching Dharma around the world. In particular, I would like to thank him for compassionately giving the many inspiring teachings included in *The Heart of the Path*. Any merit created in the process of producing this book is dedicated to Rinpoche's long life and good health and to the success of his many activities to benefit sentient beings and the teachings of Buddha. While Rinpoche's kindness is a debt that I could never repay in this and many other lifetimes, my editing of this book is a small effort toward repaying that kindness.

Chenrezig Institute
November 2007

Lama Yeshe and Lama Zopa Rinpoche in Auckland, New Zealand, 1975

1. Why Do We Need a Guru?

~જ≈~

The root of the path

IN THE LAM-RIM, or graduated path to enlightenment, the first meditation outline is *the root of the path: how to devote to the virtuous friend.* Why is guru devotion the root of the path to enlightenment? Enlightenment is like a ripe fruit, the path to enlightenment is like the trunk of a tree, and guru devotion is like the root of the tree. From the root of guru devotion, the trunk of the path grows in our mind and bears the fruit of enlightenment. Whether or not we can start to develop the path to enlightenment in our mind in this life is determined by our practice of guru devotion.

Proper devotion to the guru, or virtuous friend, is the root of all success, from success in this life up to enlightenment, just as the trunk, branches, leaves and fruit of a tree depend upon its root. Or we can think that guru devotion is like the fuel in a car or a plane, without which the vehicle cannot take us where we want to go. Without guru devotion, nothing happens—no realizations, no liberation, no enlightenment—just as without the root of a tree there can be no trunk, branches, leaves, or fruit. Everything, up to enlightenment, depends on guru devotion.

Guru devotion is the root not only of ultimate success, achieving full enlightenment and bringing sentient beings to the ultimate happiness of liberation and enlightenment, but also of temporary success and happiness. This practice is the foundation of the development of the whole path to enlightenment, as well as the foundation of all happiness. Since everything comes from the practice of guru devotion, it is called *the root of the path.*

Wise practitioners, those who know how to practice Dharma skillfully, give their full attention day and night to this point of correctly devoting to the virtuous friend. His Holiness Serkong Dorje Chang, who lived at

Swayambhunath in Nepal, once told his monks, "If you do the practice of devoting yourself to the virtuous friend well, everything will be fine, even if you don't study. You can relax and have a good time, just eating and sleeping. You can enjoy life." Rinpoche expressed the very heart of Dharma practice. If we practice guru devotion well, we can enjoy life in the best way, because our practice brings all success and stops all obstacles.

The answer to how quickly and easily we will achieve realizations of the path to enlightenment depends on our finding a qualified virtuous friend, and after having found him,[9] how well we devote ourselves to him. Before devoting ourselves to a guru, we should check him well; then after we have made the Dharma connection, we correctly devote ourselves to him with thought and with action. Devoting *with thought* means seeing the guru as a buddha, an enlightened being, by looking at him in that way; and devoting *with action* means carrying out the guru's advice, serving and making offerings to him.

The main meditation subject of guru devotion is actually contained in devoting to the guru with thought. Using scriptural quotations, logic and our personal experiences of the guru, we look at the guru as a buddha, as having ceased all faults and possessing all good qualities. At the beginning we use analytical meditation with quotations and logic to prove to the mind that doesn't see the guru as a buddha that he is a buddha, thus transforming this mind into the pure thought of devotion.

At first, when we are not actually doing analytical meditation on guru devotion, that feeling of devotion quickly disappears. However, through meditation, after some time the experience becomes stable. When we have some experience, some feeling in our heart that our guru is a buddha, even if it lasts just a short time, it is a sign of having received the blessings of the guru. When we then come to spontaneously and constantly see the guru as a buddha, we have developed the realization of guru devotion.

Devotion brings blessings. From guru devotion, we receive the blessings of the guru in our heart, and from those blessings, realizations of the path to

---

[9] Or her. Unfortunately, the only impersonal third person pronoun the English language offers us is "it," and that doesn't seem appropriate for a human being, much less a guru. It's too cumbersome to write "him or her" every time and alternating the two seems overly PC. Using "them" is just grammatically incorrect although becoming increasingly popular. Since most gurus are male, we've settled on "him"; if you have a female guru you're thinking of, read "her." However, in non-guru instances of him or her throughout this book we have in fact alternated the two. [Publisher's note.]

enlightenment manifest from within our mind. Our devotion makes it possible for us to achieve enlightenment, to cease all the faults of our mind and to complete all the realizations. This then enables us to do perfect work for the numberless other sentient beings, freeing them from the oceans of samsaric sufferings and bringing them to liberation and enlightenment. This is why guru devotion, this experience of seeing the guru as a buddha, is the root of the path to enlightenment.

Through the practice of guru devotion, looking at our guru as inseparable from a buddha or our own special deity, the blessings of the guru enter our heart. Devotion is the opening through which the nectar of the guru's blessings enters us. Without guru devotion practice, the nectar of the guru's blessings doesn't enter our mind and this makes it very difficult for us to generate realizations of the path to enlightenment. Just as a seed cannot grow without water, our mind cannot develop without blessings. Without blessings, our mind is like a hot desert where nothing grows. No matter how much we meditate on the path, no matter how much we squeeze, nothing will grow.

The guru's blessings transform our mind from being hard and unsubdued into being soft and subdued. Even from our own experiences, we can tell that what the teachings say about the blessings of the guru is true and have complete faith in it. When we have strong guru devotion in our heart, if we meditate on perfect human rebirth, we feel its preciousness very easily; if we meditate on impermanence and death, we feel the transitory nature of life very strongly and easily; and the same thing happens if we meditate on compassion, emptiness or any other lam-rim topic. In a state of strong devotion, our mind is also calmer, more subdued. Our delusions arise only with difficulty and are easy to control.

When our devotion degenerates or disappears, our delusions arise very strongly and are more difficult to control; it is also more difficult to have any feeling for impermanence and death, compassion or bodhicitta. We can check this from our own experiences. At times when our mind is very hard and skeptical, with no devotion, do we find it easy or difficult to meditate on lam-rim? And at times when we feel strong devotion, how do we feel when we meditate on the path?

When we have strong meditation experiences, ones that change our mind, we feel even more deeply the kindness of the virtuous friend and develop more devotion toward him. That developing realizations depends on guru devotion is not simply something made up so that gurus receive more respect, service and offerings. We can clearly see the truth of this from our own experiences.

Without the foundation of the devotion that sees the guru as a buddha, there is no basis for Dharma practice. It is like trying to taste artificial fruit. The blessings of the guru enable us to achieve the realizations of the graduated path to enlightenment. On the basis of the three principal paths, we then practice tantra and achieve the generation and completion stages of Highest Yoga Tantra. We are then able to achieve enlightenment in this life, or within three or sixteen lifetimes.

Achieving tantric realizations especially depends on guru devotion. By practicing the lower tantras—Action, Performance and Yoga tantras— we can achieve enlightenment in one lifetime, but only by obtaining the "immortality" *siddhi*, which enables us to live for thousands of years and thus achieve enlightenment. However, without needing to prolong our life in this way, by practicing Highest Yoga Tantra we can achieve enlightenment in the brief lifetime of a degenerate time,[10] even within a few years. (The term *brief lifetime* is used because life is much shorter in a degenerate time.) It was mainly by doing special guru yoga practice that the great yogi Milarepa, as well as many other Tibetan yogis and Indian *pandits*, were able to achieve tantric realizations within a few years and thus achieve enlightenment in one brief lifetime.

In Highest Yoga Tantra, guru yoga is practiced as the heart of the path. To achieve enlightenment in this brief lifetime, we have to cherish guru yoga practice like our own life. It is only then that practicing the Six Yogas of Naropa and other tantric techniques becomes the quick path to enlightenment. Otherwise, if we don't cherish guru yoga as more precious than our own life, no matter how many years we meditate on the Six Yogas of Naropa, nothing will happen. With strong guru yoga practice, however, we can succeed in the Highest Yoga Tantra path and achieve the unified state of Vajradhara in this life, just as those past great yogis did.

Guru yoga is the fuel that makes Highest Yoga Tantra the quick path to enlightenment. If there is no fuel in a plane, the people in the plane can't reach the place they want to go; if there is fuel, they can. The guru yoga practice in Highest Yoga Tantra is special fuel, more special than that of the Hinayana, Paramitayana and even the lower tantras.

[10] A degenerate time, or age, [Skt: *kaliyuga*] has five characteristics: short lifespans, scarce means of subsistence, mental afflictions, strong wrong views and weak sentient beings.

Why do we need a guru?

In order to do the practice of guru devotion, we first have to have clear in our mind why this practice is important. Why do we need a guru? We might think, "Achieving liberation and enlightenment is fine, but why do I need a guru to do it? As long as books on the subject are available, I can read them, then practice. Why do I need a guru?"

You might think that to generate the path to enlightenment, it's enough to read Dharma books and study by yourself. However, generally speaking, you can't clearly understand the meaning of Dharma teachings, especially the hidden meanings that need clarification through commentary, without the explanations of a guru. There is a big difference between learning something from a teacher and just reading about it in a book. Listening to a teacher has a much greater effect on your mind. Being able to parrot the words written in books doesn't mean that you really understand a subject.

Even to gain just an intellectual understanding of a subject we have to depend on a teacher. And our goal is to have not just an intellectual understanding of the path to enlightenment but experience of it. Without experience of the path we can't have a clear, complete understanding of any of its points. Having experiences or realizations of the path to enlightenment depends on receiving the blessings of the guru within our own mental continuum. The clear, strong feeling in our heart and deep benefit to our mind are what are meant by the blessings of the guru. Without a guru, we can't achieve realizations. This is why it's not sufficient to have just intellectual knowledge, like that gained from studying with professors in a university.

In *Collection of Advice from Here and There*, when someone asked which was more important, the lama's advice or the major scriptures, Lama Atisha answered,

> Even if you can recite the whole *Tripitaka* by heart, even if you know the entire Dharma, if you don't have the guru's advice, there will be a gap between you and the Dharma when you practice.[11]

---

[11] The first piece of advice in "Collection of Advice from Here and There," or *Kadam Thorbu*, compiled by Chegom Sherap Dorje. For the complete text, see "Sayings of the Kadam Masters," *The Book of Kadam*, pp. 559–610 or *The Door of Liberation*, pp. 83–122.

Even if we can recite by heart all the sutras and tantras or have studied them at university and can explain them all intellectually, it doesn't mean much in terms of realization because generating within our mind the paths revealed by the teachings has to depend on receiving the blessings of the guru. Receiving the nectar of the guru's blessings depends on our having the devotion that sees the guru as a buddha. Without the blessings of the guru, there is no way we can have realizations, no way we can actualize the three principal paths and the two stages of tantra. For this reason, we need a guru.

Just to gain an intellectual understanding of Dharma from a teacher in order to write a book or get a degree, we don't need to do the guru yoga practice of regarding him as an enlightened being. However, if our aim is not simply to obtain a degree in order to get a job but to benefit our own mind— to transform it through subduing our delusions and develop it in the path to liberation and enlightenment—it's different. This is a specific, special aim.

The point to understand is that the purpose of having a guru is not just to gain an intellectual understanding of Dharma. We need a guru for a special reason, to receive the blessings that enable us to develop our mind in the path to enlightenment. If we miss the point of having a guru, we can make many mistakes and many problems can arise. Just as we can run off the road if we don't concentrate when driving a car, if we don't concentrate on the main aim of having a guru when trying to practice Dharma, we can create many problems for ourselves.

In America and other countries in the West, people involved in teaching meditation have held meetings to discuss whether guru devotion is necessary in meditating on the path to enlightenment. Some people think that while the subject of guru devotion might have been practiced in olden times in Tibet, it is not necessary nowadays. (This discussion might also have come about because of problems happening in relation to gurus in the West in recent years.) The people who say these things have missed the real purpose and importance of the practice of guru devotion; they have missed the usefulness and richness of it in life and the benefit, as infinite as space, that is gained from it. They have missed the very point of guru devotion. Guru devotion appears to them to be something cultural, without much value or importance. They think that it's not necessary to practice guru devotion, that you can meditate on the path without it. People who say these things don't understand the real purpose of guru devotion and how it is essential for realization of the path to enlightenment.

We can't do the practices of listening to or reflecting and meditating on teachings on the path to enlightenment on our own. If we didn't need a teacher to study and actualize the whole path to enlightenment by ourselves we wouldn't need to rely upon a teacher even to learn such things as languages and handicrafts. We would be able to learn everything by ourselves without anybody else's help.

Kadampa Geshe Potowa, a lineage lama of the lam-rim, said,

> Even to learn worldly crafts, things we can understand by seeing them with our eyes, we need a teacher to show us. So how is it possible that we, who have just come from the lower realms and are entering a path where we have never been before, could travel it without a guide?

We need a teacher to learn even the ordinary activities of this life, such as learning the alphabet, fixing a bicycle or baking a cake. We even need somebody to teach us how to clean a room professionally. Even for simple things that we can learn how to do by watching somebody else, we need a teacher, somebody who knows how to do them.

Even to go to a place we haven't been before, we need a guide, someone to explain to us how to get there. So, how is it possible for us to follow the path to enlightenment without a guide? We have just come from the lower realms and are trying to go along a new path, the path to liberation and enlightenment, where we have never been during beginningless lifetimes, so of course we need someone to guide us. We can't do it alone. Since the path to liberation and enlightenment is totally unknown to us, we need to rely upon a guru, somebody who knows the whole path. There is no way we can go to the state of enlightenment without a guru.

That is why Geshe Potowa also said,

> In order to achieve enlightenment, there is nothing more important than the guru.

In explaining why we need a guru, the highly attained yogi Khedrub Sangye Yeshe said,

> Without a helmsman, a boat cannot take you across the ocean.
> Like that, without a guru, you cannot be liberated from samsara,
> even if you have complete knowledge of Dharma.

Just as a boat on its own cannot reach the other side of an ocean, we cannot be liberated from samsara without a guru, even if we have memorized and intellectually understood all of the sutra and tantra root texts and commentaries. Even if we have acquired all possible intellectual knowledge of Dharma, even if we have a whole library of texts in our mind and can recite them all by heart, without a guru, we cannot be liberated from samsara, let alone achieve enlightenment.

To be liberated from samsara, we have to generate the path within our mind, and generating the path depends upon receiving the blessings of the guru. Even if we have complete intellectual understanding of the teachings, we won't be able to generate realizations unless we receive the blessings of the guru within our heart. This is why we need to seek and devote ourselves to a guru.

In the Hinayana, the fundamental practice to achieve liberation is to live in moral conduct—but there's no way to receive the lineage of ordination without a teacher. Also, without a virtuous friend, we can't receive the blessings in our own mind that enable us to perfectly understand the teachings.

Specifically, in tantra, there is no way we can achieve enlightenment without a perfectly qualified vajra guru planting the seeds of the four *kayas* in our mind through granting the blessings of the four complete initiations of Highest Yoga Tantra. Each initiation leaves a potential, or seed, in the mind of the vajra disciple. It is through the kindness of the vajra guru that these four initiations are given, thus planting the seeds of the four kayas and enabling us to meditate on the paths of secret mantra. If we try to practice Highest Yoga Tantra without a guru, we won't achieve enlightenment.

With respect to tantra, and even sutra, without a teacher, we can't have infallible understanding of the profound meanings of the teachings. Even if we have complete intellectual understanding of the scriptures, how can we reach enlightenment without a guru? We can't even be liberated from samsara.

Padmasambhava, the second Buddha, explained why we need a guru in the following way:

> If you don't recognize the guru as a buddha, your mind cannot be liberated by the blessings. Therefore, reflect on the qualities of the guru and then make requests to him.

In the first part of this verse Padmasambhava explains why we need a guru and in the second part how to develop the devotion that sees the guru as a buddha once we have found one.

Padmasambhava is saying that if we don't recognize, or realize, that our guru is a buddha, we don't have devotion, and without guru devotion, no blessings will enter our heart. If we don't have the root of the path to enlightenment, the devotion that sees the guru as a buddha, the door of the blessings is closed and there is no way for us to receive blessings from the guru. Guru devotion opens the door of the blessings.

It is guru devotion that enables us to receive blessings in our mental continuum, which then makes it possible for us to develop our mind, to generate the realizations of the path by listening, reflecting and meditating. The blessings that enable us to liberate our mind come from our devotion. This guru devotion is not just some external pretence of devotion; it is the heart-felt devotion that comes through recognizing that the guru is a buddha. This realization comes by purifying obstacles and accumulating extensive merit, then meditating on the guru devotion section of the lam-rim teachings.

What we want is to liberate our mind from all our delusions and obscurations and to achieve enlightenment. To do this, we need to liberate our mind from all our wrong conceptions, which prevent achievement of liberation and enlightenment, and to generate all the realizations of the path. Actualizing the whole path and thus completely liberating our mind depend solely on receiving the blessings of the guru within our mental continuum. The guru's blessings enable us to generate the path to enlightenment and that path liberates our mind from all delusions and obscurations, even the subtle obscurations that prevent our mental continuum from becoming omniscient mind. If we don't receive the blessings of the guru, our mind can't be liberated from all our delusions and obscurations.

Our mind is liberated from obscurations through actualizing the remedy of the whole path to enlightenment, which depends on receiving the blessings of the guru within our mind, which in turn depends on having the cause of blessings, the devotion that sees the guru as an enlightened being. The more we are able to see the guru as a buddha, the more blessings we receive.

Just as a seed cannot produce a sprout without water, there is no way for us to generate the path to enlightenment within our mind without blessings.

To experience the path within our mind, we have to receive the blessings of the guru. Unless we receive the blessings of the guru, our mind cannot be liberated from wrong conceptions. And if our mind is not liberated from wrong conceptions, we cannot achieve the state of enlightenment or fulfill all the wishes of sentient beings, freeing them from all their sufferings and obscurations and leading them to the peerless happiness of the state of enlightenment. Without the blessings of the guru, we cannot accomplish this extensive benefit for other sentient beings.

How do we receive the blessings of the guru? We have to train our mind in the devotion that sees the guru as a buddha and then make this devotion stable. Our own devotion makes it possible for us to receive the blessings of the guru in our heart. To do this, as Padmasambhava says, we need to *reflect on the qualities of the guru*. We should think of the qualities that we can now see and also of all the other qualities of a buddha, even those that we can't see with our present obscured mind. We should think that our own virtuous friend, the one with whom we have made actual Dharma contact, has all the qualities that a buddha has, which means looking at our guru as a buddha. We should also think about the relevant quotations and lines of reasoning in the sutra and tantra teachings, but especially in the lam-rim.

We should look at our guru only from the side of his good qualities and not from the side of his faults. Looking only at the guru's good qualities means seeing the guru as a buddha, as having ceased all faults and possessing all good qualities. (It doesn't matter whether or not the guru actually is a buddha.) In this way, we will see only qualities and no faults, because reflecting on the guru's qualities helps to stop thoughts of the guru's faults. Devotion will then develop and this devotion will cause us to receive the blessings of the guru. With the devotion that sees the guru as a buddha, we receive the actual blessings of buddha within our heart. In this way the root of all the good things up to enlightenment is established within us. This is the psychological method that enables us, as disciples, to succeed in all our wishes for happiness.

With that guru devotion, we then make requests to the guru to grant us blessings to pacify all our obscurations and to generate all the realizations of the path. We make requests to develop our own mind in the path to enlightenment. The ultimate request is, recalling the qualities of the guru, praying for our own body, speech and mind to become one with the guru's holy body, holy speech and holy mind. The main way to receive blessings is to request to receive all the qualities that the guru has.

Receiving blessings from the guru depends not on our physically being with the guru but on how much devotion toward the guru we have. Even if we spend our whole life physically living with our guru, it's not certain that we will be receiving his blessings. If our mind is empty of devotion, we won't receive any blessings, just as a flower hidden under a rock won't grow because it can't receive the rays of the sun. On the other hand, even if we are physically distant from our guru, if we have great devotion we will be mentally close to him and receive his blessings—like a flower in open sunlight.

His Holiness Trijang Rinpoche gave this advice to a nun who was a student of Lama Yeshe but said that she felt very distant from Lama. I don't know whether she understood or benefited from this advice, but it was very effective for my mind.

Manjushri's advice to Lama Tsongkhapa

How can we quickly achieve realizations of the whole path to enlightenment? When Lama Tsongkhapa asked Manjushri this question, Manjushri advised,

> To train your mind in the actual body of the graduated path to enlightenment, you should attempt to purify your obstacles and accumulate merit, which are the necessary conditions. Then, you should make single-pointed requests to the guru inseparable from the deity in order to receive blessings within your heart. If you attempt to strongly and continuously practice in this way every day, realizations will come without any difficulty.

Purifying the obstacles that interfere with achieving realizations of the path is normally explained in terms of Vajrasattva recitation and meditation, but there are also many other purification practices.[12] The necessary condition of accumulating merit is normally explained in terms of the seven-limb practice, mandala offerings and so forth; there are also many other means to accumulate merit.[13]

---

[12] Other purification practices include prostrations to the Thirty-five Buddhas of Confession, Dorje Khadro fire pujas, Samayavajra meditation and recitation and making tsa-tsas. See also note 52.

[13] Other means to accumulate merit include waterbowl offerings, refuge practice, tsog offerings and guru yoga.

The practice of guru devotion itself brings great purification, purifying all our past negative karmas created in relation to sentient beings and to Buddha, Dharma and Sangha. Devoting ourselves to the virtuous friend in thought and action is the most powerful way to purify all our past negative karmas. Many eons of negative karma can be purified in one day, one hour or even one minute.

To grow crops in a field, in addition to planting seeds in the ground we need the essential conditions of water and minerals; seeds cannot grow on their own. And if they are burned by fire, eaten by insects or taken away by birds, again they cannot grow. Similarly, without the essential conditions of purification and accumulation of merit, our realizations cannot grow.

In *Liberation in the Palm of Your Hand*, Pabongka Dechen Nyingpo advises that purifying negative karma and collecting merit is more important than meditating on the path to enlightenment. I think that this is true. When we do many prostrations with strong visualization, our mind usually starts to change and powerful devotion, compassion or renunciation can begin to arise. Of course, it all depends on the heaviness of our negative karma and obscurations. Some people need to do a lot of preliminary practices to really have a strong experience of the path. For others, simply starting the preliminary practices can change their mind.

The guru is the supreme merit field. Why is the term *field* used? Because a field is something we depend upon for our survival and our enjoyment. We plant seeds in a field, the seeds grow and we then receive crops. It is similar with the guru. Like planting seeds in a field, through doing prostrations, making offerings, making requests and so forth, we accumulate merit, from which we receive all happiness: the happiness of this and future lives, liberation from samsara and great liberation, or full enlightenment. We receive all our past, present and future happiness and success in dependence upon the holy object of the guru.

Making single-pointed requests to the guru means transforming our ordinary impure mind, which sees faults in the guru, into the pure mind of guru devotion, which sees the guru as a buddha, whether or not he actually is an enlightened being. By looking at him as a buddha, we will then see him as a buddha.

While we are training our mind in the meditations of the steps of the path to enlightenment, we need to make strong single-pointed requests to the guru out of guru devotion. Single-pointedly praying with guru devotion causes us to receive the blessings of the guru. Just as a seed needs to receive water in order to grow, we need to receive the blessings of the guru for the realizations of the path to grow within our mind. The potential for these realizations, including omniscient mind, has been in our mind for beginningless rebirths. Receiving blessings is the condition that causes this potential to manifest in realizations of the path, from guru devotion up to enlightenment.

We need to do strong practice of purification and collection of merit and put effort into guru devotion. Even if in the beginning our mind is stubborn and we find it hard to feel devotion, with strong, sustained practice of the preliminaries and of guru devotion, our heart will open and we will start to feel devotion.

Unless our mind is ripened by purifying obscurations and accumulating merit and by receiving blessings through making requests to the guru, no matter how hard we attempt to meditate on the path, we will be extremely slow to generate realizations. If our mind is ripened, however, realizations will come quickly and easily.

The actual body of the practice is training our mind in the steps of the path to enlightenment, but it is only with all these necessary conditions that we can succeed in actualizing the path. This is how the Dharma has been practiced by all the lineage lamas of the path to enlightenment, by all the past yogis and pandits, including Guru Shakyamuni Buddha himself. All the lineage lamas, down to my present gurus, have practiced the path and actualized realizations in this way

Take Milarepa, for example. It was by correctly devoting himself to his guru Marpa that Milarepa achieved enlightenment not just in one life but in the brief lifetime of a degenerate time. Milarepa actually achieved enlightenment within a number of years, as did Gyalwa Ensapa, Chökyi Dorje and many other Indian and Tibetan yogis. There are many similar stories about the guru devotion practice of the Kadampa geshes and past yogis and lineage lamas, as well as about present practitioners.[14]

From Manjushri's advice to Lama Tsongkhapa, we can understand that realizations don't come simply from listening to teachings on a subject. Of course, disciples whose minds are ripe are able to realize impermanence and death, emptiness or other subjects even the first time they hear teachings on them—in past lives such disciples left many imprints of the lam-rim on their mind, purified many obscurations and accumulated much merit. The minds

---

[14] See *Enlightened Beings: Life Stories from the Ganden Oral Tradition.*

of such disciples have already been prepared, as advised by Manjushri; they have purified much obscuration and accumulated extensive merit, which are the necessary conditions, and have generated guru devotion, the cause that enables them to receive blessings and realizations. Those whose minds are qualified by having gathered all the necessary causes and conditions are able to gain realizations simply by hearing the Dharma.

For the rest of us, however, from Manjushri's reply to Lama Tsongkhapa we can understand that we can't expect to understand everything simply from listening to teachings; we can't expect to feel in our heart what we hear. We can see that reading a Dharma book or listening to Dharma teachings alone is not sufficient to understand Dharma. We need all the necessary causes and conditions of purification, accumulation of merit and guru devotion.

The four general benefits of guru devotion

1. Receiving the blessings of the guru We now understand the general reason that we need to practice guru devotion. If we have guru devotion, which means seeing the guru as a buddha, we receive the blessings of the guru, and those blessings then become the cause to achieve realizations of the path to enlightenment. In this way, we are able to achieve full enlightenment. We are then able to do perfect work for all the numberless sentient beings, liberating them from all their suffering and its causes and bringing them to enlightenment. That is the ultimate goal of our life. Because that is our ultimate goal, guru devotion, the root of the path to enlightenment, becomes an essential practice in our life.

Just as rain moistens the ground so that seeds planted in a field can grow, the rain of the guru's blessings moistens the field of our mind so that realizations can grow. If we have no devotion, we have no cause to receive the blessings of the guru, and without blessings we have no cause for realizations of the path to enlightenment. This means that we can't achieve enlightenment and accomplish the ultimate goal of our life.

Receiving the guru's blessings is the first benefit of practicing guru devotion; there are three other benefits, as well.

2. Guru devotion protects our mind from delusions The second benefit is that guru devotion protects our mind such that delusions and negative thoughts don't arise, especially negative thoughts toward the guru. Having the stable devotion that sees the guru as a buddha protects us from generating anger or heresy toward the guru, which are the greatest obstacles to all happiness, from that of this life up to the bliss of enlightenment. The best protection comes from guru devotion. Guru devotion protects us from suffering and from the obstacles to achieving realizations of the path to enlightenment. Since our devotion prevents us from creating obstacles, it allows us to receive all the realizations. The main reason to eliminate obstacles is to develop realizations—without obstacles, we can develop our mind; if we are creating obstacles, we can't develop our mind. Without the protection of guru devotion, life becomes difficult.

Anger and heresy can arise when our guru does something or tells us to do something that we don't like (which means that our self-cherishing or attachment doesn't like) or that we aren't interested in. Allowing anger, heresy or other negative thoughts to arise for even a moment is very dangerous because the virtuous friend is the most powerful object in our life. Generating negative thoughts of anger or heresy toward our guru creates very heavy negative karma, the greatest obstacle to developing our mind in the path to enlightenment, to developing our potential. Generating anger or heresy toward the guru creates the greatest of all obstacles and results in the heaviest suffering, causing us to be reborn in hell and to experience unimaginable suffering there for an incredible length of time. We have to suffer in hell for eons equal in number to the moments of our anger.

Anger, heresy and other negative minds often arise, as well as the thought that the guru is an ordinary person. In *The Great Treatise on the Stages of the Path to Enlightenment*, Lama Tsongkhapa explains that simply thinking that our guru is an ordinary person becomes causes our experiences or realizations to degenerate.[15] This means it is an obstacle to the development of our mind in the path. This quotation alone is reason enough to practice guru devotion, to see the guru as a buddha.

3. Guru devotion protects our merit   The third benefit of practicing guru devotion is that, by stopping the arising of negative thoughts toward the guru, guru devotion also protects us from destroying many eons of merit, the cause of happiness and realizations.

4. Guru devotion protects us from delayed realizations   The fourth benefit is that guru devotion protects us from the delay of realizations. When we

---

[15] *The Great Treatise*, Volume One, p. 90.

generate anger or heresy for even a moment we postpone realizations of the path to enlightenment for many eons. This is the damage we cause to our own mental continuum if we generate anger or heresy toward our guru.

In summary, by helping us prevent negative thoughts toward the virtuous friend, the practice of guru devotion protects us from creating the heavy negative karmas that would cause us to spend many eons suffering in the lower realms, destroy the merit accumulated over many eons and delay our realizations. On top of that, by practicing guru devotion, we receive the blessings of the guru, the cause of realizations of the path to enlightenment.

If we don't have guru devotion to protect our mind, if we don't know the meditations on how to look at the guru as a buddha, negative thoughts will constantly arise, and we will constantly create the heaviest obstacles in relation to the virtuous friend. We will constantly create obstacles to our achieving enlightenment, liberation and the happiness of future lives. Also, we will constantly create causes to be reborn in the lower realms. Besides this, we won't receive the blessings of the guru, because when negative thoughts toward the guru are there, there's no space for devotion, just as two people can't sit in the same seat on a plane.

In a plane, just before you take off, flight attendants introduce the safety features of the aircraft. They start with how to put the seat-belt on and then show you where the life-jacket is stored and how to put it on. They also explain about the oxygen, the lights and the exits through which to escape. (This is all in case the plane lands very nicely in the water and stays afloat; then you can do all these things.) It's all for your safety, in case something dangerous happens. Here, for safety in traveling along the lam-rim to enlightenment, guru devotion practice is the life-jacket and all the other safety devices as well.

We can now see that guru devotion is the essential practice in terms of protecting our mind and attaining full enlightenment. Whether we will achieve realizations of the path and enlightenment and how quickly this will happen depend on our guru devotion practice, on our generating stable devotion and correctly devoting ourselves to the guru. Once we understand why guru devotion is crucial, we can't wait even a second to have this realization, this transformation of mind.

From this basic introduction, you can understand the importance of guru devotion practice and why all the lam-rim texts describe guru devotion as the root of the path to enlightenment. Because of Lama Tsongkhapa's skill in guiding sentient beings, he put guru devotion as the very first subject of meditation in his lam-rim teachings, before the initial lam-rim path, perfect human rebirth.

When we study lam-rim in the Lama Tsongkhapa tradition, because guru devotion is the first subject, we understand from the very beginning what brings success in attaining the whole path to enlightenment and what creates obstacles to success in achieving realizations. After first explaining what makes our practice successful and what creates the greatest obstacle to our success, Lama Tsongkhapa then explains the complete path, from perfect human rebirth up to enlightenment.

In other traditions the first meditation subject is perfect human rebirth or impermanence and death, with guru devotion coming after refuge or the faults of samsara. Of course, in some ways this makes sense, especially for people in the West. After an introduction to the four noble truths—true suffering, true cause of suffering, true cessation of suffering and true path— you understand that to achieve ultimate happiness you need to actualize the path, so of course you need somebody to teach you the path. There then comes the need of a guru. For people in the West, I think the subject of guru devotion fits very well there, after an introduction to the nature of samsara and the four noble truths, because the need of a guru, of someone who can show you the path, has been made very clear. You then feel the need to look for a teacher, a guru, and to rely on him.

Lama Tsongkhapa, however, put the subject of guru devotion first. Everything is clearly explained at the very beginning: the advantages of having a guru; the disadvantages of not having a guru; the shortcomings if, having found a guru and made a connection, you make mistakes in your relationship with him; and how to devote to the guru with thought and with action. By being introduced to guru devotion practice first, you become careful from the very beginning not to make mistakes. You then start your Dharma practice, your spiritual life, without mistakes because you have full understanding of the subject of devoting yourself to the virtuous friend. You understand that this is the root that enables you to successfully actualize the rest of the path. By being educated in this practice from the very beginning, you don't make mistakes. I think this is why Lama Tsongkhapa put this subject at the very beginning.

Unless you know the importance of correct devotion to the virtuous friend, no matter how much the rest of the path is explained to you, you won't be successful in actualizing it because, without guru devotion, you will have no way to stop obstacles and no way to receive blessings. With the practice of guru devotion, all your wishes, including your wish to quickly achieve enlightenment, will be fulfilled. Therefore, the teaching on how to devote to the virtuous friend is the most important one, more important than any other teaching. It is the root of all happiness, from now up to enlightenment.

It is very important to study lam-rim from beginning to end, and to study and learn the whole teaching on guru devotion. In the guru devotion outlines, the first outline is the eight benefits of correctly devoting to a guru. Next comes the eight shortcomings of making mistakes in your devotion. Then comes how to devote to the guru with thought, which includes meditating on the kindness of the guru, and how to devote to the guru with action. (See appendix 1.) It is very important not only to understand all these outlines, but to meditate on them and achieve the realizations. The way to do effective meditation on each of the four basic outlines is to establish a pure thought of guru devotion, seeing the guru as a buddha, after each outline.

In his lam-rim teachings, Pabongka Dechen Nyingpo mentions,

> If we are able to look at the guru only from the side of his qualities and never allow the thought of faults in the guru to arise, we will achieve enlightenment in one lifetime.

Here Pabongka Rinpoche gives the heart advice. The answer to whether we can achieve enlightenment and how quickly we can achieve it lies in our guru devotion practice.

2. The Power of the Guru

To understand why guru devotion is so important we first need to understand the power of the guru. Only when we have this fundamental understanding will we appreciate the importance of guru devotion practice. Otherwise, our guru devotion practice will be superficial; it won't come from the very depths of our heart.

In regard to the power of objects, our parents of this life, the mother and father who gave us our present body, are more powerful objects than other ordinary people. If we show some minor disrespect to our parents, because they are powerful objects, the negative karma is heavy and we can start to experience the results of that karma as problems or difficulties even in this life, and the results continue in subsequent lives. We can create the cause and also experience the resultant suffering in this life.

There are three types of karma: the karma where we create the cause in one life and experience the result in the same life; the karma where we create the cause in one life and experience the result in the next life; and the karma where we create the cause in one life and experience the result after many lifetimes, even thousands or millions of lifetimes. The karma that is created and experienced in the same life, whether good or bad, is the karma we have created in relation to powerful objects, from our parents up to the guru.

If you verbally abuse your parents—calling them blind, for example—within one or two years, you can experience some problem with your eyes, if not blindness. One geshe did an observation[16] for one of his students who

---

[16] This refers to a divination [Tib: *mo*] in reliance upon a meditational deity, usually performed with dice.

had a problem with his arm; he told him that it was the result of hitting his mother. Such stories are common.

If we do some small good thing for our parents, the good karma is also powerful and we can start to experience its good result in this life. Some of us have already had such experiences, if we could only recognize them.

Ordinary ordained Sangha, those who haven't realized emptiness, are more powerful objects than our parents, because of the power of their vows. More powerful than ordinary Sangha are absolute Sangha, which means the arhats, the *arya* beings of the Hinayana path, who have realized the wisdom that directly perceives emptiness.

One bodhisattva, even one who has only recently generated bodhicitta, is a much more powerful object than numberless arhats. Creating negative karma in relation to a bodhisattva—through criticism, disrespect or giving harm—is much heavier than doing those negative actions in relation to numberless arhats. It is mentioned by Pabongka Rinpoche in *Liberation in the Palm of Your Hand* and also in other lam-rim teachings that the negative karma of glaring or looking disrespectfully at one bodhisattva is much heavier than that of gouging out the eyes of all the sentient beings of the three realms.[17] On the other hand, the merit of looking calmly and respectfully at one bodhisattva is much greater than that of making charity of our eyes to all the sentient beings of the three realms. We can see that one bodhisattva is an unbelievably powerful object, with the power coming from the mind of bodhicitta.

A Guide to the Bodhisattva's Way of Life says,

> One moment of anger
> Destroys the merit collected
> By having made offerings to Those Gone to Bliss and charity
> For one thousand eons.[18]

This verse is referring to someone who is not a bodhisattva getting angry at a bodhisattva. When such a person gets angry at a bodhisattva for one moment, that moment of anger destroys the merit the person had accumulated over one thousand eons and also postpones his realizations for one thousand eons.

---

[17] The three realms are the desire, form and formless realms.
[18] Ch. 6, v. 1.

Also, in *The Great Treatise on the Stages of the Path to Enlightenment*, Lama Tsongkhapa explains that if someone who is not a bodhisattva gets angry at a bodhisattva, he destroys eons of merit equal in number to the number of moments of his anger and delays his realizations.

Since we don't have omniscient mind or even clairvoyance, we can't see the level of anyone's mind. Because we can't tell who is a bodhisattva, in our daily life we should be careful not to get angry at anyone; it is wise to practice patience with everyone. There is nothing certain about how a person appears externally. Because we have an impure mind with many hallucinations, it's not certain that a person is actually what she appears to us to be.

Now, one buddha is a more powerful object than numberless bodhisattvas. Criticizing or harming one buddha is much heavier than criticizing or harming numberless bodhisattvas. And the good karma of showing respect to one buddha is much greater than that of showing respect to numberless bodhisattvas.

One guru is the most powerful object of all—much more powerful than numberless buddhas. This refers to your own personal guru, or lama—someone with whom you have established a Dharma connection, not just to anyone who carries the general title of "guru" or "lama." Creating good or bad karma in relation to a guru is the most powerful of all; much more powerful than doing so in relation to numberless buddhas. By offering a small respect or service to your guru, you create great good karma—actually, the word *great* is not sufficient to describe the amount of merit you collect.

How does this power of the guru come about? It is a dependent arising; it comes about through causes and conditions. Phenomena exist in dependence upon many factors and each phenomenon has its own nature, power and function. The power created by the meeting of a guru and a disciple is a dependent arising, like two atoms meeting to produce nuclear power or two batteries meeting to produce a charge. For example, a flashlight needs two batteries to produce light; one battery is not enough but if we align the positive and negative ends of two batteries, light is produced.

How does that person become the most powerful in our life? It happens the moment we make a Dharma connection with him. The moment we establish Dharma contact with someone with the recognition of a guru-disciple relationship, that person becomes the most powerful object in our life, more powerful than numberless buddhas. Once we recognize that person as our guru, the one we will rely upon to guide us to the happiness of future lives, liberation and enlightenment, and ourselves as his disciple, that person—whether he is an enlightened or ordinary being, lay or ordained, Tibetan or Western, male or female—becomes the most powerful object for us. So, it's a mental thing. The power is created by our making that decision to recognize someone as our guru and then making Dharma contact with that recognition. The power comes from the Dharma contact, not from whether or not the person is an enlightened being. The moment that person becomes our guru, he becomes the most powerful being in our life, even if he is not a buddha or even a bodhisattva but just a very ordinary being.

When you make the decision to form a guru-disciple relationship with someone, the Dharma connection can be established by your receiving from him a teaching, an initiation, vows or simply the oral transmission of OM MANI PADME HUM or a single verse of Dharma. The Dharma connection doesn't come simply from hearing the teaching or being there for an initiation or vows, but from doing so with the recognition of the person as your guru and you as his disciple.

Basically, however, the power is created when you decide to form a guru-disciple relationship with someone, and it doesn't depend on whether you immediately receive a teaching, initiation or vows from that person. It depends on your making the decision. For example, when Milarepa made this decision and requested teachings from his guru Marpa, Marpa didn't give him teachings right away.

Before we form a guru-disciple relationship with someone, that person is not the most powerful object in relation to us but becomes so as soon as we establish the relationship. That person is not necessarily an enlightened being or powerful in relation to other people; he is not the most powerful object for those who don't have a Dharma connection with him. He has power only in relation to the people who have made Dharma contact with him.

The meeting of two atoms to produce nuclear power can be constructive, as in medical treatment and the generation of electricity, or destructive, as in an atomic bomb. The meeting of a guru and disciple is similar. If we are careful and practice guru devotion well, we can accumulate the greatest merit in the shortest time, but if we are not careful and make even a small mistake in our practice of guru devotion, we can experience the heaviest suffering for the longest time.

The negative karma we create in relation to these objects, from our parents up to the guru, is very powerful; on top of that, even though the negative karma might be very small, because karma is expandable, we can experience the resultant problem many times, not just in one life but in hundreds or thousands of lifetimes. Any positive karma we create is also very powerful and we can experience the good results of that one good karma for many hundreds or thousands of lifetimes. The way in which karma is expandable is difficult for our ordinary minds to grasp; it is something that is beyond our imagination.

Any bad karma that we create gets heavier and heavier, from our parents up to the guru, and is heaviest in relation to the guru; similarly, any merit we create gets greater and greater, and is greatest in relation to the guru. In other words, we can experience the greatest profit and the greatest loss in relation to the guru.

It is in relation to the guru that we can purify the most obscurations and accumulate the most extensive merit. Doing a small positive action in relation to our guru brings inconceivable benefit, resulting in the experience of happiness from life to life, up to enlightenment. This is why the prayer of the graduated path in *Guru Puja* says,

> Through the power of having made offerings and respectful requests
> To you, holy and perfect, pure gurus—supreme field of merit,
> I seek your blessings, saviors and root of well-being and bliss,
> That I may come under your joyful care.[19]

However, if we are not careful, the guru, like electricity, can be dangerous. Even though electricity seems insignificant, if we are not careful with it, we can endanger our own life. Even though we can obtain the greatest benefit in relation to the guru, we can also create the greatest suffering. Even a small mistake made in relation to the guru becomes a great obstacle to developing our mind in the path to enlightenment, to achieving our own happiness from this life up to enlightenment. Negative thoughts and actions toward the guru create the heaviest negative karma and are the greatest obstacles to our achievement of realizations, as well as to our temporary and ultimate happiness.

Therefore, we need a method to protect us from these negative thoughts and actions, and that method is guru devotion. We have to transform our mind into the positive thought of devotion, seeing the guru as a buddha, free from all faults and possessing all qualities. We are in urgent need of this protection.

[19] V. 84.

The pure thought of devotion that sees the guru as a buddha doesn't allow negative thoughts toward the guru to arise, which means that we then don't create the greatest obstacle to our enlightenment. By seeing the guru as a buddha, we create only the greatest merit with our body, speech and mind. This practice brings the greatest purification and the greatest merit.

3. Checking the Guru

THE FIRST POINT in establishing a guru-disciple relationship with someone is that we should examine him well at the very beginning, before making Dharma contact. Since finding a guru means finding a person we are going to devote our life to from now on, we should check carefully to see whether we feel we can devote ourselves to this person as a virtuous teacher. After analyzing well, we then make the Dharma connection. Otherwise, there is a danger that we will later criticize or renounce the guru. If we are careful to check well before we establish a Dharma connection, we will make fewer mistakes and thus experience fewer of the shortcomings of incorrect devotion to the virtuous friend. If we are not careful at the beginning, we will experience these shortcomings many times. The degree of this danger is determined by how much merit and how much understanding of guru devotion we have.

Checking carefully before establishing a guru-disciple relationship is for your own safety, like using the seatbelt in a car or an airplane. The reason that I'm talking about checking the guru is so that your journey to enlightenment will be safe.

We need to analyze at the beginning, before we establish a Dharma connection and form a guru-disciple relationship, because guru devotion involves great dedication and sacrifice from our side. It's not a matter of choosing just anybody who can teach Dharma. We should make a guru-disciple connection only after checking for the qualities mentioned in the lam-rim teachings (see chapter 4). We shouldn't make a connection for ordinary reasons, especially not for reasons put forward by our delusions. We should make the choice out of wisdom gained through analysis.

Panchen Losang Chökyi Gyaltsen, the learned, highly attained lama who composed *Guru Puja*, emphasized that it is important to first examine a person before following him as a guru. He said,

> If you cherish yourself, don't follow just anyone you happen to meet, like a dog seeking food in the street. Examine well the lama who reveals the holy Dharma, then follow him with respect.

If you cherish yourself—or, to use a Western expression, "if you love yourself"—and wish to achieve ultimate happiness, you need a guru. However, you shouldn't seek one like a dog seeking food in the street. A street dog is always looking for food and when it finds some, immediately runs to it and gobbles it up. The dog doesn't stop to check the food to see whether it is poisoned or even edible, or to chew it well, but simply gulps it down as quickly as possible.

Panchen Losang Chökyi Gyaltsen is saying that we shouldn't act like this, taking teachings from anyone we happen to meet and immediately accepting that person as our guru without checking whether he will harm or benefit us. If we take teachings and initiations from just anybody who gives them, after some time we will become confused and will soon have a problem with every one of our teachers—it will simply be a question of whether the problem is big or small. Even though we might recite a lot of mantras and prayers every day, because we won't have paid attention to the root of the path, not much will have happened in our mind—it might even have gotten worse.

If we regard everyone we meet as a virtuous friend without first checking, there is also a danger that we could meet a non-virtuous, rather than virtuous, teacher; one who will lead us away from our goal—to suffering rather than happiness. There is then a danger that we will waste not only our present precious and highly meaningful human life but many future lives as well.

Since the way this life and our future lives will turn out depends on the qualities of our guru, we should first carefully examine the person to see whether he has the qualities described in the lam-rim teachings. Even if the person is famous and has thousands of followers, we should still examine him well.

Remember the way that Lama Atisha checked Lama Suvarnadvipi before taking teachings from him. Lama Atisha was already a great scholar of the entire Buddhadharma before he went to Indonesia to receive teachings on bodhicitta from Lama Suvarnadvipi. At that time transport was very primitive, so the ship from India took more than twelve months to get to Sumatra, where Lama Suvarnadvipi lived.

Even after putting so much effort into the journey, taking many risks and encountering many obstacles, Lama Atisha and his many disciples, who were all great scholars expert in the five categories of knowledge,[20] did not immediately go to see Lama Suvarnadvipi when they arrived at the place where he lived. They rested for a few days, during which time Lama Atisha checked Lama Suvarnadvipi's qualities and practices with some of Lama Suvarnadvipi's close disciples. He inquired about Lama Suvarnadvipi's daily life and practice. Even though Lama Suvarnadvipi, the holder of Maitreya Buddha's teachings, was famous as a great bodhisattva and renowned for his learning, purity and good heart, Lama Atisha wasn't satisfied simply by his great reputation. He still took the time to check and only after he had analyzed Lama Suvarnadvipi's behavior did he take teachings from him.

Lama Atisha then spent twelve years with Lama Suvarnadvipi. After receiving the complete teachings on bodhicitta from Lama Suvarnadvipi, like one pot being filled from another, Lama Atisha then generated bodhicitta.

Unless we analyze the qualities of the person and his teachings, instead of achieving liberation and enlightenment, we will achieve something else—samsara, and possibly even the lower realms. The teaching needs to be pure Buddhadharma. If the foundations of the path to enlightenment—renunciation of samsara, bodhicitta and emptiness—are not mentioned, there is no complete path to liberation and enlightenment. Even if the word "emptiness" is used, it won't help us unless it is the unmistaken view of emptiness. Certain teachings and meditation techniques might be correct, but if they don't reveal the whole path to liberation and enlightenment, we could spend our whole life concentrating on them and not reach anywhere.

In order to practice Dharma, both guru and disciple should examine each other well. However, if we spend too much time looking for and checking the guru, there is also a danger that nothing will happen in this life. Our precious human life will finish with nothing accomplished. One disciple said to his teacher, "I want to check you as a lama for many years"; the lama

---

[20] The five major fields of knowledge are arts and crafts, medicine, languages and grammar, logic and religious philosophy.

replied, "I also want to check you as a disciple for many years." Since their checking took almost their whole lifetime, nothing was accomplished.

Once we have examined someone well, found that he has the necessary qualities and accepted him as our guru, as Panchen Losang Chökyi Gyaltsen says, we should then *follow him with respect*. This means that we should hold him in high regard and devote ourselves to him by practicing what he advises us to do and avoiding what he advises us not to do, in accord with what Buddha has explained in the teachings.

With respect to seeking a guru, many past yogis tried to find the guru with whom they had had karmic contact in previous lives and were not satisfied even if they met other gurus. Getting a very strong feeling simply from seeing a guru and finding his teachings very effective for our mind are signs of contact with that guru in past lives.

In the story of bodhisattva Sadaprarudita (see chapter 7), even though Sadaprarudita could see countless buddhas, he wasn't satisfied. He still wanted to meet the guru with whom he had a karmic connection from his past lives. He was called Sadaprarudita, which means "always crying," because he was inconsolable at not being able to find his guru. He kept searching until he found him.

4. The Qualities of a Guru

Revealing the complete path to enlightenment

WE SHOULDN'T RELY upon just anyone as a guru. In order to achieve the goal of enlightenment for the sake of other sentient beings, we should have a virtuous teacher who is able to show us the complete infallible path to enlightenment. As mentioned in *The Great Treatise on the Stages of the Path to Enlightenment*, the guru should be someone who understands the whole instruction and can lead us in the paths of the Hinayana, Paramitayana and Vajrayana. As Manjushri advised, for the disciple to become enlightened in one brief lifetime of this degenerate time, the lama should be someone who is able to lead the disciple in the complete path. It is like pulling on a *dingwa*, the square Sangha seat cover: no matter which side you pull, the whole dingwa comes. In a similar way, all the teachings of the Hinayana, Paramitayana and Vajrayana are related to each other and are instructions for one person's graduated practice to achieve enlightenment. Nothing is to be left out.

First we have to seek a qualified virtuous friend, one who can reveal the complete unmistaken path, and once we have found one, we then need to correctly devote ourselves to him. Finding a qualified virtuous friend requires past karma, accumulation of merit and many prayers. But when a virtuous friend who can reveal the whole path to enlightenment and a qualified disciple who can bear hardships meet, full enlightenment can be achieved.

Geshe Potowa said,

> If the virtuous teacher has all the characteristics, which means one who is able to lead the disciple in the complete path to enlighten-

ment, the disciple becomes a fortunate one, able to generate the whole path to enlightenment.

As Geshe Potowa emphasized, if the disciple finds a guru who can lead him in the complete path to enlightenment, the disciple has the good fortune to generate the whole path. If the guru knows only part of the path to enlightenment, the disciple can generate only part of the path.

In *The Great Treatise*, Lama Tsongkhapa also emphasizes that we shouldn't give the label "realization" to just any kind of achievement. For example, somebody might have done some meditation practice and achieved clairvoyance or some miraculous power to heal sickness or bring wealth, but if that person hasn't meditated on the lam-rim, the main road to enlightenment, and gained any realization of guru devotion, renunciation, bodhicitta, emptiness, the five Mahayana paths and ten *bhumis* or the two tantric stages, then those other attainments can't be called realizations.

Of course, ordinary people who don't know about Dharma, who don't know about the four noble truths, regard somebody who has clairvoyance and can tell them about the past and future as very special, more special than somebody who doesn't have psychic power but can show them the four noble truths. If you don't really understand or have faith in the four noble truths, you have no appreciation of someone who actually can liberate you from the oceans of samsaric suffering and its cause, karma and delusions.

We feel that somebody with clairvoyance or miracle powers is much more special than the person who really is awakening us from ignorance and liberating us through teaching us about the four noble truths, about how to be free from the suffering of samsara and its cause. We don't feel that this person who is not only liberating us from samsara but bringing us to enlightenment by teaching us about the lam-rim, the five Mahayana paths and ten bhumis or the tantric path is special; we feel such a person is kind of ordinary.

Thinking in this way is wrong. Why? Because we have had such miraculous powers numberless times but we're still in samsara. And we have achieved single-pointed concentration numberless times, so that if we placed our mind on an object it could stay there like a mountain for years, for eons. As Kadampa Geshe Chengawa said,

We have had all those powers numberless times, but they didn't bring us any special benefit, as we're still in samsara. Leave aside practicing and realizing lam-rim, I would prefer even to ask questions about what the lam-rim is to having such powers.

It is because we didn't achieve the lam-rim in the past that we're still not liberated from the sufferings of samsara and we still haven't achieved enlightenment. To achieve liberation we need to achieve renunciation of the whole of samsara, then realize emptiness and develop that realization until we directly perceive emptiness. Because this didn't happen, we're still suffering in samsara.

Lama Tsongkhapa also stresses that the virtuous friend and his way of subduing our mind should be in accord with the general teaching of Buddha. The virtuous friend should be qualified and able to lead the disciple in the steps of the path to not only liberation but enlightenment. As a Mahayana practitioner, he should be in harmony with the general teaching of the Buddha and have subdued his mind in that way so that he can then help his disciples to actualize the whole path to enlightenment.

We should examine whether a virtuous teacher has the qualities necessary to reveal the path that we wish to follow. There are qualities to reveal Hinayana teachings, qualities to reveal Paramitayana teachings and qualities to reveal tantric teachings. The different kinds of qualities are described in commentaries to the requesting prayer in *Guru Puja*[21] as well as in other teachings. With respect to the qualities a vajra guru should have, there are differences between even Action Tantra and Highest Yoga Tantra. The ten outer qualities a vajra guru needs to reveal Action Tantra and the ten inner qualities to reveal Highest Yoga Tantra are explained in the *Guru Puja* commentary by Kachen Yeshe Gyaltsen.

Some teachings mention sixteen qualities that a virtuous friend should have, others mention ten, five or another number. However, if the guru has the qualities explained in Maitreya Buddha's teaching *Ornament of Mahayana Sutras*, *Fifty Verses of Guru Devotion*,[22] the commentaries to *Guru Puja* or the lam-rim teachings, he is able to lead his disciples along the complete path to enlightenment.

---

[21] See The Union of Bliss & Emptiness, chapter 5.
[22] See *The Fulfillment of All Hopes* and two commentaries by Geshe Ngawang Dhargyey online at www.LamaYeshe.com.

Qualities of a Mahayana guru

In *Ornament of Mahayana Sutras* Maitreya Buddha mentions ten qualities that a virtuous friend should have in order to reveal Mahayana teachings:

> Rely upon a virtuous friend who is subdued, pacified,
>   and highly pacified,
> Has greater knowledge, has perseverance, is learned in scripture,
> Has realized emptiness, is skillful in teaching,
> Has a compassionate nature and has abandoned discouragement.

The first three qualities relate to the three higher trainings. *Subdued* means the guru should be living in the higher training of morality, protecting himself from negative karma. Even a lay teacher should be living in the lay pratimoksha vows. In that way, he will have tamed, or subdued, the actions of his body, speech and mind. In other words, he should have pure morality.

On top of that, the guru should be *pacified* through the higher training of concentration. He should be able to control his delusions by having realization of *shamatha*, or calm abiding. With achievement of this, it's very easy to continuously keep the mind in virtue and then very easy to develop any realization. With perfect concentration you can then develop great insight.

Highly pacified relates to the higher training of wisdom, or great insight. The great insight referred to here doesn't have to be the view of the Prasangika Madhyamaka school; it can be the view of the Mind Only school or one of the other lower schools. This is why having realized emptiness is listed later as a separate quality, where it refers specifically to the Prasangika view.

The guru should also have *greater knowledge*, or realizations, than the disciple, otherwise he cannot benefit him. In terms of this quality of a guru, Gomo Rinpoche once said something that is very effective for the mind. When Gomo Rinpoche was talking about the meaning of "lama" (which means heavier, or greater, in knowledge) before giving a Manjushri initiation to Bakula Rinpoche, Gelek Rinpoche and Lama Yeshe in Gelek Rinpoche's home in Delhi just before Lama Yeshe passed away, Rinpoche said to the three of them, "You people are very learned. I'm not like you, but I do have one thing that you don't have—the lineage of this initiation. So, by this, I am greater in knowledge." Lama later mentioned to me what

Gomo Rinpoche had said as he thought it very effective. So, if the guru has received the oral transmission of a mantra that you haven't, it means the guru has greater knowledge than you.

The guru should also have *perseverance*. *Learned in scripture* means that the virtuous friend should have a mind enriched with quotations and teachings, so that he is able to refer to many teachings by heart. Without *compassion*, even if a teacher has great knowledge, he won't necessarily help the disciple. Having *abandoned discouragement* means the teacher should have abandoned impatience, exhaustion and laziness in guiding disciples. He should not get upset or discouraged when teaching Dharma to students. If the guru has compassion, there is no thought of laziness or tiredness in guiding disciples.

Although these ten qualities are mentioned in *Ornament of Mahayana Sutras*, Geshe Potowa said,

> Even if the guru doesn't have all these qualities, he should at least have the following five: the realization of emptiness, compassion, greater understanding and qualities than the disciple, pure moral conduct and no discouragement when teaching disciples. Otherwise, the teacher cannot guide the disciple out of samsara.

With respect to the qualities of the guru, *Fifty Verses of Guru Devotion* begins by mentioning five bad qualities to avoid when choosing a guru. We shouldn't choose as a guru someone who doesn't have compassion, who has an impatient, angry nature or who has pride. Also, we shouldn't choose a person who can't control his mind, which basically means his desire. Finally, we shouldn't choose someone who is boastful, who constantly advertises to others some small quality that he has.

Qualities of a vajra master

Fifty Verses of Guru Devotion describes the perfect qualities of a vajra master who reveals the tantric teachings in the following way:

> Firm and subdued, intelligent, patient, sincere, without cunning, knowledgeable in mantras and the various activities of tantra, compassionate and loving, learned in the scriptures, proficient in

the ten principles, expert in drawing mandalas, skilled in explaining tantric teachings, calm, with subdued senses.

Patient means able to practice patience with the enemy who gives harm and also able to bear hardships to guide disciples by giving them teachings.

Fifty Verses of Guru Devotion later summarizes the basic qualities of a vajra master into five: strong compassion for others; stable faith in the Mahayana teachings; learned in the various levels of teachings (Hinayana, Paramitayana and Vajrayana); skillful in guiding disciples in the path to enlightenment; and having tamed, or subdued, his three doors.

Similar qualities of a vajra master are described in the requesting prayer in *Guru Puja*:

> You are wise, patient, honest,
> Without pretense or guile, your three doors well subdued,
> You have both sets of ten qualities, know tantra and rituals,
> And are skilled in drawing and explaining:
> Foremost vajra holder, I make requests to you.[23]

As above, *patient* means able to bear harms from others and hardships; *free of hypocrisy* means that the guru doesn't try to hide his personal faults or pretend to have realizations that he doesn't have.

Lama Tsongkhapa advised that the virtuous friend who gives tantric initiation and reveals tantric teachings should have at least three qualifications. First, he should have received the full initiation of the deity and be living well in the samayas of his ordinations. If the guru is ordained, he should be living well in his pratimoksha ordination and abstaining from the ten nonvirtues. If the guru is not ordained he should be keeping the basic pratimoksha lay precepts. The virtuous friend should also be keeping the pledges of his bodhisattva and tantric ordinations.

Second, he should know the ten principles and be expert in the methods of giving initiations through having seen the traditional practices of the lineage lamas. He should know the ten outer principles,[24] which are related

---

[23] V. 45.

[24] The ten outer principles that a vajra master should know are: 1) how to meditate on the mandala with and without form; 2) how to maintain meditative stabilization as the deity within the mandala; 3) how to do the various hand gestures for offering adornments to the deities; 4) how to perform ritual dance; 5) how to assume a variety of postures such as the

to Action Tantra and the other lower tantras, and the ten inner principles, which are related to Highest Yoga Tantra.

The ten inner principles that a virtuous teacher who reveals Highest Yoga Tantra teachings should be expert in are: protection wheels; giving the vase, secret, wisdom and word initiations; making ritual tormas; mantra recitation; wrathful pujas; consecrations; and self-initiations.

A Vajrayana guru should be skilled in drawing protection mandalas, which are worn on the body to protect from harms, and able to dispel obstacles through meditation on protection wheels. In addition to understanding the tantric root texts and commentaries, he should understand how to do all the tantric rituals, such as drawing mandalas, reciting mantras, doing mudras, consecrations and performing various pujas, including wrathful ones. He should be expert in making ritual tormas, or offering cakes. This seems to indicate that tormas are not a Tibetan tradition but actually come from tantric scriptures.

A vajra master should also be expert in the seven different types of mantra recitation that come in the tantric sadhanas: verbal recitation, mental recitation, vajra recitation, samaya recitation, circling recitation, wrathful recitation and recitation one-pointedly concentrating on syllables.

If he cannot succeed in certain tantric practices using peaceful methods, he should be expert in the wrathful tantric methods to subdue evil beings who disturb holy beings or harm sentient beings or the teachings. He should be able to split the evil being from its helpers, such as protectors or devas, and then able to separate its consciousness from its body and transfer its consciousness to a pure realm. He should be able to do these wrathful actions with the thought of renouncing self and cherishing others.

He also needs to be expert in doing consecrations and performing self-initiations.

Third, he should have done the retreat of the deity and received permission from the deity to give the initiation—or at least, the deity should not have objected to his giving the initiation. One has to be very careful in making the decision to give an initiation because it can be dangerous in the present time and also very dangerous to the fulfillment of wishes in the future.

---

vajra position; 6) how to recite mantras; 7) how to conduct peaceful, increasing, powerful and wrathful fire pujas; 8) how to make outer, inner and secret offerings; 9) how to perform peaceful, increasing, powerful and wrathful activities, as well as how to give protection and invite different kinds of guests; and 10) how to conclude rituals and send guests back to their different dwelling places.

Unless we first do retreat and complete the recitation of the number of mantras required to generate power or to gain permission from the deity, we cannot do any of the various actions associated with tantric deities, such as giving initiations and blessings and performing the fire puja. We also cannot do the various tantric actions of peace, increase, control and wrath that are needed to complete Dharma practice and achieve enlightenment for the sake of other sentient beings. If we have not received initiation and done the retreat, our actions don't have power. In previous times it was sufficient to recite the main mantra of a deity 100,000 times, but nowadays, in this degenerate time, when even the power of mantra has degenerated, we need to recite the main mantra 400,000 times.

A vajra master, whether ordained or lay, should have at least these three qualifications as mentioned by Lama Tsongkhapa. Lama Atisha also explained this in the text *Request of the Tantra*. While many other qualifications are mentioned in *Fifty Verses of Guru Devotion* and other texts, Lama Tsongkhapa described the minimum ones.

Fifty Verses of Guru Devotion and some other tantric texts mention sixteen qualities that a tantric guru should have. In this degenerate time, however, it is extremely difficult to find a perfectly qualified guru with every single one of these qualities. Because of this, Lama Atisha advised his heart-son Dromtönpa that since it is impossible to find a virtuous friend with every single one of the sixteen qualities, one should follow a virtuous friend with at least half, a quarter or an eighth of these qualities. At the very least, the virtuous friend should have more good qualities and knowledge than the disciple.

The text *White Lotus* explains:

> In the future quarreling time, one will not see the guru other than as having a mixture of qualities and faults. There will be no one who doesn't create any negative karma at all. In short, examine well to find someone who has more qualities than you, then, my sons, devote yourself to that one as a spiritual friend.

Because of the degenerate time, the guru always has a mixture of qualities and faults and there is no one who only accumulates virtue.

Also, in this degenerate time, because our own mind is obscured by gross delusions, even if the virtuous friend were perfect, an enlightened being with only good qualities and without a single fault, we couldn't see him in that way because of our obscurations. It is extremely difficult for us to see the guru as having only good qualities. We see a mixture of good qualities and faults. Lama Tsongkhapa said that in the quarreling time it will be difficult to see a virtuous teacher without faults.

The essential qualities

Although the texts explain all these many different qualities to look for in a guru, the very essence is that our guru should at least be someone who emphasizes cherishing others more than cherishing self, because we then have the opportunity to develop bodhicitta, the root of the Mahayana path, and thus achieve enlightenment. Otherwise, if our guru doesn't emphasize cherishing others, we will have no opportunity to develop bodhicitta. In essence, we should choose as our guru somebody who emphasizes cherishing others through the practice of loving kindness, compassion and bodhicitta.

Failing that, choose a spiritual teacher who emphasizes liberation from samsara rather than samsaric pleasures. If our virtuous teacher doesn't emphasize cherishing others, he should at least be someone who looks at samsaric perfections as suffering and emphasizes liberation, because in this way we have the opportunity to achieve liberation.

At the very least choose a spiritual master who regards working for the happiness of future lives as more important than working for the happiness of this life. If our spiritual teacher doesn't emphasize this, he can't guide us even in the path to the happiness of future lives, which means to a good rebirth. If aimed only at the happiness of this life, our practice won't even become holy Dharma. Even if we're meditating every day, there's the danger that what we do will become purely non-virtue, purely attachment to the happiness of this life. If our teacher doesn't emphasize detachment from this life's pleasures and working for long-term happiness, the happiness of future lives, there's the danger that we'll waste our life completely caught up in meaningless activities for the happiness of this life.

Whether our teacher is ordained or lay, the very essence is that he should emphasize these three things: by emphasizing bodhicitta, he is able to bring us to enlightenment; by emphasizing liberation from samsara, he is able to bring us to liberation; and by emphasizing letting go of clinging to this life and working for the happiness of all the coming future lives, he enables us to achieve the happiness of future lives. Those who know how to practice lam-rim regard these as the main qualities to examine before establishing a samaya relationship with a guru. Otherwise, without these qualities, even if a person is very scholarly and has great knowledge, it will be difficult for him to successfully guide disciples to enlightenment.

If the guru has at least the very basic qualities that I have mentioned, it will help us to avoid the danger of later engaging in the heavy negative karma of generating anger, heresy or other negative thoughts toward the guru, and also of giving up the guru.

The fundamental quality

Among all the many different qualities to consider in choosing a guru, the fundamental thing to examine is whether the person emphasizes the practice of morality, or ethics. As described in the first verse of the requesting prayer in *Guru Puja*,[25] the fundamental point according to Lama Tsongkhapa's teaching is living in the morality of ordination. However, whether the virtuous teacher is lay or ordained, the basic quality is that he himself should live in morality and emphasize the practice of morality, because otherwise there is no basis for realization. Disciples who don't practice morality, which means protecting karma, can't achieve even the happiness of a good rebirth in their next life, let alone liberation from samsara. Just as you can't hold liquid without a container, you can't receive the body of a happy migratory being—a human or deva—in your next life without living in morality. Without the practice of morality, you can't even be protected from the lower realms. If the guru is someone who emphasizes morality, he's able to protect the disciple from negative karma, the obstacle to achievement of enlightenment, liberation and the happiness of future lives. The disciple is then able to achieve temporary and ultimate happiness.

Tibetans who know the essence of lam-rim practice don't decide on their gurus by checking how famous or learned they are because they know that successful practice has to do with samaya. Those who know how to correctly devote themselves to the virtuous friend, as Lama Atisha did with Lama Suvarnadvipi, check the lifestyle of the person and his practice, including

---

[25] Source of virtue, great ocean of moral discipline,
 Treasury brimming with jewels of much hearing,
 Master, second buddha clad in saffron,
 Elder, Vinaya-holder, I make requests to you. (V. 43.)

how he devotes to his virtuous friends. On that basis, they then decide. A person could be famous and very learned but have some corruption in the samaya with his gurus. Even though one could learn intellectually from such a person, it would be difficult to complete the practice and gain real benefit. Real benefit doesn't come from just learning the words, like in school or university, but from subduing the mind.

For Lama Ösel, Lama Yeshe's reincarnation, the most important factor in his life and what will determine his success in benefiting the world is the guidance of his virtuous friends. This is why at different times over the years I have made many observations to choose his virtuous friends; it is my biggest responsibility. I have mainly been choosing on the basis of the person's practice, not because of his reputation of being learned or famous.

As a child, Lama Ösel learnt Tibetan prayers and Tibetan writing from an ascetic monk, Geshe Thubten, who was one of Lama Yeshe's best friends. While His Holiness the Dalai Lama gave Lama Ösel his very first lesson in the Tibetan alphabet, Geshe Thubten taught him the rest of the letters, spelling and writing. Geshe Thubten and Lama Yeshe were in the same class at Sera Je Monastery and had a very good samaya bond between them, though they were not in a teacher-disciple relationship. This is why we requested Geshe-la to teach Lama Ösel the alphabet.

Lama Yeshe often used to praise Geshe Thubten, saying that he really knew Dharma. Even though some monks were able to debate well and were regarded as learned, Lama would sometimes say of this one or that, "Oh, his understanding of Dharma is just superficial—he doesn't have any deep understanding."

In the observations, Geshe Thubten came out many times as beneficial, but another reason I chose him is that Geshe-la himself is a very good practitioner, an ascetic monk with a very good understanding of Dharma and very good samaya with his gurus, especially Geshe Rabten Rinpoche.

Being learned is not the most important quality of a teacher. It is not enough that the virtuous friend has vast intellectual knowledge or can teach well. Having knowledge alone doesn't mean that a person can benefit others. Of course, the virtuous friend also needs knowledge, but that is not the only thing that can bring real benefit. The main thing to check is the quality of his samaya. Even if someone is very learned and capable, if he has broken samaya with his virtuous friends, no matter how great his learning or reputation, it will be difficult for him to really benefit the minds of his disciples. We are talking here about benefit that is deep and long-lasting, not just making someone happy and excited for an hour. We are talking about long-term benefit and success, up to enlightenment, which is the greatest benefit.

If the virtuous friend is a good practitioner with pure samaya, even if he isn't very wise or knowledgeable, he can benefit his disciples; disciples who correctly devote themselves to that virtuous friend can become learned, develop realizations and benefit many sentient beings.

An additional qualification

I want to specifically add one extra qualification to the usual ones explained in the teachings. If you are about to make a new Dharma connection, these days you should also examine to make sure the person is not somebody who opposes the wishes of His Holiness the Dalai Lama; in other words, make sure the person is not a practitioner of the spirit.[26] If you are about to make a Dharma connection with someone for the first time, check this point so that you don't run into problems later.

For a long while, I tried not to get involved in talking about the issue of the spirit in public but responded only to individual people who wrote to me about it. I never engaged in public debate on this issue, apart from at the Gelugpa meeting in Delhi, where I mentioned that we should follow His Holiness's wishes. However, I recently made some protective guidelines for all the FPMT centers; one of them is that before inviting a teacher, the center should check whether or not the person opposes His Holiness the Dalai Lama, whether or not he or she is practicing the spirit. This is for the protection of individual students as well as the organization.

This doesn't mean that the gurus who practiced the spirit in the past are bad or that you should become careless about the advice of those gurus. It is mentioned in both sutra and tantra teachings that we shouldn't create the heavy negative karma of criticizing or giving up the guru. Be careful not to lose faith in any of your gurus. It is not that the guru has made a mistake. This is the appearance of your karma, of your impure mind, at this time. Or you can think that these gurus have purposely manifested in this way, because showing faults is the only way they can communicate with you and

---

[26] The spirit is Dorje Shugden. His Holiness the Dalai Lama has asked his followers to stop the practice of this spirit. For further details see *The Fourteen Dalai Lamas*, pp. 209–10. See also Rinpoche's advice on the spirit on www.fpmt.org and www.LamaYeshe.com.

guide you to enlightenment. You don't have to criticize your gurus who do the practice. It doesn't have to bring conflict into your life or destroy your devotion. The main reason we practice guru devotion is to benefit ourselves because we disciples want profit and don't want loss. Our aim is to achieve the highest profit, enlightenment.

If you have gurus who practiced the spirit in the past but have now passed away, if they were existing in the same aspect now, they would also have stopped the practice. His Holiness himself did the spirit practice for a short while, but after many experiences and signs and a lot of analysis, His Holiness advised against this practice. And His Holiness is not the only one who is saying this. Many other high lamas, holders of the entire Buddhadharma, have given similar instructions to their monasteries.

After checking his own experiences and in many other ways, His Holiness came to the conclusion that it would be of greater benefit to individuals, as well as to the world, to stop doing the practice. His Holiness himself stopped and also advised others to stop. Many other great teachers have already stopped doing this practice, even though they had practiced it before.

Even though various monasteries and groups of people have asked His Holiness to change his mind, His Holiness reached this decision after many years of analysis and will never change from this view. His Holiness has kept on insisting in his teachings that he will never change from advising against this practice.

Geshe Lobsang Tsephel[27] told me that when he went to see His Holiness Trijang Rinpoche to ask for advice on the issue of the spirit, His Holiness said that when you visualize the merit field, you visualize the guru first; the guru is the highest one. After the guru, you visualize the buddhas, then the bodhisattvas, the arhats, the dakas and dakinis, and then the Dharma protectors come at the very end. Rinpoche said, "You should listen to what your guru, His Holiness the Dalai Lama, says. Who is more important, the guru or the protector? The guru is more important. Even when you visualize the merit field, the guru comes first." It is a mistake to think that what the spirit says is more important than what the guru says.[28]

My point of view is that we should stop this practice, not because we are

[27] Geshe Lobsang Tsephel, abbot of Ganden Jangtse College, is the director of Land of Compassion Buddha near Los Angeles, California.
[28] This spirit used to be referred to as a protector but Lama Zopa Rinpoche says it is more appropriate to call it a spirit.

careless about the advice of other gurus, but because this is the advice we have been given by His Holiness the Dalai Lama, the Buddha of Compassion.

Guru Shakyamuni Buddha himself made the prediction that the Dalai Lamas, incarnations of Chenrezig, would be Dharma kings working for sentient beings in the Land of Snow, Tibet. When Buddha was in India, he made this prediction to one of the bodhisattvas who usually accompanied him:

> When the teaching of Buddha degenerates in India, at that time you will be Chenrezig, the Buddha of Compassion, and the sentient beings in the Snow Land will be objects to be subdued by you. At that time you will lead the sentient beings of Tibet to have faith in Buddha, Dharma and Sangha, and you will then spread Buddhadharma like the rising sun.

During one of His Holiness's visits to Deer Park, Geshe Sopa Rinpoche's center in Madison, Wisconsin, His Holiness said in a teaching, as His Holiness often does, "I have no realization of bodhicitta or emptiness or anything else, but I have strong faith in them." Later, during a group interview, somebody asked His Holiness, "You say you don't have any realization, so how is it possible for us? We have no hope!" As this was expressed strongly, His Holiness had to respond in some way, so he let slip from his holy mouth as a kind of private comment, "Actually, I remember that I was with Shakyamuni Buddha in India."

His Holiness the Dalai Lama is also an incarnation of Dromtönpa, Lama Atisha's great Tibetan translator, an embodiment of the Buddha of Compassion. Dromtönpa is known to be in the line of reincarnations.

No other lama can benefit the world as much as His Holiness can. His Holiness is the source of the peace and happiness of sentient beings in this world. Millions of ordinary people, even non-Buddhists, not only in the East but also in the West, can see that His Holiness is someone whose holy body is filled with great compassion and wisdom. His Holiness is able to bring unbelievable peace and happiness to others. Simply seeing His Holiness has inspired many thousands of people to have faith in Buddhism. We know the positive effect, the incredible peace and happiness, that comes by seeing his holy body, hearing his holy speech or reading His Holiness's teachings. Anyone who sees and especially hears His Holiness definitely plants seeds of enlightenment. Simply seeing His Holiness brings great purification.

Even though there are many Buddhist traditions and many holy beings in this world, no one else benefits the world the way His Holiness the Dalai Lama does. There are many religious leaders in the world, but there is no one like His Holiness, who can benefit sentient beings so much. Even though there are many Buddhist leaders, there is no one like His Holiness who can benefit so much to the world. Even among the high lamas, there is no one like His Holiness, who can benefit so much to the world. And even among the incarnations of the Dalai Lamas, of whom there are now fourteen, there hasn't been anyone like this incarnation. This fourteenth Dalai Lama has benefited the world the most, and more and more in the West. The previous incarnations benefited the East but this one is now benefiting the whole world. His Holiness is the one who has the greatest impact in bringing peace in this world, in changing negative thoughts into positive.

What differentiates Buddhism from other religions is compassion for sentient beings without any discrimination. Because of that compassion, one stops giving harm to other living beings and, on top of that, tries to benefit others. In His Holiness, people see the best example of what Buddhism talks about, compassion as well as wisdom. By seeing His Holiness, even though they may not have read any books on Buddhism, they develop some interest in what a Buddhist is.

In fact, simply seeing the holy body of His Holiness plants the seed of enlightenment and inspires people to develop compassion and wisdom. Even people who don't understand what enlightenment or liberation is can feel that His Holiness is a pure being. Listening to His Holiness speak, people get a very broad view of Buddhism in a very short time, in half an hour or an hour. The quickest way to learn about Buddhism is to listen to one of His Holiness's public teachings.

His Holiness has taken responsibility for the entire Buddhadharma, not only for the Hinayana teachings and the Mahayana Paramitayana teachings, but also the Mahayana Vajrayana teachings. His Holiness has taken responsibility for the preservation and spread of the entire teaching of Buddha. His Holiness is the one who is able to preserve these teachings in this world and spread them in the most extensive and quickest way.

Because of His Holiness the Dalai Lama's guidance, all the monasteries that were destroyed in Tibet have been re-established in India and the monks have been able to continue their extensive studies. Just like in Tibet, those monasteries, especially Sera, Ganden and Drepung, have been able to produce many qualified teachers to spread Buddhadharma in the world with depth and clarity. After all the trouble in Tibet, the whole Dharma has still been preserved and is being spread to others, especially the young. This is totally by the kindness of His Holiness the Dalai Lama. It has all come about because of his compassionate guidance.

Even though there are many other monasteries, without Sera, Ganden and Drepung and the tantric colleges as centers of learning, Buddhism would be lost in this world. Without these monasteries there would be no place in the world to learn extensively and in depth, studying with many learned scholars. The same applies to monasteries of the other traditions. Their survival, their ability to re-establish and continue their traditions, is solely by the kindness of His Holiness the Dalai Lama, who, after escaping from Tibet, requested permission from Prime Minister Nehru for the Tibetans to live in India.

For the Tibetan people, of course, His Holiness is the sole object of refuge. On top of that, His Holiness has taken full responsibility for the Tibetan people, who have a particular karmic connection with Chenrezig. The reason that so many people in the West have been able to meet His Holiness and hear teachings and receive advice not just one time but many times is that they also have a connection with the Buddha of Compassion. It is not just the Tibetan people. However, there is a particular connection with Tibetans, with His Holiness guiding them not only in a spiritual way by teaching Dharma but also by guiding the whole country.

It is now similar with Western people. You should know that every day you are being guided by Chenrezig. It is because of His Holiness that Buddhism has been able to spread to the West. If His Holiness hadn't come out of Tibet but had instead decided to leave this world, Buddhism wouldn't have spread in the rest of the world. You wouldn't have been able to meet Buddhism and make your lives meaningful. It would have been impossible; it would never have happened if His Holiness had stayed in Tibet or had passed away.

Without His Holiness's existence in this form in this world, we would have a human body, but our mind would be like that of an animal, with no understanding of Dharma. Everything we did in our daily life would then be negative karma. We would have no understanding of reincarnation and karma, no understanding of how the motivation can make an action virtuous and the cause of happiness or non-virtuous and the cause of suffering. Our attitude, if not one of anger, would usually be one of attachment to this life. Therefore, even though we might not be killing people or stealing, every single thing we did twenty-four hours a day would be only negative karma, the cause of suffering. Without the existence of His Holiness in a human form that is able to spread Dharma and without His Holiness being outside Tibet, we wouldn't have had this chance. Right now we would have a human body but the mind of an animal.

We are receiving guidance from His Holiness the Dalai Lama, from Chenrezig, all the time. Every time we generate a motivation of bodhicitta, every time we meditate on bodhicitta, we are receiving guidance from Chenrezig; we are experiencing the kindness of Chenrezig. Every time we purify our past negative karma and every time we collect merit, we are receiving guidance from Chenrezig.

A patient's recovery from a sickness doesn't depend only on a knowledgeable doctor diagnosing her illness and giving a prescription for the correct medicine; from her side the patient has to take the medicine. Only then can she recover. In a similar way, even though there is an actual living Buddha of Compassion, the freedom or independence of Tibet is not only up to the Buddha of Compassion but also depends on the karma of the Tibetan people. From their side the Tibetan people have to put effort into creating the cause for that. If it were solely up to the Buddha of Compassion, not only would there be no suffering Tibetan people; there wouldn't be any suffering sentient beings at all by now.

Because His Holiness has unbelievable qualities, His Holiness is able to bring benefit as limitless as the sky to the teaching of Buddha and to sentient beings. His Holiness has taken responsibility for sentient beings in general and for those of this world in particular. His Holiness has also been carrying all the heavy responsibility while Tibet has been having a very difficult time. His Holiness carries so many responsibilities, for the peace and happiness of all the sentient beings in this world, for all the teachings of Buddha and for the independence of Tibet.

That is why we should support His Holiness and follow His Holiness's advice. The more support we offer, the more His Holiness can benefit sentient beings with all his oceans of qualities. Since we ourselves don't have those qualities, though we do have the potential for them, we cannot benefit in the way that His Holiness the Dalai Lama can. But if we offer our support and don't cause any obstacles, His Holiness can benefit not only Tibetans and the sentient beings in this world but all sentient beings.

If people do exactly what His Holiness wishes, which means following his advice in relation to the issue of the spirit, it helps His Holiness to have a longer life, so that His Holiness can benefit sentient beings even more. The whole purpose of our life is to benefit sentient beings as extensively as possible. We can't benefit sentient beings the way His Holiness does. Even if we teach Dharma courses, only sixty or seventy people come, but when His Holiness gives teachings, many thousands or even hundreds of thousands of people come. The quickest way to liberate sentient beings is to support His Holiness. His Holiness will then be healthy and have a longer life, and sentient beings will receive extensive, deep benefit and will quickly become enlightened.

That is the reasoning I use to follow His Holiness's advice. The reason is not a narrow one but as vast as the limitless sky. It doesn't involve thinking of yourself and your own happiness, but of all sentient beings and what can most benefit them.

5. The Qualities of a Disciple

BASICALLY, a disciple's achievement of enlightenment depends upon both the guru and the disciple. The guru should be someone who is perfectly qualified to lead the disciple in the complete path to enlightenment, but if the disciple doesn't have the fortune to be led in this path, she won't become enlightened. If the guru is perfectly qualified and the disciple also has the fortune to be led in the complete path, enlightenment comes very easily.

The Seventh Dalai Lama, Kelsang Gyatso, said:

> If a perfectly qualified guru meets a disciple who is a fit receptacle, enlightenment comes very easily, like printing a *tsa-tsa* in clay.

When you make a tsa-tsa from a perfect mold, the image of buddha comes out easily and perfectly in the clay, without any details missing. In a similar way, enlightenment comes easily and perfectly to a qualified disciple.

A perfectly qualified guru is one with all the necessary qualities to guide a disciple in the complete path to enlightenment. A disciple who is a fit receptacle is one who is able to bear hardships in order to practice the advice given by the guru, in order to practice Dharma.

In *Ornament of Mahayana Sutras* Maitreya Buddha describes the qualities of a disciple in the following way:

> The disciple should be impartial and intelligent and yearn for teachings. A disciple who is a fit receptacle is also one who is

able to bear hardships to accomplish the Dharma taught by the guru. One who is lazy and cannot bear even small hardships cannot accomplish the Dharma taught by the guru. When a disciple who has great will to achieve enlightenment in one brief lifetime, like the great Milarepa, and whose mind and body are both strong and able to bear hardships of hunger, thirst, heat and cold meets a perfect guru, such a disciple can achieve enlightenment in one brief lifetime.

In *Liberation in the Palm of Your Hand*, Pabongka Dechen Nyingpo mentions five qualities that a disciple should have. A good disciple is: impartial, intelligent, hardworking, has great respect for her guru and listens carefully to her guru's instructions.

If we're impartial, we're able to examine and understand other views. If we're willing to check both sides of an argument, we have the opportunity to learn through clarifying what is right and what is wrong.

If we're biased toward our own wrong beliefs, on the other hand, we never even allow ourselves to examine other views and thus have no opportunity to learn. We don't listen to what is said and don't allow ourselves to examine and understand the teachings. For example, if we take reincarnation to be complete nonsense, no matter how much it is explained using logic and quotations, we won't even take the time to understand the teachings on reincarnation. We will stubbornly hold to our own wrong view. If we don't have an impartial mind, the teachings won't benefit us because we won't take them to heart. Stuck in our own philosophical view, we won't practice the teachings taught by the virtuous friend, so it will be difficult for the virtuous teacher to guide us.

A disciple who is intelligent means one who is able to discriminate right from wrong.

Also, the tantric text *Net of Illusion* mentions that a disciple should like meditation and virtue, have devotion to the spiritual master and like to perform the daily practice of making offerings.

6. Who to Regard as Guru

Taking teachings

WE ESTABLISH a Dharma connection with someone when, on the basis of the recognition that that person is our guru and we are his disciple, we then receive even a single verse of teaching from him. Making the very first Dharma contact depends on our merit and our past karma.

It is said in the teachings that simply hearing Dharma from somebody doesn't establish Dharma contact and make that person your guru. You can hear Dharma from someone and study with him without necessarily regarding him as your guru; you make a connection with him, but not a guru-disciple connection. However, once you have taken a teaching by thinking of yourself as a disciple and the other person as your guru, even if it is only a teaching on one verse of Dharma or the oral transmission of one mantra, Dharma contact is established, which means you have formed a guru-disciple relationship, even if you didn't find the teaching effective for your mind.

With respect to accepting someone as a guru, if from the very beginning you don't have any wish to make a guru-disciple connection, you can listen to that person's teaching as if you're learning from a professor in a university. Generally, you can learn Dharma, especially sutra teachings and explanations, from someone just out of educational interest, to acquire knowledge, like studying with a professor or learning Buddhist history at school. Simply hearing the Dharma from someone doesn't mean you have established a guru-disciple relationship with that person because you do this all the time in Dharma discussions with your friends. When you discuss points with a friend who knows how to explain them, you don't regard that person as your guru. You are just helping each other.

While you can listen to Dharma teachings for educational purposes, you need to make the distinction clear from the very beginning as to whether or not you are going to devote yourself to the person as a virtuous friend. However, after some time, if you feel strong devotion in your heart or you see that you have benefited a lot from someone's teachings and want to establish a guru-disciple relationship, you can then devote yourself to that person as your guru. At that time you can make the decision. *Devote* means devoting your life to your guru by following his guidance in accordance with the explanations of Guru Shakyamuni Buddha in the sutra and tantra teachings, which is also the way that Lama Tsongkhapa and all the lineage lamas of the four traditions explained and practiced guru devotion. Whether or not you can devote yourself to someone mainly depends on your own attitude, your own way of thinking.

What do you do if in the past you have heard teachings from various people but don't remember making a particular decision to recognize them as your guru? If you don't remember any particular benefit to your mind from those teachings and didn't take them with a determination to establish Dharma contact, you can leave those teachers in equanimity. This means that you don't need to regard them as your guru but you also don't need to criticize them. Also, if somebody tells you that you don't need to devote yourself to him as a virtuous friend you can leave the matter in equanimity. But if listening to someone's teaching has benefited your mind, if you can, it is better to regard that person as your guru.

This is the advice the great bodhisattva Khunu Lama Tenzin Gyaltsen gave me when I checked with him about how to regard two of the teachers I had when I was young. When I was a child in Solu Khumbu, I lived part of the time with my mother and the rest of my family in Thangme, the village where I was born, and the rest of the time in Thangme Monastery with my first alphabet teacher, Ngawang Lekshe, who was also one of my uncles. The monastery was about a fifteen-minute walk up the hill from my home.

My uncle and many other monks and lay people were disciples of Lama Döndrub, a Nyingma tantric practitioner, or *ngakpa*, the head of the monastery, from whom they received many initiations and teachings. Like a puppy, I went along with my uncle and the other monks to whatever was happening. It was a little like going to the movies or to a party. I went along because something was happening and everybody else was going.

At that time I was a small child, perhaps four or five years old, and not yet a monk. During the many teachings, initiations and oral transmissions,

I sat on someone's lap and, of course, slept most of time. I could hear the words but I had no understanding of their meaning. I didn't even know the names of the initiations. I remember only certain physical activities, such as circumambulating and blowing a conch shell—I blew it but it didn't make any noise.

I just sat on someone's lap and watched the faces of the lama, seated on a high throne, and of the monk who read the text. Though I don't remember a single word of any teaching, I remember very well the lama's face. Simply seeing the lama benefited my mind. We used to call him "Gaga Lama"— *gaga* means grandfather in the Sherpa language. I enjoyed looking at the old lama, who looked like the long-life man, with white hair and a long white beard. (He has since passed away and reincarnated.) He was a lay lama, a married tantric practitioner, not a monk. He was a very good lama, with an incredibly kind heart, and I liked him very much. When he did pujas in the morning he would use a drum, and when I heard the drum I used to go to see him. I would open the curtain at the door and wait. The lama would then come down with popcorn or some other present. We should get presents like that again and again.

When the lama himself gave a teaching, he would sit very straight and never moved—not like me! He would speak, then always look at a particular spot on the ceiling. Sitting in the lap of one of the monks, I stared at the lama's face and looked wherever he was looking. I looked at the spot on the ceiling, wondering why he always looked at the same place, but there was nothing there—just the painted wood of the ceiling. At other times a senior monk, one of the lama's closest disciples, would read the oral transmission from the text, with the lama sitting on the throne, sometimes in the aspect of sleeping. I don't know why the oral transmission was given in this particular way; it seemed to be the custom.

Sometimes the lama would drink some *chang*, or barley beer, from a nice glass jar that had probably been offered to him by a Western trekker. The glass would be full of chang, with the barley grains at the bottom, and the lama would use a glass tube to drink from it. While his disciple was reading the text, the lama would sit there, sipping the beer from time to time, and sometimes showing the aspect of sleeping. Because I was in the front row looking at the lama as he drank the chang, he used to pass the jar down to me and I would drink a little.

In Solu Khumbu, Bhutan and other parts of the Himalayas, some of the monasteries had a mixture of monks and married lay practitioners. There was corruption in some of the monasteries, where it had become the custom for monks to drink beer. The lama himself was a lay tantric practitioner and drinking alcohol is not harmful to a highly realized tantric practitioner; it only helps him or her to have quick attainment of the tantric path. Alcohol and other intoxicants cannot harm yogis who have realizations of clear light and the illusory body because they have control over their chakras, winds and drops. They are beyond danger from alcohol and beyond non-virtuous actions.

I remember the part of drinking the beer very clearly but I don't remember a single word that the lama said, even though I was there during many initiations when the lama spoke a lot about Dharma. It was like receiving an initiation in a dream and not remembering anything when you wake up. Nothing stayed in my mind. Of course, imprints may have been left, but I remember nothing in particular that benefited my mind.

Even though, because I was a child, I had made no particular decision to form a guru-disciple relationship with Lama Döndrub and I hadn't understood a single word of his teachings, I visualized this lama in the merit field for some years. Later, when Khunu Lama Rinpoche came to Nepal, I went to ask him several questions about guru yoga practice. Even though I had been visualizing this lama as my guru for some years, I asked Rinpoche whether or not I should regard him as my guru. Rinpoche said, "If you remember that the teaching benefited your mind, it is better to regard him as your virtuous friend." But Rinpoche also said that since I didn't remember anything at all, I didn't need to recognize him as my virtuous friend. Rinpoche added that there was no need for me to criticize the lama—I could just leave the matter in equanimity. After that, I didn't visualize this particular lama in the merit field any more.

Khunu Lama Rinpoche's advice was that if we have received teachings from somebody, we should check whether or not the teachings have benefited our mind. Even if we didn't listen to a teaching with the idea of forming a guru-disciple relationship, if the teaching benefited our mind, it is better to regard that person as a virtuous friend, if we can. If we can't find any benefit to our mind, we can leave the matter in equanimity; we don't need to criticize that person.

This advice is practical, because it is good to be careful in any case. Even if someone is not our guru, he could still be a holy being, a buddha or a bodhisattva. If the person is a holy being, we create heavy negative karma if we have negative thoughts toward him or harm him. Just to be careful, to protect our own happiness, it is better to leave the matter in equanimity.

In *Collection of Advice from Here and There*, Langri Thangpa advises, "Since you don't know other people's level of mind, you shouldn't criticize them."[29] Just because someone doesn't appear to us to have great attainments, it doesn't mean that this is actually the case. What appears to us and what actually exists are not the same.

The text later says, "If you have generated bodhicitta, it is shameful to criticize others." As we have taken bodhisattva vows, we shouldn't criticize others. Also, if, out of anger or another negative mind we criticize someone who has received an initiation from the same vajra guru, we incur the tantric root fall of criticizing a vajra brother. If we aren't careful, we receive this root fall of the third tantric vow.

It is also mentioned in *The Great Treatise on the Stages of the Path to Enlightenment* and other lam-rim teachings that your realizations degenerate if you criticize a fully ordained monk, even if you don't have a guru-disciple relationship with him.

Generally, in the teachings of Kadampa thought training we are advised to practice looking at anybody who mistreats us as our guru. This is done to control our anger and thoughts to retaliate so that we don't create more negative karma. Any harmful action done to us by others appears as a teaching if we look at them as our guru. The thought-transformation teachings even advise us to look at all sentient beings as our guru or as Guru Shakyamuni Buddha. This is mainly to control our own mind, not so much because the sentient beings themselves are in fact buddhas. If we train our mind in this way, we naturally respect other sentient beings, and since anger and other negative thoughts won't arise, it protects us from creating negative karma. We train ourselves to think of sentient beings as precious and the source of all happiness, just like the guru. It is similar to practicing pure view in tantra, where we see all sentient beings as the deity.

It is excellent to look at everyone as our guru. But if we can't manage that, we still have no need to criticize anyone. We shouldn't criticize anyone, unless it somehow benefits that person.

From Nepal I went to Tibet and lived there for a few years. I was there until about nine months after China took over Tibet. I became a monk in Tibet at the monastery of the great yogi Domo Geshe Rinpoche, the guru

---

[29] See *The Book of Kadam*, p. 594, or *The Door of Liberation*, p. 116.

of Lama Govinda, who wrote *The Way of the White Clouds* and *Foundations of Tibetan Mysticism*. I was ordained as a novice monk by the abbot, Thubten Jinpa, a very good, very subdued geshe. I also can't remember anything that the abbot said at the time of my ordination. The only thing I can remember clearly is sitting in front of the abbot and other people giving me a lot of *khatags*.

My first retreat, which I did in Tibet just before escaping, was on *Lama Tsongkhapa Guru Yoga*, but I had no idea at all what I was doing. I hadn't received any teachings. Though I now regard him as a guru, Losang Gyatso, the monk who took care of me in Tibet and helped me to become a monk in Domo Geshe's monastery, didn't explain any Dharma to me. He just verbally taught me *Praise to the Twenty-one Taras*, which I didn't know by heart before that. When I checked with Kirti Tsenshab Rinpoche, Rinpoche said I should regard him as a guru because he verbally taught me the prayer, even though he didn't specifically give me any Dharma teachings or vows. Losang Gyatso gave me a text on *Lama Tsongkhapa Guru Yoga* but at the time I didn't have the capacity to understand it. I believed that I finished reciting 100,000 *migtsemas*. I then did a *tsog* offering, which Losang Gyatso had arranged beautifully. That same night we escaped from Tibet.

At that time the Communist Chinese were publicly torturing the heads of monasteries, leaders of the people and anybody who had a name as somebody important. When we heard that they were within a day or two of reaching the monastery where we lived, Pema Chöling, a branch of Domo Geshe's main monastery, we escaped that night through Bhutan to India. I went with Losang Gyatso together with some monks from Pema Chöling and some other monks that we met on the road. From Pema Chöling, which is near the border of Tibet, we had to cross only one mountain to reach Bhutan. There we met up with many monks and benefactors, then went to Buxa Duar in West Bengal.

Buxa Duar was the concentration camp where Mahatma Gandhi and Prime Minister Nehru were imprisoned when India was under British rule. This is where the monks from Lhasa and other places who wanted to continue their study were sent. Those who didn't want to study went to work building roads in different parts of India, especially at first along the border with Tibet. There were about 1,500 monks at Buxa. Because of the heat and unhygienic conditions, many monks got TB and many of them passed away.

We didn't have to stay in Buxa, as Domo Geshe Rinpoche had also founded a branch monastery in Darjeeling. As this monastery was well established, we didn't have anything to worry about. However, while all the other monks from Domo Geshe's monastery were allowed to go to the Darjeeling monastery, the head policeman of the camp, Tashi Babu, who was Indian but possibly of Tibetan origin, wouldn't allow Losang Gyatso and me to go to Darjeeling. I don't know why he didn't let us go. He had no reason to stop us—he wasn't being paid any money to do it. I thought that maybe the abbot or one of the staff of Sera Je Monastery went to the police, but that doesn't seem to have been the case. Whether it was the buddhas or the Dharma protectors, something made that policeman stop me from going away and made me stay at Buxa. I think it might have been the action of the special deity, because that is how I got the chance to meet my perfect gurus, Geshe Rabten Rinpoche and Lama Yeshe. I had this chance and the chance to study a little of the philosophical subjects and hear lamrim teachings through the kindness of this policeman.

Before I met Geshe Rabten Rinpoche, Losang Gyatso took me to another lama that he somehow knew. I went to him for teachings for an hour or so for just two or three days and studied with him one verse from the very beginning of *dura*, the preliminary debating subject. After two or three days, for some reason—perhaps because I belonged to Sera Je and he was from Drepung Monastery—he said, "I can't be your teacher. You should go to Geshe Rabten, who is from Sera Je College." He said that Geshe Rabten Rinpoche was a very good teacher and that it would be good for me to take teachings from him.

I also checked with Khunu Lama Rinpoche about whether I should regard this lama as my guru. Rinpoche said that generally it is good to regard such a person as a guru, but since he had said that he couldn't be my teacher, which was like giving me permission not to regard him as a guru, Rinpoche said that I didn't need to devote to him as a guru. Again, Khunu Lama said that I also didn't need to generate any negative thoughts toward him. Because of Rinpoche's advice, I don't include this lama among my gurus.

When I asked Kyabje Chöden Rinpoche about this point, Rinpoche said that the teacher also has to recognize you as a disciple.

It was very kind of this lama to introduce me to Geshe Rabten Rinpoche, a great hidden yogi. Geshe Rabten was very learned, a good teacher, pure in morality, very kind and good-hearted, and renowned in all the monasteries. Geshe Rabten Rinpoche's way of devoting to his virtuous friends was also incomparable. Geshe Rabten had two root gurus, His Holiness Trijang

Rinpoche and the lama who took great care of him in his home monastery. Geshe Rinpoche's way of guiding disciples, as well as his way of teaching and talking, was unbelievably skillful, exactly in accord with each disciple's wishes and capabilities.

That I now have a little bit of interest in meditation is by the kindness of Geshe Rabten Rinpoche because he was the first guru to explain Dharma to me. Since Geshe Rinpoche was talking a lot about calm abiding, my first interest was in calm abiding.

The first time I went to see Geshe Rabten Rinpoche to take teachings, I went with Losang Gyatso and took a tea offering in a thermos and some other offering. Geshe Rinpoche and many disciples were crowded into a courtyard outside one of the buildings, a long prison block with many gun-slots in the walls and doors and windows covered with bars and barbed wire. The courtyard was also not a very pleasant place. All the walls were barbed wire, so you couldn't lean on them without cutting yourself. And all the monks' seats were crowded tightly together, with Geshe Rinpoche sitting up on a high seat.

Lama Yeshe was sitting down below Geshe Rabten, with a big pile of texts on his table. Because I was very small and had the name "incarnation," Lama lifted me up and put me on Geshe-la's bed. During the teaching, Lama sometimes looked at Geshe-la's face with great devotion. I could see that he was extremely devoted to Geshe Rabten.

I took teachings like this several times, but Geshe Rabten had many disciples and was very busy. As he had to teach various classes to different levels of monks, including many senior ones, he didn't have much time to teach me on my own. Geshe-la sent me to one of his disciples, Gen Yeshe, a very good debater, who was from the same area in Tibet as Geshe Rinpoche. From Gen Yeshe I heard for the first time about the kindness of the mother from the seven techniques of Mahayana cause and effect.[30] There were no texts, so Gen Yeshe explained it orally and I wrote it down in my own writing, as I hadn't learnt how to write properly from anyone. He also taught me a little about the visualizations in *Lama Tsongkhapa Guru Yoga*.

Gen Yeshe was very learned and very humorous and joyful. He was also

---

[30] The six causes are recognizing all living beings as our mothers, remembering their kindness, wishing to repay their kindness, developing the affection that sees them as lovable, cultivating compassion and the special attitude, and the one effect is bodhicitta.

a great teacher, similar to Lama Yeshe. However, my time with Gen Yeshe was very short. Rather than be at Buxa, he wanted to live an ascetic life and go on pilgrimage around India. He didn't stay at Buxa long but left to wander around India. After some time he became a lay person, then showed the aspect of sickness and passed away in India.

I then went to Lama Yeshe for teachings. Chöphel (pronounced "Chombi"), the leader of my class and later a cook at Kopan Monastery, first brought me to take teachings from Lama Yeshe, as he had been taking teachings from him for a long time. Geshe Rabten Rinpoche actually wanted me to take teachings from one of his close disciples, Geshe Thubten, a well-educated and very good monk, but somehow my karma was different. My manager, Losang Gyatso, also had Geshe Thubten in mind.

Even though my manager was saying that I should study with Geshe Thubten, Chombi insisted that I take teachings from Lama Yeshe. We used to walk together sometimes around the hills or go to the river to bathe, and one day he simply led me to the gate of the monastery. I said, "I don't want to go any further! I don't want to receive teachings from Lama Yeshe. I want to go back home." Chombi said, "Oh, come, come, come." He insisted so much that I went a few more steps with him. Again I said, "No, I don't want to go." I walked a few more steps, then again said, "No, I don't want to go. I want to go back." Carrying on like this, I finally ended up outside Lama Yeshe's room. Again I told him, "I don't want to go. I want to go back."

I waited outside while Chombi went inside to see Lama. I hadn't brought any offerings with me as I had simply accompanied Chombi on a walk. Chombi himself piled up some rice in a bowl, offered it with a scarf and a few rupees and asked Lama if I could take teachings from him. I think Lama asked whether Geshe Rabten Rinpoche had agreed to it or not and Chombi said that he had, even though that wasn't exactly what Geshe Rabten Rinpoche had in mind. As Chombi had already made the offering, I reluctantly went inside.

Lama Yeshe had a tiny room in the jungle, with a window at the back with a nest of ants. There was almost nothing in the room—it was practically empty. There was a small stove made out of an Indian butter tin with a hole at the bottom for firewood and only two pots. There were also some texts covered with plastic and a hard split-bamboo bed with some Bhutanese woven material on top. That's all. It was extremely simple.

That first day, because I bore the label "reincarnate lama," Lama again put me next to him on his bed. I think that Lama putting me on his bed at the very beginning might be why there has been the karma for me to sit on a throne.

I didn't understand anything at all, maybe because I hadn't come with a good motivation. Lama was teaching about cause and effect, but debating the subject. He was so quick that the question came in my mind, "Why can't he teach slowly?" The next day was better, but that first day I couldn't understand anything at all.

I think there was strong karma from many past lives for Lama Yeshe to guide me. I didn't come with the intention of receiving teachings and was even rejecting the idea, but the karma was very strong. My impression is that even though I really didn't want to go that first day, there was strong karma from past lives, so that past-life karma led me.

His Holiness Serkong Dorje Chang, an embodiment of Marpa who lived and passed away in Nepal and has now reincarnated, is another of my virtuous friends. Many FPMT students met and received blessings from Serkong Dorje Chang and he also ordained one as a nun. I visualize Serkong Dorje Chang in the merit field, even though I never received any particular initiations or formal teachings on a particular text from him.

While I was at Buxa Duar I heard many stories about Serkong Dorje Chang performing the actions of a yogi, peculiar actions that didn't fit the minds of ordinary people. Serkong Dorje Chang would simply disappear; sometimes his attendants would lose him. Rinpoche would be there one minute and gone the next, suddenly appearing somewhere else. I heard that in the early times Serkong Dorje Chang had been imprisoned by the Nepalese authorities for something that wasn't his fault. Even though nobody had opened the door, Rinpoche was not in his prison cell the next day; he was back home in his monastery.

After Lama and I went to Nepal I had a great wish to meet Serkong Dorje Chang. One day I went to visit Rinpoche on top of the hill at Swayambhunath with Lama, Zina Rachevsky, our very first Western student, and Clive, from London, one of Zina's friends from Darjeeling who was teaching Lama English. Zina was very interested in meeting lamas from the different traditions. When Lama and I were living with her, as she was always going to see lamas, Lama compiled a list of Dharma questions for her to ask.

When we reached the top of Swayambhunath hill we asked around for Serkong Dorje Chang. When we got to the two-story house we'd been directed to, a very simple-looking monk was coming down the steps. I asked him where Serkong Dorje Chang was and the monk said, "Oh, wait here a little while." The monk went off to urinate, I think, then returned and went back upstairs.

We then went upstairs to meet Serkong Dorje Chang's manager. Later, when we entered the room to see Serkong Dorje Chang, the monk sitting on the bed turned out to be the simple monk we had seen coming down the steps.

Normally, if you asked Serkong Dorje Chang questions about Dharma, he wouldn't answer. But if it was the right moment and you had good karma, Rinpoche would show a peaceful aspect and maybe talk for a while. Otherwise, Rinpoche might show a wrathful aspect.

It must have been quite an auspicious day, because when Zina asked a question about how to practice guru devotion, Rinpoche gave a brief but unbelievably profound teaching. The teaching was so deep and my obscurations were so thick that I couldn't comprehend what he said at all. His voice was magnificent but the only thing I understood was that if the guru is sitting on the floor, you should think that Guru Shakyamuni Buddha is sitting there. That's all I could understand. I was supposed to be the translator but the teaching was so rich that I didn't understand it.

In the Western way, Zina then asked Rinpoche to read something from the texts that he had in front of him, but Rinpoche refused, saying, "No, no, I'm completely ignorant—I don't know anything." But at the beginning of the interview he had given incredible advice.

Rinpoche would often say things like this and act as if he knew nothing. However, after being in his presence I have not the slightest doubt that Rinpoche was Yamantaka. Even though in appearance Rinpoche seemed to be an ordinary monk, if you sat in front of him you became certain that he was Yamantaka. You didn't need to use any logical reasoning or quotations. No matter what aspect Rinpoche showed, it didn't change my conviction that he was Yamantaka.

As soon as anyone entered the room, Rinpoche could immediately see every single thing about them, past, present and future. He could even tell me the dreams I had had some days before. Sometimes, when people came to ask Rinpoche for observations, before Rinpoche started to throw the dice, Rinpoche would tell the person about their life. One man from Mustang, who had killed someone, came to Rinpoche for an observation and before he threw the dice Rinpoche said, "Oh, you killed a human being." The man was shocked, because he didn't expect to have his life revealed.

People seeing Rinpoche circumambulating the Swayambhunath Stupa would likely think he was just a simple monk, someone who didn't know much more than how to recite OM MANI PADME HUM. But if it was the right moment, Rinpoche would suddenly tell one of the other people circumambulating something like, "You're going to die in three years—you should purify yourself by doing prostrations to the Thirty-five Buddhas."

In the early times in Tibet, Serkong Dorje Chang gave initiations and teachings. Rinpoche had taken his geshe degree at the same time as the great yogi Trehor Kyörpen Rinpoche, from Drepung Monastery. One time Serkong Dorje Chang was to give a Kalachakra initiation. It had already been announced and many people were planning to come. His Holiness Serkong Tsenshab Rinpoche was very worried about how Serkong Dorje Chang was going to give even the preliminary lam-rim teaching to the people.

His Holiness Serkong Tsenshab Rinpoche, one of His Holiness the Dalai Lama's gurus, was the son of the previous incarnation of Serkong Dorje Chang, one of the great yogis of the Gelugpa tradition, who passed away in Tibet. A highly attained yogi of the completion stage of tantra, Serkong Dorje Chang was highly respected; he was one of the few lamas permitted by the Thirteenth Dalai Lama, who was very strict, to have a wisdom consort for quick completion of the tantric path.

Serkong Dorje Chang is the incarnation of Marpa, Milarepa's guru; Serkong Tsenshab Rinpoche is the incarnation of Marpa's son, Tarma Dodé; and Tsechok Ling Rinpoche, who in his past life was the guru of His Holiness Ling Rinpoche, His Holiness Trijang Rinpoche and many other high lamas, is the incarnation of Milarepa. Serkong Dorje Chang mentioned this directly from his own holy mouth to one of the monks from his monastery. One evening as this monk was accompanying Rinpoche back to the monastery after finishing a puja in a benefactor's house, Serkong Dorje Chang said to him, "In reality I'm Guru Marpa, Serkong Tsenshab Rinpoche is the son of Marpa and Tsechok Ling Rinpoche is Milarepa. We are actually like this." When Rinpoche showed the aspect of being happy, he would tell his monks stories of his past lives and other amazing things.

His Holiness Serkong Tsenshab Rinpoche fled Tibet with the incarnation of his father, Serkong Dorje Chang. When they reached the place in southern Tibet where Milarepa had built the nine-story tower they were surrounded by Chinese and there seemed to be no way to escape. Serkong Dorje Chang, Serkong Tsenshab Rinpoche and Changdzö-la, their attendant, who had been offered to Serkong Tsenshab Rinpoche by his father,

slipped quietly inside the tower, then went upstairs, where there were statues of Marpa and Marpa's secret mother, Dagmema. Serkong Tsenshab
Rinpoche had a *damaru* that had belonged to Marpa and a mala that had
belonged to the wisdom mother. Rinpoche kept them with him all the
time. Rinpoche then offered the damaru to Marpa and the mala to Dagmema, with the prayer, "Father and Mother, please understand our situation. Whatever happens in my life is up to you." It was an intense situation,
with the Chinese army all around and no way out.

At that time Changdzö-la, who heard Rinpoche call Marpa and Dagmema "Father and Mother" discovered why His Holiness Serkong Tsenshab Rinpoche is called *thug-tse*, "the holy heart-son." He is Marpa's son.
His Holiness the Dalai Lama also used to address Serkong Tsenshab Rinpoche as "thug-tse."

Also, many years ago in Tibet, when His Holiness the Dalai Lama was
invited to China, Serkong Tsenshab Rinpoche and some other learned
geshes accompanied His Holiness. When His Holiness and his party
reached Kham, many people came looking for Marpa's son to get blessings. Changdzö-la, not knowing that they meant Serkong Tsenshab Rinpoche, said, "We've never heard of Marpa's son—there's no such person in
our group." Changdzö-la told me that he later found out that many people
called Rinpoche by that name.

To return to the story: Serkong Tsenshab Rinpoche told me that the
night before Serkong Dorje Chang was to begin the Kalachakra initiation,
he instructed him on how to explain the lam-rim as the motivation for the
initiation.

The next day Serkong Dorje Chang talked about the eight freedoms and
ten richnesses as the motivation for the initiation, but when he meant to
say "long-life god" he instead said "long-life man." One learned geshe who
had come for the initiation was disappointed. Just because he thought Rinpoche had given a wrong explanation of what a long-life god is, the geshe
left; he didn't take the initiation. His Holiness Serkong Tsenshab Rinpoche
told me that during the actual Kalachakra initiation, Rinpoche gave an
unbelievable, extensive commentary.

So, while great yogis might show some mistakes, at the same time they
show things that ordinary people cannot. His Holiness Serkong Tsenshab
Rinpoche often used to say that he thought Serkong Dorje Chang embodied the meaning of "yogi."

Serkong Dorje Chang showed the aspect of being epileptic in his later life, but no matter what aspect he showed externally, Rinpoche was a great yogi. The Tibetan government would ask Rinpoche to do important wrathful pujas. Because Rinpoche was the real Yamantaka, he was qualified to do those wrathful pujas that are dangerous for ordinary people to do. On the days of the pujas, the monks would request, "Please, Rinpoche, don't have a fit today." They were scared that Rinpoche would have an epileptic fit at an important part of the puja and everything would fall apart, because Rinpoche was the main one performing the concentration to quell the evil-doer and transfer their consciousness. On those days Rinpoche would say, "Hey, if I can't do even something like this, how can I be called 'Dorje Chang'?" And on those days Rinpoche wouldn't have a fit.

Every morning before Rinpoche drank his first cup of tea, he liked to make a tea-offering to the protectors. He would also offer tea in a big bowl to all the lineage lamas of the lam-rim by reciting the requesting prayer *Opening the Door of Realization* from *Jor-chö*. And whenever Rinpoche traveled, he would always carry with him a small photo frame with pictures of all his gurus; he kept it tucked inside his *dongka*.

One time, years ago, His Holiness the Dalai Lama sent the Lower Tantric College monks to consecrate the Boudhanath stupa because some fire had come from the top of it. I think somewhere in the texts it mentions that if something evil is happening in Nepal, fire will come from the stupa to dispel the negative forces. Also, since it is because of Boudhanath stupa that Buddhism was spread and preserved in Tibet for so many years,[31] the consecration of the stupa is important. During the puja, His Holiness Serkong Tsenshab Rinpoche was the main master and Serkong Dorje Chang and I were also there. Serkong Dorje Chang took the framed picture of all his gurus, with brocade around it, out of his dongka and put it on the table to be consecrated as well.

When Lama and I first arrived in Nepal from India with Zina, we all stayed in the Gelugpa monastery in Boudhanath for about a year. The original building was built by a Mongolian lama, but the monks who lived there came from a monastery in Tibet founded by Kachen Yeshe Gyaltsen, a great pandit and yogi who was a tutor of the Eighth Dalai Lama. He established

---

[31] The four men who completed the building of the Boudhanath stupa were later born in Tibet as the Dharma king, Trisong Detsen; his minister, Selnang; the great yogi, Padmasambhava; and the abbot, Shantarakshita. For further details see *The Legend of the Great Stupa* by Keith Dowman, Tibetan Nyingma Meditation Center, Berkeley, 1973.)

the monastery with pure *vinaya* practice and discipline, though I don't think there was much debating of philosophy.

About three months after we arrived the monks from the monastery invited us to take part in a *nyung-nä* they were planning to do. The benefactor of the nyung-nä had invited one of his gurus, a Nyingma lama from Swayambhunath, to give the Eight Mahayana Precepts, but the monks didn't want to take the Mahayana ordination from that lama because you have to regard as your guru anyone from whom you take the Eight Mahayana Precepts. The monks instead invited Serkong Dorje Chang to the monastery to give the precepts.

We went downstairs early in the morning to begin the nyung-nä. When Serkong Dorje Chang came in, he sat on one of the monks' cushions, not on the throne. Someone brought him the text for the Eight Mahayana Precepts, which he opened. As the motivation Rinpoche then said, "If you want to practice Dharma, if your guru tells you to lick *kaka*, you should immediately get down and lick it, while it's still hot." Rinpoche made accompanying slurping noises. Rinpoche then said, "That is the real Dharma practice!"

After Rinpoche had said this, he closed the text and left. That was all the motivation he gave for the Eight Mahayana Precepts. There was no repeating of prayers—nothing! He said this, then left.

As Rinpoche hadn't performed the actual ceremony, we took the Mahayana ordination of the nyung-nä from the altar, even though there were other lamas there.

I found this teaching extremely powerful for my mind, like an atomic bomb. It was just a few words, but it was heavy with meaning. Rinpoche gave the very heart of the practice. Because that teaching was so beneficial, I feel devotion to His Holiness Serkong Dorje Chang. Even though that was the only teaching I ever received from him, I regard Rinpoche as my guru and visualize him in the merit field.

Do we need to formally request someone to be our guru?

You don't normally need to request someone to be your guru. Forming a guru-disciple relationship depends more on your making the decision in your mind than on your personally asking that person's permission to attend an initiation or teaching. In Tibet, if you were planning to attend an initiation or teaching from a lama for the first time, the tradition was to go see that lama and ask his permission to attend. You would just quickly ask, "Can I take these teachings?" The lama would then check and accept or reject your request.

Before listening to teachings from someone for the very first time, if there's time, you can make a request to attend the teachings; however, because there are often hundreds or thousands of people involved, there's not usually enough time for each person to personally request permission. For example, thousands of people receive teachings from His Holiness the Dalai Lama. Not everybody can go to see His Holiness and ask, "Please be my guru."

However, when His Holiness Ling Rinpoche gave some particular initiations and teachings, it seems that people would go to ask permission to attend them. They didn't go to see Rinpoche, but just asked his attendant whether they could receive the initiation.

After the teaching has happened and the connection has already been made, there is no need to ask the person to be your guru. This would be like requesting your mother to be your mother or your father to be your father after you had already been born.

Taking initiations

Simply sitting in a line of people during an initiation doesn't mean that you receive the initiation and the person giving it becomes your guru. Receiving initiation has to do with the mind, not the body. It's a mental action.

Just being where an initiation is being given doesn't mean that you receive the initiation and establish Dharma contact. If you don't take the initiation, just being there doesn't establish Dharma contact. Many other creatures— flies buzzing around, ants, fleas and other bugs, and sometimes dogs—can also be physically there while an initiation is happening and hear all the words of the explanations of the visualizations. If you simply sit there and don't do the visualizations, you haven't received the initiation. Even if you drink a whole bucket of vase water and eat a mountain of tormas, that alone doesn't mean you have received the initiation.

In certain cases you might have to be present at an initiation to ensure harmony within a Dharma center, where various lamas are invited because students have different wishes and different karma or because of your responsibility within an organization. If you have no intention of following the person giving the initiation as a guru and don't do the visualizations, simply sitting there in the group of people doesn't mean that you receive the initiation. If you know what to do and how to think, there will be no confusion. Your mind, not your body, takes the initiation.

Meditation centers in the West generally invite many different lamas to give teachings. One reason for this is that people have different karma. Each time a lama comes, there are different people who have a karmic connection with that particular lama, and even though many other lamas might come to the meditation center, until that particular lama comes, those people don't meet the Dharma. Each individual student has to be clear from the beginning whether or not he wants to make Dharma contact with a particular lama.

It's possible that someone could sit in an initiation and not do any of the visualizations at all but that the lama could do the meditations in relation to that person, such as visualizing them as the deity. The initiation can then become the giving of a blessing to that person. The person can receive the blessing but doesn't necessarily take the lama as a guru because he hasn't done the visualizations explained. He receives the blessing, but in the manner of having a puja done to give him protection. If from his side he hasn't done the visualizations or regarded the lama as his guru, he hasn't received the initiation.

However, if you decide to take an initiation, do as much as you can of the meditations and visualizations explained, which are always based on seeing the lama and the deity as inseparable. At the end generate faith that you have received the initiation. If you do all this, you receive the initiation and establish a Dharma connection with the person who has given it. You should regard that person as your guru because he has planted in your mind the seed of Dharma, the seed of the four kayas of Highest Yoga Tantra, which ripen your mind to practice the path. Even if you had no particular thought to accept the person as your guru, if you do the meditations and visualizations, you have taken the initiation and that person becomes your guru.

If you treat an initiation like a horse race, with everyone racing to get there first, problems can arise later, especially if you haven't heard complete lam-rim teachings on guru devotion or if these teachings somehow haven't touched your heart. If you later regret taking the initiation and the lama becomes an object of criticism, almost like your enemy, you will burn many eons of merit and unnecessarily make your life difficult. After a connection has been made, things won't work out if you damage the root of your practice through not having thought deeply about the meaning of the lam-rim.

Taking vows

I think that you should regard as your guru anyone who has granted you a lineage of vows: refuge, pratimoksha, bodhisattva or tantric vows, or even the Eight Mahayana Precepts. Whether that person is lay or ordained, Tibetan or Western, male or female, you must regard him or her as your guru. If you do the visualizations when you take the vows, I would say that you have established a Dharma connection with that person, even if at the time you didn't have any thought of forming a guru-disciple relationship.

With respect to the vows and ordinations you've already taken where, because of your lack of understanding of the lam-rim, you didn't regard the person as a guru, you have to regard those teachers as your guru as you have made Dharma contact. You mightn't have known the important points of this practice of guru devotion, but if you have taken the Eight Mahayana Precepts or any other vows, which are all based on refuge, from someone, I think you should regard that person as your guru.

As I have already explained, at the beginning you can listen to teachings without having to regard a teacher as your guru but I don't think you can do the same thing with vows or initiations. I don't think that any valid lamas would say that you can take a full initiation from someone without regarding him as your guru; I don't think that they would accept that in relation to any of the vows either.

If you have taken *gelong* or *getsul* ordination, you have to regard as your guru not only the abbot but also the *lobpön*, or preceptor. If you have taken gelong ordination, you have to regard as your guru both the *lekyi lobpön*, who gives the twenty-one pieces of advice to the gelongs (though sometimes the abbot does this) and also the *sangdön lobpön*, who comes outside to ask you questions about whether you have any particular sicknesses and so forth and to give you advice.

When I took gelong ordination, His Holiness Ling Rinpoche was the abbot; His Holiness Serkong Tsenshab Rinpoche was the lobpön; and the chant leader at the Tibetan Temple in Bodhgaya, a very good old monk, was the sangdön lobpön.

Some geshes say that you have to regard even the monk who reads the sutra at *sojong* as your guru because he is asked to say that prayer as the representative of Guru Shakyamuni Buddha, but such a person doesn't commonly have to be regarded as your teacher.

If you take the oral transmission of even one verse of a prayer or one mantra, the person giving it also becomes your virtuous friend—not simply by your hearing the oral transmission but by your taking it to receive the blessing.

Otherwise it would mean that we could achieve enlightenment without a guru—which is impossible. It would mean that we could achieve realizations of the lam-rim and tantric paths without needing a guru to grant initiations and vows. There is no one who has ever achieved enlightenment in that way.

In the strict interpretation, you should regard as your virtuous friend even someone who teaches you the mudras found in tantric practices or how to draw mandalas. In the monasteries in Tibet, strict practitioners of lam-rim would learn such things only from someone with whom they wanted to have a Dharma connection. However, it's possible to discuss such things as friends, without any particular recognition of a guru-disciple relationship.

Should we regard our alphabet teacher as our guru?

Tibetans traditionally regard the person who teaches them the alphabet as their guru. I include both of my alphabet teachers, who passed away many years ago, among my gurus, for example. Both of them were my uncles and both were fully ordained monks at that time. I had two alphabet teachers because I was naughty.

The uncle who first taught me the alphabet, Ngawang Lekshe, lived in the Thangme monastery, very close to my home. I was very naughty and didn't study well. I think I understood the alphabet, apart from one syllable that I couldn't seem to learn. I was like the arhat Chudapanthaka, or Small Path, who couldn't memorize the two syllables "si" and "dam." When he learnt "si," he forgot "dam"; and when he learnt "dam," he forgot "si."[32] My teacher used to teach me the alphabet in the courtyard and when he went inside our room to prepare food I scratched out the letter that I was finding hard to learn.

When I was put in the monastery by my mother I often used to run back home. After one or two days my mother would again send me back to the monastery with somebody, who would carry me up the hill on his shoul-

---

[32] See *Liberation in the Palm of Your Hand*, pp. 106–12, for the long version of this story. (Page references in these notes are to the 2006, blue-covered edition.)

ders. After one or two days there I would again escape. When my teacher went inside our room to cook our food after teaching me the alphabet outside, I would quickly run back home. I think it was because at home I got to play all the time; there was nothing particular I had to do.

At home I had some friends I would play with. One of my best friends, who played with me every day, was mute, and there were a few other children. We would play in a field where there was water and would come back home when my mother shouted from the window that lunch was ready. We would return for the meals.

Many times when we played, I would sit on a higher seat and pretend to be a lama and my friends would pretend to be disciples or benefactors. Near our house was a large rock with mantras carved into it and I would sit a little way up the rock and pretend that I was giving initiations to my friends by putting things on their heads. Since we didn't know the prayers we would just make some noise. The one pretending to be the benefactor would make an offering of food by mixing some earth with water and putting it on a small piece of flat stone. We would pretend to do pujas and things like that.

One time when everything was covered with snow, I was playing in the courtyard, blowing through a plant and pretending I was playing a trumpet in a puja, when the thought came to escape from my teacher. I ran down the mountain. At that time I was wearing some pants that my mother had given me. I hadn't had pants before—they were a kind of one-piece overall made of very cheap prayer-flag fabric dyed red; at that time in Solu Khumbu good cloth was very hard to find. Inside where the top and bottom met, there were a lot of lice and eggs.

I didn't know how to open the pants to go to the toilet. So that day when I ran from the monastery all the way down to my mother's house, I came down with kaka in my pants. When I arrived, my mother was outside with some people. She then took off all my clothing and cleaned everything up.

Because the monastery was close to my home and I kept running away every few days, my mother sent me to another part of Solu Khumbu, Rolwaling, an isolated place reached only after crossing dangerous snow mountains. Looking back now, I can see it was extremely kind of her.

I lived in Rolwaling, which has many holy places of Padmasambhava, for seven years with my second alphabet teacher, Aku (which means uncle) Ngawang Gendun, who taught me to read. We would get up at dawn, recite our prayers, then read texts. One time we had to read *The Diamond-Cutter*

Sutra over and over. We sometimes had to read all of the *One Hundred Thousand Verse Perfection of Wisdom Sutra* for benefactors who requested us to read it.

Except for meal times and when I would go outside to pee, when I got to goof off a little bit, I read texts almost all day long. We would read the whole afternoon, stopping some time before sunset. One time when I thought my teacher had gone far away I stopped reading and just turned some pages over. When he came back after ten or fifteen minutes he could see I hadn't actually been reading but had been sitting there just playing around, so he beat me. It was normal to be beaten with dried bamboo but when my teacher hit me on the head with the bamboo stick it shattered into pieces. He then spanked and beat me here and there.

I don't remember what I had done, but one time when it was raining, he made me take off my clothes and put my mouth in the water where it had collected on the flat stones in the courtyard. Another time (again I don't remember what I had done), my teacher took me outside and rubbed my backside on some nettles. I don't remember feeling much pain or really suffering.

Anyway, looking back now, I think I experienced unbelievable purification from my teacher getting me to read all those texts and from beating me. Even though I had no understanding of the meaning of the texts, I definitely think that repeating the texts over and over again for many months left positive imprints on my mental continuum. Due to the kindness of those teachers in my childhood in letting me read those texts and thus leave positive imprints and due to all their beatings, I think I purified many heavy negative karmas.

Western students have asked whether there is any difference between learning the English alphabet and the Tibetan alphabet. In Tibet, students regarded their alphabet teacher as a virtuous friend because the teacher usually taught the alphabet so that the students could learn Dharma—and this was also the student's motivation for learning it. There was normally a Dharma motivation from both sides. This is different from learning the alphabet in a Western school, but if you learn the Tibetan alphabet with the intention of studying Dharma, I think you should regard your Tibetan teacher as your guru.

Should you look at the teacher who taught you the ABC as your guru and visualize him or her in the merit field? According to Lama Yeshe's definition, the person who teaches you the alphabet becomes your guru if you learn the alphabet with the aim of practicing Dharma. I think it's not necessary to visualize in the merit field the teacher who taught you the English alphabet because her reason for teaching you was not so that you could practice Dharma. Of course, there is nothing wrong with looking at your mother, father, teacher or whoever else taught you the alphabet as your guru. It's profitable to do so.

When we were in Buxa, this issue was discussed in relation to two schools there, where some of the monks started to learn English and Hindi. There were three teachers all together: a Chinese-looking Tibetan, who taught English to the young incarnate lamas and the monks; an Indian shopkeeper; and a Ladakhi monk. At that time there was discussion as to whether to regard these teachers who were teaching the English and Hindi alphabets as gurus. According to Lama Yeshe's explanation, we didn't need to regard them as gurus since we weren't learning English and Hindi for Dharma purposes.

The importance of visualizing every guru

Since correct devotion to the virtuous friend is the root of the whole path to enlightenment, we need to take good care of our relationships with all the gurus with whom we have had direct Dharma contact. When we don't practice correctly in relation to even one of our gurus, even if all our other gurus are happy with us, if we don't change our attitude and confess our mistake, we can't generate realizations no matter how much we meditate.

It is important to have a good relationship and practice correctly with every single one of our gurus. If we practice guru devotion correctly only with those we like and ignore or practice incorrectly with those we don't, there is no way we can subdue our mind and achieve realizations of the path, no matter how much practice or retreat we do. If we leave a guru out of our visualization because we dislike or can't relate to him, we don't have the chance to develop guru devotion toward that person, and no matter how much devotion we feel toward our other gurus, nothing will happen in our mind. We should keep count of the number of gurus we have and visualize all of the gurus with whom we have made a Dharma connection when we meditate on guru yoga in the lam-rim or in *Six-Session Guru Yoga*, *Lama Tsongkhapa Guru Yoga* or *Guru Puja*.

As the lam-rim teachings mention, if somebody asks us how much money we have in our purse, we're immediately ready with the answer but if somebody asks us how many gurus we have, we're not sure. That's because we always count our money carefully and take more care of it than we do our gurus. Being unclear about the number of gurus we have shows that we haven't paid much attention to the practice that is the root of the path to enlightenment.

If we leave out from our visualizations even one guru with whom we have Dharma contact, no matter how much we practice, study or do retreat, there's no way to really subdue our mind and no way to achieve realizations of the path. It is vital not to leave anybody out; otherwise, we can't develop our mind. We shouldn't forget even the gurus who have given us just the oral transmission of a verse of teaching or a mantra, let alone those who have given us vows and initiations.

The importance of visualizing every single guru is illustrated by the story of Drubkhang Gelek Gyatso, a highly attained lam-rim lineage lama who wrote many extensive scriptures on sutra and tantra. Je Drubkhangpa's biography, which explains how he practiced lam-rim, especially bodhicitta, is very interesting and very inspiring. The cave where he did many years of meditation is high on the mountain above Sera Monastery in Tibet.

When Je Drubkhangpa began to meditate on lam-rim, he spent many years meditating, but nothing happened. There was no change in his mind, no realizations. Wondering if something was missing from his practice, he went to consult his root guru.

His guru said, "When you visualize the merit field, have you forgotten anyone with whom you have made a Dharma connection? Go back and check whether you have left out any of your gurus."

When Je Drubkhangpa checked, he found that he had left out the teacher who had taught him the alphabet when he was still a child living at home. Je Drubkhangpa saw his alphabet teacher, a monk who later broke his vows, as bad-tempered and cruel. Because he didn't like this teacher, Je Drubkhangpa found it difficult to develop devotion toward him and didn't visualize him among his other teachers. He visualized all his other teachers in the merit field.

When Je Drubkhangpa went back and explained this to his guru, his guru advised, "This is the problem. This is why you haven't been able to have any realizations during all these years. You must now completely change your attitude and meditate on this guru as your root guru in the center of the whole merit field. Visualize him as Lama Losang Thubwang Dorje

Chang,[33] the principal figure of the merit field. Until you develop devotion, look at him as the essence of the entire merit field."

As soon as Je Drubkhangpa did this meditation, everything changed. He started to develop devotion toward this teacher and realizations then came very easily, one after another, like falling rain.

Je Drubkhangpa's story is a great teaching for us, showing us the importance of ensuring that no guru is left out of our visualization of the merit field so that we develop devotion toward all our gurus. If we have used the methods for intensive purification and for collection of extensive merit and have done many retreats but still nothing is happening to our mind, it means that something is wrong; there's something missing in our practice. We then have to check our practice of guru devotion. We might not have analyzed well exactly how many gurus we have and left one out or we might not have paid attention to the heavy negative karmas we have created in relation to particular gurus. If we find that we have left out one of our gurus, we have to change the situation by putting strong effort into developing devotion to that guru. Otherwise, nothing will happen; our listening, reflecting and meditating won't be successful in transforming our mind into the lam-rim path.

We should remember all those with whom we have a guru-disciple relationship and visualize them all in the merit field, even those with whom we have made mistakes in the past and created negative karma through breaking samaya, renouncing the relationship and so forth. We should now change our attitude and, looking at every one of them as an embodiment of our own deity or Shakyamuni Buddha, devote ourselves correctly to them with thought and with action.

We should feel that all our gurus are the same in essence, just different in aspect. This is one of the meditation techniques to develop guru devotion. We don't find many faults in some of our gurus and feel much devotion toward them; however, with one or two of our gurus we might find it difficult to generate devotion because we see them as full of faults. As explained by Kachen Yeshe Gyaltsen, a technique to develop devotion also toward that guru is to think that he is the embodiment of the guru for whom you feel the strongest devotion and in whom you don't find faults. After you see

---

[33] Lama Losang Thubwang Dorje Chang is the principal figure of the *Guru Puja* and *Jorchö* merit fields. *Lama* refers to the root guru, *Losang* to Lama Tsongkhapa, *Thubwang* to Shakyamuni Buddha, and *Dorje Chang* to Vajradhara. The main figure of Lama Tsongkhapa has Shakyamuni Buddha at his heart, who in turn has Vajradhara at his heart.

that guru as buddha, you then think that your other gurus are manifestations of that guru.

If we wish to achieve enlightenment quickly we have to know the important points of guru yoga practice, such as the necessity of visualizing all our gurus. Not understanding how to practice or making mistakes in our practice will block our realizations.

How many gurus should we have?

It is not necessary to have just one guru, like having one boyfriend or girlfriend. Westerners sometimes think that they can't have many gurus but should have just one. Or they take initiations and teachings but still think that they haven't met their guru. This is a mistake.

You can have many gurus or you can have just one guru and be satisfied with that. It depends on how well you are able to practice guru devotion. Lama Atisha, who had 152 gurus, said that he didn't do any action that wasn't wished by all those gurus. Somebody who has enough merit and knows how to practice guru yoga can have hundreds, millions or billions of virtuous friends. There is no danger in such a person regarding anybody as their virtuous friend. Kadampa Geshe Sungpuwa, while traveling on pilgrimage from Kham to Lhasa, would take teachings from anyone he met along the way who was giving teachings. If a crowd had gathered by the side of the road to receive teachings from someone, Geshe Sungpuwa would go there, listen to the teaching, and then regard that person as his guru. Ra Lotsawa and Dromtönpa, on the other hand, had very few gurus.

There is a debate about whether it is wiser to have few or many gurus. The conclusion is that if you can practice guru devotion well, you can devote yourself to everyone who gives you a teaching and have hundreds of gurus without any problems. But if you can't, it's better to have fewer gurus, so that you create less negative karma—the more gurus you have, the more obstacles you create. You will make Dharma contact with one person, then generate negative thoughts toward him; you will then make contact with another virtuous friend, then again generate negative thoughts toward that person. For some people, the more gurus they have, the more obstacles they create to their enlightenment.

If you find guru devotion difficult to practice, you should make Dharma connections only with teachers with whom you think you can maintain guru devotion. By having fewer gurus, you will create fewer obstacles to the happiness beyond this life up to enlightenment. Basically, it depends on your own capacity, on your own mind. If you have a lot of superstition and always look at the negative rather than the positive, you should be careful.

There is a saying that if you can't practice guru devotion, you receive as many negativities as the number of gurus you have. But there are also advantages in having many gurus—if one guru doesn't have the lineage of a particular teaching or initiation that you need to benefit yourself or others, you can take it from another guru. In this way you can receive all the teachings.

It is fine to plan to have only one guru in your life but you may not be able to always be in the same place as that guru and he may not always have time to teach you. If you don't find other gurus to study with, your understanding may not develop quickly.

Generally, whether you have one guru or a hundred, how quickly you generate real understanding of Dharma and realizations of the path depends on your individual skill and practice.

Who is the root guru?

With respect to the root guru, anyone from whom you have directly received teachings can be called a root, or direct, guru, whereas the lineage lamas are indirect gurus. However, a common definition of the root guru is the one among all your gurus who has most benefited your mind, the one who has been the most effective in directing your mind toward Dharma.

You don't necessarily have just one root guru; you can have more than one. Among Lama Atisha's 152 gurus, for example, he regarded five as his root gurus, including Lama Suvarnadvipi and Dharmarakshita. Lama Suvarnadvipi was the guru from whom Lama Atisha received the complete teachings on bodhicitta over a period of twelve years and in whose presence Lama Atisha generated bodhicitta. Whenever he heard someone say the holy name of Lama Suvarnadvipi, because of the power of his devotion, Lama Atisha would immediately stand up from his seat and, with tears in his eyes, place his hands together in prostration on his crown.

In the case of tantric deity practice, the lama you visualize as the root guru in the *sadhana* is the one from whom you have received the initiation of that deity. If you have received the same initiation from many lamas, you choose the one among those many lamas who has most benefited your mind. Again, you can have more than one root guru.

We have to meditate and discover that the root guru is not separate from our other gurus. The root guru is one with all our other gurus and all our other gurus are embodiments of our root guru, the one who has most benefited our mind. Meditating in this way helps us to generate the same strong devotion to all our gurus, especially if there are any toward whom we have difficulty generating devotion. By meditating in this way, we stop the thought of seeing faults in those particular virtuous friends, which is the heaviest obstacle to developing our mind in the path to enlightenment. If we are able to look at all our other gurus as we do our root guru and generate the same strong devotion toward all of them, there will be no obstacles to realization. Realizations of the path to enlightenment will fall like rain.

Before we decide to devote ourselves to someone, we need to be very careful. We should examine, or check, well at the very beginning before we decide to rely upon someone as a virtuous friend. Once the Dharma contact has been made, however, examining is finished; it is then wrong to continue the examination. Once we have made the Dharma connection, we have to regard that person with a completely new mind, with the determination that he is Guru Shakyamuni Buddha or the deity we are practicing. After we have established a guru-disciple relationship, we correctly devote ourselves to the virtuous friend as explained by Buddha in the sutra and tantra teachings. If we are practicing tantra, we practice the special guru yoga as explained in tantra.

Generally speaking, there's a responsibility from both sides once the Dharma connection is made. Guiding the disciple is the teacher's responsibility and, after Dharma contact has been made, correct devotion to the virtuous friend is the disciple's responsibility. Once we have made the Dharma connection, by receiving a teaching with the recognition that that person is our guru and we are his disciple, we have to live our life with a totally new attitude toward that person and not with our old thoughts. We have to look at him in a totally different way; we have to look at him as a buddha. Even if we saw faults in that person before, from the time of establishing Dharma contact, we have to change our way of looking at him. We have to decide at the very beginning that no matter what happens, we are going to practice guru devotion toward that person. We have to change our concept and look at him as a buddha. In this way, our mental continuum is protected from the negative karmas and pollution of degenerating samaya. Otherwise, we will be totally destroying ourselves. Every day we will be creating hell.

Once we have listened to teachings with recognition of someone as our virtuous friend, whether that person is lay or ordained, male or female, there can be no question of changing our mind. It shouldn't be that as long as the person is sweet to us and we like him, we regard him as our virtuous friend but when he is no longer sweet to us we don't regard him in that way.

Be careful at the beginning, because once the relationship has been established nothing can be changed unless the guru gives you permission to no longer regard him as your guru. Once the relationship has been formed there is no heavier karma than giving up the guru, renouncing the guru as an object of devotion. It is a much heavier negative karma than committing the five uninterrupted negative actions. Among all heavy karmas, this is the heaviest.

This applies once a guru-disciple relationship has been formed, whether or not we have taken a tantric initiation from that person—though I'm sure the negative karma is greater if the person is our vajra guru. Also, even if we haven't taken a tantric initiation from the lama that we have given up, if we have taken tantric initiation from other lamas, we have to keep the tantric vows, and we should be very careful not to receive the heavy negative karma of the first tantric root fall,[34] which is the heaviest. Otherwise, no matter how many eons we practice mahamudra or other secret, profound paths, we will have no result. It will be extremely difficult to develop our mind once we make a mistake in this important point of guru devotion practice.

We have to be clear about what we're going to do at the very beginning so that there will be no problems or confusion later. As Lama Yeshe used to say, we have to make it "clean clear." We need to be clear about the way we intend to study Dharma teachings, whether as part of a guru-disciple relationship or as in a university. Otherwise, if we are not clean clear in the beginning before we establish Dharma contact, we may later create much negative karma. When problems happen later, we will be like an elephant sunk in mud. We will have already accumulated so much negative karma that it will be difficult to finish purifying it.

If we're not clear about the very root of the path to enlightenment, the very root of all realizations, no matter how much we study or understand Dharma, it will be difficult for us to complete the practice and really experience the path. If we're not clear about this point, our life will become a mess.

---

[34] The first tantric root fall is despising or belittling one's guru.

I thought to mention these points about who to regard as guru as it may help people who are unsure about the practice of guru devotion to have a clear understanding in regard to their past and future relationships.

His Holiness Trijang Rinpoche, Dharamsala, India, 1971

7. The Benefits of Correct Devotion to a Guru

ONCE WE HAVE found a guru who can reveal the infallible path, it is extremely important to follow him perfectly. All the important points of how to devote to a guru as explained in the sutras are condensed into four outlines:

1. The benefits of correctly devoting to a guru
2. The shortcomings of not devoting to a guru or of devoting incorrectly (chapter 8)
3. How to devote to a guru with thought (chapters 9–14)
4. How to devote to a guru with action (chapter 15)

These key guru devotion meditations are outlined in *Liberation in the Palm of Your Hand* and *The Great Treatise on the Stages of the Path to Enlightenment*.

There are eight benefits of correctly devoting to a guru and eight shortcomings of not having a guru or of devoting incorrectly to a guru. If you don't have a guru, you don't have the karmic cause for enlightenment and you don't experience the eight benefits of correct devotion. Not having a guru is itself a shortcoming and there are then eight shortcomings of incorrectly devoting to a guru.

The Essence of Nectar says,

> Devoting with thought and action
> To the holy virtuous friend who reveals
> The perfect, unmistaken, supreme path to enlightenment,
> Has inconceivable benefits.

1. THE BENEFITS OF CORRECTLY DEVOTING TO A GURU

The first meditation outline explains the great benefits, or advantages, of correctly devoting ourselves to a virtuous friend, which are condensed into eight points:

(1) We become closer to enlightenment
(2) We please all the buddhas
(3) We are not harmed by maras or evil friends
(4) Our delusions and negative actions naturally cease
(5) All our realizations of the paths and bhumis increase
(6) We will never lack virtuous friends in all our future lives
(7) We will not fall into the lower realms
(8) We will effortlessly accomplish all our temporary and ultimate wishes

(1) WE BECOME CLOSER TO ENLIGHTENMENT

When we meditate on the benefits of guru devotion, the first benefit is that we become closer to enlightenment. This first benefit has two divisions:

(a) We become closer to enlightenment by practicing the advice given by our guru
(b) We become closer to enlightenment by making offerings to and serving our guru

Every time we follow any of our guru's advice, including by living in vows, doing Dharma practices and serving others, we become closer to enlightenment. Each time we do what we have been told to do, we become closer to enlightenment. And it is the same with each offering we make to the guru and with each service we offer. We become closer to enlightenment each time we follow our guru's advice, make offerings or offer service to him because we thus perform the most powerful purification and collect the most extensive merit. In this way our level of mind continuously gets higher and higher and we become closer and closer to enlightenment, or to the guru—these two are actually the same thing, as we become closer to the absolute guru, the *dharmakaya*. We should be aware of these two ways of becoming closer to enlightenment in our daily life.

(a) We become closer to enlightenment by practicing the advice given by our guru

Without a guru, there is no way we can end our samsara. If we never meet a guru, the time of our achieving enlightenment will never come. But if we rely upon a guru who shows the infallible path, our own samsara, even though it is beginningless, can have an end. By meeting a guru and following his advice, we will quickly achieve enlightenment.

By following the Paramitayana path revealed by the guru, we can achieve enlightenment more quickly than the hearers and self-conquerors,[35] followers of the Hinayana path. By following the teachings of the Action, Performance and Yoga Tantras revealed by the guru, we can achieve enlightenment much more quickly than by following the Paramitayana path. And by practicing the path of Highest Yoga Tantra shown by the guru, we can achieve enlightenment extremely quickly, in one brief lifetime of this degenerate time—much more quickly than by practicing the paths of the lower tantras.

Guru yoga practice is the very heart of the Highest Yoga Tantra path. As Manjushri advised Lama Tsongkhapa, tantric practice especially is based on cherishing guru yoga more than our own life. If we protect our practice of guru devotion more than our life, it will be possible for us to accomplish enlightenment within a few years, as did the great yogi Milarepa, King Indrabhuti, Gyalwa Ensapa and many others.

The reason we have the commitment to recite *Six-Session Guru Yoga* once we have taken a Highest Yoga Tantra initiation is that nothing works without guru yoga. The main factor that makes the tantric path a quick path to enlightenment is guru yoga practice, cherishing our gurus more than our own life.

As said in *The Essence of Nectar*,

> The great unification is difficult to achieve
> Even with hundreds of efforts for oceans of countless eons;

---

[35] Skt: *shravaka* and *pratyekabuddha* (also translated as solitary realizer).

But it can be attained in one brief life of a degenerate time
If we rely upon the power of the guru.

The verse of prostration in *Six-Session Guru Yoga* also mentions,

I prostrate at your lotus feet, my jewel-like guru, whose kindness
instantly grants me great bliss.

This is similar to the way the kindness of the guru is described in the abbreviated *Calling the Lama from Afar:* "Magnificently glorious guru, who is the wish-granting jewel." (See appendix 2.)

The jewel mentioned in the verse from *Six-Session Guru Yoga* is also the wish-granting jewel, which fulfils all wishes. The guru is likened to a wish-granting jewel because there is nothing in the world to compare to its value. It is not really a comparable example but it is what we can find among material objects to give us an idea of how the guru fulfils all our wishes for happiness, up to enlightenment.

Through the kindness of our guru in having taught us Dharma, we are granted the great bliss of the dharmakaya, or enlightenment, and even that is granted instantly. Why is the term *instantly* used? If we achieve enlightenment in one brief lifetime of a degenerate time, it is like achieving it in an instant when compared to the incredible length of life of a god or hell being. The length of a day is different in the human, god and hell realms. One morning in the god realm of Tushita, for example, is equal to fifty human years. And the higher the god realm, the longer the length of a day. The length of life of the gods of the desire realm—the worldly gods situated on the levels of Mount Meru, such as the Four Guardians—is five hundred years, but this is equal to nine million human years. Even if it took us nine million human years to achieve enlightenment, it would be like achieving enlightenment in only one life in terms of the gods of the desire realm. We think it is a long time to take to achieve enlightenment but it is very short compared to the length of their life.

Even though the length of life of a being in the Realm of Thirty-three, the highest god realm of the desire realm, is very long, it seems very short when compared to the length of life of a being in the first hot hell, Being Alive Again and Again. With the eight hot hells, the lower the hell, the longer the length of life. The longest length of life, that of the eighth hot hell, Inexhaustible Suffering, is one intermediate eon. How long is an intermediate eon? One great eon is made up of twenty intermediate eons, and there are four great eons in the history of a world system: evolution takes one great eon; the world system exists for one great eon; it decays over one great eon; and then is empty, with everything having disappeared, for another great eon.

According to the time frame of the lowest hot hell, Inexhaustible Suffering, taking many millions, or even billions, of years to achieve enlightenment would be very short. One day for the beings in even the first hot hell, Being Alive Again and Again, is nine million human years. So, even if we were to take nine million years to achieve enlightenment, according to the time frame of the sentient beings in Being Alive Again and Again, we would have achieved enlightenment in one day. And for beings in Inexhaustible Suffering, it would be like an instant. Even if we took billions or trillions of years to achieve enlightenment, we would have achieved enlightenment in an instant according to their time frame.

However, we don't need to talk about the lengths of life in the different hell and god realms—we just have to think about the beginningless nature of our own samsara. It is also like an instant when compared to the duration of our samsara during beginningless rebirths up to now or from now until our samsara ends. To us it seems very tedious to have to take three countless great eons to achieve enlightenment, but if we think back, we have been circling and suffering in samsara for beginningless lifetimes. The continuity of our samsaric suffering has no beginning. Even if it takes us hundreds or hundreds of billions of countless great eons to achieve enlightenment, it is nothing when compared to our beginningless samsaric lifetimes. If we think of the beginningless duration of our suffering in samsara, taking even three countless great eons to achieve enlightenment is like achieving enlightenment in an instant.

Even if we don't achieve enlightenment in this life, but take twenty or thirty lifetimes, it is nothing compared to the lengths of life in the god and hell realms, the length of time arhats stay in nirvana before entering the Mahayana path and achieving enlightenment, or the duration of our beginningless samsara.

Also, as mentioned in the first of the verses of prostration in *Guru Puja*,

> I prostrate at your lotus feet, O vajra-holding guru,
> Who is like a wish-granting jewel,
> In an instant your compassion grants me

> The supreme state of the three kayas, the sphere
> of great bliss.[36]

Since the guru has advised us how to achieve enlightenment, if we perfectly follow our guru, there is no doubt, as mentioned in this verse, that the guru's compassion can immediately grant us even "the supreme state of the three kayas, the sphere of great bliss." The guru can grant us what normally requires the accumulation of merit for three countless great eons in an instant, which means in this brief lifetime of a degenerate time.

We have had many gurus, who have given us vows, initiations and commentaries and tried as much as possible to reveal all the various sutra and tantra methods necessary to lead us to enlightenment. If from the very beginning we had practiced exactly what each of our gurus had taught us, we would have become enlightened by now or at least have reached the completion stage of Highest Yoga Tantra. Let alone not achieving the three kayas in this life, we haven't even generated in our mind a single realization of the sutra or tantra paths. From our side, by not practicing our gurus' advice or not practicing it correctly, we have tried to pull ourselves down to the lower realms. It is we ourselves who are preventing our achieving enlightenment, the supreme state of the three kayas, in an instant.

Ask yourself, "Why don't I yet have the realization of impermanence and death? It's not because my virtuous friends haven't taught me about impermanence and death; it's only because I haven't practiced what they have taught. Forget about enlightenment—I still haven't achieved the realization of impermanence and death or any other lam-rim or tantric realization. My gurus have taught me the essence of the path, with nothing missing. If from the very beginning I had practiced exactly what they had taught I would already be enlightened or at least have high tantric realizations."

Generally, to achieve enlightenment through the Paramitayana path one has to accumulate merit for three countless great eons. It takes one countless great eon to go from the Mahayana path of merit[37] to the Mahayana path of seeing, or the first bhumi. From the path of seeing to the eighth bhumi takes a second countless great eon; and from the eighth bhumi up

---

[36] V. 18.
[37] Also translated as path of accumulation. There are five Mahayana paths, the first of which, the path of merit, has three divisions: small, intermediate and great.

to enlightenment takes a third countless great eon. If we perfectly follow the guru, however, even if we practice only the sutra path and don't practice tantra, we can still accomplish the path very quickly, as happened with the bodhisattva Sadaprarudita.[38] Even without practicing tantra, Sadaprarudita accumulated in seven years the merit that would normally take two countless great eons to accumulate by following the Paramitayana path. Without the practice of tantra, it would generally be impossible to accumulate such extensive merit in such a short time. However, Sadaprarudita followed his guru, the great bodhisattva Dharmodgata, in a very special way, cherishing him more than his own body and life. Because of the power of his special guru devotion, he was able to achieve in seven years paths that normally take two countless great eons.

Even before he met Dharmodgata, because Sadaprarudita had achieved the Concentration of Continual Dharma on the great path of merit, he was able to see countless buddhas in *nirmanakaya* aspect. Even though he could see so many buddhas, Sadaprarudita wasn't satisfied; he still wanted to find the guru with whom he had a karmic connection from past lives. Constantly tormented by this worry, he was so sad that he cried all the time, which is how he received the name Sadaprarudita, which means "always crying."

Sadaprarudita searched for a long time until he finally found his past-life guru, Dharmodgata, then devoted himself by cherishing his guru more than all the buddhas. He followed Dharmodgata by completely giving up concern for his own life. To make offerings to his guru, without any feeling of loss he even sold his own flesh to a Brahmin, who was actually a transformation of the worldly god, Indra.

At first, as Dharmodgata was in strict retreat, Sadaprarudita wasn't able to see him and request teachings. Sadaprarudita had to wait seven years before he was able to meet his guru, and while he waited, he cleaned around the temple where his guru was doing retreat. While cleaning, Sadaprarudita didn't think of food or sleep; he just thought, "When can I hear the *Perfection of Wisdom* teachings from my guru's holy mouth?" Cherishing Dharmodgata more than his own life, Sadaprarudita served him during those seven years.

When Dharmodgata finished his retreat, Sadaprarudita was finally able

---

[38] For the whole story see *The Perfection of Wisdom in Eight Thousand Lines*, chapters 30 and 31.

to meet his guru and request teachings. Before setting up the teaching throne, Sadaprarudita cleaned the teaching site. He wanted to sprinkle it with water to settle the dust but there was no water. Maras, who wanted to interfere with these Dharma activities, had caused all the water in the area to dry up. Sadaprarudita then cut himself and sprinkled his own blood on the ground to stop the dust rising. Sadaprarudita then invited Dharmodgata to give the teachings.

After Dharmodgata revealed Dharma to him, Sadaprarudita reached the eighth bhumi and achieved the patience of unborn Dharma.[39] Sadaprarudita quickly reached the eighth bhumi because his practice of guru devotion was incomparable. He was willing to sacrifice his own body and life to correctly devote himself to his virtuous friend.

In a similar way, even if we don't practice the profound path of tantra, if we perfectly follow the virtuous friend as Sadaprarudita did, we can also quickly complete the work of accumulating merit. As we have met not just tantra but the profound path of Highest Yoga Tantra, if we practice guru yoga as the heart of the path as Sadaprarudita did, protecting that practice as we protect our life, there is no doubt that we will soon finish the work of accumulating three countless great eons of merit and achieve enlightenment. It could happen even in this life.

When you meditate on this first benefit, becoming closer to enlightenment by putting the guru's teachings into practice, relate it to every single activity that you do, whether daily practice, retreat or serving others. In your daily life, every single time you carry out your guru's advice—and here we're not talking about just sitting meditation—you accumulate the most extensive merit, perform the greatest purification and become that much closer to enlightenment. Each piece of advice that you follow brings powerful purification because the virtuous friend is the most powerful object in your life. If you relate to what you are doing in this way, you become aware that you are receiving these benefits and can enjoy what you are doing.

Remember all the practices and advice the guru has given you and relate your meditation to them. This applies not only to teachings on the extensive and profound paths but also to each piece of advice you have received on how to live your daily life. Remember all the vows, commitment practices, mantras and meditations. If the guru has granted you ordination, each day that you live in those vows brings you closer to enlightenment. If your guru

---

[39] The patience of unborn Dharma is a state of attainment in which delusions no longer arise.

has given you mantras, prayers or sadhanas to recite or a meditation practice to do, each time you follow his instructions and do the practice, you are
coming closer to enlightenment. After receiving the oral transmission of
the Chenrezig mantra, you become closer to enlightenment each time you
recite it. As you complete each sadhana, you become closer to enlightenment. As you keep each of your samaya vows, you become closer to enlightenment. As you complete each preliminary practice, you become closer to
enlightenment. Each time you do the preparatory practice of cleaning your
room, each movement of vacuuming or sweeping, since it is according to
your guru's instructions, brings you closer to enlightenment.

If your guru has asked you to work in a Dharma center, whether as
director, spiritual program coordinator or something else, each day that
you work in the center makes you closer to enlightenment. You become
closer to enlightenment with each task that you do, since you are carrying
it out on the advice of your guru. Every single thing you do is a method to
achieve enlightenment. With each task that you do, you lessen your negative karma—the cause of the lower realms—and your obscurations become
thinner, so you become closer to enlightenment. For as many years as you
do the job, since you are carrying out your guru's advice, every single thing
you do is bringing you closer and closer to enlightenment.

For example, if you are building a house for a Dharma center, with each
brick that you lay and each piece of wood that you nail, you get closer to
enlightenment. No matter how many years it takes you to build the house,
all your work becomes the cause of happiness. It is the best medicine to
eliminate the root of disease and other sufferings, since it purifies the cause
of suffering, negative karma. As it brings the most powerful purification, it
is also the best preliminary practice.

Remember the great yogi, Milarepa. In Milarepa's biography, you don't
read that he did hundreds of thousands of mandala offerings, prostrations
or any of the other preliminary practices. All you hear about is how he was
beaten, kicked out of teachings and made to do only hard work. Without
giving Milarepa any teachings for many years, Marpa made him build a
tower and then take it apart three times. He had to put every stone back in
its original place, then again build the tower. From carrying all the rocks so
many times, the skin on Milarepa's back became callused and infected. His
hard work was his preliminary practice.[40]

In your daily life you become closer to enlightenment each time you are

---

[40] See p. 320–26 of this book for a more detailed story of the life of Milarepa.

able to carry out a piece of advice given to you by your virtuous friend, each time you are able to practice the teachings. If you are aware of this benefit you will see that you are gaining inconceivable merit all the time you are following your guru's advice. Your life then becomes extremely enjoyable. As time goes by, by continuously carrying out your guru's advice, you become closer and closer to enlightenment.

The sutra *Laying Out of Stalks*, which elaborates on the subject of guru devotion, says,

> For bodhisattvas who live without transgressing the words of the virtuous friend, enlightenment is close.

A root tantric teaching also mentions,

> If you offer yourself as a servant to please the virtuous friend, the virtuous friend grants you enlightenment in the brief lifetime of the quarreling time, even though it would otherwise have been difficult for you to have achieved enlightenment even in ten million eons. To whom does the virtuous friend grant enlightenment in that very lifetime? To the supreme disciple who has blazing perseverance and who is a fit object to be subdued. Those who do not have perseverance and do not put effort into practicing the teachings do not become enlightened, and that is solely the fault of the disciple.

Enlightenment is difficult to achieve and can take an uncountable number of eons in fortunate times, when the length of life is much longer and external obstacles are fewer than in this quarreling time. However, enlightenment can be granted by the virtuous friend even in this degenerate quarreling time, when the lifespan is shorter than one hundred years and the five degenerations[41] are flourishing, causing many obstacles to the practice of Dharma.

The great Indian yogi Padampa Sangye said,

---

[41] The five degenerations are the degenerations of mind, lifespan, sentient beings, times and view. See also note 10, p. 4.

If the guru leads you, you can reach anywhere you wish.
Therefore, people of Tingri, offer the guru devotion and respect.[42]

This verse is not referring to reaching a place but to reaching liberation and enlightenment. If the guru guides you, you can reach wherever you wish, even the state of omniscient mind. Whether you are able to reach the place you wish to go completely depends upon how perfectly you follow the guru. If you don't follow the guru, there is no way the guru can guide you.

During the time of the great yogi Milarepa, Padampa Sangye came to live at Tingri, in Tibet, which is one of the places where people usually stop on the way from Nepal to Lhasa. Both Padampa Sangye and Milarepa had psychic powers and they sometimes tested each other when they met in their travels. One day when Milarepa knew he was going to meet Padampa Sangye he manifested as a flower beside the road to check whether or not Padampa Sangye could recognize him. Padampa Sangye did.

The people of Tingri asked Padampa Sangye for advice, and just before he passed away he gave them many pieces of advice about how they should live their daily lives. This is one piece of advice from that text, which is like Padampa Sangye's will.

In *The Five Stages*, a tantric text on the completion stage, Nagarjuna also said:

> If someone falls down from the top of a mountain, even though he doesn't wish to fall, he will still fall. Like this, if you receive the benefit of even an oral transmission through the kindness of the guru, even if you do not wish to be liberated, you will definitely be liberated.

(b) We become closer to enlightenment by making offerings to and serving our guru

We become closer to enlightenment not only by practicing the advice given us by our guru but even by making offerings to our guru, showing him respect and serving him, as in the stories of Sadaprarudita, Milarepa and Kadampa Geshe Tölungpa. This is because in order to achieve enlighten-

---

[42] See advice number 23, pp. 47–48, *The Hundred Verses of Advice* [Tib: *Tingri Gyatsa*], the compilation of the various advices Padampa Sangye gave the people of Tingri.

ment we need to accumulate extensive merit and the supreme merit field is the virtuous friend. The first verse of the lam-rim prayer in *Guru Puja* describes the guru as the *supreme field of merit*. If we make offerings to our guru we can accumulate in a moment the extensive merit that would take an inconceivable number of eons to accumulate through following any other path. This is why we have the opportunity to achieve enlightenment in this very lifetime. It happens in dependence upon the kindness of the guru.

With respect to fields of merit, as I have already explained, there is more merit in making offerings to our parents than to other ordinary people and in making offerings to ordinary Sangha, monks and nuns, than to our parents. There is progressively more merit in making offerings to arhats, bodhisattvas and buddhas. And there is more merit in making offering to one pore of the guru than to all the buddhas of the three times. There is then no doubt at all that making offering to our own guru must accumulate much more merit—the guru is the supreme field of merit.

The *Samputa Tantra* mentions that making offerings to one pore of the vajra master collects merit superior to that accumulated from making offerings to all the buddhas and bodhisattvas of the ten directions.

A root tantric text also says:

> Making offerings to one pore of the guru surpasses making offerings to all the buddhas of the three times.

A similar point is made in one of the verses of request in *Guru Puja*:

> Even one of your hair-pores is for us
> A field of merit more highly praised
> Than all the conquerors of the three times and ten directions.
> Compassionate refuge savior, I make requests to you.[43]

The *compassionate refuge-savior* is the guru, but what are the *pores* of the guru? While the Tibetan word is the same as that for the pores of the skin, it actually refers to any being who is related to or belongs to your guru. Drogön Tsangpa Gyare said, "The pores of your guru are his disciples, wife, children, servants, relatives, neighbors and even animals, such as horses and dogs."

[43] V. 48.

The disciples referred to here are not the disciples of just anybody who is called "guru" or "lama" but the disciples of any guru with whom you have established Dharma contact. If your guru is not ordained, the guru's wife, husband or companion is also regarded as a pore of the guru. I think even your guru's close friends can be counted as his pores.

Je Drubkhangpa advised,

> Offering to the pores of the guru accumulates infinite merit, more than from making offerings to all the buddhas. When you offer, remember the guru in your heart. This is the way to practice when you make offerings to the pores of the guru.

By remembering the guru with whom you have Dharma contact, you then make offerings to his pores. For example, if you are giving a cup of tea to a fellow disciple, a biscuit to a dog that belongs to your guru or a handful of grass to your guru's horse, first remember your guru in your heart, then make the offering. Previously, when Lama Yeshe had many dogs at Tushita Meditation Centre in Dharamsala, I would try to practice with this faith, even if I was only giving them a piece of biscuit.

By making offerings to one pore of our guru in this way, even if we offer only a piece of fruit or a glass of water, we accumulate far more merit than by making offerings to all the buddhas of the three times or to all the statues, stupas, thangkas, scriptures and other holy objects in the ten directions. Our ability to accumulate all this extensive merit is due to the power of the guru.

Because making offering to even the pores of the guru has this incredible advantage, in the past, when Geshe Tölungpa drank butter tea, he would collect the residue of butter left in his bowl and send it along with his leftover food to the dogs that lived in Lo. Why did he do this? Because his root guru, Geshe Chengawa, lived in Lo, and the dogs belonged to him.

Geshe Tölungpa said, "I accumulate much more merit by giving food to the dogs in Lo than by inviting all the monks of Tölung and offering food to them." Because his guru lived in Lo, the dogs in that village were his guru's pores, so there was more benefit in offering food to them than to the monks in Tölung, who were not disciples of Geshe Chengawa. Tölung is the place near Lhasa where Lama Yeshe was born. I went there to meet Lama's relatives the second time I went to Tibet—I actually went there twice, once on pilgrimage and once to give an initiation.

How quickly we become enlightened depends on how quickly we are able to finish accumulating the merit of fortune and the merit of wisdom. Whether we are concerned about our own happiness or the happiness of all sentient beings, we should take every opportunity to collect merit, even a small amount. And it is easy to accumulate infinite merit just with the beings around us in our everyday life. We don't need to go anywhere special; we have incredible opportunities all around us. There is no doubt about this if you live in a meditation center, where there is often a virtuous friend and also the pores of that virtuous friend. But even if you live in your own home, through making offerings to the pores of the guru, you still have many opportunities to accumulate inconceivable merit, more extensive merit than from making offerings to all the buddhas and bodhisattvas and all the holy objects of the ten directions, as Vajradhara explained in some of the root tantric texts. By generating faith in these points and putting them into practice, we become wise in practicing Dharma, in accumulating merit.

In the large Tibetan monasteries most of the monks are disciples of our own gurus. There are actually very few Tibetan monks and nuns who haven't received teachings from His Holiness the Dalai Lama and we should remember this when we make any offering to a monastery. The merit of making offerings to one such monk is unbelievable, far greater than making offerings to numberless holy objects, and in a large monastery there could be a thousand or more monks who are disciples of our gurus. Even if we offer just a small packet of tea by remembering our guru and thinking that all the monks are disciples of this same guru, although that packet alone couldn't provide tea for all the monks, when added to other tea we are able to make offering to all the thousands of monks in the monastery. We then accumulate unbelievable merit.

It is similar in a meditation center in the West, where even if there are no Sangha, there are still many pores of the virtuous friend. Nowadays more and more students have received teachings from His Holiness the Dalai Lama. Therefore, if from time to time you make offerings of money, food or drink to the students at your center, who are disciples of the same guru, you collect limitless skies of merit. The offering can be made during pujas or other practices or simply as an offering. That is up to you.

I'm not saying that you shouldn't make offerings to the Tibetan monasteries. Of course, by making offering to the Sangha, those with higher ordination, you collect more merit; but at your own Dharma center there are so many students of your own gurus. You have so many incredible opportunities to collect merit; you don't have to make offerings only far away in the East. As I have mentioned, by making offerings to the guru's pores you collect more merit than from having made offerings to numberless buddhas. Can you imagine that?

Also, your offering doesn't need to be only food. It can include supporting the meditation center itself, through a building project or something similar. You are then helping all the students of the center and everyone who comes there to learn Dharma. This naturally becomes an offering.

When I go to Solu Khumbu, because I have the important name of "incarnate lama," the Sherpas often make a material offering of money or something else to me on behalf of someone who has died. They collect the offering by working hard day and night, with much sweat, worry and exhaustion. In turn, I make offerings of the money to the monasteries where there are many pores of the guru so that their offerings aren't wasted. Unbelievable merit is accumulated and again all that merit can be dedicated to the benefactors and to all sentient beings. In this way, the merit from their offering is increased, like investing money in a bank and getting interest. Also, I don't pollute my mind by enjoying those offerings.[44]

I often tell the cooks and managers in monasteries and Dharma centers that I rejoice in their work, because they have a great advantage in accumulating merit. If they know how to practice, they have the opportunity to accumulate unbelievable merit every day, each time they serve drink or food to the disciples of their gurus.

Many years ago at Kopan the cook, Chombi—the one I mentioned first brought me to take teachings from Lama Yeshe—used to get discouraged. He would come to my room and say, "I'm always so busy cooking that I never have time to practice Dharma. I'm always creating negative karma while you're always sitting on your bed saying prayers and meditating." I wasn't sure whether he was joking or serious, but he then said, "After this you will go to a pure realm." He was making his own projections.

I told him, "I just sit here doing nothing—you're the one who actually practices Dharma. Look at how much merit you accumulate every day." Since he had received many initiations and teachings, I told him, "Remember what it says in *Guru Puja*. Making offerings to one pore of the guru brings much more merit than making offerings to the buddhas of the three times. Each

---

[44] A mental pollution comes from using money given on behalf of a dead person for other than Dharma purposes.

time you offer tea in the morning you accumulate unbelievable merit as there are so many disciples of Lama Yeshe in this monastery. At breakfast time you accumulate so much merit, then again at lunch time, at tea time in the evening and then at dinner time. Even in one day you're accumulating unbelievable merit. You should understand this and be happy. You've heard more teachings than I have, so you should think in this way. Actually, you practice Dharma much more than I do—I just sit on my bed doing nothing."

Even if they don't have time to do prostrations, count mandala offerings or sit down to say prayers, I think that cooks in monasteries and Dharma centers accumulate much more merit by offering service. If you give even a candy, a cup of tea or a glass of water to one disciple of your guru, by remembering that guru and then making the offering, in that moment you accumulate more merit than by making offerings to all the buddhas of the three times. Since there is so much merit from making offerings to one pore of the guru, there can be no doubt about the merit of offering breakfast, lunch, dinner and tea to hundreds of fellow disciples. Even if only one or two people actually serve the food, since all the people in the kitchen work together to produce it, they can think in the same way. They should motivate by remembering the guru, offer the food to the pores of the guru, then dedicate the merit to others.

Although the cook himself couldn't afford to invite all those disciples to his home and offer them all meals and cups of tea, in a monastery or Dharma center other people give him this incredible opportunity to perform purification and accumulate extensive merit in such a short time. However, you can still do this practice even if you don't have the chance to be a cook, manager or kitchen worker. Whenever you give anything to a fellow disciple, remember the guru in your heart and that this person is a pore of that guru and then make the offering. That action then becomes a highly skillful method to achieve enlightenment.

If making offerings to the pores of the guru creates more merit than making offerings to all the buddhas of the three times, there can be no doubt that there is much more merit in actually making offerings to the guru. By making offerings to our guru, we collect the most extensive merit. By offering a glass of water or even a candy to our guru, we collect more merit than from having made offerings to numberless Buddhas, Dharma, Sangha, statues, stupas, thangkas and scriptures.

Basili Llorca, Lama Ösel's attendant when he was first at Sera Je Monastery, told me that every morning when Lama Ösel went to receive teachings from Geshe Thubten, he always took along something, usually one of his toys, as an offering. I told Basili that it was a very good practice to continue. Geshe-la was also very happy to see Lama Ösel doing that. Although I don't do this all the time, as I think Lama Ösel did, I try as often as possible to take an offering when I go to see one of my gurus. Since it's an opportunity that comes rarely, it's good to take it. When we have the opportunity to accumulate the most extensive merit from the merit field of the guru, as mentioned here in the eight benefits, we should take it. This doesn't mean that I'm campaigning for you to bring offerings to me, by the way.

When you make an offering to a virtuous friend, it is good, if you are familiar with it, to remember the second *Guru Puja* merit field, where every single part of the guru's holy body is meditated on as different aspects of buddhas and bodhisattvas. For example, the five aggregates are the five Dhyani Buddhas. Or you can think that the guru's holy body is like the assembly of all the buddhas. When you make the offering, think that there are numberless buddhas in each pore of the guru's holy body. This guru yoga practice is very effective for your mind and it also makes your mind very happy.

You become closer to enlightenment every single time you make an offering by thinking of your guru—for example, when you do a mandala offering or make offerings during a sadhana or *Guru Puja*. Whether you are in your own meditation room or somewhere else, each time you make an offering to your guru, either directly or in meditation, you become closer to enlightenment.

Sakya Pandita, an embodiment of Manjushri and one of the five principal lamas of the Sakya tradition,[45] said,

> All the merit you accumulate by practicing the paramita of charity for a thousand eons—giving to other sentient beings not only your head and limbs but even the merit you receive by offering your body in this way—is accumulated in an instant with the path of the guru. Therefore, offer service and feel happy.

The path of the guru refers to practicing guru yoga by making offerings to our guru, whether to the actual or visualized guru. Sakya Pandita is saying that the merit we'd accumulate by practicing the six paramitas, such as the

---

paramita of charity, for thousands of eons is accumulated in an instant by making offerings to the guru. This means that even by offering one bucket of water for the guru to bathe we're able to collect all the merit collected over thousands of eons by giving not only our own body, our most cherished object, to other sentient beings, but even the merit we have accumulated through those actions. The merit we accumulate in an instant by making offerings to our guru is unimaginable.

Sacrificing ourselves by making charity of our body and even our life to other sentient beings for one thousand eons, a great length of time, is incredible. But, as far as finishing the work of accumulating merit is concerned, simply offering one glass of water to a virtuous friend accumulates as much merit. Pabongka Dechen Nyingpo used the example of offering a bucket of water for the guru to bathe, but by offering the guru even a glass of water or a cup of tea, we accumulate in that second an inconceivable amount of merit.

Sakya Pandita then concludes, *Therefore, offer service and feel happy.* We should offer service to the guru and, by remembering the advantages of our service, feel great happiness. For example, just by cleaning our guru's room we become closer to enlightenment. We create infinite merit and this infinite merit is received through the kindness of our guru, through our having a guru-disciple relationship with him.

Sakya Pandita is giving this advice with compassion, as if to someone he feels very close to and wants to save from suffering. The heartfelt nature of his advice is very evident in the Tibetan.

If we make one tiny offering—a stick of incense, a flower or even a grain of rice—to a statue of a buddha, even without bodhicitta or some other virtuous motivation, in that second we accumulate infinite merit. It's hard for our ordinary mind to understand the unimaginable results, including enlightenment, we create by making one tiny offering to even a statue of a buddha, let alone to an actual buddha. Why does it have this unimaginable result? Because of the power of the holy object, because a buddha's power and qualities are inconceivable. This is why there are unimaginable good results from a single action of circumambulating, prostrating or making offering to a statue of a buddha. And there is no need to mention the unbelievable merit we accumulate from making offering to numberless buddhas. Now, Pabongka Dechen Nyingpo says that such merit cannot be compared to the merit from serving our guru, whether actual or visualized, by offering him a bucket of water to bathe.

Padampa Sangye also said,

> If you take care of the guru, who is much more precious than
> the buddhas, you will achieve whatever realizations you wish to
> achieve in this life, people of Tingri.

If we see a statue of a buddha as more precious than the holy body of our
guru, which we regard as an ordinary being's suffering samsaric body, we
will find it very difficult to generate realizations of lam-rim and extremely
difficult to generate realizations of tantra. But if we take care of our guru as
being much more precious than the buddhas, as Padampa Sangye said, we
will generate the realizations of sutra and tantra easily, like rain falling.

Kalachakra Tantra says,

> One cannot become enlightened in this life even if one makes
> offerings to the Triple Gem and saves the lives of millions of crea-
> tures for all the eons of the three times; but if, with devotion, one
> pleases the guru, who has oceans of qualities, one will definitely
> achieve the general and sublime realizations in this life.

In *The Five Stages* Nagarjuna says,

> Give up all other offerings—attempt only to make offerings to
> the guru. By pleasing the guru you will achieve the sublime tran-
> scendental wisdom of omniscience.

Also, the tantric teaching *Ocean of Transcendental Wisdom* says,

> For the wise fortunate one, serving the guru has greater meaning
> than making prostrations to all the buddhas of the three times
> for sixty million eons. If one accomplishes the work according
> to the guru's advice, all one's wishes will quickly be achieved and
> one will collect unimaginable merit. And one who pleases the
> guru with the offering of one's possessions will be liberated from
> the three realms of samsara, be born in the pure realm of nir-
> manakaya and go to the sorrowless state.

Even though samsaric perfections don't have any essence, we obtain essence from the wealth and possessions that we have by offering them to the guru. *Ocean of Transcendental Wisdom* mentions simply possessions but the offering that most pleases the guru is the offering of Dharma practice, which is implied here. The real meaning of offering is pleasing the guru's holy mind, which comes about through practicing Dharma or achieving realizations. It is Dharma practice that most pleases his holy mind, not material offerings.

A *wise fortunate one* is someone whose work accords with the guru's wishes. As said in this tantric teaching, skillfully working for the guru has greater meaning than making prostrations to the buddhas of the three times for millions of eons.

I mention these quotations because I find them very effective when I think of their meaning. They are the true teachings of Guru Shakyamuni Buddha and great yogis, and if we have faith in and practice them, we definitely receive the result. Also, these are quotations from the Buddha and from great yogis who have themselves practiced and completed the path. Because these quotations come from their personal experience, they have much power and we receive much blessing by remembering them and contemplating their meaning. We should especially remember these quotations when we find it difficult to do what the guru advises us to do and are becoming depressed. When working for the guru, it is extremely important to remember again and again the infinite advantages of doing so.

If we remember the benefits explained in the sutra and tantra teachings, the work we do becomes very effective for our mind, just like reading scriptures or doing meditation, and very enjoyable, because we are confident of the result we will receive from it. No matter how hard the work, our motivation for doing it will easily become Dharma. Otherwise, if we don't relate the practice of guru yoga to our own work, instead of working for the guru we'll be working for ourselves. Our motivation will become egocentric and after some time our mind will become empty, dry and without hope. We'll get physically and mentally exhausted and the work we're doing won't make much sense to us. Then there's a danger that we will lose our faith and generate heresy and other kinds of negative thoughts, which throw us into the hells.

When working at a meditation center we sometimes find ourselves in difficult situations. However, we can still be happy if we know how to apply guru yoga practice to that difficult situation. We can think, "This is the blessing of the guru" or "This situation has been purposely manifested by the guru to help me purify my negative karmas and obscurations." When we're finding it hard to deal with a particular person, for example, we can think, "This person has been purposely manifested by the guru to subdue my unsubdued mind, to tame my untamed mind." By relating the situation to guru yoga, we can accept it and be happy.

As explained in *Ocean of Transcendental Wisdom*, those who are able to offer service to their guru are fortunate beings. Why are they fortunate? Because from morning until night, everything they do is following the guru's advice and thus they accumulate unbelievable merit. If we are working at a job that the guru has given us—whether it is cleaning toilets, building houses or even running a business—it is easy for us to think that our purpose in being alive is to serve the guru. We exist to offer service to the guru. And we are fortunate beings, because from morning until night we take care of ourselves for that purpose. We even eat for the purpose of offering service to the guru. We are fortunate if what we are doing is carrying out the guru's advice, because our every movement, even in taking care of ourselves, becomes a method of purifying our negative karma and accumulating extensive merit.

If we have been working hard to serve our guru, we should feel great happiness. We don't need to worry that we don't have time to meditate or do prostrations or any of the other preliminary practices. Remember the life stories of Milarepa and Naropa and think, "This is my preliminary practice to purify my karmic obscurations." Doing hundreds of thousands of prostrations is nothing special. As mentioned in *Ocean of Transcendental Wisdom*, carrying out the guru's advice purifies much more negative karma and accumulates much more merit than does making many millions of prostrations to all the buddhas of the three times for millions of eons.

If you are doing some work on the advice of your guru, you also don't need to worry about not getting to do retreat. It is natural that all your wishes will be fulfilled, whether you are wishing for a long life, to do retreat, to generate the path, to be born in a pure realm or to achieve omniscient mind. Whatever wish you have will be fulfilled without hindrance; it's a natural process, a dependent arising. Following the guru's advice itself is the best puja to prevent hindrances to the fulfillment of your wishes. Generally, accomplishing the wishes of other sentient beings becomes the cause for your own wishes to be fulfilled; so there is no doubt that fulfilling the guru's wishes will cause your wishes to be fulfilled. There is no doubt that any project you have in this life, and in future lives, will be successful. It's the best cause for your own success. You can understand this from the life stories of Dromtönpa, the translator and closest disciple of Lama Atisha, and many of the Kadampa geshes and great yogis. You can also see examples of the truth of this even with present practitioners, many of whom underwent hardships in carrying out their guru's advice and experienced success later in their lives.

All your wishes are fulfilled because you collect unimaginable merit and purify so much negative karma. Purifying karmic obscurations itself prevents hindrances to your practice, thus ensuring the success of your Dharma wishes. Because of the hardships you have previously undergone in following the guru's advice, if you do strict retreat in an isolated place, you will be very successful, with no hindrances.

If we can remember how fortunate we are and the advantages of what we are doing, we can feel incredible happiness from morning until night. Even though we mightn't have realization of emptiness or of the generation and completion stages, we can still be satisfied with what we have.

If we understand guru devotion practice and all its eight benefits and are aware of them every day, there is no way that we could be other than happy to do all the hundreds, thousands, billions of things we have to do, especially when we work in a Dharma center. There is no happier life to be found on this earth. We recognize this if we know how to correctly devote ourselves to the virtuous friend. If we know even the very first benefit, that we become closer to enlightenment each time we carry out our guru's advice or make an offering to or serve him, we will know how to think. The more we have to do and the harder it is, the more we will see that there is no better, no happier life than this.

(2) We please all the buddhas

The second advantage of correctly devoting ourselves to the virtuous friend is that we please all the buddhas.

The Essence of Nectar mentions,

> When a disciple correctly follows the holy virtuous friend,
> The thought that this practitioner will quickly be liberated from
>   samsara
> Profoundly pleases the holy minds of all the Victorious Ones,
> Like a mother who sees that her son has been benefited.

There is also a reference to this in the sutra *Laying Out of Stalks*, which states,

> The holy minds of the buddhas are happy with the bodhisattvas
> who have entered the teaching revealed by the guru.

Just as a mother is very happy when she sees someone helping her beloved child, all the buddhas are pleased when we devote ourselves correctly to our virtuous friend with thought and with action, following their advice and serving them. Even though the person doesn't actually help the mother, she is still extremely pleased that they are giving help to her son. Similarly, if we correctly follow our guru's advice, which is the main service, and make offerings and so forth, all the buddhas are extremely pleased with us from their hearts. If we please our virtuous friend, all the buddhas are pleased and even the deity that we practice becomes closer to us. We are given guidance and granted blessings. Pleasing the guru means pleasing all the buddhas, and we receive the blessings of all the buddhas.

Pabongka Dechen Nyingpo explains that the virtuous friend is the form in which all the buddhas manifest in order to subdue us. If we don't devote ourselves correctly to the virtuous friend, even if we make thousands of offerings to all the buddhas of the ten directions every day, there is no way that the buddhas will be pleased with us. Similarly, if we disturb the holy mind of the virtuous friend by not following his advice but at the same time make thousands of offerings to the buddhas, there is again no way we will please all the buddhas and no way we will attain realizations or even have any good experiences.

If, however, we correctly follow the guru and then make offerings, we please all the buddhas. Why? Because the guru is the embodiment of all the buddhas. In order to subdue our mind, all the buddhas manifested in this particular aspect, in accord with our karma or, in other words, our merit. If we correctly follow our virtuous friend, even without needing to be invoked, all the buddhas living in all the directions will happily abide in our guru's holy body and accept our offerings.

The highly realized yogi Buddhajñana explained,

> I shall dwell in the bodies
> Of those who are living in this meaning

And accept offerings from practitioners.
Pleasing the virtuous friend purifies
The karmic obscurations in the minds of practitioners.

This means that Buddha himself dwells in the body of the qualified virtuous friend and accepts the offerings of the practitioners who correctly follow that virtuous friend. This pleases the buddhas and thus purifies the karmic obscurations in the minds of the practitioners.

A similar thing is said in *The Essence of Nectar,*

It is said that when a disciple correctly follows the guru,
Even if not invoked, the buddhas will happily enter
The guru's holy body, accept all the offerings,
And also bless the mindstream of the disciple.

The buddhas will accept the offerings from the disciple and also bless her mind, which means that her mind will be transformed so that it becomes capable of generating realizations.

As the guru is the embodiment transformed by all the buddhas in order to lead us to liberation and enlightenment, as I've already explained, by making just one cup of tea and offering it to our guru, in that moment we receive the infinite benefits of having actually offered tea to all the buddhas of the three times. As said in many prayers, the guru is the sublime field of merit.

Offering the guru even one cup of tea is like having actually made offering to all the buddhas, but the benefit is much greater. As Pabongka Dechen Nyingpo points out, if we make an offering to the buddhas of the three times, we gain the benefit of having made the offering but we can't be sure that the buddhas actually accept our offering with pleased holy minds. However, by making an offering to the guru we receive both the benefit of having made an offering to all the buddhas and of having the offering accepted. In this way we are able to quickly finish the work of accumulating merit.

(3) WE ARE NOT HARMED BY MARAS OR EVIL FRIENDS

If we correctly devote ourselves to our virtuous friend with thought and with action, allowing ourselves to be under the control of the virtuous friend, we won't be harmed by maras or evil friends. Because of our strong devotion, we purify inconceivable obscurations and past negative karmas and accumulate extensive merit; non-human beings, such as the devas and spirits who disturb the practice of virtue, and even human beings cannot then harm us. Even the four elements—earth, water, fire and air—cannot give us harm.

Generally speaking, someone with a lot of merit has much power and cannot be harmed by others, even though others might dislike the person and want to harm him. Such a practitioner has much success in his practice, in achieving realizations. But when a person's level of merit becomes low because he commits a heavy negative karma or stops creating extensive merit, he experiences a lot of problems in his life. Human and non-human beings are then able to harm him.

There are two types of maras: inner and outer. Inner maras are karma and delusions. Outer maras are worldly beings who cause delusions to increase, such as nagas, devas and various types of spirits; they can also be human beings, "evil friends." Someone who practices correct devotion to his virtuous friend can't be harmed by evil friends simply because he follows his virtuous friend and not the evil friends. Because of that, even evil friends can't be a bad influence and lead him in the wrong path.

Outer maras, such as the Deva's Son [Skt: *devaputramara*] and other black-side devas, dislike seeing people practice Dharma and can interfere with their practice by causing sickness, extreme desire and other problems. For example, in someone who is trying to practice charity, maras can cause miserliness to arise. Maras can cause ordained people to no longer recognize their ordination as a good thing and wish to no longer be a monk or nun. Maras can cause someone in retreat to suddenly change her mind and not want to do the retreat. The mudra of Guru Shakyamuni Buddha's right hand, with the palm resting on the right knee and the middle finger touching the ground, indicates that he has control over the Deva's Son.

There are many different types of outer maras. *Tsen* are spirits that live above the earth and can cause epilepsy, strokes and other diseases. (They are the cooperative cause, of course; the principal cause is karma.) Landlord, or local, spirits live on the earth and can drive people crazy and cause catastrophes. Spirits, nagas and *dön*, or demons, live below the earth and can cause infections. Local spirits, tsen and *gyal-gong* can possess people and make them crazy.

The teachings advise people doing retreat not to recite mantras at noon or when the sun is rising or setting because during these times maras come to distract the mind. If you do recite mantras at these times, they should not be counted as part of the retreat because your mind will be distracted and the recitation will not be perfect. I count the mantras anyway, because for me it doesn't make any difference—there's no concentration at any time.

In the sutra *Extensively Manifesting,* Guru Shakyamuni Buddha explains,

> The person who correctly follows the guru accumulates extensive merit. From that cause, he experiences the result of happiness. Ripening of merit brings happiness and eliminates all suffering. That fortunate one accomplishes all his wishes, defeats the maras and quickly reaches enlightenment. He also achieves the coolness of the sorrowless state.

Here, the coolness of nirvana is contrasted with the heat of samsara. Samsara, which is only in the nature of suffering, is hot, like a fire; nirvana, the sorrowless state, is like a cool breeze. Those who correctly devote themselves to the virtuous friend accumulate extensive merit and thus avoid being harmed by maras and succeed not only in removing their own suffering and receiving happiness but also in removing the sufferings of others and granting them happiness.

Another sutra says,

> The fortunate being is unable to be harmed by devas or maras.

The Essence of Nectar also explains,

> At that time, because the blessings of all the buddhas
> Enter the opening of the devotional mind,
> One isn't harmed by multitudes of maras and delusions.

Here *maras* might be related to the outer maras and *delusions* to the inner maras. As one isn't overwhelmed by the inner maras, the delusions, one is also not overwhelmed by outer maras. It is because of our disturbing thoughts and karma that we are harmed by outer maras. Having wholehearted devotion enables us to receive the blessings of the guru and we are then unable to be harmed by inner and outer maras. We are able to conquer all our enemies, the maras, especially the inner maras of the disturbing thoughts and the subtle mara of dual view. In this way we are then able to achieve buddhahood, with completion of all the qualities of cessation and realization.

(4) ALL OUR DELUSIONS AND NEGATIVE ACTIONS NATURALLY CEASE

If we correctly devote ourselves to a virtuous friend, all our delusions and vices naturally stop. We realize the advantages of devoting ourselves to a virtuous friend and also look at unsubdued minds and wrong conduct as our enemy. As we understand what is to be practiced and what is to be abandoned, we are able to give up wrong conduct. Either because we follow our teacher's example or because we practice correct devotion from our own side, all our disturbing thoughts and negative actions are naturally stopped. When we are following a guru, we allow ourselves to be under his control instead of that of our delusions.

Those who correctly devote themselves to the guru cannot be led in the wrong way because, as said in the sutra *Laying Out of Stalks*,

> It is difficult for one who is guided by a virtuous friend to be overwhelmed by karma and the unsubdued mind.

The Essence of Nectar also mentions,

> If one always devotes to the virtuous friend,
> All delusions and wrong conduct spontaneously cease.

If a guru is living an ascetic life, with no interest in worldly activities, the disciples who take teachings from and live with that guru will automatically follow his example and also live an ascetic life. The disciples will also be content, have little desire and turn their back on the eight worldly dharmas. Because of the teacher, the disciples will naturally become pure Dharma practitioners, leaving behind all concern for happiness, comfort, food, clothing and reputation. When the thought of worldly concern is left behind, the disciples will tend not to generate delusions and create negative karma.

If a teacher is strict in the practice of virtue, rather than eating, sleeping and enjoying himself all the time, he will always attempt, day and night, not to waste his time. He will stay up late at night attempting to practice virtue. His disciples will also continuously attempt to practice virtue and not spend much time on the pleasures of this life. If a virtuous teacher is a great learned being who has done extensive listening and reflecting, his disciples will also have extensive understanding of what is to be practiced and what is to be avoided. If the teacher is strict in moral conduct, abstaining from vices with his three doors, his disciples will also naturally be careful in moral conduct. Good disciples will automatically be like their teacher, renouncing even small vices. In this way, delusions and wrong actions naturally cease.

In a similar way, if the guru does much practice of bodhicitta, renouncing the self and cherishing others, his disciples will also automatically follow that example, naturally practicing the good heart. This is shown by the examples of Lama Suvarnadvipi and his disciples, such as Lama Atisha; Lama Atisha and his disciples, such as Dromtönpa; and Geshe Potowa and his disciples, such as Geshe Sharawa.

If we understand the eight benefits of correctly following the guru and the eight shortcomings of incorrectly following the guru, which actually form part of the subject of karma, we understand the vices of body, speech and mind from which we should abstain. Looking at vices and the unsubdued mind as our enemies, we will then be able to renounce them and practice their remedies.

(5) ALL OUR REALIZATIONS OF THE PATHS AND BHUMIS INCREASE

The fifth benefit of correctly following the guru is that all our realizations of the paths and bhumis will effortlessly increase, even in each second. If we follow the virtuous friend correctly, even if we don't meditate much, realizations will spontaneously, effortlessly, be generated.

The quickest way to achieve realizations is to do what most pleases the holy mind of the virtuous friend, which means following his advice. We normally have such questions as "How can I have realizations quickly?" or "How can I develop my mind quickly in the path to enlightenment?" but somehow we don't think of this section of the lam-rim, which is the answer. Our answer is normally not this basic one but that we need to do more retreat or some other practice. We don't know or we forget that it is guru devotion practice that made it possible for the past and present practitioners to achieve realizations quickly. We think that some other practice will enable us to achieve realizations quickly, but it doesn't work.

Correctly following the guru and serving him increases realizations hour by hour, minute by minute, second by second, and our obscurations are purified in a similar way. The reason we are not enlightened now is that we have obscurations. If we had no obscurations, we would be a buddha now. It's simply a question of our having obscurations.

The Essence of Nectar says,

> Realizations of the paths and bhumis are generated and increase.
> The white dharmas spontaneously develop,
> So one achieves extensive happiness in this and future lives.

Also, the *Perfection of Wisdom* says,

> Finding the profound meaning of the *Perfection of Wisdom*, emptiness, depends on only the virtuous friend. By depending on the virtuous friend, one approaches the paths and bhumis.

And Lama Tsongkhapa says in *The Great Treatise on the Stages of the Path to Enlightenment,*

> The multitudes of realizations increase higher and higher in one who never transgresses the bodhisattva's conduct and always sees the guru as a buddha and is mindful of the advantages of offering service and the disadvantages of generating heresy, thinking, "If I generate heresy, I will be born in the hells" or "If I act in this way it will harm my achievement of enlightenment."

There are many stories of Kadampa geshes, other past great yogis and even present meditators who have correctly followed the virtuous friend and increased their experiences and realizations of the path to enlightenment.

Take Lama Atisha's disciples, for example. Gönpawa always meditated. Lama Atisha would even go to Gönpawa's hermitage to give him teachings, rather than Gönpawa go to Lama Atisha. Dromtönpa was always busy translating for Lama Atisha and doing other work. And the monk, A-me Jangchub Rinchen, cooked for and served Lama Atisha. (I used to think that there was a printing error in the text and that the cook was actually a nun, Ani Jangchub Rinchen, but Ribur Rinpoche explained that the cook was a monk, A-me Jangchub Rinchen.)

A-me Jangchub Rinchen was worried that he didn't have time to meditate or do retreat because he always had so much cooking to do. When he told Dromtönpa of his concerns, Dromtönpa replied, "I have no other thought in my mind except to offer service to Lama Atisha." That answer completely satisfied A-me Jangchub Rinchen and his problem disappeared.

One day, alone in his hermitage, Gönpawa thought to himself, "Because I meditate all the time I must have a much higher level of realization than Dromtönpa, who is always busy translating for Lama Atisha and never has time to meditate or do retreat. And I should definitely have more realizations than A-me Jangchub Rinchen, who is always busy cooking for Lama Atisha."

Lama Atisha, with his clairvoyance, immediately discovered what Gönpawa was thinking in his meditation room. He called Gönpawa, Dromtönpa and A-me Jangchub Rinchen together and sat them down in front of him. He then checked to see whose mind was most developed. Lama Atisha saw that Dromtönpa's level of realization was the highest, much higher than Gönpawa's, and even A-me Jangchub Rinchen had higher realizations than Gönpawa.

Even though Gönpawa had not been busy working but had been meditating all the time, his level of realization was the lowest of the three. Even though Dromtönpa and the cook were extremely busy and had no time to meditate, they purified their minds by bearing hardships to serve Lama Atisha. This is why their level of realization was higher. Because we have buddha-nature, if we purify our mind, realizations will manifest from within it.

Before coming to central Tibet and becoming Lama Atisha's translator, Dromtönpa lived in Kham and was the disciple-servant of his first guru, Lama Setsun, whom he served for a long time. Dromtönpa once asked Lama Atisha what had been the best Dharma practice out of all the things he, Dromtönpa, had done in his life. He told Lama Atisha about his various practices and also explained how hard he had worked for Lama Setsun. At night, armed, he guarded all the lama's animals. During the daytime, he did many other things. He made all the fires. The lama's wife used Dromtönpa as a seat while she milked the cows out in the fields. Every morning for many years Dromtönpa would clean the kitchen and take out the ashes left from the fire. While Dromtönpa was using his hands to spin yarn, he'd be kneading butter into dried animal skins to make them soft and pliable with his feet. At the same time, he'd also be carrying something on his back. For many years, he worked like this—doing many things at the same time. Dromtönpa explained all this to Lama Atisha, who said, "Of all the things you have done, only your hard work for Lama Setsun has been the real Dharma."

Dromtönpa correctly devoted himself to Lama Atisha for seventeen years. From the time Dromtönpa met Lama Atisha, he never left Lama Atisha in the dark at night: every night he offered a butter lamp in Lama Atisha's room.

When Lama Atisha was showing the aspect of old age and sickness, he became incontinent; he couldn't control his bladder or bowels and would urinate and defecate in his bed. With a continuous feeling of guru devotion and without any superstitious thought that it was dirty, Dromtönpa would clean away the feces with his hands and take them outside.

One day after he had served Lama Atisha in this way, Dromtönpa spontaneously went into a state of concentration. When he arose from it, he had suddenly developed clairvoyance and was able to read clearly all the thoughts in the minds of sentient beings—even ants—up to a distance that it would take an eagle eighteen days to fly. Dromtönpa's mind became so clear because of the purification that came from serving Lama Atisha, including cleaning up his excrement.

This didn't come about through Dromtönpa's simply understanding the words of Dharma. Dromtönpa sacrificed himself to serve Lama Atisha and by doing so he purified some of his obscurations. This is why he suddenly developed this clairvoyant knowledge.

Because Dromtönpa correctly devoted himself to his virtuous friend in this way, he became the head of the Kadampa tradition, the successor of Lama Atisha, and his holy name became renowned in the ten directions. Also, Lama Atisha's holy actions, as vast as the sky, to benefit the teachings of Buddha and sentient beings in the arya land of India and in Tibet came about only through his having correctly devoted himself to his virtuous friends.

There is a similar story about how Kadampa Geshe Chayulwa served his guru, Geshe Chengawa. Chayulwa was originally a disciple of Geshe Tölungpa, who offered him to his own guru Geshe Chengawa because Chayulwa was such a good disciple and had served him so well. Geshe Chengawa was extremely pleased by this.

Every day Chayulwa served his guru Geshe Chengawa by cleaning his room. And whenever Geshe Chengawa called, even if Chayulwa was in the middle of doing something, as soon as he heard his guru's voice he would immediately stop what he was doing and go to serve him. If Chayulwa was offering a mandala when Geshe Chengawa called him, he would stop before he had finished offering the mandala and run to serve him. If he was writing the letter *nga*, not even waiting to finish the syllable, he would immediately run to serve Geshe Chengawa.

One morning, after Chayulwa had finished cleaning Geshe Chengawa's room, he collected all the dirt in the lap of his robes and went to carry it down the stairs to throw it out. When he reached the third step he suddenly saw numberless buddhas right there, a sign that he had reached the level of the great path of merit, Concentration of Continual Dharma. When you achieve the Concentration of Continual Dharma you see countless buddhas in nirmanakaya aspect and are able to continuously receive teachings from them. Before this Chayulwa had not been able to see even one buddha. Like heaping up grain, realizations then came in his mind. That was the result of his having purified his negative karma and obscurations through offering service with a pure mind of guru devotion.

Seeing or not seeing buddhas doesn't depend on the buddhas but only on our mind. It is not that the buddhas were normally not there but on that particular day they came to the steps. The buddhas were always there, inside and outside the room, but Geshe Chayulwa saw them only when he had purified his obscurations by his strong practice of guru yoga. If we purify our mind we can see buddhas wherever we are. It's not necessary for us to be in a holy place because there is no place where there is no buddha. We don't see buddhas at the moment only because we haven't purified our karmic obscurations.

When his guru Jetsun Dragpa Gyaltsen showed the aspect of heavy sickness, Sakya Pandita nursed him day and night. He bore many hardships to take care of Dragpa Gyaltsen, going without food and sleep, day and night. Sakya Pandita completely sacrificed himself to take care of his guru, cherishing him more than his own life.

Dragpa Gyaltsen was extremely pleased with the way Sakya Pandita had dedicated himself to serving him and later taught Sakya Pandita the Manjushri guru yoga practice, involving meditation on the inseparability of the guru and Manjushri, the embodiment of the wisdom of all the buddhas. When he did this practice, Sakya Pandita actually saw Dragpa Gyaltsen in the aspect of Manjushri. All the service that Sakya Pandita offered his guru when he was sick brought incredible purification. Because he pleased his guru, he was then able to realize that his guru was Manjushri.

Sakya Pandita then achieved many realizations and became very learned. He became famous and highly respected for his learning in Tibet and China and liked everywhere, not only by human beings but even by gods and spirits. He was invited to China by the Emperor, who became his disciple. He became a great pandit, highly learned not only in the inner knowledge of Buddhadharma but in the five fields of knowledge, which include poetry, logic, handicrafts and languages. Expert in the entire Buddhadharma and confident in explaining it, Sakya Pandita was thus able to offer extensive benefit to the teachings of Buddha and to many sentient beings.

Another example of developing realizations through the practice of guru devotion is Trichen Tenpa Rabgye, one of the Ganden Tripas. When his teacher Ngawang Chöjor was very sick, Trichen Tenpa Rabgye himself almost died of worry. Because he served his teacher perfectly during his illness, Trichen Tenpa Rabgye purified great karmic obscurations and then realized emptiness, actualizing the Prasangika right view. Before that, even though Trichen Tenpa Rabgye had studied and meditated a lot on emptiness, no realizations had come.

There is also a story about Phurchog Ngawang Jampa, whose guru was Je Drubkhangpa. When Je Drubkhangpa was in a cave doing single-pointed practice on the path, Phurchog Ngawang Jampa offered service to his guru, even though he himself was a very high practitioner. Because there were no trees in the place where Je Drubkhangpa was doing retreat, animal dung had to be used as fuel for fires. Phurchog Ngawang Jampa, even though he was old, would carry heavy loads of dung up the mountain and offer them to his guru. In this way, he underwent much hardship. One day Je Drubkhangpa gave him a little of the inner offering, which he had blessed, from his skullcup. Because of his guru yoga practice, when Phurchog Ngawang Jampa drank the inner offering, it blessed his mind so that he generated an intense thought of renunciation of samsara.

Some years ago, when I was staying at Tushita Retreat Centre in Dharamsala, I offered some beautiful begonias to His Holiness the Dalai Lama. Offering the flowers was a little tricky as, although they were incredibly beautiful, they flowered only briefly and would lose all their petals within a day or so. I offered the flowers in painted butter tins, along with a money offering of thirty rupees in an envelope, on which I'd written a short request for the development of my mind. At that time His Holiness was in retreat, so I left the offering at the Private Office.

I think that His Holiness must have been pleased with the offering of the flowers, because that night I dreamt that His Holiness, seated on a throne in the temple, gave me a little inner offering from the skullcup on his table, and I drank it.

The next morning when I woke up, my mind was somehow different. Normally, I'm extremely lazy, but during that time, I think because of the influence of the many lamas there in Dharamsala, who energized me, I had a tiny bit of energy to meditate a little in the mornings. I tried to do a little lam-rim meditation as a motivation for the day and as a result, that next morning my meditation was much more effective than usual. I had a strong wish to be reborn in hell for the sake of others. I wanted to be in the hot hells right that minute. The feeling was unbearable; I couldn't suppress it. This wish was so strong that I cried out loud for half an hour, sobbing like a small child.

I think His Holiness had prayed for me the previous night; he definitely did something that blessed my mind. My mind was different. The dream and the meditation experience were definite signs of His Holiness's blessing. There might also have been some purification from having offered the flowers. From the three types of kindness of the guru, such an experience is an example of the guru's kindness in blessing the disciple's mind. Of course, the effect completely disappeared after a few hours.

After that I became very interested in buying flower seeds and planting them. When they grew well, I then offered the flowers to the lamas there in Dharamsala. I discovered that the best offering was a flower offering.

Also, when we do a Vajrasattva retreat or any other retreat that our guru has advised us to do, we sometimes have strong experiences of impermanence, feeling that our death could happen at any moment, so that we have no other thought except to practice Dharma. Or strong thoughts of loving kindness and compassion arise. All these are signs of the kindness of the guru in having blessed our mind. Even those small, transient experiences prove that if we continue our practice of guru yoga, we will definitely develop realizations. It is proof that realizations can definitely happen and can be increased.

The great Pabongka Rinpoche had a monk-attendant, Jamyang, who served him for many years, in his first incarnation and also in his second, who studied in Tibet, escaped to India and became a geshe at Buxa Duar, before showing the aspect of cancer and passing away. As soon as Pabongka Rinpoche's second incarnation became a geshe, he received all the lineages of initiations from my root guru, His Holiness Trijang Rinpoche. These lineages, including many special ones, had been passed to His Holiness Trijang Rinpoche by Pabongka Dechen Nyingpo, the first incarnation. Jamyang was also able to meet the third incarnation, who studied at Sera Monastery.

Although Jamyang couldn't even read the Tibetan alphabet, before Pabongka Dechen Nyingpo passed away he told Jamyang that later he would be able to read the *Guru Puja* text by himself, without needing anybody to teach him.

After Jamyang escaped from Tibet, he went to Buxa Duar, where he lived with the incarnation of Pabongka Dechen Nyingpo. Lama Yeshe was also living in the same building the first time I went to receive teachings from him. Lama Lhundrup,[46] who told me this story, also lived there.

Lama Lhundrup told me that when Jamyang was first at Buxa he couldn't even read the Tibetan alphabet but after some time an understanding of it came to him spontaneously. Without anybody teaching him to read, he somehow came to recognize the letters and was then able to read the whole *Guru Puja* by himself, just as Pabongka Dechen Nyingpo had predicted.

This was the result of the purification that came from Jamyang serving and correctly devoting himself to Pabongka Dechen Nyingpo in Tibet. Such things cannot be explained by Western science because it has no concept of negative karma and obscurations. Of course, Western science has a concept of ignorance, of not knowing something, but it has no concept of such things as negative karma, defilements and karmic obscurations. Without understanding these things, there's no way to explain how Jamyang could suddenly read without having been taught. It was a sign of his mind having been purified. When the mind is purified, understanding comes from within, without need of a teacher.

Jamyang's story can also be related to the first benefit of correctly devoting yourself to the guru: becoming closer to enlightenment by carrying out the guru's advice and by making offering to and serving him. Jamyang devoted himself to Pabongka Dechen Nyingpo with action—carrying out his advice, offering service and making material offerings—for many years. That itself brought great purification, purifying heavy negative karmas and making his obscurations thinner. And when obscurations become thinner,

---

[46] Khen Rinpoche Lama Lhundrup Rigsel is the abbot of Kopan Monastery, Nepal.

understanding of Dharma increases. With thicker obscurations there is less understanding of Dharma. Because of his many years of guru yoga practice, his obscurations became quite thin; therefore, without anybody teaching him the alphabet, he was able to recognize the letters and read by himself. It was a sign that he had become closer to enlightenment and also that his Dharma understanding, or realizations, had increased.

Jamyang passed away at the beginning of 1985 at Kalimpong, in India. By then he was no longer a monk. He didn't appear to be a great practitioner; he just seemed to be a happy, relaxed person who enjoyed himself. When he was passing away, Jamyang said, "I have done everything I was supposed to do, except for one thing." It seems there was only one job that he didn't finish. There weren't any stories of Jamyang being a great meditator or doing a lot of retreat, but when he passed away he stayed in the meditation state for some days, and when his holy body was offered fire at the funeral, it emitted beams of five-colored light. This was a clear sign that he would be born in a pure realm.

Kadampa Geshe Chengawa mentioned,

> A disciple who practices correct devotion to the virtuous friend, even if he is as foolish as a dog or a pig, will have no difficulty in becoming like Manjushri.

In other words, even disciples who are not intelligent and who have little understanding of Dharma can without any difficulty become like Manjushri, the embodiment of the wisdom of all the buddhas, if they practice strong guru devotion and please the holy mind of the virtuous friend. A disciple might have little intelligence, but if his devotion is strong and stable he will have no difficulty in accomplishing the guru's advice. There will then be only great joy, because of the limitless skies of benefit he gets from that.

Even though a person might be very foolish, if he has indestructible devotion he has the most important thing in life. Sooner or later this will bring him all success. This is "lucky" intelligence. Some people are intelligent and educated but because they have no merit they find it hard to understand and have faith in karma. They're of "unlucky" intelligence because they're unable to practice Dharma.

Many years ago, I was talking with one of my uncles about the Kopan monks at Lawudo, where Kopan Monastery first started. My uncle said, "It's no use. Sooner or later they'll go trekking with a rucksack on their back.

They are of unlucky intelligence." He was saying that they would come to know the English language and many other things but they would have no merit to continue to be monks and to practice Dharma.

It looks a little strange to say that generating realizations depends on devotion to the guru rather than on understanding teachings. It seems illogical but it's something that we can clearly understand through our own experiences.

When the water of devotion to the guru has dried up, our mind is like a rock. When we don't have much feeling for guru devotion in our heart, our practice becomes just words and any meditation that we do also becomes just words. Our meditation doesn't touch our heart and isn't really effective for our mind.

At other times, when we have more devotion and really feel the kindness of the guru from our heart, any meditation that we try is very effective and very powerful. When we meditate on impermanence and death, we see the vision of this life as being very short and are less concerned about this life. When we meditate for a short time on bodhicitta, such unbearable compassion arises that we are unable to suppress it. We feel from our heart the kindness of other sentient beings; we feel unbelievable compassion for the suffering of others and also have thoughts of love. Our dedication is also strengthened: right that moment we have a strong wish to immediately be born in hell for the sake of other sentient beings. We have such a strong, uncontrollable wish to do this that we cry like a baby.

When the virtuous friend is happy with us and what we are doing, experiences of the path come very easily. If we are trying to experiment on emptiness, it somehow prevents hindrances to our meditation. Our meditation is very clear, and with just one or two words we're able to recognize the object to be refuted. We suddenly recognize the unification of emptiness and dependent arising that Lama Tsongkhapa talks about so much in his teachings, especially in the chapter on special insight in *The Great Treatise on the Stages of the Path to Enlightenment*. At such times, this experience comes very easily. When we have very clear understanding of this unification, stronger devotion arises, especially to Lama Tsongkhapa and to our own virtuous friend, who created the conditions for us to see the meaning of emptiness, of which we have been ignorant during beginningless samsaric lifetimes.

Many sutra and tantra teachings say that we have to practice the path that is pleasing to the virtuous friend. Experience of the path, transformation of the mind, has very much to do with this. When our guru is very pleased with us, our mind changes very easily and very quickly has experiences. At other times our mind is more difficult to change. Through our own individual practice, this dependent arising—that our growth in life depends on the guru's holy mind—can become our scientific experience.

Pleasing the holy mind of the virtuous friend isn't just about making offerings. When you do a retreat or something else that your guru wishes you to do, it pleases his holy mind. During such times, besides the fact that your mind is very happy, many good signs appear in dreams. At night you might dream of the deity being happy with you and giving you presents, for example. The retreat is different from other times. Even from the very beginning, when you have recited hardly any mantras, the retreat is very blissful. Somehow your meditation works: it is extremely effective for your mind and you find it enjoyable. This is not external enjoyment, like the excitement you feel when you are skiing or sky surfing, where people seem to be using their precious human rebirth to try to become a bird as quickly as possible. It is not that kind of enjoyment. There is incredible satisfaction in your heart. There is so much joy even while you're doing the sadhana. Many good signs, signs of purification, happen. Everything you do becomes Dharma and no matter what you meditate on, you are able to feel it very easily and very effectively in your heart.

All these things mean that you are receiving the blessings of the deity in your mental continuum. They mean that the deity is pleased with you. Why? Because you are doing something that pleases your virtuous friend. As your virtuous friend is pleased with you at that time, you naturally become closer to the deity and all these signs of receiving blessings happen.

Another point is that if you are doing something positive, something very pleasing to the holy mind of the guru, even if you don't inform the guru about what you are doing and there is a great physical distance between you, you have dreams of the guru being extremely happy and giving you presents, blessings and so forth. Or in a dream the guru looks magnificent and smiles at you.

Also, if you are in some kind of trouble, perhaps with some risk to your life, you have visions of the guru or see him in a dream and receive guidance or help.

I'm very lazy about doing retreat and rarely do it, but many years ago, on Lama Yeshe's advice, I did a short retreat in the small hut that used to be right on the top of the hill at Kopan. I found that retreat unbelievably beneficial, unbelievably effective. I didn't have any realizations but I enjoyed myself very much. In the early mornings, even before I began the sadhana, I found whatever lam-rim subject I thought about unbelievably effective. There was a big difference from other times. This happened by the kindness of Lama Yeshe, who wanted me to do that particular retreat very much. Like a bubble bursting from water, I suddenly jumped into it.

Lama Yeshe was extremely happy when I started the retreat and at the end, when I came out of the retreat, I found that Lama had made special preparations in my room. In Bodhgaya he had bought new Tibetan carpets and a very expensive cup, which he had filled with the best Tibetan tea brought by Lama's brother from Tibet.

I was very fortunate and enjoyed myself very much, but I think this was only because Lama was very happy with me. I couldn't find any other reason that I had such a good time.

(6) We will never lack virtuous friends in all our future lives

Correctly devoting ourselves to the virtuous friend helps us not to lack gurus in future lives. In other words, by correctly devoting ourselves to our virtuous friend with thought and action in this life, we'll be able to meet virtuous friends in all our future lives. That we have been able to meet many qualified virtuous friends in this life is a result of our practice of guru devotion either in this life or in past lives; it is the result of our past good karma.

Kadampa Geshe Potowa said,

> After having made Dharma contact, we must respect the guru.
> It is natural that we then won't lack a guru in future lives,
> Because karma is never lost.

Our lack of success in developing our mind and gaining attainments is not because we haven't made a Dharma connection and established a guru-disciple relationship but because after establishing a relationship we haven't practiced correctly. Our lack of progress comes from not holding to the Dharma connections we have established and not devoting ourselves correctly to our gurus.

Some people might say that the reason they don't have attainments is that they haven't received some secret or profound teaching from their gurus or because they haven't met many gurus or many well-known ones. However, it's just that from their side they haven't practiced exactly as they've been taught. Our not having realizations is not because we don't have many gurus but because we haven't correctly devoted ourselves to our gurus with thought and action as the teachings explain. If we had practiced perfectly, by now we would have achieved enlightenment, the completion stage, the generation stage, or at least realized bodhicitta or emptiness. From our side we haven't practiced exactly what we've been taught; from the side of our gurus, they have shown us the unmistaken path and done everything possible for us.

I think that we are incredibly fortunate to have met so many qualified gurus who have revealed the unmistaken sutra and tantra paths to the happiness of future lives, liberation and enlightenment. We can understand this when we compare ourselves to those who have been unable to meet a qualified teacher and have no understanding of Dharma. So many people cannot find a guru who can teach them how to create the unmistaken cause for even the happiness of future lives, let alone enlightenment. We should appreciate how fortunate we are and how precious this opportunity is. Otherwise, it becomes commonplace, like having breakfast or lunch every day.

It's amazing, like a dream, that we have the karma even to meet such qualified teachers, let alone be able to hear complete teachings from them. We should rejoice in how fortunate we are. And because of our good fortune, we should continue to practice as much as possible.

Once we have made a Dharma connection with someone, we should look at that person in a new way, devoting ourselves to him as our virtuous friend. Geshe Potowa then gives the reason that, having made the connection, we should hold on to it and respect the guru: *karma is never lost*.

The Essence of Nectar says,

> If we please the guru properly in this life,
> Experiencing the result similar to the cause
> Will be that we will meet supreme virtuous friends in all future lives
> And hear the perfect, unmistaken holy Dharma.

As mentioned in *The Essence of Nectar* and by Pabongka Dechen Nyingpo in *Liberation in the Palm of Your Hand*, if in this life we correctly devote ourselves by looking at the virtuous friend as a buddha, whether or not from their side they are a buddha, we create the karma to actually be able to meet gurus who are like Maitreya Buddha or Manjushri in our future lives. This is experiencing the result similar to the cause. Even if a teacher is impatient or cruel, if we look at him as Maitreya Buddha or Manjushri and correctly devote ourselves to him as a virtuous friend, we will develop realizations in this life without any obstacles and in all our future lives will meet and be guided by virtuous friends with the same qualities as Maitreya Buddha and Manjushri. We will be able to find a guru with all these qualities and see him as having these qualities. This is important advice to keep in mind.

If we wish in our future lives to meet perfect gurus who are like Maitreya Buddha and Manjushri, we have to take responsibility in this life. This life is responsible for how things will turn out in future lives, whether it will be easy for us to practice Dharma and have realizations or whether we will find many obstacles and great difficulty in devoting ourselves to a virtuous friend.

Guru devotion in our future lives could be easy—with our easily meeting a perfect guru and succeeding in our guru devotion practice—or difficult—with our not even finding a guru or making many mistakes when we do. How perfectly we can practice guru devotion in our future lives depends on how skillful we are at devoting ourselves to our virtuous friends in this life. And how it is turning out in this life has to do with our past lives, with our past karma. Mistakes we have made in past lives will be reflected in this life, but that doesn't mean we have no freedom, because we can purify our negative karma—Buddha is so compassionate that he explained methods we can use to do so.

If we look at those with whom we have made Dharma contact in this life as Maitreya Buddha or Manjushri, then respect and follow them, as a result of that karma, it is natural that in our future lives we will actually meet a virtuous friend who is like Maitreya Buddha or Manjushri. We will always meet such perfect virtuous friends because that karma isn't lost. Therefore, it is important not to look at our present virtuous friends from the side of their faults but only from the side of their good qualities. We should practice guru devotion well so that we don't miss this benefit.

Pabongka Dechen Nyingpo explained, "If you want to meet pure virtuous friends in the future, in this life you should devote yourself without mistakes."

If we practice this way in this life, in our future lives we will have a better karmic view, seeing the guru as having all the qualities of Maitreya Buddha or Manjushri.

Whether or not we will meet virtuous friends in our future lives and how many qualities we will see in them depend on our guru yoga practice in this life. Whether or not we are going to meet Buddhadharma again, whether or not we are going to meet the Mahayana teachings, and whether or not we are going to meet the Vajrayana teachings also depend on how well we are able to practice guru yoga in this life.

(7) We will not fall into the lower realms

If we correctly devote ourselves to our virtuous friend, any heavy negative karma we have accumulated during beginningless rebirths can immediately be purified. All the heavy negative karmas to be reborn in the lower realms, such as the five uninterrupted negative karmas, can be completely purified in the shortest time—even in an instant.

The sutra *Essence of the Earth* mentions,

> For one who is guided by a guru, even the negative karmas that would cause one to wander in the lower realms for innumerable tens of millions of eons are purified by manifesting in this life as harms to the body and mind, such as contagious disease, famine and so forth. This karma can also be purified just by receiving a scolding or having a bad dream.

This sutra is saying that if we correctly devote ourselves to our virtuous friend, we purify the heavy karmas we have accumulated in this life and during beginningless lives. Instead of our having to be born in the lower realms and experience there the heaviest suffering for an incredible length of time, we completely purify our negative karmas through experiencing disease, famine or some other difficulty in this life. All those heavy negative karmas can be purified even by having a terrifying dream or by being scolded by our guru, as in Milarepa's life story. We then don't have to experience the results of those karmas.

Marpa obliged Milarepa to build a nine-story tower, kicked him out of initiations, scolded him hard and almost beat him to death. Despite these hardships, Milarepa didn't generate any negative thoughts toward his guru. Having practiced properly devoting himself to his guru, Milarepa purified all his heavy karmic obscurations and became enlightened in that very life.

No matter how much heavy karma we have created in this and past lives, correctly devoting ourselves to the virtuous friend is the answer. What is the most powerful method of purification? Again, the answer is correct devotion to the virtuous friend, because, as I mentioned at the beginning, the virtuous friend is the most powerful among all the powerful objects.

Also, the great yogi Drogön Tsangpa Gyare, a reincarnation of Naropa, said,

> If I'm beaten by the guru, it is an initiation.
> If there is a blessing to be received, I receive it then.
> His heavy scoldings are wrathful mantras;
> If I want to eliminate obstacles, that will do it.

There are many stories of a guru purposely doing such actions to guide a disciple, as Marpa did with Milarepa.

Tsangpa Gyare was a great ascetic Kagyü yogi. I saw a set of his robes many years ago in Indiana in America. A student named Michael[47] had opened a kind of Hindu ashram, though inside it was more like a Tibetan monastery, with huge paintings of deities and Dharma protectors covering whole walls. Michael had a very old brocade dongka and a Bhutanese-style robe with straps, which had belonged to Tsangpa Gyare. The clothes still had a scented smell even though they had been taken out of an old statue a long time before. The statue had been brought from Kham, in Tibet, to Bhutan, where all the relics, including some of Padmasambhava's hair, were taken out. The robes then came to America.

Michael usually kept the robes hanging in a closet, but sometimes he would wear them, holding a *phurba* in one hand and a skullcup in the other and baring his teeth, like a protector. He liked his students to take photos of him in this pose. He said that he felt powerful when he wore the robes. Because the robes belonged to such a great yogi, I think his mind became higher when he wore them.

Pabongka Dechen Nyingpo explains that we shouldn't see the many hardships we have to bear to do the guru's work as an obligation or a burden; rather, we should see them as ornaments. Instead of letting the hardships become a burden, we should wear them as beautiful ornaments. Some African tribes put large pieces of wood in their lips or in other parts of their bodies. Even though it must be painful to decorate themselves in that way,

---

[47] Michael Shoemaker, or Swami Chetanananda; Rudrananda Ashram.

they regard it as an ornament. There are many similar examples of people being happy to bear hardships because they regard the result as ornamental. We should look at the difficulties we have to experience in serving the guru as something worthwhile and necessary. We have to realize that the more problems we experience in doing the guru's work, the more negative karma and obscurations we purify and the more merit we accumulate.

In other words, by thinking of the benefits, we should see any difficulty we experience in doing the guru's work as a good thing, something we need. No matter how many difficulties we experience, if we look at them as ornaments we accumulate much more merit and purify many more obscurations than by doing many hundreds of thousands of prostrations or other preliminary practices.

This is why Marpa treated Milarepa the way he did. For many years, Marpa didn't give Milarepa any teachings. Even if Milarepa came to the teachings, Marpa would kick him out. He scolded and beat Milarepa and only gave him work, work and more work. If Marpa had been an ordinary person, he would have been extremely cruel and devoid of compassion but because Marpa treated Milarepa like this for many years, Milarepa purified an unbelievable amount of obscurations. That is why Milarepa was able to complete all the realizations of tantra and become enlightened in one brief lifetime of a degenerate time.

Remember how Trichen Tenpa Rabgye served his guru so perfectly that he purified many of his past negative karmas and was able to realize emptiness. There are many similar stories. By practicing perfect guru yoga, a practitioner can purify the heavy negative karmas that would cause him to be born in hell and suffer there for many eons by experiencing just a headache, a toothache or some other small problem in this life. Simply having a fearful dream can purify heavy negative karmas so that they don't need to be experienced as heavy sufferings in future lives.

(8) We will effortlessly accomplish all our temporary and ultimate wishes

As a result of carrying out our guru's advice and serving him, all our wishes for temporary and ultimate happiness are quickly fulfilled. Correctly devoting ourselves to the guru establishes the root of all future happiness, including enlightenment. Everything—the works for self and other sentient beings—succeeds and we quickly become enlightened.

In the first verse of *The Foundation of All Good Qualities*,[48] Lama Tsong-khapa says,

> The foundation of all good qualities is the kind and perfect pure
>   guru;
> Correct devotion to him is the root of the path.
> By clearly seeing this and applying great effort,
> Please bless me to rely on him with great respect.

Good qualities includes not only all the realizations from the perfect human rebirth up to enlightenment, but also all our past, present and future happiness. It includes all our happiness experienced during beginningless rebirths, our present happiness and our future happiness up to enlightenment. The guru is the basis of not only the actual realizations of the path to enlightenment but also all our temporary and ultimate happiness, including enlightenment.

In short, all the multitudes of goodness we experience in this and future lives depend on correct devotion to the guru. As Lama Tsongkhapa also said,[49]

> The very root that prepares well the auspiciousness of all the mul-
> titudes of goodness of this life and future lives is making effort
> to practice correct devotion with thought and action to the holy
> virtuous friend who reveals the path. By seeing this, without giv-
> ing up the guru even for the sake of your life, please the guru with
> the offering of accomplishing the work according to his advice.

If we don't correctly devote ourselves to our gurus, including the guru who taught us the alphabet and the one with whom we usually eat and live, the root of all the multitudes of goodness will be lost. Therefore we should be extremely careful.

The tantric teaching *Ocean of Transcendental Wisdom* also mentions,

> If we practice according to the guru's advice, all our wishes are
> accomplished and we receive infinite good fortune.

---

[48] See *Essential Buddhist Prayers, Volume 1*, p. 139.
[49] *Lines of Experience*, v. 9. See *Illuminating the Path to Enlightenment*, appendix 2, p. 181.

In a requesting prayer, the great bodhisattva Thogme Zangpo also says,

> If I rely upon you with great devotion,
> Without effort, you quickly grant every temporary and ultimate
>   wish:
> To you, precious Lord of Dharma, I make request.

This verse contains all the eight benefits of correct devotion to the virtuous friend. All the realizations, from perfect human rebirth up to full enlightenment, which all come from the root of guru devotion, are also contained in *every temporary and ultimate wish*.

If we correctly devote ourselves to the virtuous friend, as Guru Shakyamuni Buddha, Milarepa and Lama Tsongkhapa did, all our wishes will be accomplished quickly and easily. This includes all our temporary and ultimate wishes; it includes all our wishes for this life, such as receiving all the conditions necessary to practice Dharma, and for future lives, such as finding a perfect human body again or being born in a pure realm, as well as all our ultimate wishes, such as achieving enlightenment for the sake of others.

If we correctly devote ourselves to our virtuous friend, all our wishes effortlessly succeed. If we do a retreat, we're able to complete the retreat and it is very successful. If we're studying, we're able to continue our studies without obstacles and study well. How much success we have in our study of Dharma, how much opportunity we get to study and to successfully complete our study, depends on our practice of guru devotion. The same applies to living in ordination.

In the monasteries, it sometimes happens that when a monk has finished studying and comes to the day of his geshe examination, even though he has a reputation for being learned, at that time when he has to debate and answer questions in front of thousands of learned monks, he can't remember the answers or answers wrongly. Even though he was in the top class, the *lharam* class, and was expected to rank first, he ranks much lower. On the day of the examination, he doesn't succeed. On the other hand, a simple monk who didn't study much or have much of a reputation for learning can be very successful on that day because he is able to remember and give the correct answers. Everything somehow works out very successfully. When you check back through the person's life, it has all to do with how well the person practiced guru devotion.

If we correctly devote ourselves to the guru, even at the time of our death, we will be successful. Without any obstacles, we will be able to apply the meditations at the time of death and succeed in peacefully transferring our consciousness to a pure realm. We often hear stories about people who were especially successful at the time of death. Even though there are good stories about how they lived, it's all related to how they correctly devoted themselves to their virtuous friends. How much we are able to succeed in our own practice and in benefiting other sentient beings depends on our guru devotion.

The Essence of Nectar says,

> In short, by devoting to the virtuous friend one temporarily
> Finds the body of a god or human, free of non-freedoms;
> Ultimately, one finishes all the sufferings of samsara
> And achieves the holy state of definite goodness.

The holy state of definite goodness means nirvana and enlightenment. These states are definite in the sense that there is no change from nirvana to samsara or from enlightenment to nirvana or samsara.

All our success in understanding the teachings and achieving realizations of the path depends on the root, correctly devoting ourselves to the virtuous friend. How much understanding and realization we are able to generate in this life and how easily they come depend on this root.

Fifty Verses of Guru Devotion also mentions that development of our mind, which means realization, depends on the guru:

> The Holder of the Vajra said that attainment depends upon the
> vajra master. By understanding this, please the guru in all things.

Another quotation from *Fifty Verses of Guru Devotion* explains the purpose of pleasing the guru:

> Do whatever pleases the guru. Abandon whatever displeases the
> guru. If you are able to do this, you will definitely achieve general
> and sublime realizations in this very lifetime.

It is also powerful just to read through the headings in this section of the eight benefits of guru devotion, then recite the following verse from *Six-Session Guru Yoga* and meditate on its meaning:

Seeing that all general and sublime realizations depend upon correctly devoting myself to you, my savior, I give up my body and even my life. Please grant me blessings to practice only what pleases you.

How extensively we can benefit sentient beings and the teachings of Buddha in this life and in future lives also depends on how correctly we devote ourselves to our virtuous friends. Lama Atisha, Dromtönpa, Milarepa, Lama Tsongkhapa and so many of the past pandits and yogis were able to offer incredible benefit to sentient beings and the teachings because of their perfect practice of guru devotion.

Lama Tsongkhapa was able to do extensive works for sentient beings and the teachings as a result of his correct devotion to his virtuous friends. Even nowadays, by studying Lama Tsongkhapa's teachings, many thousands of monks and lay people are able to understand and faultlessly generate the whole path to enlightenment. Lama Tsongkhapa made clear the subtlest points, such as emptiness and the illusory body, which are unclear in many other teachings. Lama Tsongkhapa's teachings are so clear that without any hesitation and with full confidence and joy, you feel, "If I practice this I can definitely achieve enlightenment."

It is because of Lama Tsongkhapa that the monks in Sera, Ganden and Drepung monasteries are able to study extensively the correct meaning of all the sutras and tantras. Even though Lama Tsongkhapa passed away a long time ago, the benefit of his work still continues. All this has come from Lama Tsongkhapa's correctly devoting himself to his virtuous friends.

The great Lama Atisha had 152 gurus but did not make a single mistake with any of them; his way of devoting himself to his gurus was incomparable. Lama Atisha himself said, "I have many gurus but I haven't done a single thing that those gurus disliked." In other words, not one of those 152 gurus was ever displeased with Lama Atisha.

That is why Lama Atisha was able to bring benefit as extensive as the sky to the teachings and to sentient beings both in India and Tibet. Even nowadays Lama Atisha's holy actions are still working for us, including through our hearing the lam-rim teachings, which have transformed our mind into Dharma. Even now Lama Atisha's teaching *Light of the Path*[50] is able to ben-

---

[50] See *Illuminating the Path to Enlightenment*, appendix 1, where it is entitled *A Lamp for the Path to Enlightenment*.

efit the minds of so many sentient beings in many countries, not only in the East but also in the West. Before we heard lam-rim, our mind was completely ignorant, with no understanding of what should be practiced and what should be avoided. It is through Lama Atisha's kindness that we now have a little Dharma wisdom, which enables us to discriminate right from wrong, the causes of happiness from the causes of suffering. These are all Lama Atisha's holy actions guiding us.

If Lama Atisha had not written *Light of the Path*, there wouldn't be any lam-rim teachings today in the West; we wouldn't have the chance to hear lam-rim. The lam-rim teachings given by Tibetan lamas are commentaries to *Light of the Path*. Even though Lama Atisha has passed away, his holy actions are still working for sentient beings and the teachings, even in the West, and this is the result of his guru devotion practice.

Not only in the East but even in the West, many people have read the biography of Milarepa and it's hard to find anybody who doesn't like it. People might sometimes find it difficult to relate what Milarepa did to their own life but whoever reads his biography generates the wish to be like him. That is the holy action of Milarepa; that is Milarepa working for sentient beings. Simply generating the wish to be like that is itself a cause to become Milarepa, to become enlightened. It is extremely important, because through this wish a person slowly starts to be guided. Even the holy name, Milarepa, brings great blessing; it is effective in subduing the mind. And even this power of the holy name comes from his perfect practice of guru devotion.

Lama Zopa Rinpoche and His Holiness the Dalai Lama, Dharamsala, 2005

8. The Disadvantages of Incorrect Devotion to a Guru

IF, AFTER MEETING a virtuous techer who reveals the unmistaken path, we devote ourselves to him correctly, we gain all the benefits mentioned above. Thus we can easily see that if we don't rely upon a virtuous friend at all, we don't receive those eight benefits, which itself is a powerful shortcoming. And if we have established a relationship with a virtuous friend but devote ourselves to him incorrectly and don't confess and change our negative thoughts and actions, we experience the following eight shortcomings.

2. THE SHORTCOMINGS OF NOT DEVOTING TO A GURU OR OF DEVOTING INCORRECTLY

The eight disadvantages, or shortcomings, of incorrect devotion are:

(1) If we criticize our guru we criticize all the buddhas
(2) Each moment of anger toward our guru destroys merit for eons equal in number to the moments of our anger and will cause us to be reborn in the hells and suffer for the same number of eons
(3) Even though we practice tantra, we will not achieve the sublime realization
(4) Even if we practice tantra with much hardship, it will be like attaining hell and the like
(5) We will not generate any fresh knowledge or realizations and our previous knowledge and realizations will degenerate

(6) We will be afflicted even in this life by illness and other undesirable things

(7) In future lives we will wander endlessly in the lower realms

(8) In all our future lives we will lack virtuous friends

Acting in ways opposite to correct devotion to the virtuous friend is the root of all failure, from failure to find happiness and success in this life up to failure to achieve enlightenment. One way of making mistakes is not to recognize the mistakes we are making because we haven't checked our behavior in terms of the guru devotion teachings in the lam-rim. Another way of making mistakes is simply to be careless.

For people who don't know the complete teachings on guru devotion, life becomes the continual creation of heavy negative karma. Any negative karma created in relation to the guru is the heaviest because the guru is the most powerful object, more powerful than numberless buddhas. Even if you have created one or more of the five uninterrupted negative karmas, which bring immediate rebirth in the heaviest hot hell realm without the interruption of another life, you can purify them and still become enlightened in that life. However, making even a small mistake in devoting to the virtuous friend, such as a small criticism or disrespectful action, is heavier than that. It is then difficult to achieve realizations and enlightenment, which means it is difficult for you to accomplish your ultimate goal of benefiting sentient beings.

Without understanding the complete teachings on the eight shortcomings of incorrectly devoting ourselves to a guru, we have no way to practice, no way to face and stop our wrong conceptions. How much effort we put into avoiding the eight shortcomings depends on how much we understand their importance. Doing the practice is our own responsibility.

If, on the one hand, we do a lot of Dharma practice—studying, doing preliminaries or retreat, reciting many mantras—but, on the other, continuously make mistakes in our devotion and displease our virtuous friend, we create a great obstacle. If we don't pay attention to fulfilling the holy wishes of our virtuous friend, we won't accomplish much because we will have created an obstacle the size of this earth. There is no greater obstacle than this.

If we don't know or don't apply the teachings on guru devotion, after some time our mind becomes like a rock; it can't be moved or easily changed. Nothing we meditate on affects our mind, not even the lam-rim. When the extensive philosophical teachings don't move our mind, there's still hope that listening to and studying the lam-rim will. However, if our mental state becomes like this, when we hear lam-rim teachings or read lam-rim texts, we find it difficult to have any feeling for them in our heart. This is a sign that our mind has degenerated.

The realization of guru devotion means seeing the guru as a buddha, which is made possible by looking at the guru as a buddha. Without this practice, negative minds arise because our mind has been habituated to negative thoughts during beginningless rebirths. Most of us are not habituated to positive thoughts. Some great practitioners, who practiced in their past lives and developed pure minds back then, are born with pure minds. That is a different matter. Most of us have minds that have been habituated to attachment, anger and all the other delusions during beginningless rebirths. Because of this it is extremely difficult for us to overcome negative thoughts toward the guru. So if we don't practice guru devotion we'll continue to generate negative thoughts, especially anger and heresy, toward our guru, the shortcomings of which are very heavy.

The Essence of Nectar says,

> Just as there are inconceivable advantages
> In correctly devoting to a virtuous friend,
> There are also inconceivable shortcomings
> In not devoting or incorrectly devoting to a virtuous friend.

(1) IF WE CRITICIZE OUR GURU WE CRITICIZE ALL THE BUDDHAS

If, having established a Dharma connection and accepted a guru-disciple relationship, we criticize or give up that guru, we incur the same heavy negative karma as having criticized or given up all the buddhas. Similarly, getting angry at our guru is the same as getting angry at all the buddhas. Why? As Pabongka Dechen Nyingpo explains, the guru is the embodiment of all the numberless buddhas of the ten directions and the actions of all the buddhas manifest through the guru in order to subdue our mind. Of course, since the guru is a much more powerful object than all the buddhas of the three times and ten directions, the negative karma is actually much heavier.

This first shortcoming is similar to breaking the first tantric root vow by abusing or belittling the guru but includes criticizing the guru out of anger, heresy or other negative thoughts. The Tibetan word *nyä-mö* has two aspects: the heavier aspect is giving up, or abandoning, the guru as an object of respect of our body, speech and mind; the other aspect is criticizing the guru and generating anger, heresy and other negative thoughts.

There's a difference, however, between a thought just passing through our mind and something we feel from our heart. Sometimes words such as "sentient beings don't matter" pass through our mind. I checked with His Holiness the Dalai Lama as to whether this broke the bodhisattva vow. His Holiness replied, "It's not renouncing the wishing thought but it's better to stop such thoughts because they can lead to the actual thought of renouncing bodhicitta." You could say that such passing thoughts are preparation for actually breaking the vow. It could be similar here.

It's easy to give rise to negative thoughts when things don't go according to our wishes—for example, when our guru stops us from doing something we want to do. We're not obliged to generate heresy. We can make the decision to hear things from our guru without generating heresy. But if we haven't trained our mind well in guru devotion, we're in danger of giving rise to heresy because we think that we know better than our guru. When heresy arises we can feel it in our heart. Our mind becomes like a hot, barren desert.

Among all the tantric root falls and other negative karmas, giving up the guru is the heaviest one. This non-devotional thought is the heaviest obstacle to our achieving realizations of the path to enlightenment, and without realizations we can't really offer true, deep benefit to other sentient beings.

It is more than simply getting angry at our guru and abusing him, though abuse can easily happen when we get angry. When I wrote to His Holiness Ling Rinpoche to ask the definition of the first tantric root fall, Rinpoche replied that it doesn't mean simply getting angry at the guru but giving up the guru as an object of respect by thinking, "What use is this person to me?" We experience this shortcoming if, after establishing a guru-disciple relationship, we abandon the guru as the object of our respect.

A tantric text says,

> The vajra master is equal to all the buddhas; therefore, we should never belittle or criticize the vajra master.

This is related to the explanation that the virtuous friend is the essence, or embodiment, of all the buddhas. If we serve or make offering to our virtuous friend we are serving or making offering to all the buddhas. On the other hand, if we criticize or give up our virtuous friend, it is the same as criticizing or giving up all the buddhas.

The Essence of Nectar says,

> It is said that the actions of all the Victorious Ones
> Appear in one's own guru.
> Disrespecting him is thus disrespecting all the Victorious Ones.
> What could have a heavier ripened aspect result than that?

Leave aside criticizing or disrespecting the lama who reveals Dharma by sitting on a high throne, even doing so to your everyday teacher, the one who taught you to read and with whom you live, becomes in fact criticizing or disrespecting all the buddhas of the ten directions. Remember the story I told earlier about how Je Drubkhangpa failed to achieve realizations because of his disrespectful attitude to his alphabet teacher. When you meditate, if you forget to visualize the gurus from whom you have received teachings with the recognition of a guru-disciple relationship, even though you have no negative thoughts toward them, that itself becomes a big obstacle to your attainment.

Once you become someone's disciple, even making a threatening gesture with your fist or saying something bad behind your guru's back is the same as disrespecting all the buddhas of the ten directions. This applies to any disrespect you show, not only with your speech but also with your physical gestures.

The tantric text *Commentary on the Difficult Points of the Krishnayamari Tantra* mentions,

> A person who does not regard as a guru
> Someone from whom they have heard even a single verse of teaching
> Will be reborn as a dog for one hundred lifetimes,
> And then as a human being of low caste.

Even when, after many rebirths, the karma to be born as a dog is finished and the person is again born as a human being, he is born in a low caste, which means that he will not be respected and will have little power or freedom to extensively benefit other sentient beings. Though the commentaries by Pabongka Rinpoche and other lamas say that one is born as a human being of low caste, His Holiness Song Rinpoche said that one is then born as a scorpion. You can use whichever is more effective for your mind.

This happens once you have made a Dharma connection if you forget to devote yourself to that person as a guru, either through lack of understanding of the guru devotion teachings or through failure to pay attention to him, even though you don't generate anger or heresy toward that guru or give him up. The same applies to the situation where you later decide that you don't like a particular guru with whom you have made a Dharma connection. Because you don't like the person you don't devote yourself to him and leave him out of the visualization when you do lam-rim meditation.

Just imagine if our human body slowly started to change into that of a dog. We would be so worried! If one day we suddenly started to grow a dog's nose we would immediately go to hospital to have an operation. Since we couldn't stand to have a dog's nose for even a day, there is no doubt about how we would react if the rest of our body turned into that of a dog. How could we bear to be a dog for a whole life? We couldn't, especially after having had this human body, with its incredible capacity to think deeply, understand and communicate. As human beings, if someone explains to us that virtue is the cause of happiness, we immediately understand. But with dogs, cows, horses, sheep and other animals, even if it were explained to them for eons that virtue is the cause of happiness, there would be no way that they could understand the meaning of virtue.

This verse is not referring to just anybody from whom you hear a teaching. Even when you have a Dharma discussion with your friends you can hear many explanations that are beneficial for your mind. Or you can hear teachings when somebody gives a lecture on Buddhism. It is not talking about that kind of thing. This verse is describing a situation where first you have the recognition of yourself as a disciple and the other person as your guru, then, with that recognition, you receive a teaching—even a single verse—but fail to regard that person as your guru. This can happen because either you don't know the lam-rim teachings on guru devotion or you have heard or read them in the past but don't actually practice them.

Here we are not talking about your generating anger or heresy toward that guru or intentionally giving him up but either your knowing about the practice and not doing it or simply forgetting to do it. The karmic consequences of not devoting yourself to that guru are rebirth for one hundred lifetimes as a dog and, after that, rebirth as a person of low caste or a scorpion.

(2) EACH MOMENT OF ANGER TOWARD OUR GURU DESTROYS MERIT FOR EONS EQUAL IN NUMBER TO THE MOMENTS OF OUR ANGER AND WILL CAUSE US TO BE REBORN IN THE HELLS AND SUFFER FOR THE SAME NUMBER OF EONS

The most dangerous thing is generating anger or heresy toward our guru. If we become angry at our guru we will destroy eons of merit we have accumulated in the past equal in number to the moments of our anger, and for the same number of eons will be reborn and suffer in Inexhaustible Suffering, the lowest and hottest of the hot hells, which means we will experience the heaviest suffering. If we are angry at our guru for even one moment, we create the karma to be born in hell for one eon. The longer we have to be in hell, the more distant we will be from temporary happiness, the result of virtue, and the ultimate happiness of liberation and enlightenment.

Also, our realizations of the path will be delayed for the same number of eons as the moments of our anger. If we are about to realize renunciation, bodhicitta, emptiness or some other realization and get angry at our guru, our realization will be delayed for eons equal in number to the moments of our anger. Even if the merit has been dedicated, the experience of the result of that merit is delayed for that number of eons.

The Essence of Nectar says,

> However many moments one is angry at the guru
> Destroys merit accumulated for eons equaling that number
> And one will be born in hell for the same number of eons,
> It is said in the *Kalachakra Tantra*.

The *Kalachakra Tantra* itself explains,

> One destroys the merit accumulated over eons equal to the number of moments one feels angry at the virtuous friend and for the same number of eons one experiences intense suffering in the hells and so on.

According to the Vaibhashika, the first of the four schools of Buddhist philosophy, there are sixty-five moments in the duration of a young person's finger snap. This means that generating anger or heresy toward the virtuous friend for the duration of a finger snap brings rebirth in the hell realms for sixty-five eons. According to the Prasangika Madhyamaka school, however, there are 365 moments in the duration of a finger snap, so generating anger or heresy toward the virtuous friend for the duration of a finger snap brings rebirth in Inexhaustible Suffering for 365 eons. This is much longer than the entire time it takes a world system to evolve, which is eighty intermediate eons. It takes twenty intermediate eons for the world to evolve; it then exists for twenty intermediate eons, decays over twenty intermediate eons and remains empty for twenty intermediate eons. Being empty means that there is nothing in the particular space where that world system had existed. A new one then starts to evolve in the same place.

During all those eons you are in hell, a whole world system will have evolved, existed, degenerated and become empty several times over. During all that time, if, before you died, you hadn't confessed and purified the mistakes you had made in relation to your virtuous friend, you would still be in the hell, Inexhaustible Suffering.

Even when this world had completely disappeared, your own karma to be in hell would still not have finished. From there you would again reincarnate in hell in another of the numberless universes and continue to experience suffering. This is something to keep in mind. Simply meditating on this point is very effective because you can then easily control your disturbing thoughts and avoid creating the heaviest negative karmas, which destroy your liberation and enlightenment and interfere with even your temporary happiness.

The tantric text *Self-Arisen and Self-Manifested* explains,

> One should not go against the good advice; if one does, one will fall into a hell state. Criticizing the virtuous friend or fabricating his faults is like having killed a hundred thousand ordained beings. It is only the cause of the Inexhaustible Suffering hell. Even if one thinks that the vajra master is bad-tempered, one has to suffer for sixty eons in Inexhaustible Suffering.

Criticizing the guru is only cause to be born in the hot hell Inexhaustible Suffering, where your body is red-hot and one with fire, like the wick of a candle; the only way that it can be discriminated as a sentient being is by the sound of its screaming. One tiny spark from the first category of the hot hells, Being Alive Again and Again, is said to be seven times hotter than the fire at the end of time, which melts even mountains; and the fire at the end of time is sixty or seventy times hotter than all the fire energy of the whole earth right now. Even a tiny spark from Being Alive Again and Again is unbearably hot and each category of hell is twenty times hotter than the one preceding it.

Thus criticizing the virtuous friend is cause only for rebirth in the Inexhaustible Suffering hell. Simply generating for the duration of a finger snap the thought that your vajra master has great anger, for example, throws you into Inexhaustible Suffering for sixty eons.

A Guide to the Bodhisattva's Way of Life mentions that one moment of anger destroys the merit accumulated by practicing charity and making offerings to the tathagatas for a thousand eons.[51] If we get angry at a bodhisattva for one moment we destroy the merit we have accumulated over one thousand eons, and even if the merit has been dedicated, it postpones the result of that merit, which means happiness and realizations, for a thousand eons. Before getting angry for that one moment we might have been ready, through having accumulated powerful merit, to generate the realization of emptiness or bodhicitta that very day, but after that moment's anger our realization gets postponed for a thousand eons. This shows just how harmful anger can be.

Since the guru is the most powerful of all holy objects, much more powerful than a bodhisattva, getting angry at a guru destroys much more merit and postpones realizations for many more eons. It becomes the heaviest obstacle. Here we're not talking about just anybody recognized as a guru in the world but our own guru, a person with whom we have established a Dharma connection.

The destruction of our merit is an incredible loss because we put so much effort and material expense into collecting merit in this life and from life to life. We have to put in a lot of effort to transform our mind into virtue and to then produce a virtuous action. We find it difficult to make an action become virtue, or Dharma, even though the action might appear to be Dharma. When we are meditating, reading scriptures or making charity to sentient beings, our action might appear to be Dharma, but its appearing to be spiritual doesn't mean it actually is spiritual. It depends on our

---

[51] Whatever wholesome deeds,
   Such as venerating the buddhas and generosity,
   That have been amassed over a thousand eons
   Will all be destroyed in one moment of anger. (Ch. 6, v. 1.)

motivation, not on what we are doing externally. If our mind is pure, our action becomes pure. Otherwise, our actions might appear to be Dharma but they're not actually Dharma.

If it is dangerous to allow anger to arise toward our guru for just a moment there's no doubt about the result of being angry at our guru for hours, days or months. We can't comprehend all the disadvantages we would have to experience; it's something that our mind can't grasp. By remembering this shortcoming, we should try to control ourselves as much as possible when we are in danger of generating negative thoughts, especially those of anger, toward our guru.

Purifying our mistakes

If we have been angry at a virtuous friend, criticized or given him up, harmed his holy body, gone against his advice or disturbed his holy mind, we can definitely purify the negative karma we have created to be born in hell (see appendix 3). It's not that the negative karma is so heavy that it can never be purified, like in Christianity, where once people are born in hell they are stuck there forever, with no opportunity to change from that realm. Karma is a dependent arising, as is the mind that creates hell. Because karma depends on causes and conditions, it can be changed through other causes and conditions. If it did not depend on causes and conditions but existed from its own side, it could never be changed. The only good quality that negative karma has is that it can be purified.

There are many ways we can purify the negative karmas we have created in relation to the guru. The lam-rim teachings advise that if the lama is living, we should immediately confess our mistake to him with strong repentance. The best way to purify is, on the basis of confessing our mistake, to then do something that pleases the holy mind of that guru, whether by following some advice that he has given us, offering him service or something else like that. By recognizing our mistake we change our attitude and actions. No matter what heavy negative karma we have created, we can purify it, and this is the best and quickest way to do so.

By knowing his personal characteristics, we do whatever is most pleasing to that particular guru. If we know that certain things please a particular guru, we do those things. Some lamas, for example, don't like to be praised; they show a displeased aspect when they are praised but straight talking makes them happy. Pleasing the virtuous teacher seems to be the best, quickest way to pacify obstacles to our temporary and ultimate wishes. Pleasing him is like opening the door for realizations within our mind. Any time we accomplish something that pleases our guru, much purification is done, the level of our mind becomes higher and we become closer to realizations.

To purify our mistakes we can also perform "passing Dharma," which means that by remembering our guru we make offerings of food and tea to fellow disciples of that guru. This is regarded as powerful purification, purifying any negative karma we have accumulated with that guru.

We can also purify with Vajrasattva and especially Samayavajra practice, tsog offerings and by making offerings to that guru. While Vajrasattva is a general practice of confession and purification, Samayavajra is a specific practice to purify the heavy negative karmas created in relation to the virtuous friend. We can also purify negative karmas by reciting the prayer of the Thirty-five Buddhas with prostrations, because reciting the name of the last buddha purifies broken samaya with the guru. It seems that the thirty-fifth buddha, King of the Lord of Mountains Firmly Seated on Jewel and Lotus, specifically dedicated that his name help sentient beings to purify degenerated samaya with the guru. We can also purify by reciting mantras, reading the *Perfection of Wisdom* scriptures and so on; six different methods are mentioned in the lam-rim teachings.[52]

The best, most powerful purification of mistakes we have made with a guru comes from following that guru's instructions, whether to do retreat, work or something else. Pleasing the guru's holy mind by fulfilling his wishes brings much more purification than reciting the Vajrasattva mantra for many months. Of course, it also depends on how we recite the mantra.

Phurchog Ngawang Jampa said,

> If you have broken samaya with one guru, you cannot generate realizations, even if you attempt not to break samaya with any of your other gurus. If the guru is living, confess to him. If the guru has passed away, confess to the pores of that guru.

---

[52] The six methods of purification are reciting mantras of buddhas' names; reciting the Vajrasattva mantra; reading sutras on emptiness; contemplating emptiness; making offerings; and making statues and paintings of buddhas or building stupas.

Making a mistake with one guru is the same as making a mistake with all of our gurus. Gomo Rinpoche explained that disregarding the advice of one guru pollutes our relationship with all our other gurus.

If our guru has passed away or for some other reason we can't see him, we can purify our negative karmas by confessing them to his closest disciple if our guru was ordained, or to a member of his family, such as his spouse or child, if he was a lay person. We can also confess in front of our guru's relics—hair, bones, nails, ashes, robes or other possessions—by placing them on the altar, thinking of them as the guru and making strong confession in front of them. This is how the Kadampa geshes confessed their mistakes.

If we don't purify the mistakes we have made with the virtuous friend in this life, even if we do meet a virtuous friend in our future lives we will again make the same mistakes, which is creating the result similar to the cause. If we don't purify with the remedy of the four powers[53] in this life and don't change our attitude, we will repeat our mistakes again and again and will have no development of mind from life to life. This will interfere very much in our work for self and for others.

Even if we are able to purify the karma to be born in the hells by doing powerful confession and purification, however, our realizations of the path will still be delayed because we have destroyed such an enormous amount of merit. This is why the practice of correct devotion to the virtuous friend is emphasized so much in all the teachings of Buddha, and especially in the Mahayana tantric teachings.

(3) EVEN THOUGH WE PRACTICE TANTRA, WE WILL NOT ACHIEVE THE SUBLIME REALIZATION

If we make mistakes in our guru devotion practice, even if we practice tantra, we can never achieve enlightenment. No matter how well we understand the tantric path and no matter how many eons we meditate on it, we can never achieve the sublime realization. Until we purify the negative karmas accumulated in relation to the guru, no matter how much we practice tantra, there will be no enlightenment.

The Essence of Nectar says,

---

[53] The four powers that make confession effective in purifying negative karma are the power of regret, the power of the object of reliance, the power of the antidote and the power of making the determination not to commit the negative karma again.

> Even one who has created heavy negative karmas
> Such as the five uninterrupted actions and so on,
> Through tantra, can achieve sublime realization in this very life.
> But anyone who abuses his guru from the heart,
> Will achieve no realization at all, even if he practices for eons.

The reference for this is the *Guhyasamaja Root Tantra*, which says,

> Those who have committed heavy negative karma
> Such as the five uninterrupted actions and so on,
> Can achieve the great ocean of Vajrayana, the sublime vehicle.
> But those who have scorned their guru from the heart
> Will achieve no success in their practice.

Even those who have committed the five uninterrupted negative karmas and so on, which includes the ten non-virtues, can practice tantra and still achieve the sublime Vajrayana, which means enlightenment, in that life. But those who have criticized their guru from the heart, even if they practice tantra, won't have any achievement. Sometimes a critical thought just comes and goes, but here, *from the heart* means something serious.

If we are careless in our relationships with our gurus but on the other hand do hundreds of thousands of prostrations and other practices, nothing will happen in our mind. No realizations will come even if we do retreat on secret, profound tantric meditations for many years in an isolated place. We will have no experiences; our mind will still be the same as before. We will not have even a good sign in a dream.

After death, any sentient being who has committed one of the five uninterrupted negative karmas—killed her mother or father or an arhat, caused blood to flow from a Tathagata or caused disunity among the Sangha—will immediately be reborn in hell, without taking another life in between. Even the heavy negative karmas of having killed a human being, incurred a root fall and so forth cause one to be born straight away in hell. However, by practicing tantra, even beings who have committed such heavy negative karmas can achieve enlightenment in that life. But the person who has criticized her master from her heart—no matter how much she practices tantra—won't achieve any realizations in that life.

This doesn't mean that a person who has criticized her guru from the heart cannot accomplish the Vajrayana at all in any life, that it is impossible for her to ever become enlightened. It might look like that from the words, but if it were like that, it would mean that it wouldn't be true that in time all sentient beings will definitely become enlightened.

I asked Zimey Rinpoche about a similar quotation in *The Great Treatise on the Stages of the Path to Enlightenment*, where it says that if you break a bodhisattva root vow you can never become an arya being in that life. Rinpoche said, "It means that you can't become an arya being in that life if you don't purify the bodhisattva root fall." Rinpoche said that it doesn't mean that once you have made such a mistake you can never achieve enlightenment, though it sounds like that. It means that you can't become an arya being if you don't confess and purify the mistake. If you confess and purify it, it changes the situation.

The whole point is that it is different if you change your attitude, confess your mistake and attempt not to make the mistake again. Otherwise, if you don't change your attitude and don't try not to repeat the mistake, no matter how much you practice tantra you will never achieve the sublime realization. This outline is very important to remember, especially if you feel you have made these mistakes.

By transforming your attitude into the devotion that sees the guru as a buddha, you can purify those shortcomings. If you stop your incorrect practice, do confession to purify all your past negative karmas and again accumulate extensive merit by practicing correct devotion from that time, there is a possibility of achieving enlightenment by practicing tantra in a short time, even within a few lifetimes. But as long as you don't change your attitude and remain critical of your guru, you can't accomplish any realizations even if you practice tantra without sleeping or eating for years and years.

If you don't correctly devote yourself to the virtuous friend, the root of the path to enlightenment, no matter how many eons you do strict retreat on the second stage of tantra, you can't achieve enlightenment. Nothing will happen in your mind. Since the general realizations of lam-rim and the particular realizations of tantra won't happen, you can't achieve enlightenment. But it is not saying that even if you practice tantra forever, you will never achieve enlightenment. It is not that once you have made a mistake, you can never achieve enlightenment. Of course, every sentient being can become enlightened in time, because there is buddha-nature. However, if you have abandoned the guru as an object of respect, you probably can't achieve enlightenment in this life.

(4) Even if we practice tantra with much hardship, it will be like attaining hell and the like

If we have criticized, become angry at or made some other mistake in relation to our guru, as long as we don't confess our mistake or revive the samaya, even attempting to practice tantra for many years by undergoing hardships such as foregoing food and sleep will be like attaining hell and the like. (*And the like* could refer to difficulties in this life as well as to the other lower realms.) This means that even if we endure many hardships—not eating, not sleeping, not speaking, not seeing anybody and reciting mantras and meditating day and night—to do many years of retreat in a solitary place, nothing will change in our mind if we have made mistakes in relation to one of your virtuous friends.

However, it is not saying that all this intensive practice becomes the cause of the lower realms. And it is not saying that you are not collecting merit. Even though such heavy negative thoughts are arising, you may be collecting merit by performing various practices such as making prostrations and offerings to buddha, for example. Of course, even from the power of the object, such actions become virtue. However, the mountains of negative karma from your negative thoughts toward the guru are so heavy that the good karma you collect becomes insignificant.

Negative thoughts toward the virtuous friend are the greatest obstacles to realizations, so unless you change these negative thoughts, no matter how many hundreds of thousands of preliminary practices you do, it will be like achieving hell. Until you purify the broken samaya, until you change your mind, until you stop creating that heavy karma, no matter how long or how hard you practice tantra, it will be like achieving hell. There is no way to achieve realizations.

It is explained in the root tantra *Ornament of the Vajra Essence*,

> For those who have criticized their master,
> Even if they practice tantra for thousands of eons
> By avoiding all sleep and distractions,
> It will be like attaining hell.

Lama Tsongkhapa said,

> Without being careful at all in regard to despising your guru, if

you then try very hard to do listening, reflecting and meditating, it will be like opening the door to the lower realms.

The Essence of Nectar says,

> The person who intentionally abuses and despises
> The virtuous friend who reveals the path,
> Even if he puts effort into trying to realize the meaning of tantra,
> Giving up sleep, dullness and distractions,
> It is, a tantra explains, like working for hell and so on.

No matter what hardships you bear to practice tantra— living in solitude and giving up eating, sleeping and talking—it will be like opening the door to hell rather than to realizations.

Again, this is not referring just to getting angry at your guru but to giving him up as an object of respect of your three doors. The result mentioned implies that you have made the determination to renounce the guru as an object of respect, gone against his advice and broken samaya.

The distractions referred to are those that distract you from doing a practice or a retreat session. (A person who is living in pure Dharma practice has given up the works of this life and is free from distraction, which comes from the attachment that clings to the happiness of this life.) Instead of being busy with Dharma practice, you pass the time just gossiping about worldly things and praising yourself and putting others down. You don't get to recite even OM MANI PADME HUM. Because your present happiness seems so important, you have no thought of future happiness, of great ultimate happiness. You are under the control of the thought of worldly dharmas. Even if you give up those things, don't eat, don't gossip, don't do business, don't travel, don't enjoy entertainment, but live in retreat on a mountain with fires around you so that you don't fall asleep, if you have intentionally abused or despised your guru, it is as if you are accomplishing the hells.

If you don't change your thoughts and actions, no matter how hard you practice not just tantra but even Highest Yoga Tantra, the quickest path to enlightenment, because of the mistakes you have made in relation to the virtuous friend, it will be like achieving hell rather than enlightenment. If you have ingested a deadly poison and continue to ingest it, it can become so strong that even taking its antidote has little power to benefit you and you move in the direction of sickness and death. It's similar with this particular result of making mistakes in your guru devotion.

(5) WE WILL NOT GENERATE ANY FRESH KNOWLEDGE OR REALIZATIONS AND OUR PREVIOUS KNOWLEDGE AND REALIZATIONS WILL DEGENERATE

The fifth shortcoming of incorrect devotion is that we will be unable to achieve new scriptural understanding and realizations, and even those qualities we have generated within our mind will degenerate. In this way, incorrect practice of guru devotion is most harmful for the development of our mind. Our previous experiences of compassion, emptiness, renunciation, impermanence and so forth will be lost. Our faith will also degenerate. We will also forget things—we won't even remember very much of the teachings.

The Essence of Nectar says,

> If one is devoid of devotion for the sublime object, the guru,
> Qualities are not generated and those generated degenerate.

Remember the great yogi Milarepa's life story. For a long time Milarepa's guru, Marpa, didn't give him teachings but only hard work, scoldings and beatings. Marpa's secret mother, Dagmema, felt compassion for Milarepa, so without asking Marpa's permission she advised Milarepa to go to Lama Ngokpa, one of Marpa's disciples, for teachings. After Lama Ngokpa gave Milarepa many profound teachings and initiations, Milarepa then did retreat. But no matter how much meditation Milarepa did, nothing happened, not even a good sign in a dream.

When Milarepa discussed this with Lama Ngokpa, Lama Ngokpa asked him, "Did you get permission from Marpa to come here?" Lama Ngokpa was checking whether Milarepa had done anything wrong in relation to Marpa. After Milarepa explained the situation, Lama Ngokpa went to apologize to Marpa, taking all his possessions except for one goat with a broken leg as offerings to Marpa. Milarepa then returned to Marpa. Milarepa hadn't had any good signs because he hadn't gotten Marpa's permission before going to receive teachings from Lama Ngokpa.

There is also the story of Je Drubkhangpa, which I have already mentioned. Je Drubkhangpa meditated on the lam-rim for many years but didn't generate even a single realization because he failed to visualize his alphabet teacher in the merit field. After Je Drubkhangpa visualized this teacher as the principal figure in the merit field, realizations came like rainfall.

Even though Krishnacharya, a great yogi of Chakrasamvara, traveled from place to place by flying in the sky surrounded by many dakinis playing music, he didn't achieve the supreme realization of enlightenment in that life because he disregarded a small piece of advice from his guru Jalandhari: when Krishnacharya had wanted to go to Oddiyana, one of the twenty-four holy places, to do the special tantric practices that are done just prior to enlightenment, Jalandhari advised him against it. However, Krishnacharya insisted that he wanted to go to Oddiyana, ignored his guru's advice and went anyway.

Many inauspicious things happened along the way. Jalandhari, an embodiment of Chakrasamvara and Vajravarahi, manifested in various forms to protect him but Krishnacharya didn't realize it. He met many transformations of Chakrasamvara and Vajravarahi in ordinary forms, but because he had left without his guru's permission, he didn't recognize them as deities.

At one point, Krishnacharya came to a huge river, where an old woman with leprosy was waiting to cross. When Krishnacharya went to cross the river, the old lady asked, "Will you carry me across on your back?" Not realizing that she was an aspect of Vajravarahi, Krishnacharya ignored her and crossed the river.

A little later one of Krishnacharya's disciples, the novice monk Kusali, came along. When the leper woman asked him to carry her across, Kusali felt intense compassion for her. Even though she was very ugly and covered with leprous sores, he immediately picked her up and started to carry her across the river on his back. When he reached the middle of the river, however, the old woman suddenly transformed into Vajravarahi and, embracing Kusali, took him in that same body to the pure realm of Vajrayogini. Kusali's impure karma, which prevented his seeing the old woman as Vajravarahi and made him see her as an ordinary being, was purified by sacrificing himself to carry her across the river.

If Krishnacharya, Kusali's teacher, had picked up the woman when she asked, he would have been taken to Vajrayogini's pure realm and achieved enlightenment first. Even though Krishnacharya was a great yogi, going to Oddiyana against his guru's advice became a hindrance to recognizing the leper woman as a manifestation of Vajravarahi. So, Kusali became enlightened before his guru Krishnacharya, who instead became enlightened in the intermediate state, after passing away at the holy place of Devikoti.

If we have obscurations, even if we meet someone who is a manifestation of Vajrayogini, Tara or some other deity, we won't believe it. Even if we have had dreams or some other sign, because the person has an ordinary appearance, we will see her as an ordinary person. The belief that she is ordinary will be so concrete that we won't recognize her as a deity or have faith in her, even when she is right there talking to us. Our concept that she is ordinary, solid as a rock, will interfere with our quick enlightenment.

There is also the story of one high lama, Labsum Gyaltsen, the head of the Sakya order and a lineage lama of the Vajrayogini path. One day in the street Labsum Gyaltsen saw a terrifying woman with fangs and pendulous breasts. He didn't recognize that the woman was actually Vajrayogini. Thinking that she might be a spirit, he tried to dispel her with a wrathful aspect. She then said to him, "Guiding Labsum Gyaltsen didn't happen this time. So, see you later."

There are many similar stories. We do meet such transformations, especially when we go to holy places, but our success in recognizing them as deities is determined by our having created the cause through correctly devoting ourselves to the virtuous friend.

Milarepa's disciple, Rechungpa, always served Milarepa, but when Milarepa refused to give him permission to go on pilgrimage to Lhasa, Rechungpa still insisted on going. Milarepa told him three times not to go, but Rechungpa didn't listen and went anyway. Rechungpa had previously been a monk, but in Lhasa he met a woman, married her and got into a lot of trouble. His wife often beat him. For example, when making soup, she would stir it, then beat Rechungpa on the head with the wooden spoon such that he would end up with soup all over him, with vegetables hanging from his ears. Rechungpa said, "I have received many initiations, but never before the initiation of the wooden spoon; and I have worn many ornaments, but never before ornaments made of vegetables."

Rechungpa's wife once gave him a blue turquoise but when a beggar came to beg for the turquoise, Rechungpa gave it to him. When Rechungpa went to see Milarepa on his return from Lhasa, Milarepa asked him what had happened to him. However, before Rechungpa could explain, Milarepa showed him the blue turquoise. The beggar had actually been an embodiment of Milarepa. I think Milarepa took the turquoise so that later he could prove to Rechungpa that he knew what had happened in Lhasa, in case Rechungpa didn't tell him. Rechungpa was surprised to see the turquoise.

Milarepa told Rechungpa, "Because you disregarded my advice three times, you cannot achieve enlightenment in this life. You will first have to be born as a great geshe for three lifetimes." If Rechungpa had not gone against Milarepa's advice, he would have received sublime realization in that life.

If we make mistakes in devoting to the virtuous friend, qualities of understanding and realizations that we had generated previously degenerate. For example, in previous times in India, a master of low caste had a disciple from a high caste who had the power to fly. One day while flying in the sky, the disciple saw his guru down below seated on the ground. He thought, "Not even my guru has such power as this." As soon as this pride arose, his power degenerated and he fell to the ground. (It doesn't say whether he fell on top of his guru.) This happened because he had the thought of faults in relation to his virtuous friend. Even though he had the power to fly, that power immediately degenerated.

There is also a story about Naropa. Tilopa had told Naropa, even though he was a great pandit, not to debate with the Hindus. But there came a time of great danger when a Hindu pandit wanted to debate with the Buddhists. A kind of bet was made, in which they gambled with the religion of all the people in the country: if the Hindu won, everybody in the country would have to become Hindu; if the Buddhist won, everybody would have to become Buddhist. Since Naropa couldn't bear the thought of the Hindus winning and all the Buddhists having to become Hindus, he decided to debate with the Hindu pandit.

At one point in the debate Naropa's mind suddenly went blank and he couldn't think how to answer the Hindu's point. He then thought of his guru Tilopa and made a mental request to him for help. Tilopa immediately appeared in space in front of Naropa and blessed him; he was then able to continue and win the debate. Later Tilopa explained that because Naropa made the mistake of going against Tilopa's advice not to debate with the Hindus, even though Naropa could have become enlightened in that lifetime, instead he would become enlightened in the intermediate state.

Manjushri had predicted that two novice monks from a place near Tibet called Khotan had the karma to achieve the sublime realization of enlightenment in that life. The two young monks walked for many months to reach central Tibet to receive teachings from the Dharma king Songtsen Gampo. When they neared the place where Songtsen Gampo lived, however, they heard stories of how the king punished many people by having their heads cut off and saw for themselves all the heads piled up on the ground.

In reality, Songtsen Gampo was an embodiment of Chenrezig, the Buddha of Compassion. Chenrezig manifested as the king and also as the judges who decided the punishment for the people who had created negative karma. All the many people who were executed were also manifestations of Chenrezig; they were not ordinary people. To stop the Tibetan people killing, stealing and performing other non-virtuous actions, the king made laws known as the sixteen human Dharmas and the ten deva Dharmas.[54] Basically they were laws in accord with the Dharma that encouraged people to abandon the ten non-virtuous actions. To stop the people in Tibet creating non-virtuous actions, Chenrezig manifested as the king, the judges, the executioners and also the many criminals. They were all embodiments of Chenrezig. The big pile of heads was to frighten people, but in reality there was no killing of ordinary people. It was all a way of guiding sentient beings.

The two novice monks didn't understand this; they didn't realize that even the people who were executed were the creations of Songtsen Gampo, not ordinary beings with a separate mind. Chenrezig manifested as all these beings to protect the Tibetan people from creating negative karma through harming others. However, it would be easy for anyone who didn't know the real situation to see what was happening as evil.

After having received Dharma teachings from Songtsen Gampo, the monks generated heresy because they thought that he was killing ordinary people. They then left to return home. If they had stayed and continued to receive teachings from Songtsen Gampo, they had the karma to become enlightened in that life; but because they generated heresy, their enlightenment did not happen, and they went back home with only a sack of gold. Even though they had the incredible merit necessary to be enlightened in that life, instead of achieving sublime realization, the only attainment they had was just one sack of gold.

There are many such stories, even nowadays, of monks who created negative karma in relation to their teachers, then later were unable to continue their practice and experienced many difficulties. The incarnate lama who lived in the room next to where Lama Yeshe and I lived in Buxa Duar, just separated from us by a curtain made of flattened bamboo and cloth, had a fight with his teacher, and later experienced many problems in his life.

---

[54] For a list of the sixteen human Dharmas see *Liberation in Our Hands, Part Two*, pp. 269–70, n. 115.

Later, at a train station, he was bitten on the foot by a small dog that had rabies. He then went crazy and died.

The scripture *Connection to the Present Buddha's Valid Cognizer* mentions,

> If a disciple harbors a grudge or dislike toward the guru, there is no way for him to achieve qualities. If one does not generate recognition of and respect for the guru as the founder of the Buddhadharma, Guru Shakyamuni Buddha, as well as for the practitioners of all three vehicles and the bhikshu who hasn't revealed Dharma, there's no way to accomplish the Dharma that wasn't received before and not to lose what was received before. If one does not show respect, the Dharma is degenerated.

Here it says that it's important to recognize and respect not only the guru as the founder of the Buddhadharma but also the practitioners of the three vehicles, even those who haven't generated any paths, and even a fully ordained monk with whom you haven't had Dharma contact. If you don't generate respect, you don't receive understanding and realizations of the words and meaning of Dharma and that which you had received before degenerates. Not showing respect is the cause of degenerating your Dharma. For example, you will remember less and less of the teachings and commentaries you have received, even if you have studied them.

Having a mind that is forgetful or foolish, finding it very difficult to comprehend even a simple Dharma subject, is the result of negative karmas accumulated in relation to holy objects. It can also be the result of making polluted offerings, such as making offerings on the altar or even to the actual virtuous friend without covering your mouth and not blessing offerings with OM AH HUM. Any time we make an offering we should bless it by saying OM AH HUM; otherwise, interferers, which are different types of spirits, take the essence of the offering. In that way, many obstacles, or pollution, happen to the mind, making it unclear and unable to understand the teachings. It causes you not to understand even the meaning of the words of teachings on emptiness, for example. It is also difficult to have clear visualization and your concentration doesn't last. When you try to concentrate, you are very distracted. You can also suddenly generate heresy and disrespect to the Dharma.

In *Liberation in the Palm of Your Hand*, Pabongka Dechen Nyingpo warns that evil friends can also cause our knowledge and realizations to degenerate.

Lama Tsongkhapa said,

> If one wonders how to recognize a non-virtuous friend, it is someone who doesn't help to stop the wrong conduct and natural vices one had before and helps to increase new wrong conduct.

Also, the scripture *Beyond the Sorrowless State* says,

> Bodhisattvas are more scared of evil friends than they are of a crazed elephant. The difference between the two is that the latter destroys only the body and the place while the former destroys the body of Dharma. Besides that, the crazed elephant cannot throw one into the evil-gone realms, while evil friends will definitely throw one into the evil-gone realms.

(6) WE WILL BE AFFLICTED EVEN IN THIS LIFE BY ILLNESS AND OTHER UNDESIRABLE THINGS

The sixth shortcoming is that even in this life we will be harmed by disease and many other undesirable things. We will experience one torment after another. *Fifty Verses of Guru Devotion* mentions thirteen different ways someone who has made mistakes in their devotion to the virtuous friend can die:

> The great fool who criticizes the vajra master will die from an epidemic, cold disease, a demon, a fever or poison. That person may be killed by a king, fire, poisonous snake, water, wrathful dakinis, thieves, spirits or malignant fiends. After being killed in one of these ways, he then goes to hell.

Being killed by a king is just an example—it also includes being killed by other human beings. Wrathful dakinis, who have different levels of tantric realizations, can become unhappy when a disciple generates heresy or breaks the samaya relationship with his guru and become a condition of untimely death.

The Essence of Nectar says,

In this life disease, demon harms, untimely death and so on happen.

It is very easy for the fortune of those who have degenerated or broken samaya with their guru to go lower and lower. There is then more possibility of their receiving harm from the elements, nonhuman beings, such as spirits, and even human beings. They may also die by suicide. Even if there's no one who kills them, they kill themselves. They have a terrible death. Even though they might have great Dharma knowledge and be expert in all five philosophical scriptures,[55] they end their life in a sad or terrifying way.

With respect to experiencing undesirable things as a result of making mistakes in guru devotion, there is a story about Acharya Buddhajñana. One day while Buddhajñana was teaching to a large gathering of his disciples, his guru, the great yogi Saukarika, a swineherd, passed by the teaching place. Buddhajñana saw his guru but pretended he hadn't and continued teaching. Later, after the teaching was over, Buddhajñana went to see Saukarika. As Buddhajñana was making his prostrations, Saukarika asked him, "Why didn't you prostrate to me earlier?" Buddhajñana replied, "Oh, I didn't see you." Both of his eyes immediately dropped out onto the ground. Saukarika blessed both of Buddhajñana's eyes but was able to restore only one of them.

His Holiness Song Rinpoche said that yogis immediately experience the results of such actions whereas ordinary beings don't. We ordinary beings accumulate the karma and even though we don't experience any immediate result, we will experience the hells in our future life. We might be comfortable right now, with nothing bad happening to us, but all our negative karma is waiting to be experienced in the lower realms in the life after this.

Lama Yeshe once told me to sleep above him in the upper berth in a train from Pathankot to Delhi. Because Lama gave me permission, I stayed up there but didn't feel comfortable about it. When I fell asleep that night, I dreamt there was an earthquake, with a huge crack appearing in the earth. I thought, "It's not right!" and sat on the floor instead.

Also, a novice monk made a mistake in devoting to his guru, Kadampa Geshe Neusurpa. Neusurpa commented, "Before he dies he should make

---

[55] The five major philosophical scriptures are Maitreya's *Ornament of Clear Realizations*, Dignaga's *Compendium of Valid Cognition*, Chandrakirti's *Entering the Middle Way*, *Vinaya* and Vasubandhu's *Treasury of Knowledge*.

confession to me, but he won't make any confession." At the time of his death the disciple screamed out that he was being crushed by all the mountains of Neusur. He experienced unbearable fear, with the vision that he was being burned alive, with the mountains of Neusur crushing him.

Lobpön Yeshe Zangpo, a nyung-nä lineage lama, had a skin disease that wouldn't respond to any treatment. When he tried going to some hot springs, the water just became hotter and hotter until he felt that he was being boiled alive. He then did a Red Yamantaka retreat but even that didn't help much. Later he asked a lama to help him. The lama checked with Tara, who said that since the disease was the result of mistakes made in devotion to the virtuous friend in a past life, Yeshe Zangpo should make confession. Only after he made confession was there any improvement in his condition.

The practice of confession is extremely important generally in purifying obscurations and pacifying obstacles to the generation of realizations of the path to enlightenment and specifically in curing serious disease. In the case of a heavy disease where nothing else helps, confession can be very powerful. If you do the confession strongly and perfectly, you can purify all the negative karmas you have created, which are set up in your mental continuum waiting to be gradually experienced in the future.

As I mentioned before, as a child, I lived for seven years in Rolwaling with my uncle, Ngawang Gendun, who was my second alphabet teacher. The Rolwaling valley has a river running through it and mountains all around. On one side of the river there is a monastery and a large stupa with a road running around it; on the other side there is a green meadow where Western trekkers used to camp. Tourists, guided by Sherpa porters, would sometimes come there in the summer and the autumn. The guides sometimes brought the trekkers to my teacher's house, and once or twice we went down to see them in their tents.

The river was quite wide but the bridge crossing it to the meadow was rather narrow, just two tree trunks tied together. One day I wanted to give some potatoes to some Westerners in their camp. My teacher told me not to go but I think I pushed for his permission. Somehow I really wanted to give the potatoes to the Westerners. My teacher put some potatoes in a brass container that was used for serving rice or chang, the local beer, and off I went, alone. I stepped onto the bridge, and when I reached the middle, the bridge tilted (in my view, anyway) and I fell down into the water.

My head bobbed up, then went down again. According to what my teacher later told me, I was first facing upriver, then later downriver. I was carried along by the river, with my head coming up from time to time, all the while getting closer and closer to a dangerous place where the river was very deep. One time when my head came up, I saw that my uncle was running down the mountain toward the river from the monastery, which was quite a distance away. He was wearing simple cloth pants and holding them up as he ran to catch me.

At that time the thought came into my mind, "What people call 'Lawudo Lama' is now going to die. This is going to end." I didn't have much understanding of Dharma at that time and I had no idea of emptiness, but this thought came. I felt no fear. I would find it difficult if death came now, but at that time my mind was completely comfortable. There was no fear at all—just the thought, "What people call 'Lawudo Lama' is going to die."

I was about to reach the deep water, where it would have been very difficult to rescue me, when my uncle finally grabbed me. I was dripping wet. My teacher said, "I told you not to go!" I think my falling down and dropping the container and the potatoes must have been a shortcoming of not listening to my teacher.

I later heard that one of the Western tourists came down to the river with his camera and was taking pictures as I was being carried along by the water.

(7) In future lives we will wander endlessly in the lower realms

The seventh shortcoming is that in our future lives we will be reborn and die in the lower realms for an inconceivable length of time. One after another, endlessly, we will experience the sufferings of the lower realms. We will wander in the lower realms for an incredible length of time; it will be difficult to see the end of our suffering.

The Essence of Nectar says,

> In future lives, one will wander endlessly in the evil-gone realms.

After we have established a Dharma connection with a teacher—even if we have received only the oral transmission of a few syllables of a mantra or one verse of a teaching with the recognition of a guru-disciple relationship—there is no doubt that the heaviest negative karma is criticizing or renouncing the guru.

The *Vajrapani Empowerment Tantra* mentions that Vajrapani once asked Guru Shakyamuni Buddha, "Bhagavan, what is the ripened aspect result of despising the guru?" This refers to criticizing or renouncing the guru.

Buddha replied, "Don't ask me that, Vajrapani. If I explained the shortcomings of having made mistakes in devotion to the virtuous friend, all the devas and other worldly beings would be terrified." He added, "The bodhisattvas, who have great compassion for sentient beings, would vomit blood."

In other words bodhisattvas, who have so much compassion for sentient beings, wouldn't be able to stand the shock of hearing about the heavy suffering such a sentient being would have to bear for an unbelievable length of time. The bodhisattvas would find it unendurable, like a mother who knows the son she loves very much is being tortured. They would vomit blood from their holy mouths and pass away.

Buddha then continued, "But steel yourself, and I will tell you a little, O Lord of Secrets. The person who has made mistakes in devotion to the virtuous friend by having criticized him, renounced him and so forth will be born after this life in the hell realm that I have described for the person who has committed the five uninterrupted negative karmas. He will abide there for infinite eons. Therefore, one should never belittle, criticize or give up the vajra master."

This means he would be born not only in a hell realm, but in the lowest hot hell, Inexhaustible Suffering, which has the heaviest suffering in samsara, and abide there for infinite eons. His body would be one with fire, like a piece of burning wood, with the hottest fire coming from the ten directions. He would experience unbearable suffering and only by hearing the sound of his screaming would one know that a sentient being was there.

However, when Kyabje Chöden Rinpoche was teaching on *The Great Treatise on the Stages of the Path to Enlightenment* at Land of Medicine Buddha,[56] Rinpoche said that one is reborn in the vajra hell, not in the eighth hot hell, Inexhaustible Suffering. According to Rinpoche, the vajra hell is something different and the suffering there is even greater.

Buddha would only explain a small part of the result, that such a person

[56] An FPMT center in Soquel, California.

would have to abide in hell for an inconceivable number of eons, because it is too terrifying to explain in detail.

I mentioned earlier the quotation from the tantric text *Self-Arisen and Self-Manifested*, which explains that the negative karma of criticizing the vajra master, this most powerful object, is so heavy that it is like having killed one hundred thousand Sangha. There are many similar quotations.

In going over these outlines, you can see that having killed a hundred, or even a thousand, people is not really so shocking. The negative karma of a butcher who has actually killed many thousands of animals but hasn't accumulated heavy negative karmas in relation to a virtuous friend is light compared to these negative karmas. The negative karmas of killing are easier to purify. Mao Zedong's case may be a little different because he destroyed the teachings of the whole of Tibet and killed many holy beings, though they were not his gurus.

Another tantric teaching explains,

> You should never belittle or abuse the vajra master, the one who brought you into the mandala. You should never disturb the holy mind of the vajra master. If, out of ignorance, this has happened, it will definitely throw you into a hell realm.

Because that negative karma is so heavy, even if you participate in some enjoyment with a person who has criticized her vajra master from her heart, it takes away your own realizations and causes the experiences you have developed to degenerate. It becomes the root of the pitiful suffering of the lower realms.

Lama Tsongkhapa said that if you enjoy entertainment, such as having a meal, with someone who has criticized her guru from her heart, you won't achieve realizations. Let alone you yourself disturbing your guru's holy mind or criticizing him from your heart, even sharing a meal with someone who has done so means that you won't achieve realizations. This is how heavy this negative karma is. There is no heavier karma than this, not even the five uninterrupted negative karmas. Anyone who eats with that person, talks with that person or otherwise associates with that person cannot achieve realizations.

In a commentary to the Yamantaka initiation, the Thirteenth Dalai Lama explained that even eating or drinking with someone who has broken samaya with one of your gurus causes you to go to the lower realms. The pollution degenerates your mind and causes you to be reborn in the lower realms.

People with broken samaya pollute the place where they are. Even keeping in your room objects that belong to someone who has broken samaya with one of your gurus pollutes your mind. Strict practitioners would not keep even Dharma objects belonging to such a person in their house because they would be scared that the pollution would become an obstacle to developing their mind in the path to enlightenment and cause their mind to degenerate. I'm not saying that I'm a good practitioner, but in the past, because I had heard so many teachings about these shortcomings, whenever a Tibetan who had criticized His Holiness the Dalai Lama or some other high lama gave me a picture of a deity, I would put it outside in a high, clean place or give it away. The picture itself was a holy object, so it had to be respected; but because the pollution could have so much effect on the mind, I had it put outside or gave it away.

His Holiness Song Rinpoche, who was the actual Heruka, used to mention something similar during initiations. Rinpoche explained that even drinking water in the area where a person with broken samaya lives causes you to go to the lower realms. Rinpoche was referring to the pollution from that person's degenerated samaya. There is no doubt about the result for the person who has broken samaya, but the negative effect is so great that it even degenerates the minds of the other people around them, even though they themselves didn't create that same negative karma. They incur much pollution just from being near that person that they are reborn in the lower realms.

My kind guru Serkong Dorje Chang also said that even drinking water from the same valley where there is a fellow disciple who has scorned your own guru causes you to be born in the hells.

When one of the gurus of quite a high lama in Lhasa was jailed by the Tibetan government, even though it was said that this lama had the power to help his guru, he didn't help him. This lama later wrote a very clear scripture on the vinaya, one that the monks found very useful to memorize. But when Geshe Lekden, whose practice of guru devotion is excellent, was abbot of Sera Je College, he didn't want the monks to receive pollution from this text, even though it was so well written. Geshe Lekden said that since this lama didn't help his guru to get out of prison, the Sera monks might get pollution from the text. He was so concerned about the degeneration of their practice and the development of their mind that he had all the texts collected so that they could no longer be memorized. Serious practitioners who know the point of guru devotion practice are very careful about such things.

Besides being harmful for us to criticize or belittle our virtuous friend, we should not even see a person who has done so. When a disciple of Chag Lotsawa who had degenerated samaya came to a teaching being given by the great Nyingma yogi, Lingrepa, Lingrepa was immediately unable to move his mouth. He was unable to teach the Dharma and had to leave.

Also, if you have broken samaya by criticizing or abandoning your guru and then become a teacher, there is a danger of your polluting your disciples.

(8) IN ALL OUR FUTURE LIVES WE WILL LACK VIRTUOUS FRIENDS

The eighth shortcoming of making mistakes in our devotion to the virtuous friend is that in all our future lives we will lack a virtuous friend. Even if the country where we live has thousands of qualified teachers—Tibet or India, for example—we won't be able to find a guru. We will never meet a virtuous friend, someone to guide us to liberation and enlightenment. Endlessly we will have to wander in samsara and experience suffering.

Why will we lack a virtuous friend in all our future lives? Because even though there are numberless buddhas and bodhisattvas, without the guru we cannot achieve enlightenment. That is the whole point. No matter how many buddhas there are, they can benefit us only through this ordinary aspect of the virtuous friend, which manifests according to our karma. We don't have the karma to see all the buddhas and to communicate with and receive teachings directly from them. The numberless buddhas do work for us, but only through the aspect of the guru.

The Essence of Nectar says,

> If, by chance, one finds the body of a happy migratory being,
> Because of experiencing the result similar to the cause
> Of not having respected the guru,
> One will be born in unfortunate states without freedom
> And one won't even hear the words "holy Dharma" or
>   "virtuous friend."

The result of disrespecting the virtuous teacher is that in all future lifetimes we will not find a virtuous teacher, so we will not hear the holy Dharma. Not meeting a virtuous friend in the future is experiencing the result similar to the cause of having disrespected or made mistakes in relation to the virtuous friend. In life after life we will be born in places where there is no freedom to practice Dharma, where we will not meet a virtuous friend. (This is the opposite of the sixth advantage of correct devotion to the virtuous friend, where we meet a virtuous friend in life after life.) As we don't meet a virtuous friend, we don't meet the Dharma.

Also, if we don't attempt in this life not to make mistakes in relation to our virtuous friends, the cycle will go on and on. Each complete karma, whether virtuous or non-virtuous, has four results, one of which is creating the result similar to the cause. The habit of making mistakes leaves impressions on our consciousness and when we meet virtuous friends in our future lives we will make the same mistakes we made in the past. This is creating the result similar to the cause. Even if we meet a guru in future lives, we will make the same mistakes again. We will go on and on in this way, creating the heaviest possible obstacles.

Karma is expandable, more expandable than, for example, many millions of seeds coming from planting one seed. If we generate negative thoughts toward our virtuous friend or the teachings in this life, these become the cause for the same things to happen for many lifetimes. Going against our guru's advice in this life becomes the cause of going against our guru's advice in many future lifetimes. Even though it takes only a short time to commit the mistake in this life, we will experience the result for a long time, making the same mistake over and over again in many future lifetimes. Even if we are able to take vows, we will break them again; it will be very difficult to keep them purely. If we think of the long-term disadvantages we will be careful in this life to put all our effort into practicing purely.

It's also helpful to think that all the failures in our Dharma practice—degenerating our vows, going against our guru's advice, ending our relationship with our guru—are the results of our own past karma.

Therefore, it is unbelievably important in this life to put all our effort into correctly devoting ourselves to our virtuous friends. If we don't, we will repeat the same mistake again and again, and this is incredibly harmful. It is very important to think of the long-term disadvantages, not just of those in this life. Without needing to think of the lower realms, we can think of the shortcoming of making the same mistake again for many lifetimes.

Purifying any mistake and making the determination not to repeat it help to stop experience of the same thing in our future lives.

It is very helpful to know these important points and feel repentance. We should feel great regret about any negative karmas we have accumulated in the past by having made mistakes in our devotion to our virtuous friends, as if we had swallowed poison. Because of our strong repentance, the thought not to repeat our mistakes will naturally arise and we will have a strong wish to purify our negative karmas.

If those who have criticized or abandoned the virtuous friend don't confess and purify their mistakes, it will be extremely hard for them to find even the body of a happy migratory being in their future lives. And even when, at last, they do receive the body of a happy migratory being, because of experiencing the result similar to the cause of disrespecting the virtuous friend, they will be reborn in a state where they have no freedom to practice Dharma. They will be born in a family or place where they cannot hear even the words "holy Dharma" or "virtuous friend."

For example, in Dharamsala in India, where His Holiness the Dalai Lama and many other lamas live and give many teachings, not everyone comes to the teachings. Even though they live close to the lamas, even in the same town, many people never come to listen to the Dharma. Tibetans and over the past years people from Singapore, Hong Kong and Taiwan, as well as, of course, the West, have come to listen to His Holiness's teachings. But even though the Indian people who live there in Dharamsala all the time don't have to buy an airplane ticket to come to the temple where His Holiness gives teachings, due to karma, they don't come. His Holiness, an actual living buddha, is there, but they still somehow can't realize it. They have no interest in or are unable to come to the teachings.

The way we devote ourselves to our guru is extremely important; it determines whether we accomplish the multitudes of goodness in this life and in future lives. Therefore, it is important that we don't do improper, or inauspicious, things, as when Milarepa offered Marpa an empty copper pot. Because of this inauspicious action, Milarepa experienced difficulty in obtaining the means of living when he was doing retreat. For Milarepa's sake, Marpa skillfully beat the empty pot with a stick to fill it with sound. Because of that auspicious action Milarepa become famous all over the world, both in the East and West. Marpa also filled the pot with butter and made a light offering. Because of that, Milarepa received all of Marpa's advice and in that very lifetime completed the realizations of the path and achieved omniscient mind. These various auspicious and inauspicious actions brought different results in Milarepa's life.

Also, when Marpa went to India to see Naropa, Naropa created a manifestation of Hevajra and his mandala, then asked Marpa, "Are you going to prostrate to the deity or to me?" Marpa chose to prostrate first to the deity. Because of this inauspicious mistake, Marpa's blood lineage ceased. When Marpa's son, Tarma Dodé, was killed, he didn't have a wife or children. Marpa tried very hard to find a dead human body to transfer Tarma Dodé's consciousness into, but could find only the body of a dead pigeon. From that time there was no blood lineage, even though Lama Marpa had a wisdom mother and eleven sons. Marpa said that this was because he had made prostration to Hevajra rather than to his guru.

Also, during Lama Tsongkhapa's time, his disciples didn't make a painting of Lama Tsongkhapa on the walls of Ganden Monastery. Because of that inauspicious mistake, Ganden, although the mother monastery of the Gelugpa tradition, didn't have the great, far-reaching prosperity of the other monasteries, Drepung and Sera. Many learned monks came out of Drepung and Sera, but not as many came from Ganden. Ganden also had fewer monks and suffered the most destruction by the Chinese.

Our practice of guru devotion in this life is incredibly important because the greatest profit and the greatest loss are related to correctly devoting ourselves to the virtuous friend and to making mistakes in relation to the virtuous friend respectively. If we are careful from the very beginning, when we first establish Dharma contact, to correctly devote ourselves to the virtuous friend, we will experience fewer shortcomings later.

We need to understand and study well the lam-rim teachings on the benefits of correct devotion and the shortcomings of incorrect devotion and then to practice as perfectly as we can. Practicing guru devotion correctly in this life determines whether or not we meet a virtuous friend in our future lives and whether or not that virtuous friend will be perfectly qualified. The success of all our future lives will be determined by our guru devotion practice in this life. We must be most careful about these points in order to protect ourselves from all these dangers and shortcomings, now and in the future, and in order to have success, now and in the future.

By knowing the benefits of correct devotion to the virtuous friend, we see the importance of relying upon the virtuous friend and all the profit to be gained from doing so. If we don't know the shortcomings, we won't be careful in correctly devoting ourselves to the virtuous friend because we won't see the importance of it. In that way we will create more obstacles. By understanding the shortcomings, we see how correctly devoting to the virtuous friend is an extremely important root practice. We see how extremely important it is to be careful, because if we do this practice well, there will be no obstacles to the success of our temporary wishes or to our accomplishment of the path to enlightenment. There will be no obstacles to our achievement of the three great purposes: the happiness of future lives, liberation and enlightenment.

We also know about these eight benefits and eight shortcomings from our own experience; they describe the failures and successes in our own life. For example, we may try to do retreat, but after some time many disturbances arise and we fail to complete it. Or we may be living in ordination with great ambition to work for the teachings and sentient beings like Lama Tsongkhapa, Lama Atisha or Guru Shakyamuni Buddha, but it doesn't turn out that way. The wish is there, but it doesn't happen because there are many obstacles. Even though we may have all the conditions to practice Dharma, many obstacles arise, and we fail. Such experiences are due to having made mistakes in our practice of guru devotion in past lives or this one. Because we didn't practice guru devotion well in past lives we experience shortcomings in this life and many lifetimes to come, even though we meet the Dharma. Because we have made the same mistakes for many lives in the past, we create the result similar to the cause in this life. Even on those rare occasions when we meet a virtuous teacher and the teachings, we make the same mistakes again in our practice.

However, even if we have made many mistakes, it is very important to make the determination not to make them again. Making a strong determination to put guru devotion into practice now and in the future is the remedy that prevents mistakes happening again.

It is emphasized that everything, from the happiness of this life up to enlightenment, is dependent on this root of guru devotion. That is why guru devotion is emphasized so much for the completion of the practices of listening, reflecting and meditating. Our understanding of and feeling for the eight advantages of following the guru correctly and the eight disadvantages of not following the guru correctly determine how beneficial our practice of guru devotion will be for our mind. With more understanding we will have more feeling in our heart and our guru yoga prayers won't be just words. We will be able to do guru yoga practice by mixing it with our own mind.

Using every means, especially quotations and strong reasoning, meditate again and again on the advantages of devoting to the virtuous friend and the shortcomings of not doing so or of making mistakes in devoting to the virtuous friend. If you do this, the wish to devote to the guru will arise and you will feel great happiness in devoting yourself to the guru.

The Essence of Nectar says,

> In short, if the way one devotes to the guru is wrong,
> One won't have the opportunity to achieve higher states or
>   liberation
> But will wander forever in samsara, in general,
> And the lower realms, in particular.
>
> Since the benefits and shortcomings are beyond conception,
> And even the roots of the multitudes of goodness appear here,
> From now on, without running to the object of superstition,
> Why don't I devote to and respect the virtuous friend?

H.H. Ling Rinpoche and H.H. Trijang Rinpoche, Dharamsala, ca 1974

9. The Importance of Devotion

THERE ARE TWO WAYS of devoting ourselves to the guru: with thought and with action (chapter 15).

3. HOW TO DEVOTE TO A GURU WITH THOUGHT

Devoting to the guru with thought has two divisions:

(1) The root, training our mind in devotion to the guru
(2) Developing respect by remembering the guru's kindness (ch. 14)

If we meditate on these two outlines, using quotations and logical reasoning as effectively as possible, we will be very happy to devote ourselves to the virtuous friend. Remembering the qualities of the guru causes devotion to arise and remembering the kindness of the guru causes respect to arise.

(1) THE ROOT, TRAINING OUR MIND IN DEVOTION TO THE GURU

Training our mind in devotion to the guru means using quotations and logical reasoning to prove to this mind that does *not* see the guru as a buddha that the guru *is* a buddha. It means training our mind in this meditation. Our ultimate goal is to bring all sentient beings to enlightenment. To succeed in this, we ourselves need to achieve enlightenment first; to do this we need to actualize the path; to do this we need the blessings of the guru. Since the cause of receiving blessings is our devotion, we need to look at the guru as a buddha. Otherwise the only thought that will arise in our mind will be, "I will take teachings from this lama." The guru will then be just like a teacher in school from whom we simply learn words and we will then have nothing more useful than intellectual knowledge to rely upon.

Strong devotion is what makes it easy to correctly devote ourselves to the virtuous friend. The stronger our devotion, the more we are able to dedicate our life to serving and following the advice of the virtuous friend. And the more we follow the advice of the virtuous friend, the easier it is for us to achieve realizations of the path to enlightenment. Therefore, we have to train our mind in guru devotion, transforming our mind into the pure thought of devotion, which means looking at the guru as a buddha. Whether from the guru's side he is a sentient being or a buddha, from our side we have to transform our mind into the pure devotional thought that sees him as an actual buddha by looking at him as a buddha.

Whether or not the teacher from his side is an enlightened being, if we disciples from our side don't look at him as a buddha, we will never see that teacher who revealed Dharma to us as a buddha. The key point is that if we don't look at the guru as a buddha, we will never see the guru as a buddha. That's why we need to practice guru devotion.

This outline is extremely important because all the realizations of the rest of the path have to be generated by devoting ourselves to the guru. (I prefer the expression "devoting to the guru" to "relying upon the guru" as *relying upon* makes it sound as if we just relax and leave it all to the guru. Devoting implies more action from the side of the disciple. On the basis of devoting, an action of mind, we then do something.) Unless we generate the devotion that sees the guru as a buddha, there is no way we can generate any other realization.

I will explain various techniques for training the mind to see the guru as a buddha, as described in the lam-rim teachings and by various lamas who have actualized the path. Various reasons are used to prove to our ordinary mind, which sees guru and buddha as separate, that they are one. Looking at them as one then transforms our mind into devotion. If you can't understand through one method, you can use another.

The root, training our mind in devotion to the guru, has three divisions:

(a) Why we should look at the guru as a buddha (chapter 10)
(b) Why we are able to see the guru as a buddha (chapter 11)
(c) How to see the guru as a buddha (chapter 12)

In the practice of guru devotion, the most important thing is training our mind in devotion, or faith. As I explained at the very beginning, guru devotion, seeing the guru as a buddha, is called "the root of the path" because just as the trunk, branches, leaves and fruit grow from the stable root of a tree, all the realizations of the graduated path to enlightenment grow from stable devotion to the guru. If there is no root, nothing can grow. Just as a tree depends on its root, all the realizations from perfect human rebirth up to enlightenment depend on guru devotion. If we have the stable root of guru devotion, all realizations come quickly.

Whether or not we will be able to generate the realizations of the path to enlightenment in this life or in future lives depends on whether or not we cultivate the root of the path, guru devotion, within our heart. Receiving realizations depends on receiving the blessings of the guru, and the blessings of the guru come from guru devotion. This is the whole answer. If we have this root, we will be able to attain the path from the beginning up to enlightenment. If we don't have this root, we can't generate any lam-rim realizations.

Devotion, or faith, is necessary generally for practicing Dharma and particularly for generating the realization of guru devotion. Along with recognizing all sentient beings as our mother, seeing the guru as a buddha is one of the most difficult realizations to generate. Even though it's very difficult, if we don't attempt to realize this, we can't generate the rest of the path to enlightenment.

Generally, faith has to be the preliminary to all virtuous actions. The sutra, *The Ten Dharmas,* explains,

In those who have no devotion, the white dharmas do not grow.

White dharmas refers to the scriptural understanding and realizations of the path to enlightenment. If a person doesn't have devotion, the white dharmas can't be generated.

The Ten Dharmas continues,

Just as a sprout cannot come from a burnt seed, no white dharmas can come from those who have no devotion.

The minds of those who don't have devotion or have lost it are burned by anger and heresy. Like burnt seeds, their minds don't have the potential to grow the green sprout of scriptural understanding or realizations of the path.

The sutra, *The Lamp of the Three Jewels,* explains,

> Faith is generated first, giving birth like a mother;
> It protects all good qualities.

Just as a mother gives birth to her children, faith gives birth to all good karma and all realizations of the path. And with faith, all good qualities are protected and increased. This is easy to understand. When we lose our faith, or devotion, we also lose the good qualities and good experiences we have achieved. When we have little faith in karma, we are more careless about our actions and vows. When we have little faith in our guru, we are more careless in our devotion to him and make more mistakes. On the other hand, when we have strong faith in karma, we take more care to decrease our non-virtuous actions and increase our virtuous actions. And when we have strong faith in our guru, we are careful in our devotion to him.

When we feel strong guru devotion, we find it easy to have feeling for whatever lam-rim meditation we are doing. Any meditation we do—even meditating on emptiness—is very effective. Even though for many years the words of the *Guru Puja* prayers or the lam-rim teachings and meditations mightn't have made any sense to us, suddenly the same words make incredible sense. Each word has unbelievable meaning; each word is a profound commentary, deep and rich. As we read the words, we feel them strongly in our heart. We have the confidence that if we put some effort into meditating, we could really attain realizations.

However, when the moisture of devotion evaporates, all our prayers and meditations become just dry words. Even though we recite prayers that praise the guru's qualities, we have no feeling for them in our heart. There is no connection between our mind and the meaning of the words. Everything feels very dry. No matter how much we try to meditate, our mind is very dry, like a rock. A rock can be under the ocean for hundreds of years but still no water will penetrate it.

The teachings say that the fact that guru devotion is the root of the path is proved through our own experiences. All we have to do is check what happens during the times our mind becomes like hard, dry ground because we have no guru devotion. It becomes very difficult to feel anything when we try to meditate on lam-rim. Even though we might normally feel strong loving kindness and compassion toward others, those feelings are lost; they disappear. Our mind feels distant from loving kindness and compassion. By checking our experiences, we see very clearly that when the teachings say that guru devotion is the root of the path, it is not something made up so that gurus will receive offerings.

The Lamp of the Three Jewels also explains,

> Faith eliminates pride and increases respect.
> It eliminates doubt.
> It liberates you from the four great rivers.
> Faith signifies the city of happiness.
> With faith, your mind becomes calm and clear.
> Faith is the sublime treasure.
> Generating faith, like possessing legs,
> Enables you to reach wherever you wish to go.
> Faith is the root of moral conduct.
> Like a hand, it gathers virtue.

Faith[57] can refer to general faith—in Buddha, Dharma and Sangha, for example—but here it refers especially to faith in the guru. *The four great rivers*[58] refers to the continuous stream of disturbing thoughts, which has no beginning. *Moral conduct* refers to the moral conduct of abstaining from negative karma, the moral conduct of working for sentient beings and the moral conduct of performing all virtues together, which means trying to do every practice with all six perfections.

If you have devotion, you have less pride. Your mind also becomes calm and clear. When you have no devotion, your mind becomes confused and disturbed. The lack of devotion obscures your mind so that you can't concentrate for even a few seconds. Generating devotion is also likened to possessing legs, because it allows you to reach anywhere you want to go: the happiness of future lives, liberation and enlightenment.

Like a hand collecting grain, this positive mind of devotion makes it very easy to collect extensive merit. It happens naturally, twenty-four hours a day.

---

[57] In general there are three kinds of faith: believing, or pure-hearted, faith; lucid, or understanding, faith—faith based on logical conviction; and yearning, or aspirational, faith. See *Liberation in Our Hands, Part Two*, p. 31, n. 23.

[58] The four great rivers are those of ignorance, views, desire and worldly existence. See *The Three Principal Aspects of the Path*, pp. 87–88.

With devotion you purify inconceivable defilements and negative karmas. Every day the level of your mind goes higher and higher. Why? Because with guru devotion, twenty-four hours a day, your life is naturally dedicated to accomplishing your guru's advice or serving your guru.

Those with indestructible devotion are the most fortunate of beings. All success comes to them. Because of their strong devotion they are under the protection of the guru, so evil beings—nonhuman beings, such as spirits, and human beings—cannot harm them. They attain realizations and at the time of death they go to a pure land.

I think if you have strong faith, or devotion, you are the luckiest person because you're able to abide by your guru's advice twenty-four hours a day. No matter what difficult situation you are in, there is no hardship because of your devotion. But if there's no devotion, you find it very hard to do even a small thing. Everything becomes a problem. With devotion, there are no problems. You happily and easily abide by your guru's advice, whether it is to do Dharma practice or offer service. No matter what difficulties there are, with the devotion that sees the guru as a buddha, you feel incredible joy twenty-four hours a day. You see how fortunate you are. It's like a dream. You are able to live your life in virtue. You are constantly collecting extensive merit and constantly purifying heavy negative karmas. And you are constantly receiving blessings.

When you meditate on the guru and buddha as being one by looking at them as one, when you train your mind in that pure thought of devotion, you are then able to actually realize that the guru and buddha are one. That stable guru devotion brings success. You will be able to follow all your guru's advice without any doubts or difficulties. It makes it very easy and enjoyable to follow your guru's advice, which is the most beneficial thing in life. Because you see all the benefits, instead of having doubts and feeling it a burden on you, you see following your guru's advice as the greatest thing to enjoy in your life. When you feel it is a burden, you find it very difficult to follow even a small piece of advice.

Kyabje Chöden Rinpoche made the point that the advantage of looking at the guru as buddha is that you are able to accomplish the guru's advice without any difficulties at all. With that guru devotion you're able to achieve all the realizations of the path, liberation and enlightenment and do perfect work for all sentient beings. That is the advantage of following the guru's advice.

If you don't have strong devotion, if your devotion is unstable or artificial, everything becomes difficult. You find many problems. You can't abide by your guru's advice, and then, because of your lack of devotion, many negative thoughts arise, like grass growing in a field.

Pabongka Dechen Nyingpo said,

> In order to generate realizations of the paths and bhumis within us, we need to receive the blessing of the guru through depending on guru yoga. Whether or not we receive the blessing of the guru depends on whether or not we have devotion. Therefore, from our side, we need to train our mind in the devotion that actually sees the guru as a buddha.

Geshe Tölungpa said,

> If we have faith that the guru is the embodiment of all the buddhas of the three times, the holy body, speech and mind of all the buddhas abide in that teacher, and we, the disciples, receive the blessings of the holy body, speech mind of all the buddhas of the three times.

Also, Gyalwa Ensapa, one of Lama Tsongkhapa's indirect disciples, who achieved enlightenment within only a few years, said from his own experience,

> In short, whether we achieve great or small realization depends on whether we have meditated with great or small devotion. Therefore, may I keep as my heart practice the instruction to reflect only upon the qualities of the kind guru, source of all realizations, and not to look at faults. May I fulfill this commitment without any obstacle.

Receiving the blessings of the guru and thus receiving realizations depend on whether or not we have devotion. We can say billions of words about guru devotion but, *in short*, whether we have great or small experience of the path comes from whether we have great or small devotion to the guru. Since we are seeking enlightenment for the benefit of numberless other sentient beings, we want the realizations of the path to enlightenment, and realizations come from having transformed our mind into devotion. The guru is the source of all realizations, of all the good things, as also mentioned in the third stanza of the prostration section in *Guru Puja*.[59]

The above verse from Gyalwa Ensapa contains the very essence of guru devotion practice. We should reflect only on the qualities of the valid guru, who is the source of all our attainments, common and sublime, up to enlightenment. We shouldn't look at our guru as having faults but as having only good qualities. Among the many practices we do in our life, we should keep this instruction as our heart practice.

Since we need to live in this commitment to our gurus twenty-four hours a day, we request to be able to do this without obstacles. This is for our own benefit, for us to be able to complete the path, achieve enlightenment and enlighten other sentient beings. It's not that we practice this when we're happy but don't practice it when we're unhappy because we've been told to do something that we don't want to do. No matter what happens in our life, we should keep this as our heart practice and complete our commitment. Gyalwa Ensapa advises us to make this prayer of personal commitment to train our mind in the devotion that sees the guru as a buddha. This verse contains precious instructions that we should remember every time we meditate on guru yoga.

As a constant reminder, you should write this quotation in the beginning of your prayer book or even on the cover. Or write it on the cover of your diary. Or put it up in your meditation room or kitchen. It's good to have Dharma quotations around the house to remind you of your practice, to help you control your negative thoughts. In this way, you protect yourself from heavy negative karma and are able to have quick realizations.

To achieve the sublime realization, we must have both the devotion that sees the guru as an actual buddha and unmistaken teachings. Devotion is the basis of generating all realizations. Pabongka Rinpoche says, however, that even if our instructions are mistaken, if we believe in them, we can still achieve some small common attainments.

In India in the past a man came to request teachings from his guru. The guru was busy and said, "Marileja," which actually means, "Go away." Not understanding that his guru was telling him to go away, the man thought

---

[59] You eliminated all faults and their instincts
And are a treasury of infinite precious qualities.
Sole source of benefit and bliss without exception,
Perfect, pure guru, I prostrate at your feet. (V. 20.)

he had received an instruction and recited it as a mantra. With that word "marileja" he was later able to heal himself and also many other people of illnesses. He achieved this small attainment by having faith in what he thought was an instruction from his guru.

His Holiness Song Rinpoche used to tell a story about someone with a big nose who came to ask for teachings from a lama in Kham. The lama told him, "Your nose is like a *raksha* bead."[60] The man, not understanding what the lama had said, thought that he had been given a mantra. Satisfied that he had received a teaching, he went back home and recited "your nose is like a raksha bead" many, many times, as if he were saying a mantra.

The lama had a disease that sometimes caused him pain and no medicine could help him. His servant told him, "There's a famous, powerful ngakpa in this area who has healed many people—should we invite him here?" The lama agreed, so the servant invited the ngakpa, who came and recited "your nose is like a raksha bead" and blew in the lama's mouth. I'm sure the lama laughed at what the ngakpa said, but he was healed. The ngakpa's ability to heal people came from his faith in the power of the mantra, from the power of his devotion.

In the lam-rim teachings there is also the story of the old woman who, during a famine, recited OM VALE VULE VUNDE SVAHA, thinking that she was reciting the mantra of the deity Chunda, which enables stones to be cooked and eaten. By reciting the mantra, the old woman was able to eat rocks and remain healthy.

Later, when her son heard her reciting the mantra, he said, "Mother, the mantra you're reciting is wrong. You should be reciting OM CHALE CHULE CHUNDE SVAHA." After he taught her the correct mantra, however, she was unable to cook stones with it because she had doubts about this mantra. Even when a mantra is recited correctly, it won't work if the person has no faith in it. When she then went back to reciting the mantra incorrectly, because of her strong faith, it worked again.

In the region of Tibet called Kongpo there lived a simple-minded man. When he went to see the Shakyamuni Buddha statue in Lhasa,[61] the statue spoke to him, so he invited Shakyamuni Buddha to come to his home town. Shakyamuni Buddha said, "I will come." As he was going home, a

---

[60] A raksha bead is large, red and has a rough surface. Indian sadhus often wear malas made of raksha beads.

[61] This refers to the Jowo, the famous image of Shakyamuni Buddha in the Jokhang temple in the center of Lhasa.

Shakyamuni Buddha started floating down the river and another Shakyamuni Buddha later appeared spontaneously in stone near his home. Even now this image can still be seen.

A tantric teaching explains that even a foolish person with stable devotion will have attainments, while an intelligent person with a superstitious, intellectual mind will be far from realizations.

10. Why We Should Look at the Guru as a Buddha

———— ❧ ————

WHY SHOULD WE regard our guru as a buddha? Basically, because we the disciples want profit and don't want loss. That is the bottom line. We do it for our own sake, for our own mental development. There is no great advantage to the guru in the disciple looking at him as a buddha; it doesn't make the guru become a buddha.

No matter how many quotations and lines of reasoning we use, this is the final conclusion as to why we should look at our guru as a buddha: we want profit and don't want loss. We want the profit of all the realizations of the path to enlightenment, including the ultimate profit of full enlightenment, so that we can liberate other sentient beings from all their suffering and bring them to enlightenment. This profit, however, also includes all the happiness of this and future lives, as well as liberation from samsara. All these levels of happiness and all the various means of achieving them are contained in this profit.

The fundamental reason that we need to look at our guru as a buddha is connected with the purpose of our life, which is to benefit other sentient beings. Benefiting other sentient beings doesn't mean bringing them just the happiness of this life by giving them money, food, shelter or medicine; it means bringing other sentient beings the happiness of all their coming future lives and the ultimate happiness of liberation from samsara and full enlightenment.

The only way we can achieve all this profit, all this success, is by transforming our mind into the devotion that sees our guru as a buddha. As a disciple, practicing guru devotion is our responsibility. If we have a certain disease and have been told which medicine to take, it is then up to us whether or not we take it. We are free to choose. In other words, we have to use our own wisdom to choose whether or not we practice guru devotion.

If we don't concentrate on guru devotion, we have missed the most important preparation for all our future lives. Our practice of guru devotion is the source of all the progress and all the problems in this life and from life to life. From our practice in this life, we receive all the benefits from life to life, up to enlightenment. This is the source of the greatest loss and the greatest profit. If we don't understand this point well or don't concentrate on it, we experience the greatest loss.

Each of us has the answer to achieving success in all our future lives. It is not that we don't have freedom; it is not that God created everything and we just have to wait for whatever comes. It's not up to God. We have the solution; we have the freedom to determine whether we are successful in this life and in all our future lives. It is in our hands. We know the root of all our failures from life to life, we know that we have the freedom to stop it, and we know that we can establish the root of all success, up to enlightenment.

If we don't want all this profit for ourselves or all this benefit for all sentient beings, it's a different matter. If we have no interest in all this but like to be in samsara and are happy to have a passport to the lower realms, where we have been resident during beginningless lives, it's a different matter.

In simple terms, if we can't correctly devote ourselves to the virtuous friend as explained by Guru Shakyamuni Buddha and Lama Tsongkhapa, it is our own loss. This loss can mean failing to achieve happiness or success in this and future lives and failing to achieve liberation and enlightenment. The greatest loss is failing to achieve enlightenment and thus being unable to liberate all sentient beings from all their suffering and obscurations and lead them to enlightenment.

Since our guru is the most powerful holy object, we can create the most merit and perform the greatest purification in relation to him. However, if we make mistakes in our practice, we then create the greatest obstacles to our enlightenment. To prevent this and to achieve all success up to enlightenment and then lead all sentient beings to enlightenment, we need to generate the devotion that sees our guru as a buddha.

As Padampa Sangye mentions,

> You should regard the guru as more exalted than Buddha. If you do that, realization will come in this life, people of Tingri.

It is not so much a question of whether in reality our guru is a buddha. As Pabongka Dechen Nyingpo mentions,

> Even if the guru is not a buddha, if the disciple looks at him as a buddha, such a practitioner of guru devotion experiences no loss, but only great profit.

The story of the old woman and the dog's tooth supports this. An old woman wanted very much to have a relic of the Buddha, so she asked her son, a trader, to bring her one. Her son forgot, but on the way back home saw a dead dog by the side of the road, pulled out one of its teeth, and when he got back gave it to his mother, telling her it was a Buddha's relic.

His mother believed it actually was the holy tooth of Buddha and prayed to it with devotion. By praying and making offerings every day, she actually got Buddha's relics from it. Tiny relic pills were born from that dog tooth. The Buddha's blessings entered the tooth so that actual Buddha's relics came from it. The dog's tooth was merely the condition; the principal cause of the relics was her devotion. The relics were born from her devotion. Through her devotion, the old woman got what she wanted. In a similar way, we can achieve enlightenment through guru yoga practice. Even if the guru from his side is not an enlightened being, if we devote ourselves to him as a buddha, we receive the blessings of a buddha through the guru.

Relic pills can also come from statues or the holy bodies of great yogis, even before they pass away, as a result of the power of devotion and of attainments. When His Holiness Song Rinpoche went on pilgrimage to Tsari, a Chakrasamvara holy place in Tibet, Rinpoche came to a waterfall that is regarded as Chakrasamvara's bodhicitta seed. When Rinpoche took off his robes and sat under the waterfall to receive blessings, relics appeared from the lower part of Rinpoche's holy body.

Also, my kind root guru His Holiness Trijang Rinpoche would sometimes manifest relics. He would pick white relic pills from his face and give them to his disciples.

One great geshe from Sera Je College in Tibet, who has now reincarnated, didn't need to go to a solitary cave in the mountains in order to meditate and achieve attainments; he did so while living in the monastery and following the full monastic schedule of debating, pujas and teaching disciples.

When not teaching his disciples, this geshe would always concentrate on one particular practice in his room and nobody entering his room would interrupt his practice. He had a Tara statue in front of him and many tiny relic pills came from the statue. Two of his disciples, the two Rongtha Rinpoches, saw the pills and later asked for some. Word spread, and more and more people came to ask the geshe for pills. As they began interrupting his meditation, the geshe then asked Rongtha Rinpoche to move the statue downstairs to the prayer hall.

This geshe was a learned, ascetic meditator, with great attainments. He had completely cut off all worldly concern. I heard that no matter how cold or wet it was, he never wore shoes; and he went everywhere very fast, almost running. Never looking around, he would go straight to the prayer hall or to the courtyard for debate. Sometimes his attendants would tease him by asking, "Who was sitting next to you today in the puja?" and he would reply, "Oh, a monk." He would go straight into the prayer hall and do the prayers or meditation; as he would never even look at the monk sitting next to him, he couldn't tell his attendants his name.

Even if our virtuous friend is not a bodhisattva but just an ordinary person—or even cruel, impatient or immoral—if we practice guru devotion by looking at him as a buddha, as in the story of the old woman and the dog's tooth, Buddha's blessings enter the virtuous friend, and we are able to develop our mind. In that way we receive the blessings that enable us to achieve enlightenment.

It is said in the teachings that even if the guru is later born in hell, if the disciple has practiced guru devotion correctly, the disciple will receive blessings and can still achieve realizations of the path; she is able to develop her mind and become enlightened. One pandit in the past even broke all the four root vows of a fully ordained monk[62] but continued to give teachings and ordinations. Many of that pandit's disciples entered the path and achieved liberation.

Geshe Potowa, speaking from his own experience, said,

> Whether the guru's blessings are great or small depends upon you, not upon the guru.

---

[62] The four root vows are not to kill, not to steal, not to lie and not to engage in sexual intercourse.

This means that if our devotion is small, the blessings we receive will be small, and if our devotion is great, the blessings we receive will also be great. Depending on whether we have great or small devotion to the guru, we receive great or small blessings. How much blessing we receive from the guru depends upon our own mind, upon how much devotion we have.

As Pabongka Dechen Nyingpo explains, the blessings we receive depend on the way we look at the guru. If we regard the guru simply as a bodhisattva, we receive the blessings of a bodhisattva. But if we look at the guru as a buddha, we receive the blessings of an actual buddha. And if we look at the guru as the embodiment of all the buddhas, we receive the blessings of all the buddhas.

Even if the guru is not a buddha, if a disciple practices guru yoga perfectly by not allowing any negative thoughts to arise, the disciple can become enlightened even before the guru, as happened with Kusali and Krishnacharya,[63] and Lama Atisha and Suvarnadvipi. Suvarnadvipi's view of emptiness was in accord with the Mind Only School, whereas Lama Atisha had realized the ultimate right view of the Prasangika Madhyamaka, as explained by Guru Shakyamuni Buddha and Nagarjuna. Even though this was the case, Suvarnadvipi was especially important to Lama Atisha because he enabled Lama Atisha to generate bodhicitta.

We can also understand that if we look at our guru as an ordinary being, as someone with delusions, he will appear ordinary to us and we will receive no blessings at all. Looking at the guru as ordinary itself blocks the blessings. If we look at our guru as an ordinary person it will be difficult for us to transform our mind; it won't give us any interest in becoming like him.

As I mentioned earlier, in the guru devotion section of *The Great Treatise on the Stages of the Path to Enlightenment*, Lama Tsongkhapa says that even having the thought that the guru is an ordinary person will cause us to lose realizations; it will degenerate our mind. Here we're not talking about generating anger or heresy but simply the thought that the guru is ordinary.

Dromtönpa once asked Lama Atisha, "Why is it that in Tibet there are many people who practice meditation but there is no one who has attained special qualities?" Lama Atisha replied, "Generating the great or small qualities of the Mahayana path happens in dependence upon the guru. Since you Tibetans only recognize the guru as an ordinary person, how could it be possible for you to generate realizations?"

[63] See p. 146–47.

Even if the guru is an enlightened being, if the disciple doesn't practice guru devotion and look at him as a buddha, she will not see him as a buddha and nothing will happen in her mind. Because the disciple does not receive any blessings, her mind will stay the same and she will not be liberated from her wrong conceptions.

As Geshe Potowa said in *Commentary to the Blue Manual,*

> Even if the actual Manjushri or Chenrezig came to you, it would not fulfill that purpose. You would not receive blessings, so there would be no profit and only loss, as with Devadatta and Sunakshatra.

This means that even if Manjushri or Chenrezig actually came to you as a guru, you wouldn't receive blessings because you wouldn't see them as a buddha. Fulfilling that purpose has to come from the side of the disciple.

Take the examples of Sunakshatra, the fully ordained monk who served Guru Shakyamuni Buddha for twenty-two years, and Devadatta, who hated and always tried to harm Buddha. During all the time Sunakshatra was Buddha's attendant, he didn't look at Guru Shakyamuni Buddha as a buddha; he didn't find a single good quality in Buddha. He only found him to be a liar, even though Buddha had become enlightened inconceivable eons before.

As proved by the stories of Devadatta, Sunakshatra and others, even if your guru is a buddha, if you don't look at him as a buddha, you don't receive the blessings; you don't receive profit, only loss. And even if your guru is not an actual buddha, if you look at him as a buddha, you don't receive loss but only profit.

As I have already explained, the bottom line is that if we want profit and don't want loss, we have to practice seeing the guru as a buddha. There is no way to achieve the profit of all the realizations of the path to enlightenment other than on the basis of guru devotion. Guru devotion, seeing the guru as a buddha, causes us to receive blessings, which then cause us to achieve realizations of the path. If this is what we want, this is what we have to do.

Many people, even those who have been Dharma students for many years and studied a lot of philosophy, miss this essential point in the guru devotion meditation. If we somehow miss this underlying reason for practicing guru devotion, we will then doubt all the other reasons. We will feel unsure when we hear the other reasons, then use wrong lines of reasoning.

Take the example of meditating on how all sentient beings have been our mother and kind. The whole point of the meditation is to change our attitude from one of renouncing others and cherishing only ourselves, which is the source of suffering, into one of cherishing others and renouncing ourselves, which is the source of all happiness. However, if we're not aware of what we are trying to achieve in meditating on the kindness of the mother, we will bring in lines of reasoning that aren't useful. For example, we might argue, "I have also been mother to other sentient beings. I have also been kind to others." This is of no benefit. It doesn't help to achieve the point but only interferes with the realization.

It is similar here. We have to know the point of practicing guru devotion, which is that we want profit and don't want loss. There is no other way to achieve realizations; there is no other way to achieve enlightenment and bring all sentient beings to enlightenment.

Geshe Rabten, California, 1978

11. Why We Are Able to See the Guru as a Buddha

The mind can be trained

IN HIS EXTENSIVE teaching on guru devotion,[64] Pabongka Dechen Nyingpo mentions the vital key to the practice,

> In short, if we wish to achieve enlightenment in one life on one body, we have to stop all thought of faults and look at the guru as only a buddha.

This is the heart advice of guru devotion practice and the quickest way to achieve enlightenment. This essential instruction is what will enable us, like Milarepa, to become enlightened in one life, which means within a number of years, on this body. Pabongka Dechen Nyingpo explains that if we wish to achieve enlightenment in one brief lifetime, it is essential that we stop all thought of the guru's faults, see only his qualities and train our mind in the devotion that sees the guru as a buddha by looking at the guru as a buddha.

Everything depends on how we as disciples train our mind. It doesn't matter whether or not the guru is an enlightened being. If we look at the guru as a buddha by focusing on his good qualities, we will see him as a buddha; if we look at him as an ordinary being with faults, we won't see him as a buddha but as an ordinary being. In other words, we see the guru as a buddha by looking at him as a buddha.

---

[64] *Abbreviated Notes from Explanatory Discourses Given on* [*the First Panchen Lama's*] Six-Session Guru Yoga, [*Chandragomin's*] Twenty [Stanzas on the Bodhisattva] Vows, [*Ashvaghosha's*] Fifty Stanzas on the Guru, *and the Root and Secondary Tantric Vows.*

I think that looking at the guru as a buddha is the point where we need to apply all our effort so that we have no regrets later. If we can practice pure appearance, seeing the guru as a buddha, we receive the greatest profit; we experience great purification and collect extensive merit, enabling us to quickly develop our mind. Otherwise, if we look at the guru as ordinary, we create obstacles to the development of our mind in the path to enlightenment. Giving rise to the thought of faults in the guru becomes an obstacle to realizations. Giving rise to the thought of the guru's good qualities causes us to generate realizations.

The basic reason that we are able to see the guru as a buddha is that it is the nature of our mind that we can train it in any way we wish. As Shantideva says, there is nothing that the mind cannot be trained to become.[65] In other words, the mind is a causative phenomenon, dependent on causes and conditions. Our mind is like a child: what it becomes depends on how we guide, or direct, it.

In his thought-training teachings, Geshe Chekawa said,

> This mind, which has many faults, has one great quality. What is that? Whichever way you train it, that's what it becomes.

Compendium of Valid Cognition, a teaching on logic, explains that with a physical activity such as jumping, we need to apply effort every time we jump; however, the more we train our mind in mental phenomena, such as in generating compassion, the less effort we require to generate compassion. After some time, we can effortlessly feel compassion. It is similar with seeing the guru as a buddha. At first we need to apply effort to generate devotion through using logical reasoning and quotations; then after some time our mind will effortlessly be in the nature of devotion.

Seeing the guru as a buddha has all to do with mental training; it has all to do with the way we train our mind. What we perceive depends on the way we train our mind. All the things around us are impermanent, changing within every second, but if we don't put effort into training our mind to see these things as impermanent, the realization of their impermanence won't come. Seeing things as impermanent doesn't come from the side of the objects—it has to come from our own mind. If we train our mind to

---

[65] There is nothing whatsoever
That is not made easier through acquaintance. (*Guide*, ch. 6, v. 14.)

be aware of the impermanent nature of life by meditating that it changes within each second because of causes and conditions and that death can happen at any moment, we see our life as being very short, and our wrong conception of permanence, our fixed idea that we are going to live for a long time, is stopped during that time. To realize the reality of impermanence we have to put effort into looking at things as impermanent.

In a similar way we can transform our mind from self-cherishing into bodhicitta, which is also a dependent arising. Depending on one set of causes and conditions, our mind is selfish, and depending on another set of causes and conditions, that same mind develops bodhicitta. Because causative phenomena depend upon causes and conditions, they can be changed and developed.

Similarly, all phenomena are empty by nature, but just knowing this fact is not enough for us to realize emptiness. We have to train our mind to recognize the ignorance that believes in true existence and the objects of this ignorance, the truly existent I and truly existent phenomena, which don't exist. With this knowledge, we then need to put effort into not following this ignorance and into looking at things as they are, which means as dependent arisings, empty of existence from their own side. In this way, the realization of emptiness will come.

It is the same with the tantric practice of seeing everything as pure. If this had to come from the side of the object, it would never happen. Even though we now see ourselves and this place as ordinary, through training our mind in tantric practice, as we achieve realizations of the generation stage and especially the completion stage, we will gradually come to see everything as pure; we will see ourselves and other beings as deities and the place as a mandala. This pure appearance doesn't come from the side of the object; it has to come from our side, from our own mind. We have to put effort into training our mind to look at everything as pure.

If we just wait for the realizations of impermanence, emptiness and pure view to happen, they never will, even though in reality objects are by nature impermanent, empty of existing from their own side and pure. If we don't put effort into looking at the I as impermanent or as empty, we will never realize its real nature. It has to come from our own side, not from the side of the object. We can't realize the impermanence and emptiness of the I without meditating on them.

Now, it is exactly the same with seeing the guru as a buddha. It is a matter of training our mind. Seeing the guru as a buddha doesn't come from the side of the guru; it also has to come from our own mind. Unless we put effort into looking at our gurus as buddhas, we won't realize that they are buddhas. By training our mind to look at our gurus as buddhas, we will then see them as buddhas. We have to practice guru devotion by putting all our effort into looking at our gurus as pure, as having ceased all faults and perfected all good qualities. If we train our mind to look at our gurus in this way, we will then see them in this way.

As explained clearly and perfectly by Lama Tsongkhapa in *The Great Treatise on the Stages of the Path to Enlightenment* and also by Pabongka Dechen Nyingpo in *Liberation in the Palm of Your Hand*, there are two techniques we can use to enable us to see the guru as a buddha. The first technique is to train our mind to focus on the good qualities of the guru; the second is to use the faults we see to develop our devotion.

Focusing on the good qualities of the guru

Lama Tsongkhapa says that focusing strongly on the good qualities of the guru naturally overwhelms the wrong conception that sees faults in the guru. The basic reasoning is that by looking at the good qualities, we will see the guru as having no faults but only good qualities—as a buddha, in other words—just as the light of the sun overwhelms that of the moon and stars.

Lama Tsongkhapa suggests that we use ourselves as an example. Even though we have many faults, focusing strongly on even one good quality that we have overwhelms any thought of our faults, so that we see ourselves as only good. Our faults become invisible. In a similar way, if we focus strongly on one fault that we have, the thought of that fault will overwhelm any thought of our good qualities so that we will see ourselves as having only faults. Our good qualities will become invisible and we will see ourselves as hopeless.

It is similar with the guru. Even though the guru has many good qualities, focusing on some small faults that he seems to have will obscure all those good qualities and we will see only faults. The devotion that sees the guru as a buddha then cannot arise. This is how we train our mind in a negative way. However, even if we see some faults in the guru, if we constantly think of his good qualities, our seeing faults will not become an obstacle to our devotion. If we train our mind to focus on the guru's good qualities, the thought of his faults will diminish, then eventually disappear.

In this way, we will see the guru as having only good qualities. By looking at the guru as having the qualities of a buddha, we will then see him as a buddha.

When considering the good qualities of our gurus, we should think of our own personal experiences of the special qualities of the holy body, speech and mind of each of our gurus, and any stories we have heard about them as well. Think of the particular qualities of that lama that are not common to ordinary people, such as his understanding, loving kindness, humility, patience or ways of guiding sentient beings. When we think of his good qualities we will find it easy to see the guru as a buddha—or at least a great bodhisattva. Using our awareness of the good qualities that we find in each of our gurus is an effective way to do this meditation.

If Lama Yeshe is our guru, for example, we can think of what Lama was able to do with his holy body, speech and mind that common people could not. We can think of Lama's incredible compassion, with only the thought to cherish others. We can also think of the benefit and happiness offered by Lama's holy body and the great effect of his holy speech in subduing other beings.

Of course, how the guru appears depends on the mind-training of the disciple. Some of Lama's students had a stable realization of guru devotion, seeing Lama as an actual buddha. By looking at Lama's good qualities, they saw him as a buddha without any hesitation. No matter what aspect Lama showed or what he did, it could never disturb their mind or change their devotion. Of course, there were others without devotion who saw Lama in a negative light and criticized him. They saw only faults because they looked only for faults.

The students with stable, unshakable devotion got all the profit of the eight benefits that I explained earlier, including constantly getting closer to enlightenment. Those who didn't practice guru devotion not only did not receive the eight benefits but on top of that, because they made mistakes in their devotion, experienced the eight shortcomings.

Of course, in the case of Lama Yeshe, even in the ordinary view Lama definitely had realizations of renunciation, bodhicitta and emptiness, as well as the Highest Yoga Tantra realizations of clear light and the illusory body. As I lived with Lama and he took care of me for more than twenty years, I have many stories to prove this.

No matter what worldly action Lama Yeshe did to accord with worldly people, all his actions were done purely for the sake of other sentient beings, to satisfy them and to direct their minds toward Dharma. He would act in accord with the way the people themselves acted, doing everything in the Western style. But he did everything purely with compassion, with the thought of cherishing other sentient beings and without the dissatisfied mind of attachment.

The great meditator Gen Jampa Wangdu told me the following story about two disciples of a teacher in Tibet, which also shows how the way the guru appears depends on the mind-training of the disciple. When the two disciples returned exhausted to their monastery from their home, which was very distant, their teacher greeted them with cold tea. One disciple got angry at his teacher. He thought, "We've come such a long way, we're exhausted, and he hasn't even bothered to heat the tea up for us." The other disciple thought, "Our teacher is so kind! He knew we'd be hot and exhausted after coming so far, so he's purposely kept the tea cold for us." The disciple who looked at the situation in a negative way had no profit, only loss. He created heavy negative karma by getting angry at and criticizing his guru. The other disciple, who thought that his guru had compassionately kept the tea cold for them, got only profit. This is a simple example of how the way the guru appears depends on how the disciple looks at him. It all depends on the disciple's interpretation.

The disciple who thought the teacher was bad received only shortcomings as a result. Besides not receiving any profit in terms of achieving realizations, liberation or enlightenment, the disciple received only a great obstacle to realization. The other student, who looked at the positive side, increased his devotion and respect by thinking of the teacher's kindness. His positive attitude brought him only great benefit, making him closer to liberation and enlightenment.

In *The Great Treatise on the Stages of the Path to Enlightenment* Lama Tsongkhapa explains,

> Even if the guru has many great qualities, if you look at some small fault, it becomes a hindrance to your achieving realizations. Also, if the guru has many great faults, if you do not look at the faults but only at the qualities and train your mind in devotion, it becomes the cause of receiving realizations.

Looking at the good qualities of the guru and generating devotion becomes the cause of achieving all the realizations of the graduated path to enlightenment. Even if the guru has many faults and few good qualities, ignoring his faults and looking at even one of his good qualities becomes the cause of attainments. And if the guru has many good qualities, looking at the few faults that he has becomes an obstacle to achieving realizations of the path. Seeing faults in the guru is the greatest obstacle to receiving blessings and to achieving realizations, which means the greatest obstacle to our achieving enlightenment and our helping all sentient beings by bringing them to enlightenment. As well as destroying our perfections, it causes the realizations we already have to degenerate and blocks the generation of new realizations.

If we don't look at the good qualities of our guru but see only his faults, even if our teacher is an enlightened being, we won't see him in that way. Even though Guru Shakyamuni Buddha had become enlightened inconceivable eons previously, the six Hindu founders and Sunakshatra didn't look at Buddha as an enlightened being. They always looked for faults so that they could complain about them to other people. When ordinary people looked at Buddha they usually saw an aura of beams for an arm span around his holy body but the six Hindu founders couldn't see any aura at all. All they saw when they met Buddha was a very ordinary monk.

If we look in the wrong way, we can easily find fault even with His Holiness the Dalai Lama. If we look for faults, we can find them. But that is not the practice of guru devotion. Looking for faults is not the disciple's responsibility and there's no profit in it.

By looking at the guru's good qualities, we train our mind to see the guru as a buddha. Afterwards, we won't find the slightest fault in him but only good qualities. At that time we will see him as a buddha. All the time—whenever we hear our guru's name, see his holy body or remember him—we'll have the thought of our guru as a buddha, an enlightened being. When this awareness arises effortlessly and spontaneously from the very depths of our heart without needing to rely on quotations or reasoning, we have the realization of guru devotion. All realizations, from the perfect human rebirth up to enlightenment, will then fall like rain.

Using the guru's faults to develop our devotion

In the second technique, we use any faults we see in the guru to increase our devotion and thus achieve realizations of the path to enlightenment. We do this by thinking that the guru purposely manifested in this aspect or made this mistake in his actions as a specific method to benefit us, to bring us to liberation and enlightenment. In his extensive commentary on guru devotion, Pabongka Dechen Nyingpo attributes this special technique to Lama Tsongkhapa.

We can develop guru devotion not only by reflecting on the good qualities of the guru but also by seeing even his faults. When we think that the guru is purposely showing faults or making mistakes in his actions, seeing the faults and mistakes causes devotion to arise; we can use them to support our devotion. Instead of becoming a problem for our mind and causing us to lose our devotion, seeing our guru's faults inspires us, causing us to think of the kindness of the guru and to increase our devotion. It becomes a special technique, like transforming poison into nectar, only causing our guru devotion to develop.

The Essence of Nectar also mentions that we should think that the guru deliberately manifests faults to subdue our mind,

> For sentient beings, it is said, the Victorious Ones
> Show themselves in any form, such as maras and so on.
> How do I know that these actions, which appear purely as mistakes,
> Are not purposely shown?

When we see a fault in our guru, we can remember that a buddha manifests various forms and does various activities when he sees that this is exactly what suits the mind of and benefits a particular sentient being. We can then think, "There must be a special reason for this mistake. Perhaps it was purposely done to benefit me or other sentient beings." In this way, seeing faults becomes a cause of devotion rather than a cause of conflict in our mind and an obstacle to devotion and thus to realizations.

The Essence of Nectar also says,

> Therefore, all the aspects of faults
> In my teacher's actions are
> Either the hallucinated appearance of my evil karma
> Or they are purposely shown.

With this technique, seeing faults in the guru, rather than making us lose our devotion, becomes a powerful cause of increasing it. It also causes us to remember the special kindness of our gurus, because without depending on these ordinary aspects, no buddhas can guide us to enlightenment. We then appreciate the faults in the human aspect of each of our gurus.

During a *Guru Puja* commentary in Dharamsala in 1985,[66] His Holiness the Dalai Lama, even though he didn't talk in detail about the outlines of the guru devotion meditation, touched on the most important point in a clear and effective way. His Holiness explained that "manifesting in ordinary aspect" itself means displaying faults. Otherwise, there is no object to label "ordinary aspect." Before hearing this my mind had been like a tight knot, but His Holiness's explanation, which has incredible meaning, released the knot. That teaching was like a key opening a door. My mind has now degenerated but at that time what His Holiness said affected me very much.

If we understand this point, any fault that appears to us in the actions of the guru becomes only a cause to develop the devotion that sees his good qualities. At the time when our seeing faults doesn't disturb our mind but instead becomes the cause of devotion, the stable root of guru devotion has been established within our heart. This way of thinking is essential to the development of our mind; it is essential to guru devotion and to all other realizations of the path to enlightenment.

When we become enlightened, we attain the dharmakaya. But sentient beings cannot see or communicate with the dharmakaya, so in order to benefit them, the dharmakaya manifests the rupakaya, holy body of form, which has the two pure aspects of *sambhogakaya* and nirmanakaya. But ordinary beings, whose minds are obscured, also cannot see the pure forms of buddha, so for them, the dharmakaya manifests various ordinary forms.

There is nothing fixed about these manifestations. The dharmakaya can manifest in whatever form fits the level of mind of a particular sentient being. There are numberless different kinds of manifestations for those whose minds are impure, obscured by karmic obscurations. Manifesting in an ordinary form means doing exactly what such a being would normally do because it is only in this way that it can help others.

Jamyang Shepa, a very high lama from Amdo, explains that when special holy beings, such as the great Indian and Tibetan pandits and yogis, reincarnated, when they were babies, all they knew how to do was suck milk from their mother's breasts, cry and make pipi and kaka exactly like an ordinary

---

[66] This teaching, given during the FPMT's Enlightened Experience Celebration II, has been published as *The Union of Bliss and Emptiness*.

baby. They did nothing new. They acted exactly like any normal child, having to learn the alphabet and everything else, even though in reality they were enlightened beings. You might then say that they weren't the incarnations of special beings, but many of those children could also remember their past lives as great beings and the great activities they had done. Those children ate, slept and experienced sicknesses and obstacles to their lives. They also became old and later passed away.

Jamyang Shepa asks, "Even though all these things happened, how is it possible that they were all only ordinary beings? How is it possible that a buddha would experience these sufferings? It's not possible." Jamyang Shepa then explains that it is impossible for even a Mahayana arya being to have a rebirth caused by karma and delusion. Those who have achieved the Mahayana arya paths, either the path of seeing or the path of meditation, have completely abandoned suffering rebirth, old age, sickness and death; they have a spiritual body. Jamyang Shepa says that these great beings eat and sleep and experience sickness and other problems like ordinary human beings as methods to subdue the minds of sentient beings. They do these actions for the benefit of sentient beings and they are all the appearances of sentient beings' karma. Jamyang Shepa then says, "Therefore, any fault that appears is not necessarily an actual fault."

Jamyang Shepa goes on to say that when a buddha appears in the form of a dog, the manifested dog will behave exactly like an ordinary dog. It will bark, wag its tail, eat kaka and all other kinds of dirty things, and also have sex with other dogs. And, of course, it will look exactly like a dog. That's what manifesting as a dog means.

When I mention eating kaka, I'm thinking especially of the dogs at Tushita Retreat Centre, where, during Lama's time, we had about thirteen dogs, a mixture of Lhasa Apso and Pekinese. Lama used to say, "I don't want to give them to other people—I love my dogs." Anyway, the dogs loved to eat kaka. In the afternoon when the dogs were released from their enclosure and allowed to run outside, they would run in just one direction, to the road around the side of the mountain, where they would find piles of kaka. They would then quickly return, all smelly and excited.

When a buddha manifests as a pig, that pig will have a pig's round nose as well as the body and tail of a pig. And it will spend its time behaving exactly the same as a normal pig, snuffling its nose into garbage with a Tantric College noise.

It is the same when a buddha has manifested in an ordinary human form.

That person behaves exactly like an ordinary human being usually behaves; he has delusions and suffering and makes mistakes in his actions, exactly like an ordinary person. That's what manifesting in an ordinary human form means.

For some sentient beings, a buddha manifests as a butcher and is exactly like an ordinary butcher, doing what a butcher normally does. For some sentient beings who have a lot of attachment, a buddha manifests as a prostitute and behaves exactly like a prostitute. Beings with ordinary minds just see the manifestations behaving exactly like those ordinary beings; they don't see anything higher than that. Buddha doesn't show a higher aspect because it wouldn't suit ordinary human beings who don't have the karma to see a higher or purer aspect.

When a buddha manifests as an ordinary bodhisattva, he acts exactly like an ordinary bodhisattva, not showing at all the qualities of someone who has achieved the higher paths of an arya bodhisattva. He never shows such special qualities to sentient beings who don't have the karma to see such an aspect but only the karma to see an ordinary being. Or even if they have the karma to see a bodhisattva, they can see only an ordinary bodhisattva.

For example, in teachings or in conversations with His Holiness the Dalai Lama, His Holiness quite often says "I don't know" or "I'm not sure," even in response to Dharma questions. If you don't have a pure mind you might think that His Holiness really doesn't know and see him as an ordinary being. Of course, if you have a pure mind that sees His Holiness as a real buddha, a real Chenrezig, you wouldn't have that thought. And sometimes, to certain people, His Holiness might show the aspect of being upset or angry. However, it's all the view of us sentient beings and, of course, it's done to benefit sentient beings, especially those particular sentient beings who needed such an aspect. Common people, who don't have the pure mind realizing that His Holiness is a buddha, might think that His Holiness is angry because they see an ordinary form with discriminating thoughts.

Since it's extremely difficult to understand somebody else's mind, we can't judge who is a buddha and who is not a buddha. It's clear that we can't use our perception to prove that someone is not a buddha. When we go to a market or an airport or a train station, we can't really tell who there is a buddha and who is not.

One time when Serkong Dorje Chang, the previous incarnation of the Serkong Dorje Chang who passed away in Nepal, went to see the Thirteenth Dalai Lama, upon entering the room he saw the Thirteenth Dalai Lama in the aspect of Chenrezig called "Resting in the Nature of the Mind."[67] Whereas somebody with a pure mind will see a deity, common people like us will see a human form, and sometimes a human form in the aspect of sickness. Some people will see an aspect that is upset or disturbed. It's totally up to us sentient beings. In reality the Dalai Lama is Chenrezig, essence of all the buddhas' compassion, but what we see accords with the quality of our mind. As most people don't have the pure mind to see the form of a deity, all they see is a human form.

We can also use the appearance of faults in the guru as a cause of devotion by remembering that there is nothing to trust in our view, which will be explained extensively in the next outline, *how to see the guru as a buddha.* We can think that any faults we see in the guru are the projections of our own ordinary mistaken mind. It is like looking at the reflection of our face in a mirror. If our face is clean, we see a clean face in the mirror; if our face is dirty, we see a dirty face. In a similar way, if our mind is pure, we see things as pure; if our mind is impure, we see things as impure.

In this technique, rather than pointing to the guru, we think that the appearance of faults comes from our own impure mind, our own impure karma. When we think that any fault we see is the view of our own mistaken mind, seeing faults in the guru doesn't disturb our mind or make us lose our devotion. If we think that the appearance of faults comes from our impure karma, there's no place for the arising of negative thoughts toward the guru; we're able to keep our mind steady in devotion, looking at the guru as a buddha. The appearance of faults doesn't disturb our devotion at all.

The Fifth Dalai Lama said,

> In the view of your hallucinated mind, your own faults appear in the guru's actions. All this shows is that your own heart is rotten to the core. Recognizing them as your own faults, abandon them as poison.

The heart referred to here is not the physical heart, but the mind, which is filled with superstitions and wrong conceptions.

This verse contains a powerful and effective instruction. The Fifth Dalai

---

[67] This is an aspect of Chenrezig, white, with one face and two arms, in a posture of ease, with the left hand resting behind on a moon disc.

Lama is saying that to our hallucinated mind, which apprehends objects in the wrong way, our own faults appear in the actions of the guru, just as a white conch appears yellow to someone with jaundice. Just as what appears on a movie screen is the projection of what is recorded on a film, all the mistakes that we see in the actions of the guru are projections of our own impure mind. They are actually our own faults. We tend to project our main faults onto others. If we ourselves make mistakes, we often project the same mistakes onto others. Someone who steals, for example, always suspects that other people are thieves.

We shouldn't think that any mistake we see in the holy actions of the guru comes from its own side without depending on our own mind. By realizing it is our own mistake, we should abandon it as poison. We should abandon the thought that the faults we see in the virtuous friend are there in reality and not simply appearing to be there.

The Fifth Dalai Lama is saying that we should abandon as poison all wrong conceptions toward the guru, all thought of faults and all clinging to the guru's ordinary aspect as true. By understanding all the appearances of faults in our guru are our own mistakes, we abandon them like poison. As soon as we're told that something is a deadly poison, we immediately throw it away. We don't want it near us. It is similar with this wrong conception, except that there is no comparison between the danger from all the poisons on this earth and that from wrong conceptions toward the virtuous friend.

As soon as there is a danger that a superstitious thought of finding fault will arise, we should protect ourselves by remembering this quotation. When it appears to us that our guru has made a mistake, it is important to remember that there is nothing to trust in our view. This is the most effective way to stop the arising of negative thoughts toward the guru. By thinking that our obscured mind is projecting our own faults onto the actions of the guru, we will protect ourselves from disrespect, anger and heresy. The main thing we have to abandon is our belief that the faults that appear to us exist in reality. Then, even though the faults will still appear to us, our guru devotion will not be disturbed. This meditation protects our mind, protects our devotion.

Also, *The Essence of Nectar* mentions,

> Until we are free from our obscuring negative karma,
> Even if all the buddhas without exception descended directly in
>   front of us,

We have no fortune to see the sublime holy body adorned with the
  holy signs and exemplifications—
Only this present appearance.

This present appearance means our view of the guru as only an ordinary
being, which means as someone with faults. Even if all the buddhas were
to come directly in front of us, because of our obscured mind, we have no
other way to see them except as having faults, delusions and suffering and
making mistakes in their actions. Therefore, how we see the guru is a projection of our own obscured, impure mind. This is similar to what the Fifth
Dalai Lama is saying.

These two quotations are making the same point. Thinking of either of
them will help us not to lose our devotion. If we keep these quotations in
mind, no matter what mistakes in the actions of the guru appear to us, nothing will disturb our devotion, which will be stable like a mountain. And if
we have realizations, it will ensure that we won't lose them.

How do we abandon this hallucinated mind that sees faults in the guru?
We do this by constantly training our mind in the awareness that the guru is
a buddha, free of faults and complete in realizations. We should constantly
think that in essence the guru is the absolute guru, the dharmakaya, the
holy mind of all the buddhas. With this awareness, no matter what the guru
does, we will constantly see the guru as a buddha. Even if we don't practice
guru yoga in the tantric way, transforming the guru into the pure form of a
deity, and even if we see the guru as ordinary, which means having faults, we
won't cling to that ordinary appearance as true.

If we practice awareness that the guru in essence is the absolute guru, we
automatically realize that every fault we see in the guru's actions of body,
speech and mind is the appearance of our own impure karma. There is nothing to blame for this appearance but our own mind.

The Fifth Dalai Lama's advice is the very essence of how to practice guru
devotion. If our mind were completely pure, we would now be seeing all
the buddhas and all existence of the three times. We have many limitations,
however; our mind is impure and obscured. If we relate everything that
appears to us to our hallucinated mind, we see that our own faults manifest in the actions of the virtuous friend. Whenever a fault appears to us,
we should immediately try to recognize this. We should practice constant
awareness that the guru is a buddha and that his holy mind is dharmakaya.

As we develop our mind in the path to enlightenment, our mind will become purer and we will see everything more purely. At the moment we see statues of buddhas as being made of brass, stone or clay; but when we enter the Mahayana great path of merit, we will see statues as the nirmanakaya aspects of buddhas, with all the thirty-two holy signs and eighty exemplifications,[68] and they will speak to us. And when we become Mahayana arya beings— in other words, bodhisattvas on the Mahayana paths of seeing or meditation—we will see statues in sambhogakaya aspect.

While we see statues as simply statues, not as something living that can speak, great yogis, who have purified their karma and have pure minds, see them as actual living deities. For example, when Lama Atisha was circumambulating the Bodhgaya stupa before going to Indonesia, Tara and many of the other statues there, and even the paintings on the walls, spoke to him. They advised him, "If you want to achieve enlightenment, practice bodhicitta."

Actually, if we have devotion and a pure mind, all the statues and paintings of buddhas can speak to us. The great bodhisattva Khunu Lama Tenzin Gyaltsen explained that all the stone statues around the outside of the Bodhgaya stupa spoke to Lama Atisha when he was circumambulating the stupa, not just the Tara statue.

Khunu Lama Rinpoche was a great bodhisattva and a great scholar, no different from the ancient pandits. He could remember the entire *Kangyur*, the collection of Buddha's teachings, and quote from any text in it. His Holiness the Dalai Lama received extensive commentary on *A Guide to the Bodhisattva's Way of Life* from Khunu Lama Rinpoche.

One time when Khunu Lama Rinpoche was circumambulating the Bodhgaya stupa, something dropped on his head from the *bodhi* tree.[69] When he licked the liquid to check what it was, he found it tasted like honey. It was nectar from the bodhi tree.

As our mind develops through correctly devoting ourselves to the guru, we will see the guru in different ways; as our mind develops, our view will change—not only our view of the virtuous friend but also of others. Pabongka Dechen Nyingpo explains that at the beginning we see our virtuous friends as ordinary beings. When we purify our karmic obscurations

---

[68] For a complete list of the thirty-two signs and eighty exemplifications see *Liberation in Our Hands, Part Two*, pp. 308–314.

[69] A descendant of the tree under which Shakyamuni Buddha became enlightened.

and achieve the Concentration of Continual Dharma on the great path of merit, we will see our gurus in nirmanakaya aspect, in the holy body of supreme transformation; and when we achieve the first bhumi, the Mahayana path of seeing, we will see our gurus in sambhogakaya aspect. Until we reach the tenth bhumi and become enlightened, we meet the guru as a separate being; but when we become enlightened, we meet the guru mentally. This means that when we become enlightened, we become the guru; our mind becomes the absolute guru, the dharmakaya.

When our obscurations have been completely purified, we will actually experience everything that appears to us as pure: the place will be a deity's mandala, the beings will be deities and all our enjoyments will be purest nectar. To our pure enlightened mind, everything will have the nature of bliss and voidness.

All this has to come from our own mind, not from outside. It comes through applying effort, through training. For us to be able to see ourselves and our environment as pure, first we have to put effort into looking at our body as a deity's holy body and our environment as a mandala. Seeing the guru as a buddha also has to come from our own mind, not from outside. To see the guru as a buddha we need to put in effort from our side.

Whenever we see faults in our gurus, we have to use the faults we see to develop our devotion, as explained by Lama Tsongkhapa and the Fifth Dalai Lama. Also, training our mind in the subsequent outlines—*how to see the guru as a buddha* and *developing respect by remembering the guru's kindness*—will cause the thought of the guru's qualities to arise very strongly and this will overwhelm the wrong conception of faults.

If we keep our mind firmly and constantly in pure devotion, in the awareness that the guru is a buddha, any fault or mistake we see will appear to us to be an act, like an actor playing a part. Even though there is an appearance of a fault, we won't really believe that it is true. It will appear to us like a mirage: there is an appearance of water but we know there is actually no water. If we look at the mind of the guru as dharmakaya, free from all faults and having all qualities, any appearance of faults won't bother us. It won't disturb our devotion.

If we can remember these points and put them into practice, our mind will be protected. Our mind will always be kept in guru devotion, seeing the guru as a buddha, undisturbed by any thoughts of faults in the guru. In this way we will protect our mind from creating the heaviest obstacle to achieving realizations of the path to enlightenment and from experiencing unimaginable eons of suffering in the hell realms. Otherwise, because of the imprints from our past lives, anger, heresy and the thought of faults will arise strongly and habitually, causing us to engage in the heaviest negative karma.

Each time the thought of seeing faults in the guru arises it becomes an obstacle to our achievement of realizations and enlightenment and causes our mind to degenerate. Keeping our mind in the devotion that looks at the guru as a buddha or at the guru's mind as dharmakaya becomes a protective wall, like the walls people build around their houses to keep out their enemies. It protects us from all thoughts of faults, which can destroy our enlightenment and all our other success.

If we don't put effort into seeing the guru as a buddha, since our mind will have no protection, concepts of the guru as ordinary and negative thoughts will arise. Understanding that seeing the guru as a buddha has to come from our own mind gives us a lot of protection, and our life—both this life and our future lives—won't be destroyed by negative thoughts. In this way we won't receive any loss but only profit, up to the ultimate profit of full enlightenment.

The more we can look at the guru as a buddha, the closer we become to enlightenment; and the more we think of the faults of the guru, the further we become from enlightenment. By thinking of the guru's good qualities, we receive only profit and no loss. By thinking of the guru's faults, we receive only loss and not a single profit. It doesn't matter whether or not the guru is a buddha, a bodhisattva, an arhat or an ordinary being. It doesn't matter what he is from his side. If, from our own side, we practice skillfully, looking as much as possible at his good qualities and as little as possible at his faults, we receive only great profit. We will be able to see the guru as a buddha and that devotional thought will then become the door through which we receive the actual blessings of a buddha. When these blessings enter us, the path to enlightenment then takes root in our mind. We then have the freedom to achieve enlightenment as quickly as we wish.

Khunu Lama Rinpoche, India, ca 1977

12. How to See the Guru as a Buddha

ONCE WE UNDERSTAND that it is possible to see our guru as a buddha, it is logical that we can train our mind to do so. In *the root, training our mind in devotion to the guru,* the third outline, *how to see the guru as a buddha,* has four divisions:

(i) Vajradhara asserted that the guru is a buddha
(ii) The guru is the doer of all the buddhas' actions
(iii) Even nowadays all the buddhas and bodhisattvas are still working for sentient beings
(iv) There is nothing to trust in our own view

For those who have accumulated a lot of merit, the first outline will be sufficient for them to realize guru devotion and they won't need to meditate on the other three outlines. Hearing the quotations from Vajradhara and Guru Shakyamuni Buddha will be enough for them; they won't need any further reasons to prove that the guru is a buddha. For people who develop devotion easily, simply hearing a quotation can be sufficient to convince them, without need of any logical reasoning. However, using logical reasoning to prove a point brings greater and more certain understanding.

If the first outline isn't sufficient to generate guru devotion, the second outline—*the guru is the doer of all the buddhas' actions*—can be used to clarify and help prove what Vajradhara said. If we can't generate devotion even with that, we add further proof with *even nowadays all the buddhas and bodhisattvas are still working for sentient beings.* If this still isn't enough to prove to our mind that the guru is a buddha, we use the most powerful reason of all: *there is nothing to trust in our own view.*

The second and third outlines can each become the reason for the preceding outline. Vajradhara asserted that the gurus are buddhas. Why did he say this? Because the gurus are the doers of all the buddhas' actions. We should specifically relate *all the buddhas' actions* to ourselves, to the fact that our gurus are guiding us from happiness to happiness to the peerless happiness of enlightenment. And why are the gurus the doers of all the buddhas' actions? Because even nowadays all the buddhas and bodhisattvas are still working for sentient beings.

For Tibetans, the four outlines as they are written are probably fine, but for Westerners it is perhaps better to turn them upside down:

(i) There is nothing to trust in our own view
(ii) Even nowadays all the buddhas and bodhisattvas are still working for sentient beings
(iii) The guru is the doer of all the buddhas' actions
(iv) Vajradhara asserted that the guru is a buddha

To start with *Vajradhara asserted that the guru is a buddha* is fine for somebody who already has devotion but meditating on the outlines in the reverse order might be more effective for Westerners. *There is nothing to trust in our own view* is the most powerful outline; it is like an atomic bomb. Starting with that one helps break our fixed wrong conceptions and the other outlines then come more easily.

Our view isn't always correct—we can't be certain that in reality things exist the way they appear and how things appear depends upon how we look at them. This is clear and logical and we can come to the same conclusion about our gurus. Even nowadays all the buddhas and bodhisattvas are still working for sentient beings, including us, and who are they? None other than our present gurus, who are the doers of all the buddhas' actions. Right after that we can think about how this is true because Vajradhara said that he would manifest as gurus. Having the quotations at the end can also be powerful.

Use whichever line of reasoning is most effective for your mind. Remembering these reasons, be aware that all your gurus are buddhas—or Guru Shakyamuni Buddha, if you find it more effective. It is important to prove to your mind that at least it is more likely that your gurus are buddhas. If you feel a separation between your guru and buddha, your practice doesn't become guru yoga. Pabongka Dechen Nyingpo explains that if you see a separation between your guru and buddha, you need to use logic and quotations to prove to your mind that the guru is a buddha.

The way to meditate effectively on each of these four basic outlines is to establish a pure thought of guru devotion, seeing the guru as a buddha, after each outline. We should also relate each of the four meditation outlines to each of our gurus. Meditating in this way will cause us to receive blessings and thus realizations of the whole path to enlightenment.

(i) There is nothing to trust in our own view *There is nothing to trust in our own view* is the most important outline in guru yoga practice; meditating on this topic is like dropping an atomic bomb on our superstitious thoughts that see faults in the guru. It is the most powerful outline for the mind because it stops the arising of wrong conceptions, the hindrances to realizations. The main way to stop the wrong conceptions that prevent our seeing the guru as a buddha is to meditate well on the teachings on refuge, especially on Buddha's qualities and actions to guide sentient beings, and combine it with meditation on how nothing is definite in our view. This outline is also helpful when dealing with other people in everyday life. When we start to get angry and think of harming others, we should remember that there is nothing to trust in our own view.

Nothing is definite in our own view refers to the fact that it is uncertain whether the way the guru appears to us accords with reality because we have so many wrong concepts, so many layers of hallucination. Our seeing the guru as an ordinary being, which means one having faults, doesn't necessarily mean that in reality he is an ordinary being. How we see our gurus depends on how they appear to us and how they appear to us depends on how we look at them, on our projections. How they appear to us depends on whether we look at them with devotion, as a buddha, or as an ordinary being.

Kuntang Jampelyang, a high Amdo lama, explains,

> Even though you devote yourself to the guru as your object of refuge of this and future lives, you hold to your own truth and not to the truth of the guru. This is the whole mistake.

How the guru and his actions appear to us is up to us. Since it is the view of our own obscured, mistaken mind, of course the guru appears to have faults, and we believe those faults to be real. We then use our seeing faults as a reason to prove that the guru is an ordinary being and not a buddha.

Kungtang Jampelyang says that the whole mistake comes from thinking that the way the guru appears to us is true and not offering the truth to the guru. We instead give the truth to ourselves, thinking, "My view is correct." We give the truth to ourselves, not to the guru. The whole mistake is that we believe our own view to be correct.

Everything that appears to us in this life, from birth to death, comes from our own mind, from our own karma. Everything is a karmic appearance. Whether good or bad, pure or impure, everything that appears to us is the creation, or production, of our own mind. If we look through red glass, we see everything as red, even white things. If we look through blue glass, we see everything as blue. What color we see depends on the color of the glass that we look through. In a similar way, in our daily life, the way we see things depends on how we look at them. If we look at something as good, it appears to be good; if we look at something as bad, it then appears to be bad. Unless we look at something as good, it doesn't appear good to us; and unless we look at something as bad, it doesn't appear bad to us.

It is also helpful to apply the twelve links[70] to the practice of guru devotion. Our body, our happiness and suffering, all the objects of our senses—everything that appears to us in this life comes from our ignorance and karma, which in turn come from our consciousness, which carries all the imprints that are actualized in this life. Ignorance is the farmer and karma is the seed that is planted in the field of consciousness. Just as a field holds the potential for a good or bad crop, consciousness holds all the impressions, or potentials, for happiness and suffering and carries them from life to life. The impressions carried by the consciousness are manifested in this life, just as crops come from a field.

As mentioned in *Treasury of Knowledge*, "All the various worlds are born from karma." All the various rebirths, happy and suffering, come from the seed of karma. Everything that appears to us in this life from birth until death comes from our karma. First we have to clearly understand that everything that appears to us comes from our own karma, from our own thoughts, present and past.

For example, as we drive along in a car, the scenery that appears to us is the projection of our mind. We're not watching appearances that exist

[70] For an explanation of the twelve links see *The Meaning of Life* or *Liberation in the Palm of Your Hand*, pp. 479–86.

from their own side, independent of our own mind. We have the habit of saying, "Oh, everything's karma," but it should not be just words. We need to understand that we are constantly watching the projections of our own mind. Even when we buy a ticket to see a show, all we are paying to see is the view of our own mind.

This explanation from the twelve links helps to make clear that how we see the guru completely depends on our own mind. Our seeing an ordinary aspect, one with faults, comes from our own mind. We should constantly meditate on the twelve links in relation to everything that appears to us in our life. The way that anything, including our guru, appears to us is simply the projection of our own past and present thoughts.

How things appear to us is completely determined by our own level of mind; in accordance with different levels of mind, there are different worlds, different views. We should be aware of this and not think that the view we have is the only way to see an object. The same object can appear in different ways to different people. Awareness of this is very helpful in dealing with problems in our daily life and in controlling our delusions, especially in controlling the thought of faults in guru yoga practice.

We need to be aware not only that the same object at the same time can appear differently to different people but that things will appear differently to us as our mind develops. When many people look at the same person, for example, they don't see that person in the same way. To some people, the person appears beautiful, to others ugly and to others average. The same object appears differently to each of us because we have different minds.

Why do we see impure appearances? Because our mind is impure. If our mental continuum were free of obscurations we would see everything as pure—ourselves in the pure form of a deity, with an enlightened being's pure holy body and mind; all other living beings in the pure forms of deities; the place as a mandala, the pure appearance of transcendental wisdom; and all our enjoyments as pure enjoyments. Everything that appeared to us would appear as pure, as it does to a buddha. If our mind were pure, we would be seeing numberless buddhas right now, because all the buddhas abide on each atom, as the *King of Prayers* says.[71] This isn't the case for

---

[71] On every atom are buddhas numberless as atoms,
Each amidst a host of bodhisattvas,
And I am confident the sphere of all phenomena
Is entirely filled with buddhas in this way. ("King of Prayers," v. 3. See *Essential Buddhist Prayers, Volume 1*, p. 249.)

us right now because our minds are obscured, or impure. How anything appears to us has to do with the level, or quality, of our own mind.

To illustrate how there is nothing certain about our view of reality, Pabongka Dechen Nyingpo uses the example from the Madhyamaka teachings of three different types of beings—a preta, a human and a god—looking at a bowl filled with liquid at the same time. When pretas look at the liquid, they see pus and blood; when humans look at the same liquid, they see water; and to the gods' perception, the liquid appears to be nectar.

When these three different beings look at the same object at the same time, it appears to them in three different ways. These three different appearances are produced by their different levels of mind, their different levels of merit. Pretas don't have enough merit, or good karma, to see anything pleasant, not even water. Since they have the karma to see only pus and blood, the liquid appears to them only in that way. For human beings, who have more merit, or better karma, the liquid appears as water. For gods, who have much more merit and thus the karma to experience greater enjoyments than humans, the same liquid appears as nectar. To buddhas, the liquid would appear as the purest, highest enjoyment.

Even though the liquid is pus and blood in the view of pretas, it doesn't mean that it is pus and blood for every living being. It's not the only possible view; there are other views of this same liquid. Humans see it as water and gods see it as nectar. All these views are determined by the mind of the perceiver.

This way of analyzing different views of the same object is extremely interesting and describes what we are constantly experiencing in our daily life. When we don't like something, whether it is a person, a place or a food, we have to be aware that how we see that object is just one possible view of it. It's not the only view that exists. That object can appear in many different ways to many different people. There are different karmic appearances. Those with pure karma have pure appearances; those with impure karma have impure appearances.

What we see in our everyday life is a production of our own karma, our own mind. This is clear. How things appear to us at the moment is our own view and accords with our present level of mind. There are different views even of the same object and these different views accord with the different levels of mind of different beings. First we must have this important point clear in our mind as it is very helpful not only in guru yoga practice but in our daily life. We shouldn't think that our own view is the only possible view and that nobody sees anything else. That is completely wrong.

We can see that the way we see an object is determined by our mind and not by the object. The same food can appear to some people as delicious, to others as unpleasant and to yet others as indifferent. When different people even see the food, some see it as good, some as disgusting and others are indifferent to it. And when they then taste the food, they also have different perceptions. It is the same food, but different people experience it differently.

It is the same with any object of the senses: how something—whether a person, a place or food—appears is determined by the perceiver's mind. For example, we might think it impossible that we could ever feel attachment to a particular person. However, at any time, for some reason we make up, our view could change; we could suddenly see that person as beautiful and attachment could arise. The object is the same—it's the same person we saw a few days ago—but our way of looking at her has changed. Or, even though we might think someone is our closest friend and that it would be impossible for us to ever be angry at her, at any time, for some reason we make up, our view could suddenly change and we wouldn't be able to stand the way she speaks or acts. This sudden change doesn't come from the side of the object but from our own mind.

There is no way to give a full and satisfactory explanation of these different views unless we relate them to the mind of the perceiver. We have to consider the perceiver's level of mind and karma. Her past positive or negative karma left imprints on her mind and these are projected as the different tastes, or even visual impressions, of the food. There is no other way to give a correct, complete answer as to why food or any other object is perceived in a particular way by a particular person.

For example, even though we might reach a place that is supposed to be a pure realm, such as Shambhala, if we haven't purified our impure karma, we won't be able to see the pure realm even though we are in the place where it is supposed to be—our impure mind will keep us away from it. This is like dreaming of being in a filthy hovel while living comfortably in a beautiful house.

Where somebody whose mind is very obscured might see an ordinary being, full of faults, somebody whose mind is purer might see that same being as a bodhisattva or a buddha. Looking at the same being at the same time, some people might see an ordinary person, some might see a bodhisattva and others might see a buddha. It depends upon the purity of the mind of the perceiver.

Realizing that everything is a creation of our mind is the most important discovery; it is the fundamental enlightenment meditation. It is the best, most immediate way to solve problems, because when we realize that every problem we have comes from our own mind, there is nothing to blame on others. Even if somebody is angry at us and abuses us, it comes from our own mind. Previously we have put the entire blame on other people, thinking that all our problems came from outside, not from our own mind.

When we find that there is nothing external to blame, there is nothing for us to do except to transform our own mind, to purify our own karma. We have to purify our present impure karma, which projects these unpleasant appearances, and accumulate more merit. Since everything comes from our mind, enlightenment also has to come from our mind. Our own mind has to create enlightenment.

We can also use the stories of present and past great yogis to show how there is nothing to trust in our own view. When sentient beings look at a buddha, even a buddha will appear in many different ways in accord with the level of mind of each individual being. Some will even see an animal, as Asanga did. Remember the story of Asanga and Maitreya Buddha. At the beginning Asanga saw Maitreya Buddha simply as a wounded dog. After doing retreat in a hermitage for twelve years to try to achieve Maitreya Buddha, Asanga hadn't seen Maitreya Buddha, so he decided to give up the retreat. As he was leaving his hermitage for the final time, Asanga saw a wounded dog in the road. Although it was actually Maitreya Buddha, Asanga saw only a wounded dog, its lower body an open wound filled with maggots.

Asanga felt unbearable compassion for the wounded dog and was willing to sacrifice himself to help it. He completely gave up concern for himself and cherished that being. In those moments, he purified the negative karma that for such a long time had blocked his seeing Maitreya Buddha. Because he finished purifying that karma, he no longer saw a dog. That ordinary, impure appearance ceased and he actually saw the holy body of Maitreya Buddha.

Asanga later carried Maitreya Buddha on his shoulders into the nearby town, shouting to all who could hear, "I'm carrying Buddha! Please come to see Buddha!" Most of the people thought he was crazy because they couldn't see anything at all, but there was one old woman who saw him carrying a wounded dog on his shoulders.

There are many stories in the lam-rim about great yogis who looked very ordinary even though they were actually buddhas. There are also many stories of enlightened beings who appeared to be ordinary beings engaging in killing and other unethical actions, as if they had no compassion. Many past yogis, including Lama Yeshe, were seen as great yogis only later, after they had passed away.

When the lineage lama Buddhajñana met his guru, the great yogi Manjushrimitra, he saw him as an ordinary family man. He saw Manjushrimitra, his head wrapped in a monk's yellow robe, plowing and fertilizing a field. His children were picking up the worms he turned up with the plow and making soup with them, which the whole family then ate. Buddhajñana saw this great master as an eccentric person.

This is similar to when Naropa first saw Tilopa—Naropa didn't think that it could be Tilopa. People commonly saw Tilopa as a beggar or a simple fisherman, even though from Tilopa's side he was an enlightened being, the actual Buddha Vajradhara. When Naropa first saw Tilopa, Tilopa was cooking live fish in a fire and eating them. When Naropa saw this he doubted that it could be Tilopa. At that time, when Naropa asked, "Are you Tilopa?" Tilopa shook his head. At a later time, when Naropa had developed some devotion and could see some of Tilopa's qualities, he began to think it was Tilopa. At that time, when Naropa asked, "Are you Tilopa?" Tilopa nodded his head in agreement. Tilopa's response was determined by what Naropa was thinking.

Also, both Krishnacharya and his disciple Kusali saw Vajravarahi as an ordinary leper woman, her skin black and oozing pus.

When Milarepa met Marpa for the first time, Marpa appeared to be just an ordinary farmer, covered in dust, drinking wine as he plowed a field. Even though Marpa was an enlightened being, the actual Vajradhara, he appeared to Milarepa to be an ordinary being.

The Guhyasamaja text *Twenty-one Small Letters* explains that both Nagarjuna and Saraha remained in their old bodies after achieving the unification of no more learning and commonly appeared to other people as ordinary beings.

Maitripa saw his guru, the great yogi Shavaripa, as simply an ordinary person hunting animals in the forest. Shavaripa's cave is the Mahakala Cave near Bodhgaya, which many people go to visit; a small monastery has been built nearby. Shavaripa wrote the praise to Six-Arm Mahakala after seeing Mahakala at that cave.

The great yogi Luipa appeared externally to be a destitute beggar but when King Dharigapa and his retinue took teachings from Luipa, they became enlightened. With his psychic powers, Luipa also taught Dharma to the creatures in that place and even they became enlightened.

The great Sakya pandit, Kunga Nyingpo, had two sons, Dragpa Gyaltsen and Sönam Tsemo, who he always held close, often in his coat, as if he were very attached to them. The people around him were upset by this and lost faith in him because he appeared to be an ordinary man living an ordinary family life.

Kunga Nyingpo, understanding what they were thinking, warned, "You mustn't give rise to wrong views about the vajra master," then said, "Look at this." He then stretched his legs out toward the people, showing them vivid mandalas of Chakrasamvara and Hevajra, complete with all the deities, on the soles of his right and left feet. When the people saw this, all their wrong conceptions of him were destroyed and they generated much devotion to him. Even though Kunga Nyingpo was the actual Chakrasamvara, the actual Hevajra, his neighbors saw him only as someone attached to ordinary family life.

Even Lama Yeshe appeared differently to different people in accord with their karma. Many practitioners with great devotion saw Lama as an actual buddha in human form. Some, who didn't have devotion, saw him as a very ordinary, difficult person.

Our not seeing the guru as a buddha doesn't prove at all that the guru is not a buddha. Our seeing faults isn't logical proof that our guru really has faults. All the manifestations that we see accord with the level of our own mind. Our own karma determines how many good qualities and how many faults we see in our guru. Our seeing beings as enlightened, or pure, depends on our purifying our karmic obscurations. Therefore, there is nothing to trust in our view of reality.

Pabongka Dechen Nyingpo explains that since we have such great obscurations, we can't see our guru as a buddha, and adds that we should be grateful that at present we are able to see him in human form, as even this is quite a high level.

The great yogi Chengawa Lodrö Gyaltsen said,

Since our karmic obscurations are so heavy,
We should be happy to see our guru even in human form.
We have great merit not to see him as a dog or a donkey;
Therefore, generate heartfelt respect, sons of Shakyamuni.

We are very fortunate to see our guru in an ordinary human form and not in the form of a dog, as Asanga saw Maitreya, a donkey or some other animal. If we saw our guru in the form of a dog, a donkey or a pig, what could we do? Even though in our karmic view we do see faults in our guru we are still lucky because we are also able to see many good qualities.

It is practical to think as Kachen Yeshe Gyaltsen explained,

> I am fortunate even to be able to find a few good qualities in my guru. If even my impure mind is able to see this many qualities, how many more good qualities there must be for someone whose mind is purer.

Think of how so many more non-virtuous than virtuous thoughts arise in our mind each day. Our mind is overwhelmed by disturbing thoughts and negative karma, which constantly obscure and create obstacles in our mind. It's a miracle that with a mind so heavily obscured by impure karma we are able to see the guru as purely as we do.

What appears to us and what we believe don't necessarily accord with reality. There are so many aspects of reality that we don't see or that we see wrongly. Even without taking LSD or any other hallucinogenic drug, we see many hallucinations in accordance with our wrong conceptions.

We don't necessarily see an object in the way that it actually exists. Our life, our possessions and all other causative phenomena are impermanent in nature, changing, or decaying, hour by hour, minute by minute, second by second, and even within each second because of causes and conditions. Because of that subtle impermanence, there is then gross change, which is noticeable, such as when people become old and wrinkled. Although impermanence is the reality of causative phenomena, we don't see them in this way. They appear to us to be permanent and we cling to our belief in that appearance of permanence.

Also, even though Guru Shakyamuni Buddha, Nagarjuna, Lama Tsongkhapa and all the other great enlightened beings have explained that there is no inherent existence, we cannot see this. Even though everything—including I, action and object—is empty of inherent existence because it is merely labeled by the mind, we don't see it that way; everything appears to us to be only inherently existent. We see everything in a completely wrong way, as existing from its own side without depending on our mind.

From morning until night, from birth until death, from beginningless lifetimes until enlightenment, everything comes from our own mind through being merely labeled. That is the nature of phenomena, but it doesn't mean that they appear that way to us; it doesn't mean that we realize this is the way they exist. Even though in reality everything exists in mere name, it doesn't appear to us in this way and we don't see it in this way. We see something else, a total hallucination. The permanent, independent, inherently existent phenomena that we see don't exist at all; they are simply not there. The way they appear to us and the way we apprehend them completely contradict reality.

Pabongka Dechen Nyingpo tells the story of a monk who, in previous times in India, one night experienced the karmic appearance of being a preta. Feeling incredible thirst, he went outside to the big river nearby but couldn't see even a drop of water. He walked across where the river should have been, put his ceremonial robe in a tree, then returned home.

When he awoke the next morning, the karmic appearance of the preta realm had finished, but as proof that his experience wasn't just a dream, he found his robe hanging in the tree on the other side of the river. For that one night the monk had experienced the appearance of preta karma. All those appearances—feeling incredible thirst, being unable to find water even though it was normally there, seeing the water the next morning—came from his own mind, from his own karma.

In *Liberation in the Palm of Your Hand* Pabongka Dechen Nyingpo suggests using some of the logical reasoning from *du-ra* and *ta-rig*, such as "a person who doesn't have the karma to directly see a guru as a buddha has no chance to see the guru as a buddha because he doesn't have a valid mind that realizes that the guru is a buddha."

By using quotations and logical reasoning, we're trying to establish the valid mind that is able to directly see the guru as a buddha. Our mind is so limited and ignorant. Since our mind is so obscured, how can we judge whether someone is a buddha or a sentient being?

We might not accept that something exists unless we can see it with our own eyes but we are ignorant about so many things. There are so many things that exist but that we don't see. When talking about reincarnation, His Holiness Song Rinpoche would say that we can't use the reason that we ourselves don't see or haven't experienced something to prove that it doesn't exist. There are numberless phenomena that exist but that we don't see. Rinpoche would say, "If it is the case that something doesn't exist if you can't see it, the back of your head doesn't exist, because you can't see it." Besides the fact that we can't judge anyone's level of realizations, we can't even see the back of our own head. We don't have the power of mind to see even our own face without taking refuge in a mirror. And unless we turn around, we can't even see what is happening behind us.

We also can't even see what is happening inside our body. Even to know whether we are healthy, we have to depend on a doctor examining us. When we have the symptoms of a sickness, we need to rely on doctors, machines and blood tests to see what is going on inside our own body. Even with gross things that exist, such as sickness, we can't see what is happening. We also don't understand our own mind, with all its mental factors. We have to depend on Buddha's teachings to learn about our mind.

Besides not having omniscient mind, we don't have even clairvoyance. We're not able to read the minds of others or see their past or future karma. We can't even remember our past life, even though our past life did exist and our present life continued from it. Even though there will be a future life, we can't see it. We can't even see the immediate future. We can't see what is going to happen tomorrow—or even tonight. We're not even really sure whether our consciousness will still be with this body one hour from now. Forget about tomorrow and the rest of the future—we can't see what is going to happen even in the next minute. We can't see anything that is going to happen in the future, not in the next hour, minute or even second. It's totally dark. Our mind is completely obscured.

Pabongka Dechen Nyingpo explains that people with various types of sickness that alter their perceptions can't see even gross ordinary things as they are. For example, someone with bile disease[72] will actually see a white snow mountain or white conch shell as yellow. ("Actually" seeing a fault in our guru is the same as "actually" seeing a white snow mountain as yellow.) Pabongka Dechen Nyingpo also mentions that someone with *lung*, or wind

---

[72] Bile disease refers to jaundice and other liver diseases.

disease,[73] will actually see white objects as blue. And someone with eye disease can actually see a shower of strands of hair.

When people take LSD, datura or some other hallucinogenic drug, they hallucinate and actually see things that are different from how they normally are. They might see the dust as worms or hear people talking even though nobody is there. But actually seeing or hearing these things doesn't mean that they exist in reality.

Generally, if everything that appeared to us were true, since Yamantaka and other deities in wrathful aspect appear to have anger, these wrathful deities should have anger. But as they are enlightened beings, we know that they don't actually have anger.

All these examples illustrate that nothing is definite in our own view, including our view of the virtuous friend. Saying that we actually see particular faults in our gurus is not logical proof that the faults exist in reality and that the gurus are not buddhas. What appears to us depends on the state of our mind. What we see is our own mental projection, our own view. If our mind is pure, we will see things purely, but the more impure, or obscured, our mind is, the more impure what appears to us will be. When we are training our mind to look at the guru as a buddha, when we see a fault in our guru, we have to think that it is the view of our impure mind. Even if faults appear to us, we don't believe that the guru actually has these faults, just as we don't believe that things are inherently existent, even though they appear to us in that way. This protects our mind so that seeing faults doesn't become an obstacle that causes us to lose our devotion, the root of the path to enlightenment.

As ordinary beings, our mind has been heavily obscured by ignorance during beginningless rebirths. In the view of such a heavily obscured mind, it would be impossible to see the guru as a buddha.

Pabongka Dechen Nyingpo says,

> Those with certain diseases are mistaken as to the objects of their perception. Since the minds of us ordinary beings are made defective by ignorance, which projects hallucinations, how is it possible for us see the guru as an actual buddha?

---

[73] Wind disease, or *lung*, refers to states in which the wind element within the body is unbalanced; it is similar to a stress- or anxiety-induced state.

We have seen that we don't necessarily see even ordinary objects in the way that they exist, and seeing the guru as a buddha is much harder than this. Since we can't see even ordinary things accurately, it would be extremely difficult for us to discriminate whether a separate being has an enlightened mind. Remembering that the way things appear to us doesn't necessarily accord with reality, we at least begin to lean more to the side that perhaps our gurus are buddhas. And if we begin to think that someone might be a buddha, we will be more careful in our actions in relation to that being.

One simple and concise reason that we don't see the guru as a buddha is that we don't have the view of a completely pure mind, the holy mind of a buddha. Omniscience is the object only of omniscience. Everything thought, known and done by an omniscient mind is the object of only omniscient mind. An arhat, or even a tenth bhumi bodhisattva, can't know every single action of a buddha's holy body, speech and mind.

Only an omniscient mind can definitely and faultlessly see the minds of other beings. Since we don't have omniscient mind or even clairvoyance, we can't judge others. We can't really say whether or not anyone else is a buddha; we can only really be sure about whether or not we ourselves are a buddha. We can see clearly and judge our own mind but we can't see and judge the minds of others. Outside of this, there is nobody that we can be fully confident about. We can only guess about the minds of others. Therefore, our not perceiving our guru as a buddha doesn't mean that our guru is not a buddha.

In *Liberation in the Palm of Your Hand*, Pabongka Dechen Nyingpo says that we can't really judge whether our friends or the dogs outside the door are gods or maras, let alone our guru. The only one we can be sure about is ourselves. If we move away from this more than one step, the rest is subject to doubt. Since we don't have omniscient mind or even clairvoyance, we can't directly see the level of anyone else's mind; therefore, other than ourselves, everything else is subject to doubt. Our own view that someone is an ordinary being because we see his faults does not alone prove that he is ordinary.

Guru Shakyamuni Buddha said, "Only beings such as I can judge the level of mind of others. If others try to judge, there will be degeneration." Since Buddha's holy mind is omniscient, he can see the minds of others but ordinary beings can't. If we try to judge others, we can create negative karma and cause our own mind to degenerate.

Remember the quotation I mentioned earlier from *The Essence of Nectar:*

> Until we are free from our obscuring negative karma,
> Even if all the buddhas without exception descended directly in
>   front of us,
> We have no fortune to see the sublime holy body adorned with the
> holy signs and exemplifications—
> Only this present appearance.

Until we have purified our mind of impure karma and obscurations, even if every single buddha actually descended directly in front of us, we wouldn't be able to see them as buddhas adorned with the thirty-two holy signs and eighty holy exemplifications, like the nirmanakaya aspect of Shakyamuni Buddha. At the moment, since our mental continuum is not free from obscuring negative karma, we don't have the fortune to see buddhas in the pure aspect of a buddha. We would have only our present view of them as ordinary beings, which is the projection of our present obscured mind; we would see them only as having faults, delusions and samsaric suffering. There is no other way for us to see the guru except in ordinary aspect.

This quotation is extremely powerful and beneficial to remember in our meditation and in our daily life. Why don't we see numberless buddhas? Because our mind is obscured by our impure karma, which blocks our seeing them. We don't see our gurus as buddhas for a similar reason.

Because our mind is impure, even if we saw all the numberless buddhas, we would see them in ordinary aspect. Even if our guru is an actual buddha, we cannot see him as a buddha. The only way the numberless buddhas can guide us to enlightenment is by manifesting in an ordinary form. If they manifested in a purer aspect than this, we wouldn't have the karma to see them. Therefore, we are very fortunate to be able to see the guru in even an ordinary human aspect.

A bandit leader from the area of Golok called Arig Tö had killed and harmed many human beings. When he came to see the Shakyamuni Buddha statue in Lhasa, not only could he not see the statue, he couldn't see even the golden butter lamps in the temple. He saw only darkness. Terribly upset, he went to one of the past incarnations of Lama Gyalsä and asked, "Why can't I see that statue? And what should I do to purify my mind so that I'm able to see it?" In accordance with this lama's advice, he did confession practices and made thousands of offerings. When he then went to see the statue, he was able to see just the throne of Shakyamuni Buddha and the butter lamps; he still wasn't able to see the Shakyamuni Buddha statue itself.

We can also think in the following way. "The whole of existence is covered by buddha; there is no place where there is no buddha. There is no existence that buddha's holy mind does not see. There is no place that is not covered by buddha's holy mind, as well as buddha's holy body. There are numberless buddhas around me here right now, but I don't see them."

We have to understand how the whole of existence is covered by buddha from the point of view of the tantric teachings, not the sutra teachings. Wherever a buddha's holy mind focuses, that buddha's holy mind together with the subtle wind, the vehicle of that mind, is on that object. Wherever there is the subtle mind of dharmakaya, there is also the subtle wind. The mind cannot exist without its vehicle, the wind, just as we cannot use electricity without its vehicle, electrical wires. Though the subtle mind and subtle wind have different functions, they are one in essence. Since a buddha's holy mind understands every object of existence, there is no object that the omniscient mind doesn't cover, and since it is inseparable from the subtle mind, the subtle wind is also there. This pure subtle mind is the dharmakaya and the subtle wind is the rupakaya. Therefore, with the unification of a buddha's holy mind, the dharmakaya, and a buddha's holy body, the rupakaya, there is no object that a buddha does not cover. This is one of the basic reasons that the whole of existence is covered by buddha.

Even if we don't believe that a buddha is on our crown, it doesn't mean that buddha is not there. There is no doubt that buddha is there. There is not even a single atom of existence that buddha doesn't cover; there is not even a single atom where there is no buddha. All the buddhas are right there, wherever we are; it's just that we don't see them. Only when our karma is pure do we see them. Our failure to see the buddhas is simply a question of our karmic obscurations. If our karmic obscurations were purified, right now we would see that we are completely surrounded by buddhas. Because the buddhas are already there, I sometimes think that there is no need to invoke them from somewhere else. The practice of invocation is for us ordinary beings, who have much superstition. Since we believe that the buddhas are somewhere else, doing the invocation helps us to generate more faith that they are there in front of us.

Pabongka Dechen Nyingpo says that, besides buddhas, there are many other beings around us that we can't see. There could also be spirits in front of us, for example. Because we can't see spirits, we can't tell whether or not there's a spirit in front of us, but we can't say that no spirit is there. We can't actually see gods, spirits, nagas or many other types of worldly beings. We might also meet buddhas, bodhisattvas, dakas and dakinis many times in our daily life, but meeting them doesn't mean that we recognize them.

Someone with pure karma can see buddhas anywhere. It is our impure karma that obscures our mind so that we don't see buddhas. When doing the preliminary practices, Lama Tsongkhapa saw all of the Thirty-five Buddhas in his retreat cave, as well as Manjushri and Maitreya Buddha surrounded by all the deities and pandits. Lama Tsongkhapa was able to see them because he had purified his negative karma. At various times, Lama Tsongkhapa actually saw an inconceivable number of deities in various aspects.

At Buddhist holy places in India, most people see just some piles of earth or the ruins of a building or a throne where Buddha once sat. Some years ago a group of people, including an old woman from Tibet, went on pilgrimage to Nalanda. No one else saw anything but the old woman saw a life-sized figure of Buddha with a golden holy body sitting there. Also, when taking teachings from His Holiness the Dalai Lama, she saw Buddha on the palm of her hand.

I also heard that one Western man who went to the Palden Lhamo lake,[74] which can give predictions, saw Vajrasattva and Chenrezig on the lake when he arrived there. Some people spend weeks there and don't see anything. It has all to do with karma.

When Lama Yeshe was giving a commentary on the Six Yogas of Naropa at Istituto Lama Tzong Khapa in Italy,[75] every morning Lama would do the middle-length Heruka Chakrasamvara Body Mandala self-initiation before going to give the commentary. One morning, at the beginning of the teaching, Lama was crying. Jacie Keeley, the American woman who was Lama's secretary at the time, told me this. Jacie saw that after Lama sat down and before he began the teaching, he was crying. She saw that something had strongly affected Lama's mind.

After Lama returned from the teaching, Jacie asked him why he had cried. Lama said, "What are you talking about? I saw my guru." Lama saw

---

[74] Lhamo Lhatso is a lake in Tibet that is associated with Palden Lhamo, the protectoress of Tibet. It is an oracle lake and is usually consulted in the search for the incarnations of the Dalai Lamas.

[75] An FPMT center in Pomaia, Italy. These teachings have been published in *The Bliss of Inner Fire*.

His Holiness Trijang Rinpoche, his main root guru, who had passed away a couple of years before. Nobody else saw Trijang Rinpoche there.

None of this comes from the side of the object; it all comes from the mind of the perceiver. It's not so much a question of whether the objects exist there or not; it's mainly a question of whether our karma is pure or impure.

Our view of things as ordinary is so powerful that we totally believe it to be true. Because our belief that other people are ordinary is so strong, it's very hard for us to see someone as an enlightened being, even if he or she is. Even if someone who is an embodiment of Tara or Vajrayogini is right in front of us, our view and conception of her as ordinary is so strong that it is difficult for us to believe that she is an enlightened being.

In former times, when Guru Shakyamuni Buddha was in India, Buddha manifested in nirmanakaya aspect, with thirty-two holy signs and eighty holy exemplifications, and ordinary people usually saw an aura of beams for an arm span around Buddha's holy body. The six Hindu founders who criticized and competed with Buddha, however, saw him as a very ordinary monk; they couldn't see even Buddha's aura.

Even if a teacher is fully enlightened, it doesn't mean that the disciple will see him as an enlightened being. Even if our guru is a buddha, this isn't sufficient; from our side, we have to look at him as a buddha. If we don't, we're like the fully ordained monk Sunakshatra, who saw only faults in Guru Shakyamuni Buddha. There is then no way for us to generate good qualities within us.

The Essence of Nectar says,

> As for the appearance of faults:
> Devadatta, Sunakshatra and the *tirthikas*[76]
> Saw the Founder, with all stains gone and qualities complete,
> As full of faults.

> Like a person with jaundice sees a white conch as yellow,
> Because the veils of my evil karma and obscurations are so thick,
> I see the faultless as having only faults.
> How is it possible that in fact they have faults and vices?

---

[76] Skt; Tib: *mu-teg-pa*. Forders—early Indian followers of non-Buddhist systems. See *Meditation on Emptiness*, p. 320 ff.

As I have mentioned a couple of times before, Sunakshatra was Guru Shakya-muni Buddha's attendant for twenty-two years but during all those years he always saw Buddha as just an ordinary being. Even though Guru Shakya-muni Buddha had become enlightened an unimaginable time before, Sunak-shatra never looked at him as a buddha; he didn't see a single good quality in Buddha during those twenty-two years and instead saw only faults. He saw Shakyamuni Buddha as only a liar. Why did he see Buddha as a liar? Because he looked at Buddha as only a liar and not as an enlightened being. Since he looked at Buddha as only a liar, that is how Buddha appeared to him. Sunakshatra said, "I served Shakyamuni Buddha for twenty-two years and I didn't see in him a good quality even the size of a sesame seed."

When Buddha went begging for alms and people made offerings to him, Buddha would explain the result of that karma. In a small village one day, a girl offered a handful of grain in Buddha's begging bowl. Buddha then predicted that as a result of her offering, in the future she would be reborn as the arhat Supranihita. Sunakshatra couldn't believe what Buddha told the girl. How could someone become an arhat just from offering a handful of grain? He generated heresy toward Buddha, thinking that Buddha was simply flattering the girl because she had made an offering to him. It didn't occur to Sunakshatra, who didn't have omniscience or clairvoyance, that Buddha was making a prediction. He didn't see Guru Shakyamuni Buddha as even sincere.

Buddha then asked him, "Do you know that from planting a small seed a huge tree that can cover five hundred horse-carriages can grow?" Sunakshatra said, "Yes, I know that." Buddha replied, "No, it doesn't exist." Sunakshatra said, "Oh, yes, it exists, because it is my experience. I know it exists." Buddha then said, "It is also my experience that by giving one handful of grain this woman can achieve arhatship." Sunakshatra then had nothing to say.

If, from our side, we don't look at our guru as a buddha, we won't see him as a buddha. If we look at only the faults, we will see only faults in our guru. We will look at him as an ordinary being and will then always see him only as an ordinary being, as Sunakshatra did. By looking at our guru as a buddha, by training our mind in this pure view, we will then see him as a buddha.

Even if our guru is a buddha, we don't necessarily see him as a buddha because what we see accords with our own karma. If we have a pure mind and pure karma, we see a buddha; if our mind is obscured by impure karma, we see an ordinary being with faults.

Our seeing faults in our gurus doesn't prove that in reality they have faults; we can't say that our gurus are not buddhas because we see that they have anger, attachment, ignorance and other delusions. How things appear to us very much depends upon us. Even what we call a fault depends on our way of looking at it. Pabongka Dechen Nyingpo says in *Liberation in the Palm of Your Hand* that if a disciple wants to go to bed early, she sees her guru going to bed very late as a fault, but if the guru goes to bed early she sees this as a good quality. (If you're living in the same house, you're normally not supposed to go to bed until your teacher does.) This is just one simple example of how things very much depend on our own interpretation. Whether we call something a fault or a good quality depends on our own definitions.

Many times problems come from not understanding that the external appearance we cling to is not necessarily reality, which is beyond what appears to us. Even when Gyalwa Ensapa was close to achieving enlightenment, ordinary people thought he was crazy because he appeared to them to be a crazy person who couldn't control his mind. Remember how Naro Bönchung saw Milarepa. Naro Bönchung, a Bön practitioner, wanted to compete with Milarepa because he had heard so much about him. But when he actually met Milarepa, Naro Bönchung commented that Milarepa was just a skinny, blue old man who looked as if he could easily be blown away by the wind. (Milarepa's body was blue with cold because he wore no clothes.) This is how Milarepa appeared to Naro Bönchung, even though Milarepa was an enlightened being whose holy mind was enriched by realizations as limitless as the sky.

Even though Lama Yeshe acted many times as if he were angry, at certain times Lama would say, "The object is a sentient being so how is it possible that I could be angry at him?" *Sentient being* means a pitiful, obscured, suffering being. What Lama said was the reality, even though it contradicted what normally appeared to us.

Also, even though Lama Yeshe had no eight worldly dharmas, he acted as if he had clinging to this life. And even though Lama had no miserliness, he appeared to be miserly in relation to certain things. There are many stories to illustrate this and only later did we realize that what we had seen in the past didn't accord with reality and that Lama had inconceivable internal qualities. It had very much to do with our own karma, with our own interpretation.

The Essence of Nectar says,

Whatever holy body and actions are shown,
In fact there is no doubt
That all the Victorious Ones of the ten directions
Are showing the holy bodies that subdue us,
In order to guide us in the path to liberation.

The compassionate founder Shakyamuni Buddha said in the sutra *Meeting of Father and Son*:

> I will work for sentient beings by manifesting as Indra and Brahma and sometimes in the form of a mara, but people in the world will be unable to recognize me. I will also manifest in the form of women and even in the animal realm. Even though I don't have attachment, I will act as if I have attachment; even though I do not have fear, I will act afraid; even though I am not crazy, I will act crazy; even though I am not blind, I will act as if I am blind. With various forms, I will subdue sentient beings. To sentient beings with strong anger, I will manifest as having strong anger. To sentient beings with great attachment, I will manifest as having great attachment in order to guide them. Like this, I will manifest in whatever form fits sentient beings.

The sutra teachings also explain that Buddha will manifest even as someone who has generated heresy or broken all four root vows. To people who have strong attachment, Buddha will manifest as a prostitute in order to subdue them. Buddha will also manifest as a wine-seller or as an animal. Buddha will manifest as an eagle to protect other eagles, but ordinary sentient beings will simply see an eagle, not Buddha.

By using quotations and analytical reasoning, we gain definite understanding that the guru is a buddha, free from all faults and possessing all realizations. When we have the certainty in our heart that the guru is all the buddhas, that the guru and all the buddhas are mixed, at that time we have the realization of guru devotion.

First of all, we should remember the ultimate meaning of guru, which is the absolute guru. We have to realize that the guru that we see and hear is the absolute guru, the dharmakaya, the transcendental wisdom of nondual bliss and voidness, the eternal primordial mind that has no beginning and no end. Since this absolute guru is the holy mind of all the buddhas, all the buddhas are the guru. We can understand from this that the guru is all the buddhas and all the buddhas are the guru.

This is why it makes sense to say "guru-buddha." With this explanation, by simply saying "guru" we can naturally realize that it means buddha, without needing to use the extra label "buddha."

We need to see each of our gurus as all the buddhas and each buddha as all of our gurus. Flour, for example, can be made into many foods of various shapes and tastes: noodles, bread, cakes. However, despite all the different shapes and different names, it is all flour. It is the same with the guru. Spontaneously, naturally, constantly arising from the depths of our heart should be the thought that the guru is a buddha. When we visualize deities or think of a buddha, we should understand that this is the guru. This thought should be stable, not just last a few hours or days and then disappear. When this thought is stable, we have achieved the realization of guru devotion.

When definitive understanding that the guru is the embodiment of the transcendental wisdom of all the buddhas arises spontaneously, do fixed meditation on that. Do analytical and fixed meditation in this way again and again. When at the end one sees there is no buddha separate from the guru and no guru separate from all the buddhas, when the guru and all the buddhas become mixed, or one, at that time the realization of guru devotion has been generated. When water and milk are mixed, they become one, and it's still called milk.

The ultimate goal is for our own mind and the guru's holy mind to merge to become one. When we become enlightened, our own mind and the guru's holy mind merge to become one in the great bliss of the dharmakaya. On the basis of the common path, we complete the tantric path, especially the generation and completion stages of Highest Yoga Tantra, achieving the clear light, the illusory body and unification. We cease all our obscurations and develop the simultaneously born primordial mind of clear light, the transcendental wisdom of nondual bliss and voidness, and the continuation of that mind, the great bliss of the dharmakaya, is itself the guru's holy mind. At that time we become enlightened in the essence of the guru. We achieve the guru's enlightenment; our own body, speech and mind become inseparable from the guru's holy body, holy speech and holy mind.

To prepare for that, from this moment on, we should make ourselves harmonious with, or closer to, the guru's holy mind. It's important to prepare for our mind and the guru's holy mind to merge, to prepare to achieve the guru's enlightenment.

In the Lama Tsongkhapa tradition one doesn't say that one is the guru or one is a buddha or that one's own mind is dharmakaya, the deity's or the guru's holy mind, but when we practice tantra we have to generate divine pride, so we meditate in that way. Even though it's not comfortable for us to accept that our present obscured mind is the guru's enlightened mind, when we practice tantra, we have to hold the divine pride now of what we are going to become in the future. Even though the idea is not philosophically correct and could be defeated in debate, it is an effective meditation for those who practice tantra.

(ii) Even nowadays all the buddhas and bodhisattvas are still working for sentient beings   At the present time all the buddhas and bodhisattvas are working for sentient beings, including us. There is no other way they are doing that except in the forms of the teachers who are directly guiding us by giving us the three levels of vows, oral transmissions, initiations, sutra and tantra commentaries and advice. Every single word of their teaching is guiding us to enlightenment. If our gurus are not those numberless buddhas and bodhisattvas working for us, there is no one else to point out as the ones guiding us to enlightenment. Therefore, our gurus are buddhas.

> The Controlled Ones do not wash away negative karma with water;
> They do not remove the sufferings of transmigratory beings with
>   their hands;
> Nor do they transplant their own realizations into others.
> They liberate by revealing the absolute true nature.

When I introduce the concept of the buddhas and bodhisattvas working for sentient beings to Westerners, I normally recommend that they first use their own experience of compassion as an example, as this makes it easy to understand. When we feel compassion for someone, we want to help, not harm her. In other words, we try to benefit that person by doing whatever we can for her with our body, speech and mind. Even though we don't feel compassion for every sentient being, we do whatever we can to help those for whom we do feel compassion. If we did feel compassion for all sentient beings, we would try to help all of them according to our capacity. This is logical.

Now, some people have much more compassion than we do; their compassion is stronger and broader, encompassing more sentient beings than ours. These people give more help and less harm to others than we do. We can't deny the reality of this. Some people feel compassion not only for their friends but also for strangers and even enemies; they have compassion not only for those who help them but even for those who don't help them or who actively harm them.

From our own experience we can see that our compassion can be increased if we continue to meditate on the sufferings of our own samsara, the general and specific sufferings of the lower realms and the sufferings of other sentient beings. If we really look at how other sentient beings are suffering, there will definitely be a change in our mind, even while we are meditating. Such meditations affect the mind, transforming it into compassion. If we continue to put effort into the meditations, we can definitely develop stronger and stronger compassion for more and more sentient beings.

Bodhisattvas feel *great* compassion, which means compassion for all sentient beings. Not only do they wish all sentient beings to be free from suffering but they actually take upon themselves the responsibility of freeing them. Even very new bodhisattvas, ones who have just generated bodhicitta and entered the Mahayana path, have completely given up the thought of working for themselves, of seeking happiness for themselves. Their minds cherish only other sentient beings. Every single action of their body, speech and mind is focused on working for others. This is their only thought. Every single movement they make, even breathing in and out, is done for other sentient beings. Eating, walking, sitting, sleeping—everything is done only for the benefit of other sentient beings.

This reminds me of Gen Jampa Wangdu, who often used to visit Lama Yeshe and me at Tushita Retreat Centre in the evenings for a chat, and he would sometimes tell us about his life. One time he said, "For the past seven years, I have never been to anybody's house for my own purpose." Gen Jampa Wangdu didn't mean that he hadn't gone to other people's houses at all for seven years but that he hadn't gone to anybody's house for his own sake. He normally didn't tell other people about his realizations; he was just not the kind of person to make a big thing of them or talk much to other people. But Lama and I were very close to him; we were the best of friends. (This was before I received the lineage of the teachings on the pill retreat from him, which I did a couple of years before he passed away.) Because Gen Jampa Wangdu liked Lama and me very much, he would reveal more of himself to us.

Whenever Gen Jampa Wangdu came to see us at Tushita, it was the best time; we enjoyed his visits very much. The best entertainment was to hear about his own meditation experiences, as well as those of other meditators and about what he had done in the past. Geshe-la told us how he had been very naughty when he was in Sera Monastery in Tibet, never studying and only teasing and fighting the other monks.

Even though Gen Jampa Wangdu didn't say straight out that he had achieved bodhicitta, it was clear that he had generated bodhicitta seven years before. Much earlier than that he had also achieved the nine levels of calm abiding.

Since even a new bodhisattva does everything only for other sentient beings, there is no doubt about a buddha. All the buddhas have completed training their minds in compassion and have compassion for every single sentient being, including us. Their compassion cannot be developed further; theirs is the ultimate development of compassion. Therefore, all the buddhas of the three times must be working for and guiding all sentient beings. Because of their compassion, they have no choice.

Since there are beings whose holy minds have completed the training in compassion and who are working for and guiding sentient beings, if they are not our gurus, who else could it be? Our present gurus are the buddhas who are working for sentient beings, including us.

One-pointedly focusing in turn on each of your gurus, think, "This guru is a buddha." Like reciting a mantra, keep on repeating, "This guru is a buddha, this guru is a buddha, this guru is a buddha...." Recite this twenty-one times, for half a mala, or for one mala, according to the time you have. At the same time try to stabilize your mind in the devotion that sees each guru as a buddha.

We can use the same logical reasoning in relation to knowledge. There are other people with greater knowledge than we have. It's not the case that only what we know and have experienced exists and what we don't know and haven't experienced doesn't exist. There are people with more knowledge, even in terms of worldly education, and there are people with much greater knowledge than we have. Some people have the capacity to remember previous lives and see future lives and other distant phenomena. Such people have greater knowledge and a greater capacity to benefit others.

Now, there are beings who have completed all knowledge; beings who have no obstruction to directly seeing all past, present and future phenomena. The only mind that has completed all knowledge is the omniscient mind, the enlightened mind, the mind of a buddha. The omniscient mind of a buddha directly sees all existence all the time and knows the level of mind and characteristics of every single sentient being and every single method suitable to free them from suffering and bring them from happiness to happiness to enlightenment.

Since there are beings who have completed all learning and who use that knowledge to benefit sentient beings, if they are not our gurus, who else could they be? Other than our present gurus there is no one we can point out as these buddhas.

Again, by thinking of each of your gurus, repeat, "This guru is a buddha, this guru is a buddha, this guru is a buddha…." With one-pointed concentration, stabilize your mind in devotion. Stay a little while in fixed meditation on your complete determination that your gurus are buddhas.

On top of that, buddhas have perfect power to guide sentient beings. They can manifest in whatever way accords with the level of mind of sentient beings and then reveal with their holy body, speech and mind the methods that suit the level of that sentient being's mind. Since there are beings who have the complete power to benefit others and who do benefit other sentient beings, if they are not our gurus, who else could they be? There's no one else to point out as these beings except our present gurus.

Again, by thinking of each of your gurus, recite, "This guru is a buddha, this guru is a buddha, this guru is a buddha…." With one-pointed concentration, stabilize your mind in devotion.

Buddhas have all these three qualities—infinite compassion, omniscient mind and perfect power—but the main factor that causes them to guide sentient beings is their compassion. If buddhas had omniscient mind and perfect power but no compassion there would be the danger that they wouldn't guide all sentient beings. But since they have completed training their mind in compassion and have compassion for every single obscured, suffering sentient being, they have no choice but to work for every sentient being without discrimination; their holy minds are bound by infinite compassion that embraces all sentient beings. We can understand this by relating it to our own everyday experiences. If we feel even a little compassion for somebody, we don't harm her and, according to our knowledge and power, do what we can to help her.

There is no doubt that buddhas definitely work for and guide sentient beings. Even bodhisattvas, who are not yet enlightened, work for us, so why not buddhas? The only reason the buddhas achieved full enlightenment was to be able to guide sentient beings.

It is not that the buddhas simply have the wish that sentient beings be free from suffering and then do nothing about it themselves. It's not that they simply relax on their bed or at the beach and expect somebody else to do the job of freeing sentient beings from suffering. Great compassion means not only wishing all sentient beings to be free from all suffering but taking the responsibility upon yourself to free them. You then generate the special attitude, "I will work to free sentient beings from suffering and lead them to enlightenment by myself alone." After that comes bodhicitta, when you think, "For that reason I need to achieve enlightenment." So, even before generating bodhicitta, you have the attitude of taking responsibility upon yourself for all sentient beings.

Therefore, there is no doubt that enlightened beings, who have completed the development of compassion for all sentient beings, are working for us, guiding us. We should first make this point clear through use of quotations and logical reasoning, before considering our gurus. On the basis of certain faith in this, we can then consider our gurus. The subject of guru devotion will then have taste and meaning.

It is also helpful to remember the four reasons that a buddha is a worthy object in whom to take refuge: a buddha is free from all fears; a buddha is skillful in guiding sentient beings away from all dangers and liberating them from all fears; a buddha has compassion for all sentient beings, without discriminating some as close and others as distant; and a buddha works for all sentient beings, regardless of whether or not a sentient being has benefited him. In other words, a buddha's helping a sentient being doesn't depend on whether or not that sentient being likes or has made offerings to him. Therefore, the buddhas definitely have compassion for and guide us.

Also, since buddhas guide even animals, who are dumb and mute, they must guide human beings. We, who have received not only a human rebirth but a perfect human rebirth, are intelligent and can communicate, so we are easy to guide. Since we can not only hear and understand the words of Dharma but have faith in Buddhadharma as well, there is no doubt that the buddhas must be guiding us. And who are these buddhas who are guiding us? None other than our present gurus.

Again recite, "This guru is a buddha, this guru is a buddha, this guru is a buddha..." and again transform your mind into guru devotion, seeing the guru as a buddha. Do fixed meditation by keeping your mind for a little while in that pure thought of devotion.

Since the buddhas have all these qualities of omniscience, compassion and power and never lie, they must be working for sentient beings. The numberless past, present and future buddhas are working for sentient beings, which includes us. If our present gurus are not the buddhas who are leading us to enlightenment, who else is? There is nobody else to point out. We then reach the conclusion that our gurus are buddhas.

We should come to this same conclusion, that our gurus are buddhas, with this and the subsequent outlines, *the guru is the doer of all the buddhas' actions* and *Vajradhara asserted that the guru is a buddha*. When we come to the conclusion that our gurus are buddhas and our mind is transformed into devotion, we should hold that experience for some time in fixed, or single-pointed, meditation. First we do the analysis; second, when we have proved the point to our own mind and our mind is transformed into the devotion that sees the gurus as buddhas, we keep our mind in that state for as long as possible. With this transformation, we will experience much joy, as the nature of that mind of devotion is peaceful and pleasurable.

We should then continue the experience, not only during the meditation session but after we stand up and walk out of the meditation room at the end of a session. We shouldn't think that our ordinary life has nothing to do with what happens on our meditation cushion. The main point is to continue the experience, keeping our mind during the rest of the day in that state of devotion we achieved during our meditation session in the morning. We should live our life in that state of mind, in that experience of the path.

This is called "taking the essence all day and all night." It makes our life meaningful twenty-four hours a day because with this devotion we are constantly accumulating merit. Everything we do is done out of devotion and directed toward that devotion. This itself brings the greatest purification and accumulates the most extensive merit.

Keutsang Jamyang Mönlam said,

> The buddhas and bodhisattvas who descended in the past are still working now for sentient beings. If you are truly able to recognize this fact, they are all gathered in the qualified guru.

This means that even at this present time the buddhas and bodhisattvas are working for sentient beings, including us, through the aspect of our guru. If we are able to recognize it, the root guru that we visualize on our crown or in our heart is all the buddhas and bodhisattvas who are working for us and for other sentient beings. This present guru embodies all of them.

In *Liberation in the Palm of Your Hand* Pabongka Dechen Nyingpo says,

> My guru said that there is a complete buddha sitting on the crown of each sentient being.

(iii) The guru is the doer of all the buddhas' actions During our beginningless lifetimes until now, all the virtuous teachers we have met—those who gave us ordinations, initiations and teachings—are one being, the absolute guru, who has manifested in various aspects, with different names and forms. When the sun or moon rises, billions of reflections spontaneously arise in all the bodies of water on the earth—in oceans, rivers, ponds and even dew drops. Like this, effortlessly, spontaneously, buddhas work for sentient beings, by revealing the various means that suit them. All our virtuous teachers are the dharmakaya, the absolute guru, from where all the buddhas, Dharma and Sangha come. The absolute guru, the dharmakaya, the holy mind of all the buddhas, which is bound by infinite compassion that embraces all sentient beings, manifests in, or through, the ordinary aspects of our gurus.

If you analyze the meaning of the prayers in *Guru Puja* you will see that the whole practice is based on this meditation that the guru is the doer of all the buddhas' actions; and the doer of the actions of the buddhas has to come from the dharmakaya.

The Essence of Nectar says,

> The virtuous friends who reveal the path
> Are like the one moon in the sky, reflected
> Without effort and at the same time
> In all the waters of this world.

> A sutra says, The transcendental wisdom of the buddhas
> Appears without effort in the holy bodies of

Sambhogakaya, nirmanakaya and ordinary virtuous friends
To the pure and impure objects who are to be subdued.

In our past lives we have been guided by many different virtuous teachers, with many different aspects, but we shouldn't think that they are separate from our present virtuous teachers. Our gurus enabled us to plant the seed of Dharma in our past lives; they guided us from the lower to the upper realms, including our present perfect human rebirth, by allowing us to create good karma. During beginningless lifetimes, these virtuous friends have been leading us from happiness to happiness to enlightenment. These same gurus who are guiding us in this life have guided us in the past and will still be guiding us when we are bodhisattvas on the tenth bhumi, about to achieve enlightenment.

The dharmakaya, the holy mind of all the buddhas, the transcendental wisdom of nondual bliss and voidness, is the absolute guru. This dharmakaya is eternal, with no beginning or end, and it pervades all phenomena. Because this holy mind is bound by infinite compassion that embraces all the numberless sentient beings, whenever the karma of a sentient being ripens, without even a second's delay, it manifests in a form that accords with the karma of that sentient being.

For those with pure minds, such as higher bodhisattvas, it manifests in the sambhogakaya aspect of a buddha. To lower bodhisattvas, those who have achieved the Mahayana great path of merit, it manifests in nirmanakaya aspect. It also manifests in ordinary human forms to guide sentient beings. It can manifest as an ordained or lay person, as male or female, as a child, as rich or poor. It can manifest in a beggar's form to enable others to accumulate merit through making charity. For those with strong attachment, it can manifest in the form of a prostitute. The dharmakaya can also manifest in animals, spirits and various other forms. There is nothing fixed about the way it manifests. It can manifest even in material objects, such as bridges or water, in accord with the characteristics and needs of sentient beings. However, even though it manifests in all kinds of forms, they are all one in essence.

When an actor wears the costume of a king, a beggar, a farmer or a trader, we recognize that the same actor is appearing in the different costumes. Remember how Shakyamuni Buddha guided sentient beings in various manifestations and also how Chenrezig subdued the sentient beings of

Tibet by manifesting as the king, the minister, the translator, the judge and so forth.

Many lam-rim texts, especially *Liberation in the Palm of Your Hand*, use *the guru is the doer of all the buddhas' actions* as the main logical reasoning to prove that the guru is a buddha.

In *du-ra*, four different conditions are explained: the immediate condition;[77] the self-condition, which could be the cause—for example, a seed produces its own result, a sprout; the causal condition;[78] and the condition of seeing—for example, compassion is generated by the condition of seeing the sufferings of sentient beings. Since the object that you have seen becomes the condition for generating compassion, suffering sentient beings are the condition of seeing.

All the teachings and other Dharma activities of our gurus are regarded as coming from the self-condition of the dharmakaya, just as a sprout comes from its seed. From where do all the teachings that guide us to enlightenment come? They come from the self-condition, dharmakaya. And in whom does the dharmakaya abide? There is no one to point out other than our virtuous friends.

Also, the self-condition of all the virtues we have accumulated in our mind is the dharmakaya, and in whose mind does this self-condition of dharmakaya abide? In the guru's holy mind. Therefore, our gurus are buddhas.

This is the main logical reasoning normally used by His Holiness Ling Rinpoche and His Holiness Trijang Rinpoche, and it seems to be the same in *Liberation in the Palm of Your Hand*. Somehow I find this one hard to understand. It seems that when your mind is ready, which means more purified, you are able to feel that it is true, but when your mind is obscured, you cannot feel it.

Our mind is so obscured that no matter how much the buddhas want to manifest to us in the aspect of a buddha, we don't have the karma to be able to see them in that pure form. In order to subdue us, the buddhas perform their actions by revealing the ordinary aspects of our virtuous friends, which suit our own fortune, or merit. Since we don't have the fortune to actually meet buddhas in the aspect of buddhas, the buddhas show aspects

---

[77] The immediate condition in generating compassion, for example, would be the moment of consciousness immediately prior to generating a motivation of compassion.

[78] The causal condition in generating compassion could be the suffering of other sentient beings or the same as the immediate condition.

that are similar to ours, then teach us Dharma. Pabongka Dechen Nyingpo says that even from this we can realize that the guru is a buddha and that the actions of all the buddhas come to us through the guru. Even if we could see an actual buddha, there is no higher action they could do than our gurus' present action of revealing teachings.

Since all we can see are impure aspects, the buddhas can't appear to us in any other way than as ordinary beings, which means ones having faults. There is no meaning of *ordinary being* other than that.

If the buddhas manifested in purer forms than we now see, we wouldn't have the karma to see them and receive teachings from them. Because our mind is obscured by impure karma, we can't see a buddha's holy body or hear a buddha's holy speech. And if the buddhas manifested in forms lower than we now see, such as in the forms of animals, it would be difficult for us to recognize them and have faith in them. We also couldn't communicate with or receive teachings from them. Therefore, in order to guide us, the buddhas have manifested in the ordinary forms of our virtuous friends, which exactly suit the level of our mind and our karma. In other words, our gurus are the ones who do the activities of all the buddhas, just as ambassadors act on behalf of their country. For example, the many American ambassadors around the world act on behalf of the American government and the American government works through those ambassadors.

The buddhas have to manifest in the ordinary forms of our gurus because they have no other way to directly guide us through teachings, advice and other methods. Through communicating with us, these ordinary aspects prevent us from being born in the lower realms, liberate us from samsara and lead us to enlightenment. Since these present ordinary aspects are the only ones that can directly guide us to enlightenment, the numberless buddhas are unbelievably kind to take these ordinary aspects in order to make it possible for us to see them and receive their teachings and guidance. Otherwise, we'd be totally lost.

After we have generated the definitive understanding from the very depths of our heart that all our gurus are buddhas, when we trace back, we find that the buddhas are the base of transformation of our gurus. And, if we trace even the buddhas back to their source, they are transformations of Vajradhara, so all our gurus are transformations of Vajradhara. Vajradhara is our own guru. If we wonder where Vajradhara came from, the great bliss of the dharmakaya manifested in the aspect of a deity. If we trace the base of transformation of our own gurus back to its source, it is the dharmakaya, the transcendental wisdom of all the buddhas. And what is that? That is the absolute guru. The transcendental wisdom of all the buddhas, which is of one taste in the sphere of the dharmakaya, manifests in the ordinary aspects of our gurus, the holy bodies of transformation.

As Pabongka Dechen Nyingpo says in *Calling the Lama from Afar*,[79]

> The play of various emanations, suiting the dispositions of the many to be subdued, is itself the behavior of the sambhogakaya of the kind lamas. I beseech you, Lama, nirmanakaya, please look after me always without separation, in this life, future lives and the bardo.

> The play of the inseparable three kayas, appearing in the form of the lama, is itself one with the very essence of all kind lamas. I beseech you, Lama, the inseparable three kayas, please look after me always without separation, in this life, future lives and the bardo.

The Essence of Nectar says,

> Therefore, whatever appears to me,
> In fact their essence is that they encompass in one
> Each and every one of the infinite Victorious Ones of the infinite
>   fields,
> Having ceased all faults and perfected all qualities.

The lineage lamas taught another practical technique for seeing the guru as a buddha and all the guru's actions as the actions of all the buddhas. When a medium invokes a spirit, as soon as the medium thinks of the spirit, the spirit immediately enters the medium's body and speaks through the medium. When the spirit speaks, we don't say that the medium is speaking; we say that the spirit is speaking, even though it is using the medium's body to do so. Until the spirit leaves the medium, we always relate any action that is performed to the spirit, not the medium.

It is similar with Dharma protectors. An oracle whose body is qualified to receive the transcendental wisdom of a Dharma protector can invoke

---

[79] See appendix 4.

that protector just by saying its name or reciting a prayer. The protector immediately enters the oracle's body and then gives predictions or blessings or performs healing. We say that the protector is giving us predictions; we don't say that the oracle is talking to us. Even though we see the ordinary human body of the oracle and not the form of the protector, in our mind we realize that during the time the protector is within the oracle's body, it is the protector that is giving predictions and blessings and performing the other activities, not the oracle.

If Dharma protectors and even ordinary worldly spirits, who are not free from karma and delusions, immediately come when we think of them, why not the buddhas? Of course the buddhas come. As soon as we think of a buddha, buddha is there. As soon as we generate faith that our guru is a buddha, buddha is there.

Wherever we have faith that a buddha is, buddha is there. There is a saying, "Whenever we think a buddha is on the palm of our hand, on our crown, in our heart or in front of us, a buddha is there." A tantric root text also says that a buddha abides wherever we have faith that a buddha is, whether on the muscles, veins, sinews, joints or other parts of the body. For example, in the *Guru Puja* merit field, we visualize many buddhas and bodhisattvas—the deities of the Guhyasamaja mandala—on the holy body of the guru. We should recognize that the guru's holy body is covered with buddhas; every atom is covered with buddhas. With faith in this, we receive the blessings of the holy body, speech and mind of all the buddhas through the guru's holy body.

Since even an ordinary spirit immediately enters the medium when the medium thinks of the spirit, as soon as we think that the guru is a buddha, there is no doubt that buddha is immediately in that holy body. Otherwise, buddhas wouldn't have even the ordinary psychic powers that spirits have.

Since the buddhas have omniscient mind, infinite compassion for all sentient beings and perfect power, of course they will come as soon as we think of them. A buddha has omniscient mind, and all existence is covered by omniscient mind. There is no object that is not covered by omniscient mind. So, of course, when we think that our guru is a buddha, buddha will definitely be there.

Just as all the actions of an oracle's body, speech and mind during the time a Dharma protector is in the oracle's body are the actions of the protector, all the actions of the guru's holy body, speech and mind are the actions of the buddhas, whether they are giving us teachings or scolding or beating us. All the activities of the buddhas are performed through these ordinary aspects. Whether we see good qualities or faults in our gurus, it is all the act of the buddhas.

If we examine this way of meditating on guru devotion carefully, it will become clear that the guru is a buddha and all the guru's actions are the actions of the buddhas. The gurus, who reveal the teachings and guide us in peaceful and wrathful ways, are the doers of all the buddhas' actions.

In *In Praise of Dependent Arising*, Lama Tsongkhapa explains that the highest action of a buddha is revealing the teachings to sentient beings. Of the infinite variety of buddhas' activities to guide sentient beings, the highest activity is revealing Dharma. Giving teachings is the best way to free sentient beings from their sufferings and lead them to liberation and enlightenment. Our present gurus are the ones performing the highest activity of the buddhas; they are the ones revealing the various teachings that are needed to liberate us and lead us to enlightenment.

Simply by giving us the oral transmission of the mantra OM MANI PADME HUM, our guru definitely takes us to enlightenment. Receiving the oral transmission plants the seed of the whole path to enlightenment by leaving an imprint on our mind. Sooner or later, in this or future lives, when we have accumulated enough merit, this imprint will enable us to actualize the path that is contained in OM MANI PADME HUM. Because of the planting of this seed, even later in this life, we will be able to understand the teachings more clearly and deeply. And this imprint eventually enables us to experience the whole path to enlightenment.

Even if it doesn't happen in this life, in our next life the seed planted by receiving the oral transmission of OM MANI PADME HUM will sprout and we will become expert in the meaning of that mantra and the path it contains. Remember the story of Vasubandhu and the pigeon. In the past, a pigeon used to sit on the roof of the hermitage of the great Indian pandit, Acharya Vasubandhu, while he was reciting the *Treasury of Knowledge* text. After some time, the pigeon died. When Vasubandhu checked what rebirth this pigeon had taken, he discovered that it had been reborn as the son of a family that lived in the town down below his cave. Since Vasubandhu knew that this boy would become his disciple, he went down and asked the family if he could take care of the child. The family agreed to give the child to him. The child became Vasubandhu's student and later a monk called Acharya Sthiramati (Lobpön Loden), who wrote four commentaries to the *Treasury of Knowledge*, the words of which he had heard recited by Vasubandhu when he was a pigeon sitting on the roof of Vasubandhu's hermitage.

There are many such stories that show the incredible results from simply hearing the words of the Dharma. Just by hearing the words of the *Treasury of Knowledge*, this pigeon became expert in this teaching in his next life. Therefore, we should listen to oral transmissions by concentrating on the sound of the words, remembering that listening brings great benefit.

If even the guru who simply gives us the oral transmission of OM MANI PADME HUM takes us to enlightenment, there is no doubt about the others who give us vows, initiations and commentaries and perform other Dharma activities. Our gurus give us the three levels of vows—pratimoksha, bodhisattva and tantric—oral transmissions, initiations, sutra and tantra commentaries and personal advice. Their actions definitely lead us to enlightenment. The lam-rim teachings explain that these are the actions of the buddhas, of the dharmakaya, the holy mind of all the buddhas. Therefore, since their holy mind is dharmakaya, our gurus are buddhas.

Everything our gurus do for us protects us from delusions and karma, the cause of suffering, and thus from suffering. Every single thing that they do, even scolding us, purifies our negative karma. Everything they do also plants seeds of the path to enlightenment in our mind, causing us to achieve realizations of the path. By planting seeds in our mind, they definitely bring us to enlightenment.

So, if our present gurus are not buddhas and if their actions are not the actions of the buddhas, there's nobody else to point out as the buddhas that bring us to enlightenment. Therefore, our gurus have to be buddhas.

When we have transformed our mind into the devotion that sees our gurus as buddhas and their actions as the buddhas' actions, we should maintain that experience for a while by doing fixed meditation on the conclusion that each of our gurus is a buddha and the doer of the actions of all the buddhas.

Also, if the actions of our gurus—giving us vows, oral transmissions, initiations, commentaries and instructions—are not the actions of the buddhas guiding us to enlightenment, we have to conclude that all our gurus are ordinary beings and ordinary beings are revealing Dharma to us and guiding us to enlightenment. After promising to guide us, the numberless past, present and future buddhas have disappeared. If these ordinary beings are the ones guiding us to enlightenment, it looks as if all the buddhas are sleeping or taking a holiday. Something is wrong with the way the superstitious mind thinks because it comes to the conclusion that the numberless buddhas of the past, present and future are not working for and guiding sentient beings.

This would mean that the buddhas don't have omniscient mind, don't have compassion for us or don't have the perfect power to guide us. Or it means that there is no such thing as a buddha. According to this way of thinking, it looks as if the particular sentient beings who are teaching us are much more capable and skillful in guiding us than the enlightened beings of the three times. There is no way this could be true. A buddha has omniscient mind, infinite compassion for all sentient beings and the perfect power to guide them. Only a being with all these three qualities receives the name "buddha."

The buddhas having to rely on ordinary sentient beings, our gurus, to accomplish their works for sentient beings would be like a king having to rely on beggars for his food. And, since ordinary sentient beings would then be more powerful and skillful than the buddhas in accomplishing the works for others, there would be no need to attempt to achieve enlightenment.

Also, if even an ordinary person with a compassionate, sincere nature doesn't deceive us, how is it possible that the buddhas would deceive us? There is no way that buddhas, having trained their minds in compassion, would promise to guide us and then not guide us. There is no way the buddhas would lie to or cheat sentient beings. Their great compassion would never allow it because the function of compassion is not to harm sentient beings. Harm to sentient beings comes out of delusions and buddhas have no delusions—even arhats don't have delusions.

Since there is no doubt that buddhas have infinite compassion for all sentient beings, the buddhas definitely have to guide us. Since the actions of our virtuous friends are guiding us to enlightenment, if they are not the buddhas guiding us, there is no one else to point out.

Again reach the conclusion that your gurus must be buddhas and that they are the doers of all the buddhas' actions. Do fixed meditation on this conclusion, keeping your mind in the devotion that looks at each of them as a buddha.

The actions of all the buddhas are received in the mind of the disciple through the guru. During a retreat or at other times when we are doing powerful Dharma practice, we might dream that our guru is very pleased with us and gives us a present or some advice. The interesting question is,

Why did this dream happen? Even though we haven't directly informed our guru about what we are doing, at times when we perform some great purification or some practice of great benefit to the teachings or to other sentient beings, we dream that our guru is very happy with us. This happens when we have done something very positive, something that is very pleasing to all the buddhas. Because we did something that brought great purification or accumulated extensive merit, we pleased all the buddhas.

At other times, when we have committed or are in danger of committing a heavy negative karma, we might dream of our guru being upset or ill or scolding us, even though he doesn't directly know that we have done anything wrong.

Such dreams of the virtuous friend have deep meaning and can be related to the sutra and tantra teachings on guru devotion. They help us to understand that the ordinary aspect of our guru is the manifestation of all the buddhas and that all the buddhas are working through this aspect to guide us. Through the aspect of the guru, the buddhas can communicate with us even in dreams.

Sakya Pandita said,

> Even though sunbeams are very hot,
> Without a magnifying glass, they can't ignite a fire.
> It is the same with the blessings of the buddhas:
> Without the guru, they cannot enter the disciple.

Dawö Rinchen, a disciple of Gyalwa Götsangpa, said a similar thing:

> When the intervening obscurations are purified,
> The power of the sun focuses on the tinder
> By the dependent arising of the clear magnifying glass.

> When the thought of faults is purified,
> The blessings of the buddhas of the ten directions
> Enter the mind of the disciple
> By the auspiciousness of the perfectly qualified guru.

In Solu Khumbu in the past, when there were no matches, people made a fire by using a flint and a stone to give a spark, which would then cause some dry grass or leaves to catch fire. Sakya Pandita used the slightly different example of a magnifying glass. No matter how hot the sun is, if there is no magnifying glass, the sun cannot make a fire. Like that, no matter how many buddhas there are, without the guru in this ordinary aspect, the buddhas can't guide us. No matter how many qualities and how much power they have, the buddhas have to depend on this guru in ordinary aspect. Only through this aspect can they cease our delusions, the cause of suffering, and the defilements on our mental continuum, then bring us to liberation and enlightenment.

Even if the sun is shining and we have dry grass or tinder, without a magnifying glass we can't start a fire. When sunbeams hit tinder through a magnifying glass, however, fire comes effortlessly. In a similar way, the blessings of all the buddhas, who are like the sun, come through the guru, who is like a magnifying glass, to the minds of the disciples, who are like the tinder. Even though the fire comes about through the beams of the sun passing through the magnifying glass, the actual function of producing fire comes from the magnifying glass. Like a magnifying glass, the guru burns the delusions in the disciple's mind.

Without these gurus in ordinary aspect, there is no way that we can receive the blessings of the buddhas; there is also no way that we can receive the buddhas' actions of teaching and so forth. Even though the buddhas have omniscient mind, compassion and perfect power, they cannot destroy our disturbing thoughts and develop our mind without the gurus. All the buddhas can guide us only through our gurus. Therefore, even though there are numberless buddhas, without the ordinary forms of our gurus' holy bodies, we would be lost. These aspects become so important and so precious to us because without them there is no way for us to receive guidance.

The sutra *Stainless Sky* also mentions,

> We should regard the virtuous friend as more precious than the tathagatas. Why? Even though buddhas are very compassionate and skillful beings, without the self-condition of the guru, the buddhas' actions cannot enter the mental continuum of the sentient beings, who are the objects to be subdued.

Just as the sun can perform the function of burning tinder only in dependence upon the self-condition of a magnifying glass, all the past, present and future buddhas can perform the function of guiding sentient beings to enlightenment only in dependence upon the guru. Even the buddhas themselves cannot happen without the guru; they are born from the guru. As Buddhajñana explains, "Before the guru there is not even the name 'buddha.'" Therefore, we should regard our gurus as more precious than all the buddhas of the ten directions.

Another effective way to meditate is to think of the guru as being like a rope and ourselves as being down in a deep pit of fire. Being in samsara is like being in a fire. When we have fallen into a fiery pit, the people standing at the top of the hole can't rescue us without a rope. In a similar way, without the guru, all the buddhas of the three times and ten directions can't guide us to enlightenment.

Correctly devoting ourselves to the guru is like grabbing hold of the rope that is sent down to us by the buddhas. If we hold onto the rope, there is no doubt that we can be saved from the fiery pit. If we hold onto our gurus, if we correctly devote ourselves to our gurus, there is no doubt that we can be saved from the sufferings of samsara, particularly those of the three lower realms, and also from the lower nirvana.

Not devoting ourselves correctly to our gurus is like ignoring the rope that is sent down to us. If we don't grab hold of the rope, we can't be saved. Even though there are numberless buddhas, if we don't devote ourselves to our gurus, no matter how much we devote ourselves to those other buddhas, they have no means to directly guide us. If we don't correctly devote ourselves to our gurus, these aspects in whom all the buddhas of the three times have manifested in order to guide us, there will be no method to save us from samsara and guide us to enlightenment.

(iv) **Vajradhara asserted that the guru is a buddha** In the second chapter of the tantric text *Two Investigations*, Vajradhara says,

> In the degenerate time, I, who am called Vajrasattva, will abide in the form of the spiritual master. With the aim of benefiting sentient beings, I will abide in ordinary forms.

In the tantric text *Vajra Tent*, Vajradhara says,

> In the future degenerate times, I will manifest as a child and in various forms as a means.

In the same text, Vajradhara also mentions,

In the final five-hundred-year period,[80] I will manifest in the holy body of the leader of disciples At that time you should believe it is me and generate devotion.

Another tantra says,

At the end of time the All-Pervasive Lord[81] himself will manifest in the ordinary body of the holy virtuous friend and guide the transmigratory beings of the degenerate time.

While these quotations come from tantric texts, there are also quotations from the sutras. Once on a high mountain in south India where Guru Shakyamuni Buddha was teaching, bodhisattva Amoghadarshi asked Buddha, "At the moment we can receive teachings from the Buddha, but what shall we do in the future when you have passed beyond sorrow? Who will guide us?" Guru Shakyamuni Buddha replied, "Amoghadarshi, in degenerate times in the future, I will manifest in the forms of spiritual masters and abbots. In order to ripen the minds of sentient beings, I will also show birth, old age, sickness and death. Don't worry that you will not meet me in the degenerate times. At that time I shall manifest as the abbot or as the teacher."

In other words, Guru Shakyamuni Buddha said that in the future he would take ordinary forms and manifest experiencing the samsaric problems of birth, old age, sickness and death. Amoghadarshi asked this question on behalf of all sentient beings and Buddha's reply was meant not only for Amoghadarshi but for all sentient beings.

Also, in the sutra *Great Gone Beyond Sorrow* Buddha explains,

Even though I have shown passing beyond sorrow in this great land of Dzambu, in the end I have not gone beyond sorrow completely. Even though I have shown being conceived in a mother's womb in this land of Dzambu, it is just for my mother and father to recognize me as their son; my holy body wasn't born from the gathering of attachment. My holy body does not have suf-

---

[80] Shakyamuni Buddha predicted that his teachings would endure for ten 500-year periods.
[81] This is an epithet of Vajradhara.

ferings of hunger and thirst, but in order to fit with the beings of this world, I also show hunger and thirst. Other than that, I also show myself as an ordinary being to individual beings. I have had profound wisdom for countless eons. Even though I have passed completely beyond the world created by grasping, I show walking, sitting and other conducts. I show having headaches, stomach aches, backaches and boils. I wash my legs, hands, face and mouth, and clean my teeth with a tooth stick. Even though individual ordinary beings believe I have all these problems, my holy body has none of these problems.

There are many such quotations where Guru Shakyamuni Buddha said that he would manifest for the benefit of sentient beings. Even though Buddha himself has no suffering, he manifests having suffering; even though Buddha has no faults, he manifests having faults.

Also, in the past when Shakyamuni Buddha was the bodhisattva Brahma Samudraraja, he generated bodhicitta and made five hundred special prayers in the presence of his guru Ratnagarbha. He prayed, "In the future quarreling time of the five degenerations, when the lifespan of human beings in this world will be one hundred years, I will guide and subdue the sentient beings of that time, who the other thousand buddhas of the fortunate eon found too difficult to subdue." Buddha voluntarily took this responsibility upon himself. This quotation, usually found in the section on the kindness of the guru, can also be related to this outline.

Now, our age is the quarreling time and we are the sentient beings for whom Buddha generated great compassion and promised to guide. There is no doubt that Buddha must be guiding us. We should ask ourselves, "Who is the Buddha that is guiding me to enlightenment in this quarreling time?" The Guru Shakyamuni Buddha who is guiding us is none other than our present gurus, who are showing us the path to enlightenment. There is no one else to point out except our gurus. Therefore, our gurus are definitely Guru Shakyamuni Buddha.

There are many quotations from Guru Shakyamuni Buddha and Buddha Vajradhara explaining how, in order to guide sentient beings in the future, they would manifest in the forms of virtuous friends and in various other forms. Who else can that be but our present virtuous friends? If the teachers that we have visualized in the merit field are not the embodiments of Vajradhara, who else can we point out? There is nobody else to point out as the ones guiding us to enlightenment except these virtuous friends. Therefore, our virtuous friends are definitely buddhas.

Such stories and quotations give us more feeling and make it easy for us to generate devotion, the root of the path. They help us to lean more to the side that the guru is a buddha. They help to change our mind from the wrong conception that thinks the guru is an ordinary being and not a buddha.

Meditate on this outline then come to the conclusion that each of your gurus is a buddha. Completely decide that each guru in essence is Guru Shakyamuni Buddha or Vajradhara, who promised to subdue the sentient beings of the degenerate time, who are so difficult to subdue. Once you have reached this conclusion and proved to your mind that each of your gurus is a buddha, keep your mind in that state of guru devotion.

13. Debating with the Superstitious Mind

THERE'S A BRIEF but effective technique used by the lineage lamas to meditate on the four outlines of how to see the guru as a buddha as explained in *Liberation in the Palm of Your Hand* and other lam-rim texts. This presentation helps to cut off some of the wrong views in relation to guru devotion practice. We do analytical meditation by debating with and defeating our own superstitious mind, which sees faults in the guru. We debate with our superstitious mind until it runs out of answers.

First, visualize all your gurus, without leaving any one out. Then ask your superstition, "Are all my gurus buddhas?" Just pose the question—don't put forward any reasons to prove that they are buddhas. Superstition, your opponent in the debate, will then answer, "Even though you say that all these gurus are buddhas, all you're doing is imagining it."

You then introduce the first outline of how to see the guru as a buddha, *Vajradhara asserted that the guru is a buddha*. You tell the superstitious mind, "My gurus are buddhas. Why? Because in many sutra and tantra scriptures Vajradhara says that he will manifest in ordinary forms in future degenerate times—and a buddha doesn't lie to sentient beings. In the tantric text *Two Investigations* Vajradhara says, 'In the degenerate time, I, who am called Vajrasattva, will abide in the form of the spiritual master. With the aim to benefit sentient beings, I will abide in ordinary forms.' There are similar quotations in *Vajra Tent* and many other texts. Therefore, my gurus are buddhas."

When you put forward these quotations to negate your superstition, it argues, "No, no, no! It's not like this! Even if you tell me all these quotations, it still doesn't mean that all these gurus are buddhas. It means that among all these gurus, one of them is a buddha."

You then ask, "Then which one is a buddha?" With all your gurus visualized in front of you, you check each one with your superstition, "Is this one a buddha?" Superstition replies, "No. This one is not a buddha because I see that he has faults. He is very angry (or impatient or ignorant or desirous or immoral or miserly...)." Since the superstitious mind is trying to find faults, it will definitely see some faults there.

You try another guru, "Is this one a buddha?" Superstition again responds, "Oh, no—I see many faults in this one." As you keep checking your gurus one after another in this way, your superstitious mind will point out faults in all of them. Superstition will see faults in every single guru; it's simply a question of whether the fault is large or small.

You then argue, "If you say that a guru is not a buddha for the reason that you see mistakes in his actions, since you have found faults in every single guru, there is not one buddha among all your gurus. In that case, there is not one buddha working for you. This makes you the unluckiest sentient being, because you have been abandoned by all the buddhas.

"With great compassion, the buddhas cherish all sentient beings as objects to be subdued. They cherish sentient beings more than sentient beings cherish themselves. If you had been abandoned by all the buddhas, it would mean that buddhas have partiality of mind, guiding some sentient beings but not others, and that their promises are lies.

"While Guru Shakyamuni Buddha was a bodhisattva following the path, his motivation for achieving enlightenment was to work for all sentient beings. How is it possible that after achieving enlightenment Buddha stopped working for you? It's not possible! If Buddha had this motivation even before entering the Mahayana path, he is definitely working for you now. Therefore, among these virtuous friends, there is definitely at least one who is a buddha."

If you follow your superstitious mind you reach the conclusion that what Vajradhara and Guru Shakyamuni Buddha asserted is not true, that they are telling lies and are therefore not worthwhile objects of refuge. If a buddha cheats sentient beings, it means that you can't trust anybody. There's then nobody who can save you from samsara, especially the lower realms, and from the lower nirvana; there's nobody who can guide you.

Argue further with your superstitious mind. "If none of your gurus is a buddha, they are all just ordinary beings with faults. There is then no one to point out as the buddhas guiding you to enlightenment. By revealing the teachings to you—giving you vows, oral transmissions, initiations, commentaries and so forth—these ordinary beings are leading you to enlightenment but the buddhas aren't. It leads to the impossible conclusion that these ordinary beings are more skillful than buddhas. These ordinary beings are working very hard to bring you to enlightenment but the buddhas aren't doing anything for you. Buddha is hiding somewhere or is a fairy-tale. How is it possible that the buddhas have to depend on these virtuous friends, who are ordinary sentient beings, in order to work for you? This would be like a wealthy king having to beg food from a beggar in the street. How is it possible that ordinary beings are bringing you to enlightenment but the buddhas are not doing anything to benefit you?"

If you follow your superstitious thought, you make the big mistake of concluding that a buddha doesn't have all the qualities that are explained in the teachings. It leads you to the mistaken conclusion that the buddhas don't have compassion for you, don't have omniscient mind or don't have the power to guide you. The logical conclusion you reach is that in fact, there is no such thing as a buddha. It then leads you to the conclusion that there was no Guru Shakyamuni Buddha who showed the twelve deeds,[82] including enlightenment, in India. You are then contradicting what actually historically happened. You're saying that something that exists doesn't exist.

After having achieved enlightenment, the dharmakaya, a buddha effortlessly manifests sambhogakaya and nirmanakaya forms for the sake of others. Even to guide one sentient being, a buddha can manifest billions of forms and, with various actions of body, speech and mind, guide that sentient being in accordance with her level of mind. According to superstition, it would be impossible for buddhas to work effortlessly for others under their own power; they would have to rely on the help of ordinary sentient beings, these virtuous teachers. This would mean that buddhas had not achieved enlightenment.

Continue to argue with your superstition. "Even though it is not your present experience, it is the experience of Guru Shakyamuni Buddha and other enlightened beings that a buddha is able to work effortlessly for other sentient beings without depending on the help of others. There are

---

[82] For a list of Shakyamuni Buddha's twelve deeds, see *Opening the Eye of New Awareness* pp. 91–92.

definitely such enlightened beings who can work effortlessly for others in this way. Among all their actions, a buddha's highest action to guide sentient beings to enlightenment is revealing teachings. Your gurus are doing all the buddhas' actions that bring you to enlightenment; therefore, they are buddhas."

If the superstitious mind then insists, "These gurus are not buddhas because I can actually see their faults. It's not that I've just heard about them—I've actually seen them with my own eyes," you then debate with it in the following way. "You say that none of your gurus is a buddha because you actually see that they all have faults. Does everything that you 'actually see' exist? Even though your death could happen at any time, you actually believe that your life is permanent, that you are going to live for many years. And even though the I and other phenomena don't have inherent existence, you actually see them as inherently existent, the complete opposite of reality. If you have bile disease, you actually see a white conch shell or a snow mountain as yellow and if you have wind disease, you actually see white things as blue."

Many things that we actually see don't exist. We actually see things as permanent, we actually see things as truly existent, we actually see things in dreams and hallucinations, and we believe them to be true. You can refute the superstitious mind with the many other examples I mentioned previously.

"You actually see many things that don't exist; therefore, your actually seeing faults in your gurus doesn't alone prove that in reality they have faults. Your gurus don't necessarily exist in the way they appear to you to exist. Isn't it possible that the faults you see are the projections of your own hallucinated mind?"

The superstitious mind then argues, "If the gurus are buddhas, why don't I see them that way?"

You reply, "There are many other phenomena that exist that you don't see or that you see incorrectly. You don't see things as impermanent and empty of inherent existence, even though they exist in that way. The fact that you don't see your gurus as buddhas doesn't prove that they are not buddhas. The only person you can be certain is or is not a buddha is yourself. You can't decide about anyone else."

As Lama Tsongkhapa explained, you can also think that the guru even purposely manifests the faults that you see in order to subdue your mind and inspire your guru yoga practice. On the basis of Lama Tsongkhapa's advice, put the following questions to your superstitious mind, "Isn't it possible that your guru is purposely manifesting faults for your benefit? Isn't it possible that this is a buddha showing an ordinary aspect?" When you ask such questions to the superstitious mind, it finds them very difficult to answer.

The point here is not that you are trying to prove that someone else's guru is a buddha; you are trying to convince your mind that your own guru is a buddha. I remember when Geshe Rabten Rinpoche was once debating with someone at Sera Je College about whether or not Geshe Rabten's guru was a buddha. Geshe Rabten answered by making a gesture that meant his opponent should shut his mouth. Geshe Rabten then said, "You don't need to argue about whether or not my guru is a buddha. That is my responsibility and I understand. You have nothing to say on this matter."

In relation to your own gurus you have to think, "My gurus are buddhas." There's no discussion on that—for you, that is the practice. And not just the practice but the fundamental practice. It is the foundation of all the other practices of lam-rim. In terms of my relationships with my gurus, it is like that. No matter how others might want to debate that my gurus are not buddhas, from my side there is no questioning of that.

At the conclusion of this particular guru devotion meditation in which you debate with your superstitious mind, superstition might say, "Why do you need to look at a guru as a buddha? Just because someone is a guru doesn't necessarily mean that he has to be a buddha. I am also a guru—I teach Dharma and I have disciples—and I know from my own experience that I am not a buddha. My disciples don't need to look at me as a buddha because I am not a buddha. How can I tell them that they should think of me as a buddha?"

Dr. Nick [Ribush] raised this question when we were working together on the translation of this part of the guru devotion subject, debating with the superstitious mind, for the revised version of the first Kopan course book *The Wish-fulfilling Golden Sun*. The same question is also raised by the lineage lamas when they explain how to stop wrong conceptions when meditating on guru devotion. When you hear this question, you might be struck by it and think it is true. If your understanding isn't clear, there's a danger it will affect your practice of guru devotion, causing you to lose or to degenerate what little experience of guru devotion you have.

As I explained earlier, this is similar to thinking, "Oh, I've also been mother and kind to others," when meditating on the kindness of other sentient beings. That's useless. It doesn't help you to develop bodhicitta. Your thinking that you have also been mother to all sentient beings, even though it's true, doesn't help you to realize the kindness of other sentient beings. Thinking this has no benefit, but thinking how sentient beings have been mother and kind has benefit because you then feel it unbearable that others are suffering and you're able to generate loving kindness and compassion. From that then comes bodhicitta, the thought to achieve enlightenment for sentient beings. The whole aim is to benefit others. Thinking "I have been mother to all other sentient beings and been kind to them" doesn't help you accomplish your goal of achieving enlightenment for sentient beings.

It is similar here. Even though your reasoning is true, it doesn't help you. The main point is that for you to succeed in liberating the numberless sentient beings from the oceans of samsaric suffering and bringing them to enlightenment, you need to practice guru devotion. You have to understand this point. Otherwise, the thought can arise in your mind, "This Tibetan Buddhism is very strange. I teach Dharma to others but I'm not a buddha." You can then have doubts about the lam-rim and especially about this very first and most important meditation.

You debate with the superstitious mind in the following way. "You say that your disciples can't meditate on you as a buddha because you're not a buddha. But don't your disciples need to generate devotion by stopping the thought of your faults and looking at your good qualities? Don't your disciples need to devote themselves to you as their guru with thought and with action, where 'with thought' means recognizing you as a buddha? If, because you're not a buddha, you don't guide your disciples by teaching them about guru devotion, they will have no way to protect their minds when negative thoughts arise. They will then create negative karma and experience the sufferings of hell for many eons. This means that you are throwing your disciples into the hells."

If you are teaching Dharma to others, you have to explain guru devotion as much as possible out of compassion in order to guide your disciples and protect their minds. If you explain the subject with a good motivation, there is no risk. The point is that you're explaining it for the sake of your disciples so that they can attain enlightenment.

Of course, it doesn't mean that it is always suitable to teach guru devotion. It is best to explain it when you can see that it is the right time. If you try to explain guru devotion when others aren't receptive, it can create more obstacles.

Teaching guru devotion is the responsibility of the teacher and practicing guru devotion is the responsibility of the disciple. If guru devotion is not explained, it is the fault of the teacher; if it is not practiced after having been explained, it is the fault of the disciple.

The conclusion of this particular analytical meditation on guru devotion in which we debate with our superstitious mind is not only that there is nothing to trust in our own view but also that Vajradhara asserted that the guru is a buddha, the gurus are the doers of the buddhas' actions and even nowadays the buddhas and bodhisattvas are working for sentient beings, including us. Even if we don't visualize our gurus in the aspects of buddhas, we concentrate one-pointedly on the feeling that they are buddhas. We keep our mind in that state, with recognition of our gurus as buddhas, for as long as we can.

Wrong thoughts toward the guru don't usually arise right at the beginning when we first meet the Dharma and first hear the teachings. It is after some time that many wrong thoughts arise toward the practice of guru devotion and we start to look at things in a negative way. This meditation is especially useful at that time.

Lama Zopa Rinpoche and Lama Yeshe, Kopan, Nepal, 1977

14. The Kindness of the Guru

(2) DEVELOPING RESPECT BY REMEMBERING THE GURU'S KINDNESS

THE SECOND major division of devoting to the guru with thought is *developing respect by remembering the guru's kindness*. Actually, the Tibetan word *gü-pa* doesn't mean simply respect but something more like reverence. This outline has four sections:

(a) The guru is kinder than all the buddhas
(b) The guru's kindness in teaching Dharma
(c) The guru's kindness in blessing our mindstream
(d) The guru's kindness in inspiring us to practice Dharma through material gifts

The guru's main kindness is in teaching Dharma.

When remembering the kindness of our gurus we should recall their kindness in guiding us not only during this life but during beginningless lives. Our gurus are the absolute guru, the dharmakaya; therefore, our present gurus are all the gurus from our beginningless past lives who have guided us to the point of our present perfect human body and they are the same ones who, in our future lives, will guide us to enlightenment. Each of our gurus has been kind to us during beginningless samsaric lifetimes, is kind to us in this life and will also be kind to us in the future, until we achieve enlightenment. Recognizing our guru's past, present and future kindness deepens our appreciation of his kindness.

Here it helps to understand the meaning of "unified primordial savior" [Tib: *zung jug dang pöi gön po*], an expression found in one of the requesting verses in *Guru Puja*.[83] It describes the all-pervasive Vajradhara. If we keep in mind the real meaning of guru, we can see all our past-life gurus as just one. All our gurus—those who gave us vows and teachings in all our past lives, the gurus we have now and those we will have in the future—are just one being: the unified primordial savior, the primordial dharmakaya.

All our past, present and future gurus are just one, and they guide us through the conventional guru, who appears in accordance with our karma. This is the aspect we can see and receive direct guidance from. This is all our past-life gurus, all our present gurus and all our future-life gurus.

That unified primordial savior, that dharmakaya, that absolute guru, is bound by infinite compassion that embraces every single one of the numberless sentient beings. Why is the absolute guru working for us sentient beings? Because of compassion for all sentient beings. Compassion is like a pilot who flies a plane to different places, taking people to wherever they wish to be. The absolute guru is bound by perfect compassion, by compassion for all sentient beings, without excluding even one.

When meditating on the kindness of the guru, it is good to read the relevant verses in *The Essence of Nectar* (see appendix 5) and the first few lines of the abbreviated *Calling the Lama from Afar* (see appendix 2) and relate these verses to each of our gurus. Those who have studied *Liberation in the Palm of Your Hand* can use the section in *The Essence of Nectar* to expand their meditation on the kindness of the guru; those who haven't had the chance to study *Liberation in the Palm of Your Hand* can use *The Essence of Nectar* to guide their meditation on the kindness of the guru and their practice of pleasing the guru with action. I find these verses very effective for my mind.

The words of *The Essence of Nectar* are profound and effective, as in the verse at the end of the requesting prayer to the lineage lamas:

> The compassion of all the numberless Victorious Ones
> Manifested in the holy body of the supreme virtuous friend who
>   reveals the path.
> To the kind root guru, I request,
> Please bless my mental continuum.

---

[83] Arising from the play of omniscient pristine awareness,
You are the essence of ten million mandala cycles.
Pervading lord of a hundred buddha families, foremost vajra holder,
Unified primordial savior, I make requests to you. (V. 51.)

(a) The guru is kinder than all the buddhas

This section has two parts:

(i) the guru is kinder than all the buddhas in general
(ii) the guru is kinder than Guru Shakyamuni Buddha in particular.

While in terms of good qualities the guru is equal to all the buddhas, in terms of kindness the guru is much kinder than all the buddhas of the three times. More specifically, the guru is kinder than even the present founder of the Buddhadharma, Guru Shakyamuni Buddha, who is also kinder than all the buddhas of the three times.

(i) The guru is kinder than all the buddhas in general *The Essence of Nectar* says,

> Not only are these, my saviors,
> Of the essence of all the Victorious Ones;
> In constantly guiding me with the nectar of holy Dharma,
> Their kindness is much greater than that of all the Victorious Ones.

Also, as mentioned in the requesting prayer in *Guru Puja*,

> To those untamed by countless past buddhas,
> The unruly migrators of this degenerate age who are difficult to
>   subdue,
> You show unmistakenly the good way of those gone to bliss.
> Compassionate refuge savior, I make requests to you.[84]

During our beginningless rebirths, countless buddhas have descended and led numberless sentient beings to enlightenment but we have been left out, unable to be guided by them. In his lam-rim teachings, Pabongka Dechen Nyingpo gives us some idea of how many buddhas have appeared in this world.

Between Buddha Mahashakyamuni and Buddha Rashtrapala, 75,000 buddhas appeared in this world but we were not subdued by them. This

[84] V. 46.

doesn't mean that we didn't exist in samsara at that time but that we didn't have the karma to be subdued by those buddhas. As explained in the vinaya teachings, Guru Shakyamuni Buddha made offerings to these 75,000 buddhas in the first countless great eon of his following the path to enlightenment.

Next came Buddha Bhadrakara, and between Buddha Bhadrakara and Buddha Indradhvaja, 76,000 buddhas appeared in this world but again we didn't have the fortune to be guided by any of them. When each of these buddhas descended, numberless other sentient beings had the karma to be led in the path to enlightenment and enlightened by them but we were left out; we didn't have the karma to be subdued by them. Guru Shakyamuni Buddha made offerings to these 76,000 buddhas in the second countless great eon of his following the path.

Then, between Buddha Dipamkara and Buddha Kashyapa, 77,000 buddhas appeared in this world; but even though each of these buddhas subdued numberless sentient beings and led them to enlightenment, we didn't have the karma to be subdued by them. We were left out once more. Guru Shakyamuni Buddha made offerings to these 77,000 buddhas in the third countless great eon of his following the path.

According to the general sutra vehicle, the kind founder, Guru Shakyamuni Buddha, accumulated merit by serving and making offerings to all these buddhas for three countless great eons, but specifically according to the Mahayana, as explained in *Sutra of the Moon Lamp* and other Mahayana sutras, Buddha offered service to countless times ten million buddhas, equal to the number of sand grains of the Ganges River. Even though such an incredible number of buddhas appeared, we were unable to be subdued by any of them. Yet we, who were unable to be subdued by all those previous buddhas, are now being guided by our present gurus.

Of the one thousand buddhas of this fortunate eon, three buddhas descended prior to Guru Shakyamuni Buddha. In this present eon, when the length of life of human beings in this world was 80,000 years, Buddha Krakucchanda appeared in this world and, by revealing Dharma, subdued countless sentient beings and led them to liberation and enlightenment, but we were left out, unable to be guided by him. When the human lifespan had decreased to 40,000 years, the second Buddha, Kanakamuni, appeared and, by revealing Dharma, subdued numberless sentient beings and led them to enlightenment. However, we were left out; we didn't have the karma to be guided by this buddha. When the human lifespan had decreased to 20,000 years, Buddha Kashyapa appeared and, by revealing Dharma, subdued numberless sentient beings and brought them to liberation and enlightenment. Again we were left out. Even though these buddhas appeared, revealed Dharma and enlightened countless sentient beings, we didn't have the fortune to be subdued by any of them. Our present gurus, however, are now guiding us—what could be kinder than this? In this way, our present gurus are kinder than all those numberless buddhas.

It's as if our gurus give us food when we are starving and about to die, while the buddhas give us food when we already have plenty to eat. Or our guru is like a guide who suddenly, unexpectedly, appears and leads us to safety when we are terrified, lost and alone in a dark and dangerous place surrounded by packs of savage animals, whereas the buddhas are like those who come to guide us in the daytime when we are walking happily and fearlessly in a beautiful flower garden. In other words, when we have accumulated the merit to be able to see buddhas, our mind is already in a high state that is not greatly disturbed by delusions and defilements.

In *Calling the Lama from Afar* Pabongka Dechen Nyingpo says,

> Thinking of how you show the excellent unmistaken path to me,
> an unfortunate wretched being, abandoned by all the buddhas—
> reminds me of you, Lama.

There have been numberless buddhas in countless universes, but we haven't been subdued by any of them. During our beginningless past lives, we didn't have the fortune to receive teachings directly from those buddhas and become enlightened. Numberless other sentient beings who were wandering in samsara with us have become enlightened, but we still haven't achieved any realizations. Like this, we are pitiful. We are like the bone in meat, which can't be eaten and has been cast aside. We are like the student who has been kicked out of school because he is impossible to help.

Numberless other sentient beings have become enlightened during our beginningless rebirths but we have been left out, which shows very clearly how selfish and unsubdued our mind has been. Even though our mind is like this and we are so pitiful, our guru has shown us the complete and unmistaken path to the happiness of future lives, liberation and enlightenment. Even if each guru hasn't personally revealed the whole path, all our gurus together have shown us the complete path. Therefore, they are unbelievably kind, and without wasting this opportunity, we must practice this path, on the basis of correctly devoting ourselves to our virtuous friends.

(ii) The guru is kinder than Guru Shakyamuni Buddha in particular The wheel-turning king, Aranemi, had one thousand sons, who will be the one thousand buddhas of the fortunate eon. When they generated the altruistic mind of bodhicitta, each of them vowed to subdue a particular field of sentient beings. Except for the son called Brahma Samudraraja, who would later become Guru Shakyamuni Buddha, all the rest of the one thousand sons made prayers to guide sentient beings in good times in this world. We were left out because those bodhisattvas were unable to generate the altruistic mind in relation to us. Guru Shakyamuni Buddha was the only one who specifically vowed to guide the sentient beings of the quarreling age, when the lifespan would be one hundred years and life would be very difficult because of the explosion of the five degenerations, with many wars, famines and other disasters. When Brahma Samudraraja generated bodhicitta, he made five hundred great prayers in front of his guru Buddha Ratnagarbha to be able to descend during the quarreling age and subdue the sentient beings of this time, who are so difficult to subdue and have been left out by all the other buddhas. The devas then praised this bodhisattva, saying, "You are like a white lotus among the one thousand buddhas."

In this quarreling age, Guru Shakyamuni Buddha, the founder of the present Buddhadharma, appeared in this world in the country of the aryas, India, revealed the Dharma and enlightened numberless sentient beings.

When Magadhabhadri invited Guru Shakyamuni Buddha from very far away to her house in Magadha with the invocation prayer "Protector of all beings without exception...,"[85] Buddha took the time it takes to stretch out an arm to come from where he was to her house. Even during that short period of time Buddha liberated seven thousand sentient beings in the roads and forests along the way. This was just one occasion—there were so many others. However, on all such occasions, even though so many sentient beings, including animals, were liberated, we were unable to be subdued by Guru Shakyamuni Buddha.

Guru Shakyamuni Buddha taught Dharma in Rajghir and many other

---

[85] Protector of all beings without exception;
Divine destroyer of the intractable legions of Mara;
Perfect knower of all things:
Bhagavan and retinue, please come here.

places but we didn't have the fortune to be his direct disciples and hear teachings directly from Buddha, achieve realizations of the path and become enlightened along with his other disciples. We were left out; we didn't have the karma to be subdued by Guru Shakyamuni Buddha. Now, when the Buddha's teaching is setting like the sun and everything is about to become dark in this world, our gurus are guiding us by revealing the Dharma. While Guru Shakyamuni Buddha is kinder than all the other buddhas of the three times, our virtuous friends are even kinder than Buddha.

After Guru Shakyamuni Buddha passed away, many great yogis and pandits appeared, like stars in the sky. The Seven Patriarchs—the Hearer Kashyapa, Ananda, Upagupta and so forth[86]—guided so many sentient beings, leading them in the path to liberation and enlightenment. However, we didn't have the karma to be subdued by them. Even the one arhat, Upagupta, offered unbelievably extensive benefit to sentient beings. Each time one of his disciples became an arhat, Upagupta put one stick in a huge hole, twelve cubits square by six cubits deep, that he had dug in the ground. He completely filled that huge hole with sticks. Upagupta had 1,800,000 disciples who directly perceived emptiness. Even this one arhat liberated so many sentient beings but we didn't have the karma to be liberated by him at that time.

The Six Ornaments—Nagarjuna, Asanga and so forth[87]—beautified the world and the Two Sublime Beings—Shakyaprabha and Gunaprabha—appeared, as did the Eighty Mahasiddhas: great yogis such as Saraha, Tilopa, Naropa, Indrabhuti and so forth.[88] Each one of them brought unbelievable benefit to sentient beings by leading them in the path to liberation and enlightenment. Even though all these pandits and yogis appeared and ripened the minds of so many sentient beings, we didn't have enough merit to be subdued by them. We were left out by all these pandits and yogis.

Even in Tibet, there were many, many great yogis. In the early times in Tibet, the trio of the Abbot (Shantarakshita), the Master (Padmasambhava) and the Dharma King (Trisong Detsen) appeared. Padmasambhava

---

[86] The Seven Patriarchs are Kashyapa, Ananda, Shanavatsa, Upagupta, Dhitika, Krishna and Mahasudarshana.

[87] The Six Ornaments are Nagarjuna, Aryadeva, Asanga, Vasubandhu, Dignaga and Dharmakirti.

[88] For details of the Eighty Mahasiddhas, see *Buddha's Lions: The Lives of the Eighty-Four Siddhas*.

had twenty-five special followers, who achieved high realizations. They subdued great numbers of sentient beings and led them in the path to liberation and enlightenment but at that time we didn't have the karma to be guided by them.

Many great yogis appeared from the Nyingma, Kagyü and Sakya traditions. At Drak Yerpa, a holy place near Lhasa, eight great Nyingma yogis who practiced secret mantra appeared. Kunga Nyingpo and the other great pandits known as the Five Sakya Lords benefited an unimaginable number of sentient beings by leading them in the path to liberation and enlightenment. Marpa, Milarepa and many other Kagyü lamas also appeared. One teaching explains that even among the disciples of Milarepa, twenty-eight became enlightened in one life, like Milarepa himself, and thousands of others actualized the clear light and illusory body as well as other realizations of the path to enlightenment. So many great yogis appeared in Tibet but we didn't have the karma to be subdued by any of them. We were left out.

We also didn't have the karma to see and receive teachings from Lama Atisha or any of the Kadampa geshes. We didn't have the karma to see and receive teachings even from Lama Tsongkhapa and his disciples, founders of the new Kadampa tradition. An inconceivable number of sentient beings received teachings from Lama Tsongkhapa and his disciples and were led to liberation and full enlightenment. But we were left out; we didn't have the karma to be subdued by them.

Like stars in the sky, an inconceivable number of holy beings—buddhas, bodhisattvas, highly attained pandits and yogis—have appeared in India, Tibet and other places and have liberated numberless sentient beings, but we didn't have the karma to receive teachings from or be subdued by them. Having created negative karma, we were wandering in the lower realms and didn't have the fortune to be subdued by them. So far, during beginningless rebirths, we have been permanent residents in samsara, especially the lower realms.

Like a discarded bone, we have been cast aside by Guru Shakyamuni Buddha, all the Indian pandits and all the great Tibetan yogis. However, since our present gurus are guiding us, they are much kinder than all those other holy beings. If we hadn't met our present gurus we would be completely ignorant. We would be called a human being simply because we have the external form of a human. If we hadn't met our present gurus we would have had no opportunity at all to practice Mahayana Dharma, to create the cause of temporary and ultimate happiness and to abandon the cause of suffering. We would have had no opportunity to make preparation for the happiness of future lives, liberation and enlightenment.

If our present gurus weren't guiding us, what would happen to us? We would be completely lost. There would be nobody to guide us on the path to the happiness of future lives and especially to liberation and full enlightenment. Therefore, our gurus are extremely kind, kinder than all the buddhas before Guru Shakyamuni Buddha and kinder than even Guru Shakyamuni Buddha. We should think, "How extremely kind my gurus are to guide me."

In his requesting prayer, the great bodhisattva Thogme Zangpo says,

> You liberate the extremely foolish and stubborn ones,
> Unable to be liberated by the many Gone to Bliss,
> From the ocean of samsara so difficult to cross:
> To you, precious Lord of Dharma, I make request.

Relate this verse to yourself. Because you are so deeply ignorant, stubborn and difficult to subdue, you have been left out by all the buddhas. Think of yourself, recognizing your own nature, then think of the kindness of your guru in liberating you from the ocean of samsara that is difficult to cross.

As mentioned in the requesting prayer in *Guru Puja,*

> At this time when the sun-like teachings of the Sage are setting,
> You enact the deeds of a conqueror
> For the many beings who lack a savior refuge.
> Compassionate refuge savior, I make requests to you.[89]

At this time the teachings of the Buddha are like a setting sun, about to disappear from this world. However, when sentient beings are completely lost, the gurus—sole saviors and objects of refuge for us and other sentient beings—perform the actions of all the buddhas. By remembering this verse, meditate on the kindness of the guru.

None of the previous buddhas and great yogis were able to subdue us; we were abandoned, like a child left alone in a jungle full of wild animals on a dark moonless night. Imagine being a child lost in an unknown place on a

[89] V. 47.

pitch-black night; you would be terrified. With no light and nobody to ask for help, you would be in a pitiful state. While you were lost and terrified, somebody's suddenly appearing in front of you with a light would seem like a miracle. If this person was someone who you could trust and who could guide you out of the jungle, you would regard this person who saved your life as incredibly kind and precious.

This person's kindness, however, is nothing compared to the kindness of our gurus, who save us from all the sufferings of samsara, including the unimaginable sufferings of the lower realms. We have been wandering, lost, in samsara, in the darkness of ignorance with no light of Dharma wisdom and attacked by many samsaric sufferings. We have been without a guide, left out by all the previous buddhas, including even Guru Shakyamuni Buddha, and by all the past pandits and yogis. At this most difficult time, our present gurus are showing us the light of Dharma wisdom and guiding us to liberation and enlightenment. There is no greater kindness than this.

At this time when we are deeply ignorant and unable to see any buddhas or bodhisattvas, our present gurus are unimaginably kind in manifesting in ordinary forms, which accord exactly with the level of our mind. It is only through these present ordinary aspects that we can receive the guidance of all the numberless buddhas of the three times. In showing ordinary aspects, our gurus are extremely kind because they thus enable all the buddhas to guide us to enlightenment. These ordinary aspects are extremely precious because without them we have no way to receive guidance from any of the numberless buddhas.

I think that even the aspects of the gurus with whom we have a karmic connection is an essential point in this meditation—we receive the guidance of all the buddhas through the aspect of this person with whom we have a karmic connection from the past. If there were no karmic connection with this particular person, he couldn't benefit us in this way. We can understand this from our own individual experiences: when we have no karma with somebody we never establish a connection by meeting or hearing Dharma from that person.

Without these ordinary aspects, we have no way to receive teachings, no way to put them into practice and no way to achieve liberation from samsara or enlightenment. Without these ordinary aspects, we would be completely lost. We would have nobody to take care of us, nobody to guide us on the correct path to the happiness of future lives, liberation and enlightenment.

This is the only way that we can achieve enlightenment and then bring all sentient beings to enlightenment. Therefore, these ordinary aspects with faults are extremely kind and precious.

Keep on developing respect by remembering the guru's kindness. The emphasis here is not so much on external respect but on respect in our heart, on devotion. This meditation on the guru manifesting in ordinary aspect also becomes part of remembering the kindness of the guru.

(b) The guru's kindness in teaching Dharma

In his past lives as a bodhisattva, Guru Shakyamuni Buddha sacrificed what was dearest to him to receive even a single verse of teaching. For example, when he was born as King Vyilingalita, he drove one thousand nails into his holy body. When he was born as King Ganashanapala, he lit one thousand lamps on his holy body. When he was King Suvarna, he had to allow vicious *yakshas* to eat his beloved wife and son. When he was King Utpala, using his skin as paper and one of his bones as a pen, he wrote the teachings that he heard with his own blood.

Lama Atisha also went through much hardship and many dangers to receive the teachings, traveling by boat for thirteen months to Indonesia.

When twenty-one Tibetan students were sent by the Dharma King of Tibet to study at Nalanda in order to revive Dharma in Tibet, all but two of them died from the heat. The Dharma kings of Tibet, Lhalama Yeshe Ö and Jangchub Ö, had to give up the gold that had been collected to invite Lama Atisha to Tibet and Lhalama Yeshe Ö gave up even his life to spread the teachings. They persevered despite great hardships.

Without needing to bear even a small part of such hardships, we have the opportunity to listen to and reflect and meditate on the extensive and profound advice of the graduated path to enlightenment. It is only by the kindness of our gurus that we have been so extremely fortunate.

The Essence of Nectar says,

> If it's said that the kindness of teaching a single verse
> Cannot be repaid by making offerings for eons
> Equal in number to its letters,
> How can one measure the kindness
> Of having shown the complete pure path?

With respect to the kindness of the guru in revealing the teachings, Panchen Losang Chökyi Gyaltsen said,

> Even if I offer everything—my body, life and possessions—for as many eons as the number of syllables of Dharma that I have been taught, there is no way I could repay the kindness of you, the Lord, Je Chökyi.

Also, it is said that even if we made offerings for six eons we couldn't repay the kindness of being given the oral transmission of the six-syllable mantra OM MANI PADME HUM.

We couldn't repay the kindness of the guru in teaching us one verse of Dharma even if we made offerings to him for eons equal to the number of syllables in the verse. Even if we were to offer our gurus the three thousand galaxies of the universe filled with wish-granting jewels for eons, we couldn't repay their kindness in teaching us one word of Dharma. Such an offering is nothing when compared to the limitless skies of benefit we get from that one word. Therefore, there is no doubt that we can't repay the kindness of our gurus in revealing to us the whole path to enlightenment. No matter for how many eons we made offerings we could never finish repaying this kindness.

When our guru gives us teachings, every single word brings us closer to enlightenment. Every single word we hear lessens our ignorance and leaves on our mind a positive imprint, which will later enable us to actualize the path. With each word we become closer to enlightenment. Without even talking about hearing a commentary, simply hearing the oral transmission of one mantra or verse of teaching definitely brings us to full enlightenment.

Remember the story of when Guru Shakyamuni Buddha gave teachings to five hundred swans, who simply heard the words of the teachings. Right after their deaths, all five hundred swans were born as human beings because they had heard the words of Dharma. They also all became Sangha, not just living in ordination but realizing emptiness. Also remember the story I told earlier of Vasubandhu and the pigeon.

The Essence of Nectar also says,

> If a man is suffering in prison
> And someone frees him from that prison,

Then has him taken to a place of perfect enjoyments,
We definitely recognize that as great kindness.

Therefore, when our gurus have revealed to us
The methods of escaping from the three evil-gone realms,
Kindly giving us the chance to enjoy for a while
The perfections of gods and humans,

And they then show us well the highest method
For pacifying all the degenerations of samsara and nirvana,
And lead us to the exalted state of the three kayas—
Why is this kindness not supreme?

We should compare the kindness of our guru in teaching us Dharma to the kindness of a doctor or healer who cures us of cancer. If we had cancer and were afraid of dying, we would find the situation unbearable. Day and night we would look for help. If we found a doctor who could cure our cancer we would regard her as very kind and very precious. We would consider the rest of our life to be a gift from that person.

The kindness of a doctor who cures our cancer is nothing compared to the kindness of our guru. Even if our guru gives us just the oral transmission of one mantra or one verse of teaching, the benefit we receive is as limitless as space. If we do nothing about the actual cause of our cancer—negative karma and delusions—our recovery from cancer will only be temporary. We can't purify karma and delusions simply by taking medicine or having an operation.

If we were starving to death and somebody gave us food or money, we would regard the person who saved our life as very kind and very precious. However, his help cannot be compared to the limitless benefit we receive from the guru who gives us the oral transmission of one mantra or one verse of teaching. The guru's kindness to us is as limitless as space.

If we were blind and somebody donated one of her eyes to us so that we could once again see, we would regard it as an incredibly kind act. But that cannot compare with the kindness of the guru, who gives us the Dharma wisdom eye so that we can see what is the cause of happiness and what is the cause of suffering. Our guru enables us to see all the various types of samsaric suffering—the general sufferings of samsara and the particular sufferings of each realm, especially the lower realms—and their causes; he enables us to see the whole path to enlightenment. The Dharma wisdom eye given to us by our guru enables us to understand each Dharma subject, and each understanding helps us to cease the stains on our mental continuum and to develop good qualities. This kindness is as limitless as space.

Consider the example of a person who, having eaten poison, food and medicine, is close to death. If a skillful doctor comes along and treats the person by making him vomit up the poison, turning the food into medicine and transforming the medicine into the nectar of immortality, we would say that such a doctor is extremely kind.

Like such a person, we have eaten a lot of the poison of non-virtue, which makes us go to the lower realms. By explaining methods of confession and purification, the guru enables us to confess and purify the non-virtues we have created during beginningless lifetimes and to abstain from those negative actions in the future.

We have also accumulated merit, but with the aim of obtaining good health, a long life, wealth, power, reputation and other meaningless things. The guru transforms our attitude into a pure one, leading us to direct the merit we have accumulated through our virtuous actions toward the happiness of future lives. And, through pure dedications, the guru leads us to transform the merit we have accumulated for the happiness of future lives into causes of liberation and enlightenment. Therefore, there is no one with greater kindness than our guru.

Our present gurus are unbelievably kind because they are leading us to full enlightenment by revealing the unmistaken Mahayana teachings. Think of how all their actions of giving vows, oral transmissions, initiations, teachings and personal advice are guiding us to enlightenment. First of all we can think of their kindness in revealing Buddhadharma, then especially Mahayana Dharma, which enables us to achieve not only a good rebirth in our next life and liberation from the whole of samsara but full enlightenment. And if we have received tantric teachings, we can meditate on the kindness of the guru who, by revealing tantra, grants us enlightenment quickly, within one life or even within a number of years. Think how unbelievably kind to us the guru is; there's no greater kindness than this.

As mentioned in *Guru Puja*, the guru is kind in three ways.[90] There are three kindnesses according to sutra and also three according to tantra. In

---

[90] There sits my root guru, kind in all three ways, in essence all buddhas... (V. 10).

sutra, the three kindnesses are giving oral transmissions, teachings and commentaries. In tantra, they are revealing the teachings, giving the three levels of vows and imparting tantric instructions.

We can also think about the kindness of our gurus in enabling us to meet Lama Tsongkhapa's teachings, which are especially clear compared to other teachings.

The Essence of Nectar says,

> It is by the kindness of our holy instructors
> That we have met the teaching of the Jamgön Lama,
> Which is difficult to find even on searching for many thousands
>   of eons,
> And that we have confidence in the methods of his teaching.

Lama Tsongkhapa is known as the Jamgön Lama (*jam* means gentle and *gön* means savior, or protector), because he is one with Manjushri (Jampälyang, in Tibetan), the embodiment of the wisdom of all the buddhas.

Lama Tsongkhapa's teaching is specifically mentioned in the section on the guru's kindness in *The Essence of Nectar* because Lama Tsongkhapa's sutra and tantra teachings have many special qualities. To appreciate having met and found faith in Lama Tsongkhapa's teaching, we have to understand these special qualities. A prayer composed by Pabongka Dechen Nyingpo[91] and another composed by Gungtang Tänpäi Drönme[92] are commonly recited at the end of practices to dedicate merit toward the flourishing of Lama Tsongkhapa's teaching. Both of these prayers describe the special qualities of Lama Tsongkhapa's lam-rim and tantric teachings.

Realizing how fortunate we are to have met Lama's Tsongkhapa's teachings depends on studying them and also on studying other teachings, because we can't fully appreciate how special Lama Tsongkhapa's teachings are unless we compare them with other teachings. There is no doubt that Lama Tsongkhapa's teachings are special when compared to the teachings of other religions, but they are also special within Buddhism. There is no doubt about the special nature of Lama Tsongkhapa's teachings on philosophy and tantra, but we can see how even his lam-rim teachings are special

---

[91] *Prayer for Meeting the Teaching of the Great Tsongkhapa, Dharma King of the Three Realms, Giving Compassionate Refuge and Care.*
[92] *Prayer for the Flourishing of Je Tsongkhapa's Teachings* [Tib: *Lo-sang gyäl-tän-ma*]. See *Essential Buddhist Prayers, Volume 1*, p. 259 ff.

when we compare them with other Buddhist and non-Buddhist teachings. The more we understand how pure and precious Lama Tsongkhapa's teachings are, the more we will appreciate the kindness of the guru who teaches them to us.

Of course, you can achieve enlightenment through all four traditions of Tibetan Mahayana Buddhism: Nyingma, Kagyü, Sakya and Gelug. Even though in the other traditions the explanations of the most difficult subtle points might not be as clear and as detailed as those of Lama Tsongkhapa, a person who has accumulated a lot of merit in the past will still be able to have realizations of lam-rim and tantra. In some cases, however, because the teachings are expressions of the experiences of highly realized yogis, it can be easy to misunderstand them. Those with a lot of merit who practice correct devotion to the virtuous friend might have planted so many seeds to have realizations in past lives that they are still able to have correct realizations. However, Lama Tsongkhapa's teachings have remarkable clarity, especially in explaining the most difficult points of sutra, particularly calm abiding and the Prasangika Madhyamaka view of emptiness, and of tantra, particularly the means to achieve the illusory body.

Lama Tsongkhapa's teachings have remarkable clarity, especially on the most difficult points of the path where other learned masters, even those who are great meditators, make mistakes. In calm abiding, for example, there are two major obstacles to meditation: attachment-scattering thought and sinking thought, both of which have gross and subtle levels. Many meditators make mistakes in relation to subtle sinking thought, which is very difficult to recognize; they think that they are meditating perfectly when actually they are experiencing subtle sinking thought. In his teachings, particularly his lam-rim teachings, Lama Tsongkhapa gives incredibly clear explanations of calm abiding.

If you are a monk or a nun, you can meditate specifically on the kindness of your guru in having directed your life toward liberation by giving you vows and enabling you to live in ordination. On the basis of this fundamental practice, you are able to achieve liberation and end the whole suffering of samsara and its causes. Even if you don't engage in much formal practice but do nothing apart from eat, sleep and go to the toilet, you are constantly collecting merit, day and night, by living in your vows.

You can also think about all the shortcomings you would experience if you were living a lay life, which is like being caught in a fire, and see that you are protected from them. Lay people have no freedom to practice Dharma;

they are completely trapped, with many problems both inside and outside their mind. Inside the mind there are all the delusions and outside there are many obstacles. They have no time to practice Dharma because they have to engage in so many meaningless activities. Think of all the problems and distractions of the lay life, then think of the benefits of living in ordination. Meditate in this way on the kindness of the guru in giving you vows.

The Essence of Nectar says,

> It is by the kindness of our precious gurus
> That we renounce family life, which is like being in the center of a
>   fire,
> Then, living in a sage's righteous conduct in a solitary place,
> We experience the sublime taste of the nectar of holy Dharma.

A lay person can live in the eight precepts, some or all of the five lay precepts[93] or the refuge vow alone.[94] These are also the basis of achieving liberation and allow you to accumulate extensive merit. If you have taken even one of the five lay vows, because you take the vow until your death (pratimoksha vows are taken until death, bodhisattva vows until enlightenment), you continuously collect merit, day and night, from the second you take the vow until you die. While you are eating, walking and sleeping—and even if you are in a coma—you are constantly collecting merit. And if you have taken all five precepts, there is no doubt that you are constantly accumulating even more merit.

The Heaped Flowers Sutra[95] explains that the merit collected by one person living in vows who makes a tiny light offering to one buddha using butter the size of a mustard seed and a wick the size of a hair is far greater than that collected if all the sentient beings of the three realms, without living in any vows, became rich and powerful wheel-turning kings and each one of them made an extensive light offering to every one of the numberless buddhas using an ocean of butter and a wick the size of Mount Meru. Even a lay person who is living in eight, five or fewer precepts or simply in the refuge vow alone accumulates unbelievable merit by making even a tiny offering to the guru-Triple Gem or by making charity to other sentient beings. Because

---

[93] See the glossary for the eight and the five precepts.
[94] See *Liberation in the Palm of Your Hand*, pp. 380–84 for details of the refuge vow.
[95] *The Avatamsaka Sutra*, translated as *The Flower Ornament Scripture*.

we have been granted vows by our gurus, we can collect unbelievable merit in our everyday life. All these benefits we receive by living in our vows come about through the kindness of our gurus.

We can also relate the kindness of our gurus to the bodhisattva vows. If we don't live in the bodhisattva vows, there is no enlightenment; if we live in the bodhisattva vows, there is enlightenment. All the infinite merit we continuously collect in each second from the moment we take the bodhisattva vows is also by the kindness of our gurus.

Also consider initiations. Without taking a great initiation, there is no way for us to enter the door of Vajrayana; we cannot listen to tantric teachings or practice tantra. This means that we have no opportunity to achieve enlightenment quickly or to free other sentient beings from suffering and bring them to enlightenment.

There is no way we can achieve enlightenment without a qualified vajra guru planting the seeds of the four kayas in our mind through granting us the blessings of the four complete initiations of Highest Yoga Tantra. Each initiation leaves a potential, or seed, in the mind of the vajra disciple. For example, receiving the vase initiation allows us to meditate on and actualize the generation stage and leaves a special imprint on our mind to achieve the nirmanakaya. Receiving the secret initiation allows us to meditate on and actualize the path of the illusory body and leaves a special imprint to achieve the sambhogakaya. Receiving the wisdom initiation allows us to meditate on and achieve the clear light and leaves a special imprint to achieve the dharmakaya. Receiving the fourth initiation, the word initiation, allows us to meditate on and achieve the path of unification and leaves a special imprint to achieve the unified state of Vajradhara, or the *svabhavikakaya*, which is the ultimate nature of a buddha's omniscient mind. We receive all this by the kindness of our vajra gurus.

When we think about the process of the Vajrayana path from the beginning up to enlightenment and about how we become enlightened by receiving initiation from the vajra guru, it is easy to recognize the kindness of the guru and how important the guru is in order to achieve enlightenment.

We can relate to the kindness of the guru in a general and extensive way and then meditate on specific examples of the kindness of each of our gurus. We should remember the kindness of our gurus from our heart.

Besides that, we should remember that we have received a human body with eight freedoms and ten richnesses and all our present happiness, wealth and comfort through our past practice of morality, charity and so forth. In our past lives our guru gave us vows and teachings on karma and we were then able to create the causes of a human body through the practices of morality and charity. Both the result, this human body, and its cause, morality, were received by the kindness of the guru.

We can also relate the various practices we do in our daily life to the kindness of the guru. All the virtuous actions we perform, all the Dharma understanding we gain, and all the merit we collect every day come from our present gurus. For example, when we do prostrations and recite the names of the Thirty-five Buddhas, by reciting each name, we purify many eons of specific negative karmas. In the few minutes it takes to read a lam-rim prayer we plant the seed of the whole path to enlightenment so that sooner or later we will achieve enlightenment. Even during one session of Dharma practice we are able to derive so much benefit by doing prostrations, making offerings and meditating on bodhicitta and other lam-rim topics. We gain all these benefits in our daily life through the kindness of our virtuous friends. At the end of each practice we should remember that our having the opportunity to accumulate all this merit is by the kindness of our gurus. It is our present gurus who enable us to collect all our merit, cause of the happiness of future lives, liberation from samsara and full enlightenment.

One high Amdo lama, Mipham Yangchen, from whom Kirti Tsenshab Rinpoche received many teachings, said in his lam-rim teaching written in verse form that everything—even the place where we do our practice—is the manifestation of the guru. All our enjoyments and all the conditions necessary for us to practice Dharma are embodiments of the guru.

Even though we may not recognize it, all our happiness comes from our gurus. Every single good thing—past, present and future—comes from our gurus. There is no doubt that the more we learn and practice Dharma, the more we develop our compassion and our wisdom and the more we are able to benefit other sentient beings. We are able to bring deeper and deeper benefit to others. All this comes from the kindness of the guru. Every single benefit we offer sentient beings through understanding and practicing Dharma comes from the kindness of the guru.

In this life, we can not only achieve any happiness we want—the happiness of future lives, liberation from samsara and enlightenment—but we can achieve all of these three great meanings in each second. For example, if even without bodhicitta motivation we circumambulate or make offerings or prostrate to a statue, stupa or scripture of Buddha, just through the power of the holy object we create the cause of enlightenment and, by the way, liberation from samsara and all the happiness of future lives. All this comes about through the kindness of the guru.

If we hadn't met our virtuous friends and had their guidance, even though we have been born as a human being, our life would have been completely wasted. We would have had a human body but our mind would have been no different from that of an animal. It is only by the kindness of our virtuous friends that we have become an actual human being, something more than an animal. It is only by the kindness of our virtuous friends that we have been able to hear teachings and understand their meaning and thus been able to make preparation for not only the happiness of future lives and liberation but full enlightenment as well. Our ability to work for and attain these goals comes about only through the kindness of our virtuous friends.

Without our gurus there is no way that we could even leave an imprint on our mind by hearing the words of Dharma let alone meditate on the path to enlightenment or attain realizations. Not everyone has this chance—in fact, only a very small number do. Most people don't have even this opportunity to leave an imprint of the path to enlightenment. Even if we don't get the chance to meditate, at least we have had the chance to imprint our mind with the complete path to enlightenment through hearing teachings from our gurus. Even though we might not now be able to attain realizations, sooner or later, because of the imprints, we will be able to have complete understanding of the words and their meaning and be able to actualize the path. Through this, we will then achieve enlightenment.

(c) The guru's kindness in blessing our mindstream

Generating within our mind all the realizations of the path from guru devotion up to the unified state of no more learning is dependent upon the guru blessing our mind. The arising of every single virtuous thought within our mind is because of the kindness of the guru in blessing our mind.

The guru's kindness in blessing our mental continuum means that when we meditate on the lam-rim, we are able to transform our mind into that meditation: when we meditate on loving kindness or compassion, we are able to transform our mind into loving kindness or compassion; when we meditate on refuge or guru devotion, we are able to transform our mind into devotion to the Triple Gem or to the guru; when we meditate on impermanence and death, we are able to transform our mind into the thought of impermanence and death—we feel not only that death is definite and can happen at any moment but that the appearance of this life is short and that we need to practice Dharma. Even though we mightn't generate the actual realization of these meditations, we have some experience of them. We mightn't achieve the stable, spontaneous, intense experience that characterizes an actual realization, but some transformation happens in our mind when we meditate. This is regarded as the kindness of the guru in blessing our mind.

There are many stories of past great yogis and pandits who achieved sublime realizations of tantra by serving and being blessed by their gurus. Since the minds of these great yogis were blessed by their gurus, they were able to generate extraordinary realizations. Naropa, without having meditated, generated the transcendental wisdom of simultaneously born great bliss by having undergone twelve great hardships, which almost caused him to die (see chapter 18). By experiencing each of the great hardships, he received initiation from his guru, Tilopa, with realization of each level of the path occurring spontaneously at its appropriate time.

Lama Tsongkhapa said,

> If you listen, you cannot comprehend the words; if you reflect, you cannot understand the meaning; if you meditate, you cannot generate the realization in your mind. At such times, when the power of intelligence is extremely small, the advice is to depend on the power of the merit field. When listening, reflecting and meditating don't work in the right way, if you pray and make requests to the guru at that time, they will quickly and easily be accomplished. Even that is a sign that your mind has been blessed.

Lama Tsongkhapa advises that during such hard times, when the capacity of our mind is limited, we should rely upon and make requests to the special merit field of the guru. By visualizing the guru as inseparable from the deity, we rely upon a special merit field that increases our devotion and grants us blessings. By making requests to this special merit field, we accumulate merit and purify obscurations. We then hit the target, which means that our practices of listening, reflecting and meditating become successful and effective.

If, when we make requests to the guru, realizations and experiences increase in our mind, it is a sign that our mind has been blessed by the guru. When, no matter how much reflecting and meditating we do, we never generate any experience in our mind, the best practice to eliminate obstacles is to make requests to the guru. If we pray to the guru our mind gets blessed and we quickly and easily generate realizations.

Tilopa said,

> The best of all methods for spiritual progress is the guru.

Earlier I told you the story of Naropa when he was the pandit doorkeeper at Nalanda Monastery about to be defeated in debate with a Hindu. When Naropa made requests to his guru Tilopa, Tilopa descended on his crown. Naropa immediately generated extraordinary wisdom and was then able to win the debate. This was also an example of the guru's kindness in blessing the mind.

Making requests to the guru is very powerful, even in accomplishing the small works of this life, such as when we have disease or spirit harms and nothing seems to help. We can be freed from the problem by praying to the guru. Also, for the guru to bless the disciple's mind, it's not necessary that the guru actually be living on this earth, like a mother hen with her chicks.

When an ascetic meditator from Sera Me Monastery, Gen Wangdu, did *chu-len* practice[96] in Orissa in east India, he lived in the forest in a very simple house, like a tribal person living in the jungle. He just had four wooden poles with a simple roof on top. He said that at night wild animals would come and fight each other. They made such a lot of noise that he expected to see dead bodies in the morning, but there would be nothing there.

One time a bear came underneath his hut and was just about to come inside. Gen Wangdu prayed very strongly and single-pointedly to a photo of his root guru, His Holiness Trijang Rinpoche. He prayed, "If the bear comes in, let it not eat me or else eat me quickly." While he was praying, the bear left; it didn't come in. He said that from that time he had unshakable devotion to His Holiness Trijang Rinpoche.

As mentioned in the lam-rim teachings, the best way to eliminate obstacles is to pray to the guru. When we have problems, whether with our Dharma practice or even ordinary problems, we should make strong, single-pointed prayers to the guru, but by looking at him not as an ordinary being but as a buddha. In emergency situations, the usual advice given is to pray to your root guru.

---

[96] See *Taking the Essence*, Lama Yeshe's teaching on this practice, on www.LamaYeshe.com.

When Pabongka Dechen Nyingpo met difficulties and nothing seemed to help, he would recite his precious lama's name mantra seven times and pray to him. All his works would then be accomplished.

From the holy speech of Gyalwa Götsangpa,

> So many people meditate on the generation stage,
> But there is nothing higher than meditating on the guru.
> So many people recite mantras,
> But there is nothing more profound than praying to the guru.

(d) The guru's kindness in inspiring us to practice Dharma through material gifts

The other kindness of the guru is in making us happy and inspiring us to practice Dharma through giving us gifts of food, clothing and other material things. Because we like material things more than Dharma, the guru is able to guide us into the Dharma by providing us with material enjoyments; in this way we continue to follow the guru and to practice Dharma.

Sometimes we may generate negative thoughts toward the guru because we have experienced suffering in fulfilling his demands and he doesn't even bother to express his gratitude or compliment us. At such times we could have a black view of our lama, seeing him as heartless and filled with nothing but self-cherishing. By fulfilling our temporal needs, the lama can transform the situation; he can make us happy, cause us to generate devotion and stop us from creating negative karma.

Also, when we don't care much about practicing Dharma, by fulfilling our temporal needs, our guru can inspire us to transform our mind and follow his advice. When the guru gives material gifts to those no longer interested in practicing Dharma, they can be inspired to practice. When we are tired from listening to teachings, for example, after our guru gives us a cup of coffee, we are able to listen to more.

In *Lines of Experience of the Graduated Path to Enlightenment* Lama Tsongkhapa says,

> At the beginning, by meeting their temporal needs, may I gather sentient beings into my retinue then satisfy them with holy Dharma.

As it is said,

> All the happiness and perfections of the three times are received
> by the kindness of the guru.

This is so because all the merit of the three times is accumulated through the kindness of the guru in different aspects. Kindness such as this cannot be measured, even at the end of the path to enlightenment.

We might have the doubt, "All these results are not due to the kindness of a single guru—there were many different gurus at different times." When that thought arises, we should think of the basis of transformation of all our various gurus: the absolute guru, the dharmakaya, the holy mind of all the buddhas, the transcendental wisdom of nondual bliss and voidness. Like many waters coming from different places into one ocean, the holy mind of all the buddhas becomes of one taste in emptiness; the dharmakaya, the absolute guru, manifests in all our gurus in accord with our own karma. With this understanding we then see all our gurus as one being, and all our present gurus are also one with all our past-life gurus. All our past, present and future happiness is received from our present gurus.

Pabongka Dechen Nyingpo says that our own guru is the embodiment of all the buddhas and all the buddhas are manifestations of our guru. The holy minds of all the buddhas are of one taste in the essence of the dharmakaya, inseparable bliss and voidness. The guru then manifests from that dharmakaya, like a bubble coming from the ocean, which itself comes from all the different rivers that drain into it. If we understand this, we know that all the buddhas of the hundred types, the five types, the three types[97] and the one type, which means Vajradhara, are all manifestations of the guru. There is no Vajradhara and no other deity apart from the guru. In reality, there is no buddha separate from our gurus.

If the guru is pleased with us, all the buddhas are pleased; if the guru is displeased with us, all the buddhas are displeased. Attaining this one practice of guru devotion attains the practices of numberless buddhas. If we don't do this one practice of guru devotion or make mistakes in this prac-

---

[97] The buddhas of the three types are Vairochana, Amitabha and Akshobhya—essences of a buddha's holy body, speech and mind. The buddhas of the five types add Ratnasambhava and Amoghasiddhi to the previous three, and these five are related to a buddha's five pure aggregates. The buddhas of a hundred types are related to five aspects of a buddha's five aggregates, four elements, six inner bases of consciousness and five sense objects.

tice, we won't succeed, no matter how many different aspects of buddha we try to practice. But if we succeed in this one practice of guru devotion, we succeed in the practices of all the buddhas.

While we may take initiations, engage in the practices, do retreats and recite mantras of many different deities, we need to recognize that in reality we are trying to attain the guru. We can understand this by thinking of the actual meaning of the guru: the absolute guru.

After the verse on the guru's kindness in enabling us to meet Lama Tsong-khapa's teachings, *The Essence of Nectar* continues,

> Therefore, my virtuous friends are:
> Rescuers, rescuing me from the lower realms;
> Captains, taking me across the ocean of samsara;
> Guides, leading me to upper realms and liberation;

If we have studied the sufferings of the lower realms and have a complete view of all the sufferings involved, we will have a strong feeling for the kindness of the guru in protecting us from those many eons of suffering. But if we don't recognize the sufferings of the lower realms, we won't appreciate the kindness of the guru in protecting us from them.

At this point think of the entire suffering of samsara: the six, four or three types[98] of general suffering and the particular sufferings of each realm. Each realm has oceans of suffering. The guru liberates us from the oceans of samsaric suffering, like a captain taking us across the ocean in a boat to the place where we wish to be.

The more extensive our knowledge of the general and particular sufferings of samsara, the more strongly we will feel the kindness of the virtuous friend, the captain who liberates us from the oceans of samsara.

Upper realms refers to the body of a happy migratory being, of a human or god, and liberation refers to liberation from samsara and to full enlightenment, or great liberation, as well.

---

[98] The six types of suffering are uncertainty, dissatisfaction, repeatedly leaving bodies, being born over and over again, moving from high to low again and again, and having no companion; the four types of suffering are birth, old age, sickness and death; the three types of suffering are the suffering of suffering, the suffering of change and pervasive compounding suffering.

> Doctors, curing the chronic disease of delusion,
> Streams of water, extinguishing the great fire of suffering,
> Lamps, dispelling the darkness of ignorance,
> Suns, illuminating the path to liberation,

The delusions, the continuation of which has no beginning, are like a chronic debilitating disease—our virtuous friend completely cures the disease of delusion and ensures that we never ever experience it again. Even if an ordinary doctor gives us medicine to help us recover from sickness, it is only a temporary cure and does nothing to pacify the cause of the sickness, our delusions. The virtuous friend is the real doctor because he ceases the delusions, from where the 424 diseases and all other problems arise.

Remember the kindness of the virtuous friend in being the doctor who cures you of the chronic disease of delusion.

> Liberators, releasing me from the bonds of the samsaric prison,
> Rain clouds, showering a rain of holy Dharma,
> Relatives and friends, bringing benefit and dispelling harm,
> Parents, always caring for me with love.

Releasing me from the bonds of the samsaric prison means that the guru breaks the continual chain of the twelve links. And the guru, like a brother or sister, always helps us to get rid of our problems.

It is extremely effective to read these verses and to meditate on their meaning by relating them to each of our gurus.

By training our mind in the root, devotion, and remembering the kindness of the guru, we feel the guru is there in our heart—as if the guru *is* our heart. We feel that the guru is the most important, most precious thing in our life. Respect for the guru then arises, which brings us inconceivable merit and great purification. Correct devotion to the virtuous friend then comes naturally and easily. In accord with how well we have trained our mind and how much devotion and realization of the guru's kindness we have, we are happy to devote ourselves to the guru and follow his advice. Our practice of guru devotion then becomes very successful.

Six-Session Guru Yoga mentions,

Seeing that all general and sublime realizations depend upon correctly devoting myself to you, my savior, I give up my body and even my life. Please grant me blessings to practice only what pleases you.

This attitude is what enables us to achieve enlightenment quickly, even within one brief lifetime of a degenerate time, as Milarepa did. Because Milarepa had this realization, cherishing his guru more than his own life, he sacrificed himself to follow his guru Marpa. Due to his strong guru yoga, Milarepa was able to achieve enlightenment within a few years.

The kindness of the guru in Guru Puja

In the prostration section of *Guru Puja,*[99] first the qualities of the guru are described and then the kindness. It is very effective to meditate on each verse in relation to the kindness of each of our gurus.

Your compassion grants even the sphere of great bliss,
The supreme state of the three kayas, in an instant.
Guru with a jewel-like body, vajra holder.
I prostrate at your lotus feet.

Our gurus give us all the teachings of the whole path to enlightenment, both lam-rim and tantra, as well as initiations; they teach us all the most secret, profound means of achieving enlightenment in this brief lifetime. By practicing these, we can become enlightened in this life. This is like achieving enlightenment in an instant, compared to one day in even the first category of the hot hells, Being Alive Again and Again, which is equivalent to nine million human years. Compared to the duration of beginningless time and one day of a hell-being's life, our gurus grant us enlightenment in an instant. Our teachers are extremely kind in revealing to us the teachings of the entire path, which can grant us enlightenment, *the sphere of great bliss, the supreme state of the three kayas*, in a moment.

You are the wisdom-knowledge of all the infinite conquerors
Appearing in any way that subdues.

[99] Vv. 18–22.

With supreme skillful means, you manifest as a saffron-robed monk.
Holy refuge-savior, I prostrate at your feet.

This second verse is talking about the kindness of the guru in manifesting in whatever form suits our mind. Even though there are numberless aspects of buddhas, since we can't see buddhas in the form of buddhas, we can't receive teachings from them in that form. Therefore, the guru is extremely kind in manifesting in his present form, which accords with our level of mind, and guiding us by giving the various teachings.

You eliminated all faults and their instincts
And are a treasury of infinite precious qualities.
Sole source of benefit and bliss without exception,
Perfect, pure guru, I prostrate at your feet.

In this verse, when we recite the line about eliminating all faults and even their imprints, it is good to think about all our delusions, every single one of them, and to remember all the negative actions we have done out of them. We should then remember in detail all the suffering of the six realms that has resulted from these negative karmas. For example, we should remember all the various problems of human beings that result from negative karma—not only old age, sickness and death, but famine, epidemic disease, relationship problems and the many other problems. Who is it that totally eliminates all our problems and their cause, negative karma and delusions? Our gurus.

We should think especially of eliminating the negative actions and delusions that result in the unimaginable suffering of the eight hot and eight cold hells, as well as the branch hells. No matter what pain we experience from heat and cold in the human realm, it is pleasurable compared to the sufferings in the hells. Who ends all our suffering in the hot and cold hells and its cause? Our gurus.

We should also think of the hungry ghosts, whose sufferings we couldn't bear. We couldn't survive without food or even a drop of water for seven days, yet hungry ghosts experience such great suffering for hundreds of years. Who completely ends the immense suffering we have to experience as a hungry ghost? Our gurus.

We should then think of all the animals, who are extremely foolish, suffer from heat and cold and eat one another. A human being couldn't bear the suffering that animals experience; there is no way a human could bear even the hardship of not being able to explain her needs. Through giving us teachings, our gurus are the only ones who can completely end for us all the karma and delusions that bring this animal suffering.

When we recite the line, *Sole source of benefit and bliss without exception*, we should remember that every single merit we create is the action of the guru; it comes through the guru's kindness. Who gives us every single happiness of past, present and future and every single quality of a buddha's holy body, speech and mind? Who gives us all the merit that we receive? Our gurus. All the good things that we have now and will receive in the future, up to enlightenment, come through the kindness of the guru. Our gurus are treasures of inconceivable merit, source of all happiness and benefit, and the panacea of peace. This is why we prostrate at the holy feet of our gurus.

> Teacher of gods and all, in nature all buddhas,
> The source of 84,000 pure dharmas,
> You tower above the whole host of aryas.
> Kind guru, I prostrate to you.

With this verse, we should think that each of our gurus is all the buddhas; each guru is Manjushri, Tara, Vajrapani and all the other buddhas. And because each guru is all the buddhas, each guru is the source of all the Dharma, of all the 84,000 teachings. Without each of our gurus, there is no Buddha, there is no Dharma, there is no Sangha.

> To gurus dwelling in the three times and ten directions,
> The Three Supreme Jewels and all worthy of homage:
> With faith, conviction and an ocean of lyric praise,
> I prostrate, manifesting as many bodies as atoms of the world.

The objects of prostration include not only living beings, but statues, scriptures, stupas and all other holy objects. Here we should remember that without the guru there is no Triple Gem with which we can accumulate merit. Without the guru, there is not even one statue to which we can make offering and with which we can accumulate merit; there is not even one scripture we can study to leave an imprint of the path; there is not even one stupa with which we can purify and accumulate merit. Any merit we accumulate with any holy object comes solely by the kindness of each of our gurus.

In relation to holy objects, we can think, "The guru manifested in these forms to enable me to purify my mind and collect merit." It is such an easy way to collect merit, as it doesn't even depend on our having a virtuous motivation. Even if our motivation is not Dharma, simply seeing, circumambulating, or prostrating or making offering to holy objects immediately becomes the cause of enlightenment, liberation from samsara and the happiness of hundreds of thousands of future lives. And, of course, it also affects this life. Because we purify so much negative karma, it reduces the problems of this life.

The existence of holy objects makes it so easy for us to purify our heavy negative karmas and collect extensive merit, enabling us to have realizations of the path to enlightenment. We should also understand that all these holy objects exist due to the kindness of the guru. By understanding that the meaning of guru is the dharmakaya, the holy mind of all the buddhas, we see that these holy objects happened through the kindness of the guru, or through the guru manifesting in them, to liberate us from samsara and bring us to enlightenment.

As mentioned in these verses, the guru has done the work of giving us all the teachings of the complete path to enlightenment, from beginning to end. If we had practiced these teachings, if we had followed the guru instead of our selfish mind, we would already have become enlightened, or at least had some attainment of the graduated path to enlightenment.

As mentioned here and in *Six-Session Guru Yoga*, it is definite that our gurus give us enlightenment in an instant; the fault is only that from our side we haven't followed them. Our gurus have been unbelievably kind in giving us vows, thus helping to protect us from negative karmas and enabling us to accumulate merit. In this way, each of our gurus is leading us from our present state to the state of enlightenment. Each of our gurus is extremely kind.

This is the way to meditate on the kindness of the guru with these verses from *Guru Puja*. It is very effective to read or chant these verses slowly, meditating on their meaning.

15. Devoting to the Guru with Action

4. HOW TO DEVOTE TO A GURU WITH ACTION

WITH GURU DEVOTION, seeing the guru as a buddha, we are able to devote ourselves correctly to the virtuous friend with thought and we then naturally devote ourselves correctly with action. Easily and joyfully we are able to follow the guru's advice, practicing the teachings according to his instructions, which is the best way to devote to the virtuous friend with action. Correct devotion to the guru with action comes easily as a result of correct devotion with thought. How well we are able to devote ourselves to the guru with action is determined by how well we devote ourselves with thought.

Through training our mind in the devotion that sees the guru as a buddha and generating respect by remembering the guru's kindness, we hold the guru in our heart, cherishing him as the most precious person in our life. Because of this feeling, we never find any hardship in carrying out any advice he gives us, even if he asks us to do something difficult. Rather than finding it a burden, we are happy to do it and see it as the most worthwhile thing to do in our life. We know from our own experience that following the guru's advice is easier when our devotion is strong. When our devotion is weak, however, being asked to do even a small thing becomes a burden.

There are three ways to devote ourselves to the guru with action:

(1) Carrying out the guru's advice
(2) Offering respect and service
(3) Making material offerings

(1) CARRYING OUT THE GURU'S ADVICE

The main practice—and the best offering—is the first one: carrying out the guru's advice, which means following the holy wishes of the guru with our body, speech and mind. This is the best way to purify negativities and to accumulate merit. Pleasing the guru by fulfilling his wishes is itself the quick path to enlightenment.

As Milarepa said,

> I have no material offerings. My offering to my father-guru is my practice.

He also said,

> The striving and suffering I bear in my practice is an offering to please my father-guru. I repay my father-guru's kindness with my practice.

Because he was living an ascetic life, Milarepa didn't have anything material to offer; his offering to his guru was his practice. Milarepa's practice was doing everything that Marpa advised him to do after they met, including building the tower, doing retreat and actualizing the whole path to enlightenment.

Here *father* is referring to the spiritual master, who takes care of us completely and upon whom we totally rely, now and in our future lives. The virtuous friend guides us like a parent guides his or her child. Repaying the father-guru with practice means following the guru's advice, practicing the Dharma and attaining realizations of the path to enlightenment.

(2) OFFERING RESPECT AND SERVICE

Offering respect and service includes all the respectful behavior described in *Fifty Verses of Guru Devotion* and *The Essence of Nectar*, such as standing when the teacher enters the room, prostrating, bathing and offering perfumes and ornaments to the holy body, cleaning, cooking and other services. We must read *Fifty Verses of Guru Devotion* and then put those teachings into practice.

(3) MAKING MATERIAL OFFERINGS

We make material offerings if we can. The lam-rim teachings mention that while the guru doesn't seek material offerings, disciples should still make the best offerings that they can. Again, as with all guru devotion practice, making material offerings is done for our own sake, to accumulate merit.

Devoting ourselves to the virtuous friend with action in these three ways quickly purifies extensive obscurations and accumulates extensive merit. We are then able to quickly achieve enlightenment.

In *Six-Session Guru Yoga*, devoting to the guru with action is contained in the following verse, which is the very essence of the samayas of correct devotion to the guru explained in *Fifty Verses of Guru Devotion:*

> Seeing that all general and sublime realizations depend upon correctly devoting myself to you, my savior, I give up my body and even my life. Please grant me blessings to practice only what pleases you.

This means that from this moment until our enlightenment, we should try only to please our virtuous friend with our body, speech and mind.

Once we have meditated on the eight benefits of correct devotion to the guru, trained our mind in the devotion that sees the guru as a buddha and generated respect by remembering the guru's kindness, each piece of advice given to us by our guru is like a wish-fulfilling gem, because each time we follow our guru's advice we purify inconceivable negative karmas and obscurations. Following the guru's advice brings the most powerful purification, purifying the heavy negative karma we have accumulated in the past. And each time we carry out our guru's advice, we come closer to enlightenment. Everything—all the happiness not only of this life but of future lives, liberation and enlightenment—comes from following each instruction. Sincere practitioners see each piece of their guru's advice as a wish-fulfilling gem that fulfills all their own wishes for happiness and brings success in their wish to benefit all sentient beings.

It is explained in the lam-rim teachings that there is a big difference in the benefit in terms of purification and accumulation of merit between doing a retreat or some other practice because we ourselves have made the decision to do it and doing something on the advice of our guru. Following our guru's advice, no matter how hard we find it, brings much greater purification. Like a puja to eliminate obstacles, it prevents hindrances to the completion of our Dharma practice.

It is also said in the lam-rim teachings that following each instruction we are given by our guru is a cause of achieving the sambhogakaya, the holy body of complete enjoyment, since the guru's holy speech is the expression of the subtle wind.

I often tell the Kopan monks how fortunate they are because the whole monastery program from morning until night has been set up for them by their guru. During their daily life in the monastery, almost every single thing they do is following their guru's advice. Even the simple action of sweeping up a little dirt with a broom becomes a way to purify negative karmas and obscurations and accumulate merit. Once they join the monastery, everything they do—even sweeping the grounds each morning—has been arranged by the guru.

If we know all the benefits, it is a very enjoyable to be in a monastery; it is something to make the mind happy from morning until night. Every day, by following the guru's advice, we create a great many causes for temporary and ultimate happiness in this life and in future lives. There is then nothing we enjoy more than the daily work of following our guru's advice.

We should also think in a similar way if we work in a Dharma center. Doing any work that our guru has advised us to do has great benefit, making our life highly meaningful. Even if we're not doing the actual work of teaching Dharma, by working in a Dharma center we are providing the conditions for many other people to practice the holy teachings and follow the infallible path to enlightenment. If we frequently think about this in our everyday life, our mind will be very happy. We should constantly keep our guru in our heart, day and night. When we practice *Lama Tsongkhapa Guru Yoga*, Guru Lama Tsongkhapa enters and abides in our heart and we then remember him in our heart for the rest of the day. In the same way, we should constantly remember our guru in our heart and do our work for him. This itself is guru yoga practice. All the work we do from morning until night then becomes Dharma practice. It is also enjoyable and each day we are happy to be working in a Dharma center.

When we are actually living with our guru, serving our guru itself is our guru yoga practice. We don't need to seek the practice of guru yoga separately from that. We don't need to meditate separately on the holy body of the guru as we are with the actual holy body of the guru. Making prostrations and offerings to and serving our guru are the actual guru yoga practice, which we only visualize in pujas. Don't think that guru yoga practice has to do only with sitting and visualizing or reciting some prayers and has nothing to do with actual person-to-person contact.

When we do pujas, we visualize the beings in the merit field—the direct and indirect gurus, buddhas, bodhisattvas, arhats, dakas and dakinis and Dharma protectors—as different aspects of the guru, then make offerings of praise, mudras, bath and physically performed offerings. We use a vase to offer water to a reflection of the merit field in a mirror and use a scarf to represent offering robes, but these are substitutes for actually offering a bath and robes to the guru. We do all this to purify our own mind. The guru-buddhas don't need to wash; we do it to purify our own defilements and to collect merit so that we can achieve realizations of the path to enlightenment. When we actually offer a bath to our guru—filling the bath with water, washing the guru and offering robes—we are performing the real guru yoga practice of offering a bath, which we only visualize in *Jorchö* and other sutra and tantra pujas.

In pujas, we set out various offerings on the altar, then, with mudras, make the eight types of offerings[100] and the five sense offerings,[101] but offering our guru tea, food, clothes, flowers, sweet sounds and so forth is the actual practice of offering. And with these offerings we accumulate much more merit than when we visualize making the eight offerings, both actually arranged on the altar and mentally transformed, to the deity in pujas or sadhanas.

However, we shouldn't think that since we are serving the guru we don't need to do other practices. We should also try to do the other guru yoga practices as much as we can, as they are methods to quickly finish the work of accumulating merit.

While we are perfectly serving the guru who actually lives with us, all our realizations of the path naturally increase second by second. Offering service to the guru, the highest merit field, is the quickest way to complete the work of accumulating merit.

The sutra *Essence of Earth* says,

---

[100] The eight offerings are water for drinking, water for washing the feet, flowers, incense, light, scented water for the heart, food and music.

[101] The five are offerings of forms, sounds, scents, tastes and tangible objects.

> All the merit of having made offerings to unimaginable millions
> of buddhas and also of having made charity and practiced moral-
> ity are surpassed by one moment of offering service to the guru.

When we are serving our guru by cleaning his house, we should think that
the guru is all the buddhas and bodhisattvas and that we are cleaning their
abode. When we offer even a glass of water to our guru, we should make the
offering by thinking that the guru is all the buddhas and bodhisattvas of
the ten directions. Since making an offering to even a pore of the guru creates more merit than making offerings to all the buddhas of the three times,
there is no doubt about the benefit of making offerings to the actual guru.
Even though there is already this benefit, our practice will be more effective
if we meditate that the guru is all the buddhas and bodhisattvas when we
serve him because it will help us to constantly keep guru devotion in mind
and to stop negative thoughts toward the guru.

It is dangerous to practice guru yoga without understanding how to
practice correctly and the shortcomings of practicing wrongly. There is also
great danger in living with our guru and serving him if we don't know how
to practice guru yoga. In a moment we can create the karma to be in the
Inexhaustible Suffering hell for eons. Like electricity, the guru can bring
incredible benefit but can also be very dangerous.

It is also inspiring to read the verses in *The Essence of Nectar* that extensively
describe pleasing the holy mind of the virtuous friend with action. These
verses are clear and detailed. Especially effective are the verses that describe
how Naropa, Milarepa, Chayulwa and other great yogis did special practice
of guru devotion and had incredible attainments. They are mentioned as
excellent examples for us to follow.

The section of devoting to the guru with action begins,

> Every single benefit of samsara and beyond
> Comes through the kindness of the guru.
> Although I can never completely repay this kindness,
> In order to try to repay it, I will try to please him.

This means that all the happiness we experience is due to the kindness of the
guru. Even though we can never finish repaying this kindness, we shouldn't
give up all together, as we might do with a debt that we couldn't finish pay-

ing in this life. We should still attempt to repay the guru's kindness, and to do this we do the practice of pleasing the guru's holy mind.

> Just as one plants seeds in a fertile field,
> Even though the guru doesn't depend on offerings and respect,
> To quickly complete my own great accumulation of merit,
> Why don't I attempt to plant seeds in this supreme field
> By making offerings and showing respect?

Although we might work hard—planting seeds, fertilizing and so forth—to grow crops in an ordinary field, there is no expectation from the side of the field. It is similar with the supreme field of the guru. The guru doesn't depend on offerings and respect. All of my gurus are exactly like this.

The guru is the supreme field of merit because, as I've already explained, it is in relation to the guru—through following his advice, respecting and serving him and making offerings—that we collect the most extensive merit. In order to quickly complete our collection of merit we should attempt to make offerings and show respect to the guru. The real meaning of offering is not simply giving something material but pleasing the guru's holy mind. That is the best offering.

Fifty Verses of Guru Devotion says,

> Giving to the guru always becomes an offering to all the buddhas.

Offering to the guru brings a great accumulation of merit, and from such accumulation we accomplish the supreme realization.

It is also said,

> If you are wealthy, offer the best of your possessions to your guru,
> as Lama Dromtönpa and others did.

Fifty Verses of Guru Devotion also says,

> Whoever wishes to have unceasing good fortune and happiness should offer to the guru whatever is rare and extraordinary or even what is a little better than average.

From the holy speech of Lhasowa,

While we have something good to offer, if we offer something bad, we degenerate our samaya. But there is no shortcoming if we have only poor offerings or if the guru is pleased with poor offerings.

Disciples should offer whatever is the most pleasing, and gurus shouldn't cling even a little to material possessions. As Kadampa Geshe Sharawa said,

> A guru is someone who is pleased by the disciples' practice and realization and does not mentally cling in the slightest to material objects.

Whether or not we physically hear or see that the guru is pleased, the guru is someone who is pleased by our practice, not by receiving material offerings. This is how it should be. However, if we see our virtuous friend made happy by receiving material offerings, it's a mistake to think that this is wrong. That is incorrect devotion to the virtuous friend. Many times, to make a disciple happy, high lamas show the aspect of being pleased when receiving material offerings.

The previous incarnation of Pari Rinpoche, Pari Dorje Chang, a high lama of Sera Monastery in Tibet, was once offered a leg of mutton by someone who earned his living by printing Dharma texts. While the person was there in front of him, Rinpoche showed the aspect of being very pleased and said, "Oh, how thoughtful! Now I can make momos." Right after the person left, Rinpoche threw the whole leg of mutton into the toilet because it came from money obtained by printing and selling Dharma scriptures. Eating food bought with money earned by selling statues or Dharma scriptures is regarded as heavy negative karma and brings great pollution. Pari Dorje Chang didn't give the meat to other people because it would have been the same negative karma. He showed pleasure at having received the offering, then immediately threw it away. This is the skillful way that high lamas act in guiding sentient beings. Even if they accept an offering, they take it for the benefit of the disciple, so that the disciple can accumulate merit.

The Essence of Nectar continues,

> It is said that making offering to one pore of the guru
> Who has revealed to us the unmistaken path

Collects greater merit than honoring and making offering to the
multitudes of aryas:
Hearers, self-conquerors, bodhisattvas and buddhas.

This verse describes the power of the guru. Leave aside making offerings and
paying respect to our guru, even making offerings to our guru's disciples collects far greater merit than making offerings to all the numberless buddhas,
bodhisattvas and arhats, as well as all the statues, stupas and scriptures of
the ten directions. As I've already explained, we collect such merit when,
thinking of our guru, we give even a glass of water or a piece of candy to a
fellow disciple or a member of our guru's family or even give some food to
our guru's dog.

Many holy beings, such as Naropa, Milarepa,
Dromtönpa, Sakya Pandita and Chayulwa,
Gave up without a thought their body, life and wealth
For their gurus and achieved many realizations.

Without hesitation, Naropa immediately did every single thing that his
guru Tilopa mentioned he should do. He thus bore twelve great and twelve
small hardships. The twelve great hardships almost caused Naropa to die.
Each time Naropa was close to death Tilopa would come along and bless
him so that he would again recover his health. Milarepa is one of the most
inspiring examples of someone who practiced incomparable devotion to
the virtuous friend. After making unbelievable sacrifices and bearing hardships to practice Dharma, Milarepa had great success, achieving enlightenment within a number of years. I will describe the stories of Naropa and
Milarepa in more detail later (see chapter 18).

In addition, Dromtönpa, Sakya Pandita and Kadampa Geshe Chayulwa
are used to illustrate correct devotion to the virtuous friend. I described
earlier how these great yogis experienced powerful purification as a result
of serving their gurus (see chapter 7).

The Essence of Nectar continues,

Therefore, I shall strive to respect and serve with my body and speech,
Such as by offering all my cherished possessions,
Prostrating, rising, giving massages and baths,
And speaking respectfully, praising and so on.

Rising refers to rising to our feet when we see our guru.

In devoting ourselves to our guru, we should be very happy to make offerings to him. We first meditate on our guru as inseparable from our special deity. As His Holiness Song Rinpoche always advised, when we visualize the deity we should think of the guru and when we see the guru we should think of the deity. By thinking of the qualities of the guru, we manifest countless bodies, equal to the number of our past lives and make prostrations. We then offer ourselves as servants to the guru and with beautiful chants, praise him with our speech. In this way, we offer service with our body and speech.

We then offer to the guru actually arranged material offerings as well as mentally transformed ones. For example, we visualize transforming all our merits of the three times into various offerings and then offer them to the guru. This is the way to make miscellaneous offerings, both those materially arranged and those mentally transformed.

With respect to how to devote to the guru with action, the Hinayana teachings explain that in the daytime, one massages or offers perfume to the holy body, as well as robes; at night, one makes the guru's bed, offers robes and so forth. This is body service.

With respect to speech service, when one mentions the holy name of the guru, one uses a particular honorific word as a preliminary, then says the name. That is why when Theravadin monks talk about or to their abbot, they put their palms together and say "Venerable Such-and-such." The ordination text explains, "First say this, then say the holy name." In a gelong ordination, the *sangdön lobpön* asks those who are to take ordination some questions as to whether or not they have particular obstacles to ordination, then gives them advice as to how to address the abbot and other teachers. When His Holiness Ling Rinpoche or His Holiness Trijang Rinpoche were quoting from a teaching of Pabongka Dechen Nyingpo, they would always say "Kyabgön Pabongka Dechen Nyingpo." *Kyab* means refuge and *gön* means savior. A particular name that expresses the teacher's exalted qualities is used.

Speech service also means saying "I will do it" when our guru gives us an instruction. Using respectful words when we talk to virtuous teachers or ask them questions is also speech service.

Each time we offer a glass of water, a cup of tea, food or a bath to our guru, we should do so with the mind of guru yoga, looking at the guru as a buddha. When we serve our guru, if possible we should remember the second merit field in *Guru Puja*, where the guru's holy body is decorated with the Guhyasamaja mandala. We should try to look at the guru's five aggregates as the five Dhyani Buddhas and all his pores as the twenty-one thousand arhats. (Here we are not talking about ordinary arhats; they are actually manifestations of buddha.) With awareness of this, we then offer robes to our guru or perform other services. We should also think of the absolute guru, the dharmakaya, the holy mind of all the buddhas, which pervades all existence and has no beginning and no end. This is the most profound guru yoga meditation, and any service we offer our guru with this awareness accumulates unbelievable merit.

> Especially, I will attempt day and night without distraction
> To practice the complete, unmistaken graduated path:
> The best way to please my guru with my three doors.
> I will please my guru with the offering of practicing in accord with
>   his advice.
> Please grant me blessings to be able to do this.

The best way to please the guru with body, speech and mind is by attempting day and night without distraction to practice the lam-rim, the complete and unmistaken path to enlightenment. We will then definitely achieve our goal of full enlightenment. On the basis of this, we please the holy mind of the guru by following his advice. If our main goal in life is to subdue our mind and have realizations of the lam-rim and not just to be famous for our understanding of Dharma, attaining our goal depends on correctly devoting ourselves to our virtuous friend, which means following his advice. Following our guru's advice on the basis of practicing lam-rim is what pleases our guru the most.

We should read the section on respecting and serving the guru in *The Essence of Nectar* again and again and remember it when we serve our guru.

His Holiness Song Rinpoche, London, 1978

16. Is Absolute Obedience Required?

After we have met a guru, we should then correctly devote ourselves to him by practicing what he says to do and avoiding what he says not to do. However, a question can arise as to whether we should do every single thing that our guru tells us to do. His Holiness the Dalai Lama always emphasizes that we should refer to the teachings rather than to the person. This means that we have to check the guru's advice in relation to the reliable sources of Guru Shakyamuni Buddha's teachings and the teachings of Nagarjuna, Asanga and the other great pandits and yogis. These authentic scriptures are more important than the guru's advice.

If the guru's advice accords with the teachings of Guru Shakyamuni Buddha and the scriptures written by the pandits, or at least doesn't contradict them, we can follow it. If the guru's advice isn't mentioned in those scriptures, or contradicts them, we don't need to follow it. Since the advice doesn't have a pure reference, it is better to leave it in equanimity, which means that we don't need to criticize or complain about our guru.

The teachings of the Nyingma and Kagyü traditions generally advise that any time we see a contradiction between the guru's advice and the Buddha's teachings, we should think that there is an underlying meaning in the guru's advice. In his commentary to *The Thirty-seven Practices of a Bodhisattva*, Rongpu Sangye, the Nyingma lama who was the root guru of Trulshik Rinpoche and Gomchen Khampala, says that even if our guru asks us to do what looks like a non-virtuous action, we should do it immediately, without any doubt or hesitation. If our mind isn't capable of understanding the purpose, we simply think, "There must be some great meaning in what he is telling me" or "I'm sure that doing this must have some great benefit for me," then do the action without any hesitation.

However, His Holiness the Dalai Lama often advises in his teachings that it is when a special guru and a special disciple meet, as in the cases of Tilopa and Naropa and Marpa and Milarepa, that the disciple does every single thing that the guru says. For special disciples, doing every single thing the guru says to do only becomes the path to enlightenment.

Naropa, Milarepa and many other great yogis had special guru-disciple relationships in which they did every single thing their guru told them to do. However, it is different for ordinary beings. As ordinary disciples, it is more skillful for us to devote ourselves to the virtuous friend in accordance with the teachings. While some lamas emphasize that the disciples should see every action that the guru does as pure, His Holiness the Dalai Lama has a slightly different emphasis. I think that His Holiness, as the holder of the whole Buddhadharma, takes many factors into account. His Holiness emphasizes very much that we should not simply see everything the guru does as pure but that we should check the guru's advice well to see that it accords with Guru Shakyamuni Buddha's sutra and tantra teachings before practicing it.

His Holiness is not saying that we should allow negative thoughts toward the guru to arise; His Holiness does emphasize the importance of stopping such negative thoughts. The whole point of seeing the guru's actions as pure is to stop the arising of negative thoughts toward the guru so that we can successfully achieve all the realizations of the path to enlightenment. However, I think His Holiness and Rongpu Sangye Rinpoche reach the same conclusion: we do what benefits our achievement of enlightenment.

If our guru asks us to do something that contradicts the Buddha's teachings and would result in our committing a heavy negative karma and we aren't capable of transforming that action into virtue, into the path to enlightenment and bringing great benefit to sentient beings, we should skillfully and respectfully try to get the guru's permission not to do that action. Remember the advice of the Fifth Dalai Lama, who said,

> Without generating anger or heresy and thus creating obstacles that destroy your own liberation and enlightenment and with guru devotion, skillfully try to get permission from the guru not to do the heavy negative actions that you cannot transform into virtue.

Generating anger or heresy toward the virtuous friend can cause us to be born in the lower realms for a long time, destroy eons of merit equal in number to the moments of our anger and delay all realizations. Avoiding these dangers, we skillfully try to get permission not to do anything that is not in the Buddha's teachings or that we don't have the present capacity to do.

The sutras and the vinaya advise that if our guru asks us to do something that contradicts the Buddha's teachings, we can choose not to do it. The vinaya says that we don't need to do anything that is against the Dharma or against our vows. *Fifty Verses of Guru Devotion* also explains that if our guru tells us to do something that is opposite to the Dharma or that we cannot do because of our level of mind, we can respectfully explain that we can't do it or that we don't have the capacity to do it. However, we should still correctly devote ourselves to that guru as explained by Guru Shakyamuni Buddha and Lama Tsongkhapa. In other words, without losing our guru devotion or criticizing our guru but at the same time protecting ourselves, we respectfully try to get permission to excuse ourselves by explaining that we are incapable of following the guru's advice.

We explain with external and internal respect and don't allow wrong conceptions to arise even for a moment. We should constantly respect the guru: mental respect is devotion, and there are also verbal and physical respect. Without disturbing the guru's mind, we should try to get permission not to do the action. Instead of allowing anger and other wrong thoughts to arise, we should humbly and respectfully explain to the guru how we are not capable of doing what he asks, whether because it is a non-virtue or because our own capacity is limited. The essential point is not to hurt or displease the guru's holy mind. We should use whatever skills we have not to displease the guru as this is the greatest obstacle to developing our mind in the path to enlightenment.

If our guru says something that contradicts the Dharma, we shouldn't respond with irritation or anger, saying something like, "This is stupid! You don't know anything about Dharma!" We shouldn't allow our pride to become bigger than Mount Everest and arrogantly indicate that the guru is ignorant of the teachings and knows less about Dharma than we do. Even if we can't feel devotion, we shouldn't criticize the guru. We shouldn't allow anger or disrespect to enter our mind; we also shouldn't look at the guru with an angry face or speak rudely to him. Besides not having the slightest benefit, such behavior completely destroys the root of all our happiness. We should remember the eight shortcomings of incorrectly following the guru, which we will experience if we act in this way, and not allow anger or heresy to arise. We should think of our own profit and loss.

If our guru tells us to transform a mountain into gold within ten years, we can't do it. We couldn't even cover a mountain with gold leaf in ten years. There are certain things that we don't have the ability to do. It's not that we can't do them because they are negative karmas; we are simply incapable of doing them. In such cases, again we skillfully explain to our guru that we are incapable of doing what he asks.

Of course, there are also things that our guru tells us to do that aren't necessarily wrong but we don't want to do them because we're following our self-cherishing thought and other delusions. It also depends on what we like and what we don't. Our guru might make us work or study hard day and night, without giving us a break or any free time. In reality this is not a wrong path, like the guru asking us to kill someone, steal something or commit some other negative karma. When something is done that we don't like or we are told to do something that we don't want to do, even though it is not a non-virtuous action, we can generate negative thoughts toward the virtuous friend.

When our guru advises us to do something and we fail to do it, we have to explain why. Let's say that our guru tells us to be in India within a week. If our plane crashed so that we couldn't arrive in time we'd have to send him an apology from the intermediate state—I'm joking! If we couldn't make it to India within a week we would have to explain that we had the intention of going but experienced sickness or some other external hindrance; it wasn't that we were lazy. As long as we haven't purposely failed to follow the guru's advice we don't receive the negative karma of disregarding the guru's advice.

How do we explain to our guru that we can't follow his advice without losing our guru devotion? Remember what the Fifth Dalai Lama advised,

> In the view of your hallucinated mind, your own faults appear in the guru's actions. All this shows is that your own heart is rotten to the core. Recognizing them as your own faults, abandon them as poison.

We should abandon as poison seeing faults in the virtuous friend and believing those faults to be there in reality. In other words, even if our guru is doing or advising us to do something that is opposite to Buddha's teachings, we should continuously be mindful that this is a manifestation of our own faults, our own obscured, hallucinated, impure mind. In this way we won't lose our guru devotion, the root of the path to enlightenment.

We have to constantly watch our mind and think, "What I am hearing and seeing is the projection of my own impure mind and karma. In essence, the holy mind of the guru is dharmakaya." We should have constant awareness that our guru's holy mind is dharmakaya, free of all faults and complete in all realizations. What appears to be wrong advice is the result of our own negative karma and impure mind. While our mind has this recognition of dharmakaya, with our speech we respectfully explain why we aren't capable of doing what has been asked.

Even if our guru advises us to do something that is wrong, such as to kill someone, we should never at any time in any situation allow the thought of faults to arise. There shouldn't be any change in our devotion. Seeing faults in the guru is the greatest hindrance to realizations of the path to enlightenment. No matter what fault we see, the most important thing, especially when we are with our guru, is to always watch our own mind so that we never allow negative thoughts toward the guru to arise. In this way we can quickly accomplish our work of generating realizations of the path to enlightenment. Whether or not the guru is in fact a buddha, for our own sake we should be as careful as possible. If negative thoughts do arise, we should try to recognize them right away and quickly stop them. We should then confess and purify them (see appendix 6).

We should always remember that there is nothing to trust in our own view. Things don't actually exist in the way that they appear to us: things that are impermanent in nature appear to us to be permanent; things that are empty of true existence appear to us to be truly existent. We live in hallucination upon hallucination. We don't have the least clairvoyance. Since we can't even tell what is going to happen to us tomorrow, how can we judge anything? How can we judge the level of our guru's mind? We have to remember that what we see is the projection of our own impure mind.

If our guru tells us to do something that involves just a small negativity, however, if it will please the guru, it is better to do what he says. In the past I once wrote to my root guru, His Holiness Trijang Rinpoche, with a question about not eating in the evening. I don't keep that precept now but at that time I had been fasting in the evening for a long time, while I was building the monastery at Lawudo in Solu Khumbu and also while I was at Kopan. However, Lama Yeshe was concerned about my health and was insisting that I eat in the evening. I wrote to ask His Holiness Trijang Rinpoche what I should do and how I should think. As a monk I was not supposed to eat in the evening but my guru was telling me to do so.

His Holiness Trijang Rinpoche replied in a letter that if the guru asks you to do some heavy negative action that is against the Dharma, such as killing, it is wiser not to do it. Without losing faith, you skillfully try to get the guru's permission not to do the action. But Rinpoche said that if it is a matter of a small non-virtuous act, it is better to follow the guru's advice if not to do so would displease the guru, because there would be more harm from disturbing the guru's holy mind, which is a great obstacle to realization. Our main aim should be not to disturb our guru's holy mind.

Rinpoche said that in small matters it is better to listen to the guru's advice because we then don't displease the guru, a great obstacle that is much more dangerous than breaking the monk's vow about eating. Displeasing the guru is the greatest obstacle to attainment; it brings great harm in terms of long-term suffering in the hell realms and of blocking attainments of the graduated path to enlightenment.

This meant that it was better for me to accept to eat in the evening, even though it was opposite to a monk's vow, because it would please Lama Yeshe. Pleasing the holy mind of the guru is more skillful because by doing so we collect much merit and become closer to enlightenment. Pleasing the guru's holy mind is also one of the most powerful purification practices, purifying heavy negative karma from many, many lifetimes. Many tantric teachings mention that attainment comes only by pleasing the virtuous friend.

If we become too concrete about small vices, rejecting our guru's advice might disturb his holy mind, which becomes a great hindrance to our accomplishment of temporary and ultimate happiness. It is as if we incur a big wound in order to avoid a small one. There is more harm from disturbing our guru's holy mind than from incurring a small vice. We have to check which action is more harmful; we have to think of what is more profitable. Making a skillful decision depends on understanding the complete teachings on guru devotion.

We might also get confused if two different gurus give what looks to us like different advice. If our gurus appear to contradict each other, it is our own impure karmic view. Guru Shakyamuni Buddha taught that we should do what accords with the Dharma and what has more benefit. We can use our own intelligence and our own understanding of Dharma to analyze this.

Without disturbing either guru's mind, we follow whichever advice benefits other sentient beings more.

Of course, because of our own karma, our own lack of merit, it is also possible to receive wrong answers.

We need to correctly devote ourselves to the virtuous friend and we do so in accordance with what Guru Shakyamuni Buddha, Lama Tsongkhapa and the valid lineage lamas explained in the teachings. We decide whether to do what the guru tells us to do by checking his advice against the scriptures of Guru Shakyamuni Buddha and the Indian pandits. The teaching of Buddha is the main reference for how we should practice. If we act in accordance with the teachings of Buddha, we will be in no danger.

Serkong Dorje Chang, Kathmandu, Nepal, 1978

17. How the Past Kagyü Lamas Practiced[102]

❧❦

Gomchen Khampala, a Nyingma meditator who lived in Solu Khumbu, gave me a text written by his root guru, Rongpu Sangye, who I mentioned in the previous chapter. It is an incredibly moving teaching on guru devotion, with quotations from great yogis that describe how to see as positive such actions as killing, stealing, sexual misconduct, lying and so forth. It shows how to use any fault that appears to us to develop devotion within our mind.

Gomchen Rinpoche was regarded as an embodiment of the great Tibetan yogi Tangtong Gyalpo. In 1975 Gomchen-la came to Kopan when I was there teaching a course and asked me to give him the oral transmission of *Lama Tsongkhapa Guru Yoga*. He wanted me to give the oral transmission during the course, with all the Western students, which I did. When we then asked him to give a talk, he gave a talk on guru devotion (see appendix 7). Though not a scholar, he was a great practitioner who had spent years meditating in the mountains, so of course, every single word of his talk was effective.

Marpa, Milarepa, Gampopa and the other previous Kagyü lamas practiced guru yoga by trying to see every action of the guru, including all the mistakes, as pure. These Kagyü lamas generated the complete path of sutra and tantra and became enlightened in one brief lifetime through practicing guru yoga as the very heart of the path.

The previous Kagyü lamas practiced seeing the guru's actions as pure in the following way:

---

[102] See *The Great Kagyu Masters*.

> Every action done by the qualified holy guru is good,
> Every action done is a quality.
> Even if the guru acts as a butcher or kills a human being,
> It is meaningful and good:
> It is definite that sentient beings are being guided with compassion.

This verse could be referring to transferring the consciousness of an evil-doer to a pure land. There are various ways to do this, with weapons and with meditation. With the meditations of wrathful tantric fire pujas, for example, a person's consciousness can be separated from his body and transferred to a pure land.

Even if the guru kills a human being, you think that the being who has been killed is definitely being guided by him with compassion from the lower realms to better realms. If the guru does something that you find confusing, such as being careless of others or harming them, you should think, as the Kagyü lamas did, "It is definite that those sentient beings are being guided with compassion." Or think, "If they were left as they are now they would experience much suffering. Instead, their negative karma is being purified and they are being guided with great compassion to a better realm."

In ancient times in Tibet, even the executioners who cut off the heads of criminals were all in fact embodiments of Chenrezig, as were the king, the minister and the judge, even though externally they looked like ordinary people committing heavy negative actions.

Also, a butcher behind the Potala Palace, even though externally he looked like an ordinary person, was in fact an embodiment of Yamantaka.

Once a monk who was very miserly with his money died. After he had died, his close disciples searched his room to find where his money was kept so that they could use it for pujas and to make offerings to the monks in the monastery to pray for their teacher. They couldn't find the money anywhere. One disciple remembered that their teacher used to go to a spot a little distance from the monastery, where he had sometimes seen him digging. The disciple figured that the money might be buried there. When the disciple and some of the other monks went there they discovered the spot was covered with a flat stone. When they dug away the dirt they found a sack full of money hidden there but a lobster was holding it in its claws. Because of his miserliness, the teacher had been reborn as a lobster.

When the disciple went to ask Phurchog Jampa Rinpoche what to do, Rinpoche advised him to take the lobster and offer it to the butcher behind the Potala Palace. When the disciple did this the butcher seemed surprised and demanded, "Who told you to bring it here?" The disciple told him that Phurchog Jampa Rinpoche had advised him to do it. At the beginning the butcher scolded the disciple but he finally accepted the lobster. He put the lobster on his chopping block and split it in two with a knife. He then ate half and threw the other half into space.

The disciple returned to Phurchog Jampa Rinpoche to tell him what had happened. After he had explained, Rinpoche said, "Now it's all right. He ate half, and the half he threw into space signifies that the consciousness was transferred to a pure realm."

There are many similar stories illustrating that we often can't really determine what other people are. Even though we might see them as ordinary beings doing evil actions, it is hard to really trust what we see as true. It is difficult to say whether particular people are actually evil beings, as we see them.

Generally, as we can't see other beings' level of mind, we can't have the fixed idea that someone is actually an ordinary person or an evil person just because we see him doing evil actions. We may see faults in someone and decide that what we see is in fact true. But to place so much trust in our own view of something as concrete or ordinary is dangerous, as it can disturb the generation of realizations within our mind.

> Even if the guru shows the act of sexual misconduct,
> It signifies the unification of method and wisdom
> And is done to receive and increase realizations.

To receive and increase realizations could be related to the subject, the virtuous teacher, as a yogi practitioner achieving the rest of the tantric path and the Vajradhara state by quickly cutting off dualistic view. However, it can also be understood in terms of subduing the minds of other sentient beings—their intense dissatisfaction and other disturbing thoughts—and developing their realizations of the path.

The way to practice is to look at the action of sexual misconduct as pure, which stops the arising of heresy and other wrong conceptions, the heaviest obstacles to achieving the graduated path to enlightenment.

> Even if the guru cheats others by telling lies,
> He is guiding sentient beings in the path to liberation
> Through various means.

This is the way the previous Kagyü lamas thought in order to see the guru's action of lying as pure.

> Even if the guru shows the act of stealing,
> He is transforming the possessions of others into merit.
> It is a means to pacify the poverty of those living beings.

In other words, the possessions are used to accumulate merit for the sake of those sentient beings. This pacifies the karma that caused them to be poor, without the means of living. This is the advice on how to think to see the guru's action of stealing as pure.

> If the guru shows the act of scolding,
> It is reciting a wrathful mantra that definitely eliminates obstacles.
> If the guru shows the act of beating,
> It is a blessing and the source of all realizations.
> The devoted are satisfied and joyful.

Devoted, respectful disciples see being scolded or beaten by their guru as pure and only as helping them purify their negative karma; thinking that their guru's actions only benefit them makes them happy. Guru yoga practice is to not criticize the guru but remember his kindness instead and helps generate realizations.

The famous example here is Milarepa, whose guru Marpa scolded and beat him a great deal. But no matter how much Marpa scolded or beat him, Milarepa's guru devotion remained stable.

It was similar with the old monk who was Geshe Ngawang Dhargyey's attendant. When I went to school in Dalhousie[103] for six months, Geshe Ngawang Dhargyey would sometimes come up to the school on Sundays because one of the Gelugpa lamas staying there was Geshe-la's disciple.

One time Geshe-la invited me to come down to his house in Dalhousie for a meal. So one Sunday a couple of the other incarnate lamas and I went down to Geshe-la's house. I think Geshe-la wanted to give us momos but his attendant served us bread and vegetables instead. Geshe Dhargyey then scolded the old monk for about twenty minutes. He scolded him for a long, long time.

---

[103] A former British hill station in Himachal Pradesh in India.

I sat there thinking, "If I were Geshe-la's disciple I couldn't stand that!" I wouldn't have lasted long—I would have run away immediately. But this old monk was a great example of guru devotion practice. He wasn't known to be learned and I'm not sure he even had the title "geshe," but his mind was unbelievable. I thought he might disintegrate because of the scolding but there wasn't the slightest change in his face. His nose didn't become red, nor did his ears, and his eyes didn't bulge. There wasn't the slightest reaction. He kept exactly the same calm expression, as if Geshe-la wasn't saying anything.

I was there only once for an hour but I'm sure Geshe-la would have scolded him not just on that one day but over years and years. I think this old monk had great achievement.

Geshe Doga[104] told me that this monk would drink the little bit of water left after Geshe Ngawang Dhargyey had washed in the mornings. This is a proof of his unshakable guru devotion. Some monks mightn't bear the title "geshe" or have a reputation for being learned or good in debate but their practice and attainments are very inspiring.

> Even if the guru shows the act of killing a hundred human beings
>   at one time,
> It is definitely only the action of a buddha benefiting sentient
>   beings.
>
> Even if the guru shows the act of enjoying a hundred princesses,
> It is the transcendental wisdom of great bliss, the mahamudra.

Unless our teacher gives us permission not to regard him as a virtuous friend, once the Dharma connection is made, we as disciples have the responsibility to correctly devote ourselves to that guru. No matter what happens after Dharma contact is made—even if our guru commits the ten non-virtuous actions or kills millions of people—it is our responsibility to practice guru devotion. No matter what the guru does, for our own benefit we mustn't allow heresy or other wrong thoughts toward the guru to arise, as Buddha explained in the sutras and Lama Tsongkhapa explained in the lam-rim. We have to try to see everything the guru does as positive. If we allow negative

---

[104] Geshe Doga, the long-serving resident geshe at Tara Institute, Melbourne, Australia, is a disciple of Geshe Ngawang Dhargyey.

thoughts toward the guru to arise we harm our achievement of realizations and enlightenment. With a firm mind, we have to practice carefully, thinking of our own profit.

You shouldn't give up a virtuous teacher by thinking you can no longer see him as your guru because he doesn't practice Dharma or kills human beings, steals, fights with others, has much anger or doesn't live in the precepts. Even if your guru keeps a hundred wives or goes to war and kills millions of people, there is nothing to be done. You still have to practice guru devotion. It is not that you can first recognize someone as your virtuous teacher and then later decide not to recognize him any more. Once the contact is made, there is nothing to be done.

However, this doesn't mean that if your guru drinks wine, you should also drink wine; that if your guru smokes, you should also smoke. It doesn't mean that if your guru doesn't live in precepts, you shouldn't live in precepts. Even if you do see mistakes in the actions of your guru, such as criticizing other sects, you don't need to imitate him and also criticize other sects. Thinking, "My guru does it so why can't I?" is the wrong way to practice guru devotion.

Even if your guru goes to the city every night and spends his nights with prostitutes, it doesn't mean that you should do that. Perhaps if the level of your mind is like that of the Sixth Dalai Lama, you can do it. However, I'm not saying that all the gurus who act like this have this level of mind. If you have reached the completion stage, you can imitate the Sixth Dalai Lama, who went to a different brothel in Lhasa every night to sleep with prostitutes. To prove to the many people who criticized him that he did not lose any semen without control, one day he went on the top of the Potala Palace and urinated. Just before the urine hit the ground, he drew it back into his holy body.

We have to practice in accordance with the level of our own mind. Whether or not we can do what the guru does is determined by our level of mind. We can practice those actions of the guru that accord with the Dharma and also with the level of our mind. There is no need to copy exactly what the guru does, thinking, "I should do this because my guru does it," and there is also no need to criticize him. If we can see our guru's actions as pure, that is good as it benefits us; but even if we can't see his actions as pure, there is still no need to criticize him.

The great Kagyü yogi Drogön Tsangpa Gyare said,

> As long as you don't do anything inauspicious in relation to the qualified lord, it doesn't matter if you break off every other relationship. Let it happen. But if you do something inauspicious in relation to the qualified lord, even if all other sentient beings become your friends, what is the use?

Tsangpa Gyare is saying that as long as we don't make any mistake in relation to the virtuous friend, it doesn't matter if we have broken our connections to all the other people in the world. If we have to choose between breaking samaya with our guru and breaking off a relationship with an ordinary friend, even if she has been very kind and helped us a lot, it is better to end the friendship. If keeping this relationship means going against the advice of our guru or breaking or even endangering our samaya, then maintaining the relationship doesn't matter. Break it off; let it end.

However, if we make a mistake in relation to our virtuous friend, even if everyone else in the world becomes our close friend, it is of no benefit because we will have no success in our life or in developing our mind. If our guru is unhappy or displeased with us, even if everyone else in the world is happy with us, it means nothing. There is no happiness in this life, and there is no happiness in future lives, liberation or enlightenment.

As mentioned in the lam-rim teachings, if we have degenerated or broken our samaya with one guru, even if we have a good relationship with all our other gurus, we can't generate realizations. And after we have made a Dharma connection, even if we don't renounce the virtuous friend but simply leave him out or forget to devote ourselves to him with thought and action, we will experience heavy shortcomings. These are important points to consider if we are concerned about developing our mind for ourselves and for other sentient beings.

This is the way the past Kagyü lamas practiced guru yoga: they looked at all the various actions of the guru as pure. Thinking in this way doesn't allow negative thoughts and superstition toward the guru to arise. Whether or not the guru is pure, or enlightened, if from our own side we practice in this way, trying to see his actions as pure, it stops the arising of anger, heresy and other negative thoughts. Without hindrance, we are then able to quickly generate realizations of the sutra and tantra paths.

Achieving enlightenment in one brief lifetime of this degenerate time depends on how much we are able to stop negative thoughts toward the guru. In order to quickly generate realizations of the path, even if we don't have the devotion that sees the guru as a buddha, the most important thing is to at least stop the arising of negative thoughts toward the guru. We can then train our mind in the rest of the path, and there is a possibility of generating the realizations of the path.

As His Holiness the Dalai Lama often says, "Even if you can't see the guru as a buddha, the very basic thing is to stop wrong conceptions arising." In that way you don't create obstacles to your own success in the path to enlightenment. This is the whole point. For this reason, the Kagyü lamas practiced guru devotion by training their minds to look at the guru purely.

18. Exceptional Gurus, Exceptional Disciples

A s His Holiness the Dalai Lama often says, when there are special gurus and special disciples, like Tilopa and Naropa or Marpa and Milarepa, the disciple immediately follows, without question, every single word that the guru says.

Tilopa and Naropa[105]

The great yogi Tilopa, Naropa's guru, was born in Sahor, in eastern India. Tilopa had inconceivable qualities and showed many aspects, sometimes appearing in the form of a monk and at other times as a naked yogi. There were many, many Tilopas—sometimes he seemed to be everywhere.

Tilopa was an enlightened being, Buddha Vajradhara, and he used skillful means to guide Naropa in a way that purified many eons of negative karma and defilements and enabled him to reach enlightenment very quickly. Before even giving him a teaching, Tilopa let Naropa undergo twelve great hardships,[106] which endangered his life, and twelve small hard-

---

[105] See, for example, *The Life & Teaching of Naropa* and *Illusion's Game*.

[106] The twelve great hardships that Naropa underwent as a student of Tilopa were 1) jumping off a temple roof; 2) jumping into a fire; 3) being beaten after ruining the food of those refusing to give alms twice; 4) being attacked by leeches as he attempted to build a bridge; 5) being tortured by hot reeds at the hands of Tilopa; 6) chasing the vision of a man to the point of exhaustion; 7) being beaten by a minister and his followers after attacking a minister and his bride; 8) being beaten by a king and his followers after attacking a queen; 9) being beaten by an army after attacking a prince; 10) being dissatisfied with his consort and his job, as well as hitting his penis with a rock; 11) having to give his consort to Tilopa and having her beaten by Tilopa; and 12) making a mandala with sand and his own blood and

ships.[107] Twelve times Tilopa asked Naropa to do something that almost killed Naropa. When Naropa was almost dead, Tilopa would come and bless him and save his life. Tilopa would then tell Naropa to do something else and again Naropa would almost die. The things Tilopa asked Naropa to do were all very dangerous; he wasn't asking him to go to a cave and meditate. Because he underwent these hardships, Naropa became a great yogi in that life; then, after passing away, he achieved enlightenment in the intermediate state.

Tilopa's heart disciple, Naropa, was born in Srinagara, also in eastern India. Naropa became a great scholar expert in the five aspects of knowledge and achieved realizations. When Naropa was in a cemetery doing a retreat to attain the secret mantra called the "Seven Syllables,"[108] a dakini predicted to him in a dream at dawn, "O son of the race, you should go to the east, where there is a yogi called Tilo. You should take mahamudra teachings from him." It seemed that Naropa was showing the aspect of pride in his learning, so that night the dakini told him that he still had things to learn and that he should seek his guru, Tilopa.

Naropa didn't ask where Tilopa was but simply headed east. He asked some monks he met, "Have you seen a yogi called Tilopa?" The monks replied, "We haven't seen a yogi called Tilopa but there is somebody here called Muttuova Tilopa." *Muttuova* can mean "pagan." Because Tilopa had the external appearance of a sadhu, the monks might have believed he was a Hindu.

---

body parts. After each hardship, Tilopa healed Naropa of any physical problems he had, then gave him a particular teaching.

[107] Naropa experienced the twelve small hardships as visions in which 1) Vajrayogini appeared in the form of an ugly old hag and told him to go to Tilopa; 2) he leapt over a leper woman without hands and feet, who was blocking his path; 3) he jumped over a stinking bitch crawling with vermin; 4) he didn't want to associate with a man playing tricks on his parents; 5) he didn't want to help a man who was tearing the intestines out of a human corpse and then cutting them up; 6) he refused to help a man who had opened the stomach of a live man and was washing it with warm water; 7) he entreated to marry a king's daughter in order to hear of Tilopa's whereabouts from the king; 8) he refused to kill a deer with a bow and arrow given to him by a dark man with a pack of hounds; 9) he refused to eat the fish and frogs cooked alive by an old woman; 10) he refused to help a man cruelly killing his parents; 11) having actually met Tilopa, he refused Tilopa's request to kill a handful of lice; and lastly, 12) he met many one-eyed people, a blind man who could see, an earless one who could hear, a man without a tongue who spoke, a lame man running about and a corpse gently fanning itself. All twelve visions were pointing out the symbols of mahamudra.

[108] The Heruka near heart mantra, OM HRIH HA HA HUM HUM PHAT.

When Naropa finally reached the temple where Tilopa was staying, he saw a yogi wearing ragged red clothes, old and full of holes. He was sitting in line with the monks, who were eating their meal. In his left hand Tilopa was holding four or five live fish and in his right hand, burning firewood. Tilopa then burnt the fish alive.

Naropa thought, "What this man is doing is terrible!" He doubted that it could be Tilopa.

The monks didn't like Tilopa and had no respect for him. Some of the monks came to beat Tilopa with sticks, saying, "Why do you come here and sit in our line?" Tilopa replied, "If you don't like it, then you go away." He then snapped his fingers over the fish and all the fish he had burnt flew into space.

Naropa then thought, "This is wonderful! This must definitely be Tilopa."

After Tilopa revived the fish, the monks realized that he was a great yogi. They all did three prostrations to Tilopa and circumambulated him three times and then everybody apologized to him. Tilopa accepted all their apologies. Naropa thought, "This is definitely Tilopa. Now there is no doubt!"

Naropa also made three prostrations and did three circumambulations. Naropa then placed Tilopa's feet on his head and told Tilopa, "It was prophesied that I should come here. I'm requesting you to please take me out of samsara."

Tilopa didn't say anything but simply walked away. Even though Tilopa hadn't said anything, Naropa followed him. When Naropa followed Tilopa into a bamboo grove, Naropa fell into a hole in the ground and a piece of bamboo pierced his backside. Tilopa beat Naropa on the back with a piece of bamboo and then looked into his face. Again Tilopa didn't say anything and left.

Naropa continued to follow Tilopa and three days later Tilopa asked him, "Are you sick?" Naropa asked Tilopa, "Please stay here." Tilopa didn't say anything and left again. Naropa was so sick that he just remained there, lying on the ground. Three days later Tilopa returned. He placed his hand on Naropa's body and the pain went away. From that time, the name "Naropa" was given. I think it was because Naropa lay in the sand like a corpse.

Naropa continued to follow Tilopa. One time a family invited some monks for a meal and Tilopa and Naropa were sitting in line at the family's house waiting to be served. Before the food was offered to the monks, Tilopa said to Naropa, "I'm so hungry I can't stand it! I can't wait. Go now and beg some food." Without hesitation Naropa went, but the family said, "How can we give you food before it is offered to the Sangha?"

Naropa then put some food in a bowl and ran away with it. The family chased Naropa with sticks and beat him almost to death. When Tilopa looked at one of the men chasing Naropa, the man became paralyzed and couldn't walk. Naropa then offered the food to Tilopa. Tilopa came and blessed Naropa and Naropa recovered.

Another time Tilopa went up on the roof of a temple and told Naropa, "Any capable person who doesn't go against the guru's advice would jump from here." Naropa thought, "There are no other disciples here; he must mean me."

Naropa jumped from the roof of the temple and broke both his legs. Tilopa came close to Naropa and just stood there looking at him for a while. He then went away, leaving Naropa there with his legs broken. Two or three days later Tilopa came back and asked, "Are you sick?" Naropa said, "I've become like a corpse. I can't get up. I can't do anything." Tilopa again placed his hands on Naropa and blessed him. The pain went away and Naropa recovered.

One day while Tilopa was walking with Naropa he collected together some flowers, made them into a garland and gave it to Naropa. Two men were escorting a girl to her wedding. Tilopa told Naropa, "Put these flowers on her. The girl and the men will be happy and the men will give you a present. When they come to give you the present, don't take it but instead rub the girl's breasts."

Naropa went to the girl and offered her the flower garland. As he was putting the flowers around her neck, the two men went to give Naropa a present. Naropa then rubbed the girl's breasts. The two men got extremely angry, tied his hands with rope and beat him almost to death.

Tilopa came and asked Naropa, "What happened? What did you do wrong?" Naropa replied, "I did exactly what the guru said but the men who were escorting the girl tied me up." Tilopa then gestured with his hands and blessed him and Naropa was again relieved of all his pains.

On another day, the wife of King Indrabhuti invited Tilopa to be the master at a tsog puja. She arranged the tsog and invited everybody to the place to do the puja. From the place where the tsog offering was arranged, without going to see Tilopa, King Indrabhuti's wife simply requested, "O Tilopa, Sherab Zangpo, people say that you have clairvoyance. Please come to my tsog puja." She made the request simply by thinking this.

Even though Tilopa was living in a small cave many days away from the place where she had arranged the tsog, he appeared there the same day she made the request. Tilopa discovered her request through his clairvoyance and immediately went there, along with Naropa, who had also achieved psychic powers. They then offered tsog and made offerings.

Tilopa then left that place and Naropa followed him. Tilopa lay down beside a great river and told Naropa, "I'm very hungry. Go beg some food." Naropa crossed the river and went to beg for food. When Naropa returned with some rice he saw a monk lying on Tilopa's bed. He thought, "This must be an embodiment of my guru" and offered the food to the monk. When Naropa offered the food, the monk hit Naropa on the head, saying, "You're giving me food in the afternoon."[109] Naropa thought, "My guru Tilopa has manifested as a fully ordained monk. This means my guru definitely has attainments." Again he followed Tilopa.

In time Tilopa reached a forest, but when he tried to enter the forest he kept on turning back. Naropa watched, wondering what the problem was. Naropa then saw that Tilopa seemed to be having difficulty jumping across a few feet of water. Naropa also saw that there were many, many leeches in the water. Naropa thought, "Since it is so difficult for my guru Tilopa to cross this water, I'll use my body as a bridge."

Tilopa agreed to this and Naropa stretched his body across the water. Tilopa went very slowly across Naropa; it took him a long time to cross. When Tilopa had crossed over and Naropa stood up, his whole body was covered with leeches all drinking his blood. When Naropa saw this, he trembled and then fainted.

Tilopa left and returned after three days. Tilopa asked Naropa, "Are you sick?" and Naropa replied, "I feel like a corpse." Again Tilopa moved his hands over Naropa's body and all the pain went away.

At another time Tilopa and Naropa were in a cemetery. When Naropa went to beg for food, he found some that was incredibly delicious; he had never tasted food like that before. Naropa felt it would be a waste if he simply ate it all himself, so he kept some to offer his guru. When he offered the food to Tilopa, he ate it with delight, smacking his lips in order for Naropa to accumulate merit. He then told Naropa, "These vegetables of yours are delicious!" Naropa was very happy. He thought, "So far nothing I have offered my guru has satisfied him but he is extremely pleased with this

[109] Eating food in the afternoon is against a monk's vows.

offering; I'm going to get another serving." Tilopa agreed that he could go, so Naropa went to look for more of those delicious vegetables but couldn't find any anywhere.

In India, there was a custom that you could beg food once a day, but not twice. Naropa looked and looked for that delicious food but couldn't find any. Finally he found a pot of it in the house of one family, so he grabbed the whole pot and ran away with it. The men from the house chased and caught Naropa and chained him to a post so that he couldn't move at all. Tilopa then came along and asked, "What did you do wrong?" Naropa explained the whole story and Tilopa again moved his hand over Naropa's body and all the pain went away.

On another day Tilopa told Naropa, "While you are on this huge plain, don't rest, don't drink, and don't eat anything. Just keep walking." Naropa did exactly as Tilopa advised. After some time, because he was walking continuously without resting, eating or drinking, he collapsed. Naropa was about to die when again Tilopa came along and asked, "What happened?" Naropa explained, "I did exactly what my guru advised me to do." After Tilopa moved his hand over Naropa's body, Naropa again recovered.

One day Tilopa put three huge pieces of firewood together and started a fire. He then asked, "Is there anybody who can sit in this fire?" Since there was no one else around, Naropa thought, "He must be talking to me." Naropa then sat in the center of the fire. All his flesh was burnt away, leaving just the whiteness of his bones. Again Tilopa moved his hand and again Naropa recovered.

Another time Tilopa told Naropa, "You should bring that princess here," so Naropa went to get the princess. He waited outside the palace until she came out and immediately grabbed her. The king's retinue then caught Naropa and tied him up. This time, simply by thinking, "I'm doing this for my guru," Naropa was released.

On another day a minister's wife came along in a carriage. Again Tilopa asked, "Is there anybody who can capture this minister's wife?" Naropa thought, "He must be talking to me," and went to kidnap the minister's wife. The minister and his retinue caught Naropa and cut off his arms and legs. Naropa thought, "How is it possible to recover from this?" When Naropa thought this, Tilopa suddenly appeared there and said, "What did you do wrong?" Naropa replied, "I went to kidnap the minister's wife and the minister cut off my limbs." Tilopa then put together the pieces of Naropa's limbs, again moved his hand over Naropa's body and again Naropa recovered.

Throughout all these ordeals Naropa didn't generate even a single heretical thought toward Tilopa. Naropa himself said, "I didn't generate heresy toward my guru for even a moment during all those times."

In this way, for twelve years Naropa did every single thing that Tilopa advised him to do and experienced twelve great hardships. After Naropa had undergone these twelve hardships in serving Tilopa, one day Tilopa asked Naropa whether he wanted teachings. When Naropa requested initiation, Tilopa asked him to offer a mandala. Since there was nothing to offer as a mandala, Naropa urinated on the sand and made a mandala offering with the wet sand. Tilopa then threw this sand mandala offering in Naropa's face and immediately asked him to look up into space, where Naropa saw the entire Heruka mandala in beautiful colors. Tilopa transformed the actual Heruka mandala in space, transformed himself into Heruka and then initiated Naropa into the mandala.

All the twelve great and twelve small hardships that Naropa experienced in following Tilopa's advice were his preliminary practice. By doing this preliminary practice, Naropa purified his karmic obscurations and when his mind had become receptive, Tilopa's transcendental wisdom manifested in the Heruka mandala in space and he then initiated Naropa.

One day Naropa did prostrations to Tilopa, circumambulated him, and requested, "Please guide me!" Tilopa didn't answer—he just sat there looking around. Tilopa then took his shoe off and hit Naropa between his eyebrows with it. Naropa immediately fainted. When he regained consciousness he was suddenly able to see clearly all the words and meanings of the four tantras. At that time Tilopa gave Naropa special advice on the short AH.[110]

Naropa thought, "I have served my guru and now I think the guru is happy with me and keeps me in his heart. I have been blessed and I have now accomplished my work." Naropa then thought "Since I now have both scriptural understanding and realizations, what should I do? Should I teach or should I meditate?" Naropa went to ask Tilopa for his advice.

At that time Tilopa had a skull filled with hot excrement, with steam coming off it. Using a human rib as a spoon, Tilopa said to Naropa, "Eat this and then try to understand the meaning." Tilopa then left. Naropa ate the excrement without any superstition or hesitation. When he ate it, along

[110] Meditating on the short AH is part of the completion stage practice of *tummo*, or inner fire. See *The Bliss of Inner Fire* for more about this practice.

with a beautiful scented smell, he experienced the hundred tastes,[III] which he had never experienced before. Naropa thought, "Both the excrement in this skull and the human rib are dirty things but the blessing of Tilopa has made them delicious." Naropa then thought "This is telling me that if I don't practice Dharma the whole of this body is dirty. But if I practice Dharma, if I meditate, these unclean things become a blessing. Therefore, this is telling me to meditate." This is what Naropa understood.

Tilopa then came and asked Naropa, "Do you understand?" When Naropa told Tilopa what he had understood, Tilopa said, "It means exactly what you have understood."

Naropa did prostrations to Tilopa and again followed him, this time to a great city. There people were saying "A very good yogi has come" and many people came to make offerings. At that time Naropa found a big pot filled with pearls. He was very pleased. Thinking, "My guru is very kind to me and also my services are not small," Naropa went to offer the pot of pearls to Tilopa. Realizing what Naropa was thinking, Tilopa thought, "Naropa is still not a good yogi." In order to break Naropa's pride, Tilopa sat himself on an incredibly high throne of pearls. When Naropa saw Tilopa sitting on this pearl throne, he thought, "My guru Tilopa is so rich that my offering of this pot filled with pearls is nothing special." He then sprinkled the pearls in the mandala and went away.

Naropa reached the house of a blacksmith and slept there. In the very early morning when he got up to do his practice, the blacksmith thought, "It must be dawn." When he found out it wasn't dawn, the blacksmith scolded Naropa so much that he couldn't do his meditation. Naropa then got angry and asked himself many times, "Whose fault is this?" He then realized, "It's my own fault—I must cut off the root of anger." At that time Naropa was able to cut off the root of anger and to realize the unborn nature of ignorance (which means he realized that ignorance doesn't have truly existent birth). Naropa then realized that he was able to achieve this through the kindness of his guru. At that time, Naropa was able to cut the root of all dharmas, which means the root of samsara.

From there Naropa went to the great monastery of Nalanda, where there were many hundreds of pandits. Nalanda had four gates, with a pandit protecting each gate, which meant they were responsible for debating with learned Hindus. At the eastern gate was Prajnakara; at the southern gate,

---

[III] Food of a hundred tastes refers to a variety of fine foods with many delicious flavors.

Krishnacharya; at the western gate, Ratnakarashanti; but there was no pandit to protect the northern gate. The local king asked Naropa to be the protector at the northern gate.

When the king asked Naropa to be the fourth protector, Naropa thought, "In our early times together my guru Tilopa advised me not to become the pandit who protects the fourth door of Nalanda but this Dharma activity is so important that maybe it will be OK for me to do it." Naropa promised to do what the king asked. The king bowed at Naropa's feet and Naropa then initiated him and gave him teachings.

One day when Naropa was protecting the northern gate of Nalanda monastery, a Hindu pandit came to debate with him. That first day the Hindu won; Naropa couldn't seem to defeat him. The Nalanda monks thought, "Tomorrow Naropa will again lose the debate." That night Naropa prayed to Tilopa, "Guru Tilopa, please help me." Tilopa then appeared in front of Naropa. Naropa was upset and appealed to Tilopa, telling him that he had shown little compassion for him that day, "You didn't help me to win when I was debating." Tilopa replied, "I was right there in front of you but the reason you lost was that you went against my earlier advice not to debate with the Hindus at Nalanda's gates." Tilopa then said, "When you debate with this Hindu tomorrow, you should do so with your hands in the threatening mudra."[112]

The next day when Naropa debated with the Hindu he did exactly as Tilopa advised. He pointed at the Hindu with the threatening mudra and just seeing this mudra made the hearts of all the Hindus quake. They were all defeated and had to become Buddhists.

Another day a huge elephant fell dead at the northern door of Nalanda. Everybody was very worried because if its corpse were left there all the people of the northern side would become ill. But the body was so huge that it couldn't be carried away. Naropa made a big hole somewhere near the city, then made his consciousness enter the dead body of the elephant and moved it into the hole. After putting the elephant's corpse in the hole, Naropa reabsorbed his wind-mind.

One day Naropa went to bathe but left the protection amulet[113] that he normally kept on his body in a pig-sty so that it wouldn't get wet. A crow

---

[112] This is the mudra displayed by many wrathful deities, such as Vajrapani and Mahakala.

[113] A protection is an amulet containing printed mandalas, holy relics and so forth; it is sometimes wrapped in cloth and worn around the neck or on another part of the body to protect the wearer.

came and flew off with his amulet, so Naropa made the threatening mudra and just by looking at the crow like that paralyzed it. This showed that Naropa had accomplished the tantric actions.

At another time Naropa lived by begging with a skull and he would take any food from anybody. One day, instead of putting food into Naropa's skull, a group of robbers put in a knife. Naropa swirled the skull around and the knife melted into nectar, which Naropa then drank.

Naropa performed many amazing actions in correctly devoting himself to his virtuous friend Tilopa. He then gained great attainments, as shown by his doing these various actions that ordinary people cannot do. Naropa then achieved the realization of mahamudra. His holy mind attained inconceivable qualities, and he achieved enlightenment in the intermediate state.

Marpa and Milarepa[114]

Milarepa is one of the most inspiring examples of incomparable guru devotion. Milarepa had such strong devotion that nothing could affect it. By hearing Milarepa's life-story, we want to become like him. We want to have the same realizations that Milarepa had and we want to find a virtuous teacher just like Milarepa's.

I first read Milarepa's life story in Solu Khumbu when I was a small boy, maybe six or seven years old. I think when I was young my mind was probably clearer because reading Milarepa's biography was a little like having visions of the stories.

I had a strong desire in my heart to find a guru like Marpa, just as Milarepa had. When I first went to Tibet with my two uncles and was at Tashilhunpo, the Panchen Lama's monastery, I met a Sherpa monk, Gyaltsen, who looked a little like a *dob-dob*. He had a black *shemtab* that was smeared with a lot of butter and carried a long key. He didn't seem to study or go to pujas but mainly traveled back and forth between the monastery and the town of Shigatse.

We stayed at Tashilhunpo for a week. We didn't go to the pujas but when a puja had finished, we got into the line of monks to receive the money offering. I think Gyaltsen probably guided us. On the very last night before we were to leave, Gyaltsen insisted very much that I should stay and become

---

[114] See, for example, *The Life of Marpa the Translator*, *The Life of Milarepa* and *The Hundred Thousand Songs of Milarepa*.

his disciple. Both my uncles agreed that I should stay there. I didn't have the slightest desire to become his disciple! I had an unbelievably difficult time. I don't think I had any sleep that whole night, wondering how I could escape from this. I couldn't think what to do. I don't know how it happened, but fortunately the next morning my uncles allowed me to leave with them.

A little while later, in Phagri, I met Losang Gyatso, a senior monk in Domo Geshe's monastery. When I first met him he asked me whether I would be his disciple and I replied, "Yes, okay." The whole thing was up to karma. I asked Losang Gyatso, "Can you be like Marpa?" He said, "Yes."

I think I have been very fortunate to have met many virtuous teachers with the same qualities as Marpa. The problem is not that I haven't met a guru like Marpa. From the guru's side everything has been perfect; they have had everything that Marpa, Milarepa and Naropa had. The only problem is that from my own side I haven't done a single practice.

In his early life Milarepa had learnt black magic on the advice of his mother and used it to destroy his aunt and uncle and all the other people who had treated his family badly. He received instructions on black magic from a lama and did the necessary retreats. He then performed black magic while his aunt and uncle were celebrating a marriage with a crowd of people. Many people were singing and dancing upstairs, with horses and other animals downstairs. Milarepa used black magic to break the supporting posts so that the whole house collapsed; all the people, numbering more than thirty, were killed, as well as all the animals.

Milarepa later regretted his action very much and wanted to practice Dharma. The lama who had taught him black magic advised him to learn Dharma from the great yogi called Marpa. This is how Milarepa came to meet Marpa.

Even though Marpa was an enlightened being, the actual Hevajra, when Milarepa met him for the first time he appeared to Milarepa to be just an ordinary farmer drinking beer as he plowed a field, his body and clothes covered in dust.

Milarepa said to Marpa, "I have created heavy negative karma, so I have now come to practice Dharma. I have nothing to offer you but my body, speech and mind. Please give me the Dharma and also food and clothing." Milarepa asked for food and clothing because he didn't have anything at all.

Although Milarepa went to Marpa solely to receive teachings, for many years Marpa never gave him any initiations or teachings. Instead, Marpa only scolded him and gave him hard work to do. Marpa advised Milarepa to build a nine-story tower, something like a Chinese pagoda. I think this tower is still there in Lhodrak in southern Tibet. Marpa told Milarepa to build it by himself, without anyone else's help. When Milarepa finished the building there were no thanks from Marpa; he didn't say, "Oh, you've done a wonderful job! Are you exhausted?" Marpa simply told him to tear it down and return every stone to its original place. He then asked Milarepa to rebuild the tower. This happened three times. Milarepa's back became bruised, callused and infected from carrying the stones. But still Marpa wouldn't give Milarepa initiations or teachings.

Even though Milarepa repeatedly asked for teachings, Marpa didn't give him any for a long time. Since Marpa never called Milarepa to give him private teachings or initiations, whenever he was giving a public teaching Milarepa would slip inside and try to listen among the other people. But whenever Marpa would see him at an initiation or teaching sitting among the other disciples he would immediately shout at or beat him and kick him out. Instead of giving Milarepa teachings, Marpa would only scold and beat him. For years, Milarepa received no teachings from Marpa, only his wrath. There was no sweet talk from Marpa. Milarepa received no praise or thanks but only years of scoldings and beatings.

Imagine if you met a guru who treated you in that way, who scolded you in public and beat you and kicked you out if you tried to come to teachings or initiations. If you met a guru who treated you in the way that Marpa treated Milarepa, could you bear it? Comparing yourself to Milarepa helps you to understand and have strong faith in Milarepa. From this you can understand why Milarepa became enlightened not just in one life but within a number of years. You can also understand how Milarepa practiced Dharma, how he devoted himself to Marpa, and you can then understand why, even though you met Buddhadharma many years ago, there is still no change in your mind, let alone realizations of the path.

If I went to take teachings from a lama and all I received from the very beginning was scolding, I would feel extremely depressed or angry. I think I would run away—and maybe pray never to meet him again. These days in the West we would probably say that Marpa abused Milarepa. If someone these days were treated the way Marpa treated Milarepa or Tilopa treated Naropa, there would be a human rights investigation and Marpa and Tilopa would probably end up in court. However, this was Marpa's skillful means to quickly purify all Milarepa's heavy negative karma and enlighten him.

During all those years, no matter how much Marpa scolded or beat him, Milarepa never lost faith in Marpa or gave rise to anger or any other negative thought toward him for even a moment. Milarepa simply did everything that Marpa asked him to do; he totally sacrificed himself to serve Marpa. From the very first, Milarepa never generated heresy toward Marpa. His guru yoga practice was incomparable.

Milarepa practiced guru devotion with the nine attitudes explained by Lama Tsongkhapa in *The Great Treatise on the Stages of the Path to Enlightenment*, especially with the attitudes like the earth and like a faithful dog (see appendix 8).[115] Just as the earth supports mountains and other heavy things, Milarepa was able to hold all the heavy responsibilities that Marpa gave him and follow the advice he was given. A faithful dog, no matter how badly it is treated by its master, never retaliates or runs away but always stays with its master. In a similar way, no matter how badly Marpa treated him, Milarepa never became angry or retaliated or ran away; he always stayed with Marpa. Without losing his guru devotion, Milarepa always kept a positive mind. Both attitudes emphasize following the guru without feeling upset.

Even after Milarepa had built the nine-story temple three times and received much scolding and beating, Marpa still had no intention of giving him teachings or initiations. His plan was to give him even more work to do so that, in bearing more hardships, he could purify more negative karma and become enlightened more quickly. Marpa did all this out of his great compassion.

However, Marpa's wisdom mother, Dagmema, felt sorry for Milarepa. She secretly advised him to go to see Lama Ngokpa, one of Marpa's disciples,

---

[115] The nine attitudes, taught in the sutra *Laying Out of Stalks* are: 1) like an obedient child, giving up your own will and submitting yourself to your lama; 2) like a diamond, being solid in your devotion and not letting anyone split you apart; 3) like the earth itself, accepting any task your lama may load upon you; 4) like the great mountains at the edge of the world, staying unshakable in your service, regardless of any troubles that come; 5) like a hand servant, carrying out any task your lama gives you, never seeking to avoid it, no matter how distasteful it may seem; 6) like the dust of the earth, seeking the lowest position, giving up all pride, all pretension and all conceit; 7) like a sturdy vehicle, undertaking any burden your lama may give you, however heavy; 8) like a loyal dog, staying without anger, regardless of how your lama might berate or scold you; and 9) like a boat, never complaining no matter how much you have to come and go in the service of your lama. See *The Great Treatise, Volume 1*, pp. 78–80.

and receive teachings from him. As offerings to Lama Ngokpa, Dagmema gave Milarepa Naropa's crown ornaments and a ruby mala Naropa had given to Marpa.

Milarepa then went to Lama Ngokpa. For many months he meditated in a hole in the ground he had made there but no realizations happened—not even a good sign in a dream—because Marpa hadn't given him permission to go to Lama Ngokpa. Even though he had received teachings from Lama Ngokpa, Milarepa had no good signs during his retreat. When Milarepa explained to Lama Ngokpa that he didn't have Marpa's permission to be there, Lama Ngokpa knew it was a mistake and then took Milarepa to Marpa to apologize.

Dagmema kept insisting that Marpa give Milarepa teachings until Marpa reluctantly agreed. From Marpa's side he didn't want to give teachings and initiations even when he did; he wanted Milarepa to continue bearing hardships in following his advice even longer. It is said that if things had happened as Marpa wanted, Milarepa would have achieved enlightenment even quicker. That was Marpa's plan. Though Milarepa still achieved enlightenment in one brief lifetime, he took longer to become enlightened because Dagmema pushed Marpa to give teachings and initiations to Milarepa. If she hadn't pushed and things had gone according to Marpa's plan, Milarepa could have been enlightened even earlier.

From Marpa's side, there was no formal sitting on a throne and giving teachings to Milarepa. Marpa grabbed Milarepa and banged his head three times on the floor. He then told Milarepa to look up at the sky, where Milarepa saw the Hevajra mandala. Marpa, who had achieved the unified state of no more learning, transformed the mandala in space and, transforming himself into Hevajra, initiated Milarepa into it.

After Milarepa had received all the teachings and necessary instructions, Marpa then advised him to go to Mount Kailash and other holy places in the Himalayas to practice and actualize all the teachings Marpa had given him.

At the end, as Milarepa was leaving, Marpa walked a little way with him from the hermitage where Marpa lived and advised, "Just as you can't sew cloth with a two-pointed needle, you can't practice worldly dharma and holy Dharma together. If you try to do so you lose the holy Dharma."

After receiving this advice from Marpa, Milarepa went into the mountains of Tibet and followed Marpa's advice exactly, doing retreat on the Six Yogas of Naropa and other practices. Milarepa went into the mountains with nothing. He didn't have anything at all: he actually lived naked in caves and ate nothing but nettles.

Once Milarepa's sister saw him naked and felt so embarrassed that she offered him a roll of woolen cloth. Milarepa cut some pieces off the cloth and made covers for his fingers and penis. When his sister next saw him she was shocked. Because Milarepa had achieved the Six Yogas of Naropa he had no need of clothing.

He practiced the patience of voluntarily accepting sufferings, such as cold, to practice Dharma, one of the three types of patience.[116] Of course, after he accomplished the Six Yogas of Naropa, even though he was naked he didn't feel the cold. With realization of *tummo*, or inner fire, there's no such thing as feeling cold. Even if you live in an ice cave in an ice mountain, the ice is melted by your heat.

Milarepa practiced, had all the realizations and liberated himself, overcoming death. First he was afraid of death, but then he went to the mountains to meditate and actualized tantric mahamudra. He didn't realize just emptiness and sutra mahamudra but tantric mahamudra. He actualized the primordial mind of simultaneously born bliss and totally overcame the cycle of death and rebirth. In the beginning, he began to practice Dharma with fear of death, but he used that fear to practice Dharma. At the end he overcame the fear by developing his mind in the tantric path. With the primordial mind of simultaneously born great bliss, he was totally free from fear. He was able to free himself from all suffering.

As Milarepa himself expressed it, "Afraid of death, I fled to the mountains, where I realized the nature of the primordial mind. Now even if death comes to me, I have no fear."

By bearing hardships, Milarepa practiced the teachings and became enlightened; he achieved the unified state of Vajradhara in that life. Milarepa didn't possess even one dollar but he possessed a perfect human rebirth and practiced Dharma. And the Dharma practice that enabled Milarepa to become enlightened in one brief lifetime was his strong guru devotion. Milarepa correctly devoted himself to Marpa with thought and action, cherishing Marpa more than his own life. No matter how Marpa treated him, it never affected his mind; Milarepa never generated anger or heresy toward

---

[116] The three types of patience are the patience that is not disturbed by the harm done by others, the patience that voluntarily accepts suffering and the patience needed to gain assurance in the Dharma.

Marpa. He never lost his devotion; he always had strong devotion. And he put into practice every single piece of advice Marpa gave him. Because of his strong guru devotion, Milarepa became enlightened in that life.

Milarepa, after making unbelievable sacrifices and bearing hardships to practice Dharma, had great success. By renouncing the eight worldly dharmas and bearing hardships to practice Dharma, Milarepa achieved enlightenment within a number of years.

Milarepa was not a particularly great scholar; he hadn't studied in a monastery for thirty or forty years. He received the essential teachings from Marpa and meditated on them. What made Milarepa so successful was his correctly devoting himself to the virtuous friend. That's what enabled him to become enlightened within a few years and what has enabled him to enlighten numberless sentient beings since that time.

It is our obscurations that block our actualizing the steps of the path to enlightenment. If we didn't have negative karma and obscurations we would be a buddha and our mind would be dharmakaya. The whole point is that if our goal is to have realizations and actually achieve enlightenment for the sake of sentient beings, we need to purify our mind. Intellectual knowledge of Dharma alone can't bring us realizations. If that were the case, the methods these great yogis Tilopa and Marpa used to guide their disciples would have been simply forms of torture. To have realizations of the path and even to understand Dharma intellectually, we need to purify our mind.

In the stories of Naropa and Milarepa there is no mention of their doing hundreds of thousands of prostrations, Vajrasattva mantras or mandala offerings. The yogis who became enlightened in a brief lifetime of this degenerate time practiced Dharma by correctly devoting themselves to the virtuous friend. No matter how much hardship they had to bear, they didn't generate any negative thoughts. Nowadays we do many hundreds of thousands of the various preliminary practices but the best preliminary practice is to endure all the hardships these past great yogis did. This is the quickest way to achieve enlightenment.

19. What Is Guru Yoga?

⸺❧⸺

GURU YOGA enables us to practice correct devotion to the virtuous friend with thought and action but what is it? Guru yoga is a process, through logic, quotations and meditation, of transforming the mind that sees the guru as an ordinary being into the devotion that sees the guru as a buddha, a fully enlightened being, one who has ceased all faults and completed all qualities, or realizations. After proving to ourselves that the guru is a buddha, we then meditate on the guru in the aspect of the special deity that we practice.

If we visualize the deity in front of us but regard our own guru as ordinary and separate from that deity, then even though we might say that we are practicing guru yoga, what we are doing is not even a part of guru yoga meditation. Drogön Tsangpa Gyare said, "If you look at the guru and deity as separate, you can't receive blessings." This means that you can't achieve attainments.

We have to constantly see the guru as in essence our own personal deity, the one with which we have strong karmic contact. No matter how many gurus we have, we have to regard them all as embodiments of this deity. All the time, when we eat, drink, sleep or do any other activity, we practice being one with this deity. And just as we always have the divine pride and clear appearance of being this deity, we also see the guru as this deity.

On top of that, we constantly meditate that our mind, as well as our body and speech, is unified with the guru and our special deity. This is the tantric practice of guru yoga.

There are different ways of devoting to the virtuous friend according to the different Buddhist vehicles. In Hinayana practice, although the abbot who grants vows is respected and served as if he were Shakyamuni Buddha, he is not seen as a buddha. The teacher is regarded as a substitute for Buddha and is offered the same respect as Buddha. How to do so is clearly explained in the Hinayana teachings.

In the Paramitayana, the virtuous teacher is seen as in essence a buddha, as someone who has completed all the qualities of cessation and realization.

In tantra, the guru is seen as a buddha not only in essence but also in aspect. His Holiness Song Rinpoche often used to say that meditating that the essence of the guru is the deity brings greater blessings but if we also visualize the guru in the pure form of a deity, we receive blessings more quickly. In Mahayana Secret Mantra, we not only look at the guru as a buddha but also stop looking at him as an ordinary being, even in aspect, by stopping ordinary concept and appearance. We look at the guru in pure form, which means in the aspect of a buddha. *Mantra* means protecting the mind: *man* means mind and *tra* means protection. When we practice guru devotion, we protect our mind from negative thoughts about the guru and from thoughts of the guru as an ordinary being. In addition to the Paramitayana practice of looking at the guru as in essence a buddha, in the tantric practice of guru devotion we look at the guru in even the aspect of a buddha.

Pabongka Dechen Nyingpo says that in the tantric way of devoting to the virtuous friend, it's not sufficient to do it the way it is done in the Paramitayana path. In tantra, you should devote yourself to the virtuous friend as explained in *Fifty Verses of Guru Devotion*.

The fundamental practices in tantra are stopping impure conception and appearance and practicing the four purities, which means visualizing now what you are actually going to experience when you become an enlightened being. You stop the impure conception and appearance of yourself as an ordinary person and practice the divine pride of thinking of and looking at yourself as the deity you practice, with the pure vajra holy body of a buddha. You also stop your impure conception and view of your environment as an ordinary place and look at it as the pure mandala of the deity. You also have pure enjoyments and perform pure actions. You practice the divine pride of having already achieved these four purities, as if you already were that future buddha.

While holding this pure appearance, your mind is protected from impure conception and appearance, which are the basis for the arising of many delusions and the creation of negative karma, the cause of samsara. You protect your mind from ordinary, impure conceptions and appearances and look at everything as pure. When you become enlightened, everything you see will appear as pure, as in the nature of great bliss. Nothing impure appears to a buddha's holy mind. In tantra, it is not enough to look at the guru as in essence a buddha; there is the additional practice of looking at the guru in the aspect of a buddha.

We need to do the visualizations and recitation of mantra of deity practice on the basis of correct meditation on guru yoga. Pabongka Dechen Nyingpo says,

> Visualizing the deity in front of you without mixing it with the guru is never going to fulfill the meaning of guru yoga.

If we simply visualize the deity without mixing it with the guru, we haven't incorporated the meaning of guru yoga into our practice. We have missed the point. If we're meditating on the deity separately from the guru, our practice doesn't become guru yoga meditation. Simply visualizing the external aspect of a deity is not actual guru yoga practice.

Visualizing the guru as an ordinary person separate from this deity also doesn't become guru yoga meditation. If we visualize our guru but don't meditate that he is inseparable from the deity, we have again missed the point of guru yoga. We are left with the recognition of the guru as only an ordinary being, and meditating on the guru as an ordinary being doesn't become guru yoga. There is no way to receive blessings from that.

Visualizing the guru as the deity, in essence and in aspect, cuts our ordinary impure concepts and ordinary impure appearances. We are then able to have pure concepts and pure appearances, and devotion then arises. The arising of devotion causes us to receive the blessings of the guru-deity and from that we then achieve realizations.

If we do the visualizations and recitation of mantra with the understanding that the guru is the deity, we receive blessings. Otherwise, our practice is like an empty momo. Doing visualizations without guru yoga is like having a picture of the most delicious food but not eating the actual food or like having a mannequin in the shape of a friend but not having the actual friend. Leaving out the guru means our practice doesn't become guru yoga, so it doesn't become the means to receive blessings. The way that Pabongka Dechen Nyingpo explains this from his own realizations brings unbelievable blessing.

Whenever we do sadhanas and visualize either ourselves as deities or external deities, it is very important never to separate from guru yoga practice. We shouldn't visualize ourselves as a deity that has no connection to our guru. Our own mind, the deity's holy mind and the guru's holy mind—all three are one.

Thinking that a buddha is a higher or more powerful object than our guru is not the mind of guru yoga. Remember what the great yogi Padampa Sangye said,

> One should hold the guru higher than the buddhas; realization will then come in this life, people of Tingri.

Making offerings to the buddhas as something separate from the guru also doesn't become guru yoga practice. If we make offerings without the devotion that sees the buddhas as one with the guru, our practice doesn't become guru yoga practice.

Even in a temple, whenever we make prostrations or make light, scarf or any other offering to paintings or statues of buddha, we should always remember the guru and then make the offering. There are also a lot of offering practices when we do any deity's sadhana. If we make the offering each time with the guru yoga mind, if we think of the guru, we collect the most extensive merit.

As mentioned in *Guru Puja* and many other teachings, devoting to the virtuous friend with thought and action is the most powerful way to finish the work of accumulating extensive merit in order to achieve enlightenment. Achieving the dharmakaya and rupakaya depends on completing the two types of merit, the merit of fortune and the merit of wisdom,[117] and the most powerful way to quickly finish the work of accumulating extensive merit is by correctly devoting ourselves to the virtuous friend with thought and action. Since we accumulate the most extensive merit, the more we are able to devote ourselves to the virtuous friend with thought and action, the closer we become to enlightenment.

This is why the practices of listening to and reflecting and meditating on the teachings of guru yoga are essential in our everyday life. The benefits of

---

[117] The merit of wisdom, accumulated by meditating on emptiness, becomes the cause of dharmakaya, a buddha's holy mind; the merit of fortune, accumulated by virtuous activities other than meditating on emptiness, becomes the cause of the rupakaya, a buddha's holy body.

practicing guru yoga are as infinite as space, starting from the success of this life up to enlightenment. I mention the success of this life because when we practice guru yoga all the happiness and success of this life happens incidentally. Even though we are looking for happiness beyond this life and might feel detached toward the happiness of this life, the happiness and success of this life comes as a result of pure practice of guru devotion, as do all other happiness and success up to enlightenment.

Reciting the words of a guru yoga practice is not the main point; the main point is to change our mind, to transform our mind into guru devotion, the root of the path to enlightenment, which brings success in all realizations from the beginning to the end of the path to enlightenment.

It is a foundation of strong guru devotion that enables us to receive the blessings of the deity when doing retreat and deity practice. There is no other way to receive the blessings of the deity. If we leave out the practice of guru yoga, simply visualizing the deity and reciting mantras is like trying to get water from an empty container; we receive nothing.

The purpose of doing deity retreat is not just to fulfill a commitment, like doing a job we promised to do, but to receive the blessings of the deity. Receiving the blessings of the deity then enables us to have realizations of the path to enlightenment. This is scientific, and those who have done retreat can relate to this from their own past experiences. When we have no devotion to our gurus or our devotion is superficial and not from our heart, nothing much happens. We don't receive any good signs, not even a good dream. When we check our past experiences, we discover that it was during times of strong guru devotion that we had many good experiences, when we received many blessings. I think that guru devotion is the most important factor in having a successful retreat.

Guru devotion is the main factor that determines how much we can receive the blessings of the deity and gain experience by doing meditation on the path. This is especially true if we are doing something that pleases the holy mind of the virtuous friend; in that case, we can quickly have wonderful experiences and also many good dreams and other signs. We then receive the blessings of the deity and become closer to the deity.

If we don't understand the fundamental meditations on how to see the guru as a buddha or don't know how to do them properly, our practice won't be effective. It's not sufficient simply to think about our personal experience of the particular qualities that our gurus have that we and other ordinary people don't have. We need to establish stable devotion through logic and quotations. Doing the later practices on the basis of stable devotion has incredible power and brings incredible blessings. Even doing a little meditation on guru yoga will make our mind as soft as cotton-wool, and any lam-rim meditation that we then do will come very naturally. Even if we practice guru devotion only a little, perhaps simply meditating on it for a few days in retreat, experiences will be great and come very easily and quickly; it will immediately change our mind. Success will come very easily. It will not be as if the teachings hit a rock when they hit our mind.

Even if we think that we know what the guru is, unless we do the basic meditations explained in the lam-rim, using logic and quotations, many superstitions can arise and create obstacles. If we haven't proved to our mind that the guru is a buddha, we have no opponent to stop superstitious thoughts. Without an understanding of and faith in the inseparability of the guru and buddha, the essence of the practice will be lost.

After studying what Buddha taught on guru devotion in the sutras and tantras and studying the lam-rim teachings on guru devotion, we then practice devoting ourselves to the guru in accordance with all those teachings. All success in terms of not just the general happiness of this life but especially realizations of the path to enlightenment and in terms of stopping obstacles depends on guru yoga practice. Everything depends on whether or not we practice guru yoga and how we practice it. Guru yoga is the key to all happiness.

The real meaning of guru

When we think about what *guru* really means, we have to think about the absolute guru. We have to go beyond the conventional guru to the absolute guru, the real meaning of guru. And what is the absolute guru? In tantric terms, it is the dharmakaya, the transcendental wisdom of nondual bliss and voidness. It is eternal, with no beginning and no end. (This absolute guru is a little similar to the eternal God of Christianity but Christianity has no explanation of how God is eternal.) This dharmakaya pervades all existence; there's no place that the dharmakaya, the holy mind of the buddhas, does not cover.

In *Ornament of Mahayana Sutras*, Maitreya Buddha explains,

> Just as the innumerable beams of the sun mix to constantly perform the one activity of illuminating the world, in the uncon-

taminated sphere of dharmakaya the innumerable buddhas mix
to perform the one activity of illuminating with transcendental
wisdom.

Just as an inconceivable number of sunbeams always focus on the one action
of illuminating the world, in the dharmakaya the countless buddhas mix to
perform the one action of guiding sentient beings, of making the transcendental wisdom of omniscient mind appear in the minds of sentient beings.
The dharmakaya, the absolute guru, is the completely pure holy mind, the
transcendental wisdom of great bliss always in equipoise meditation directly
seeing the emptiness of all existence. Like having poured water into water,
the transcendental wisdom of great bliss is inseparable from emptiness forever. The transcendental wisdom of all the buddhas is of one taste in the
dharmakaya. The phrase *uncontaminated sphere of dharmakaya* means that
the dharmakaya is a state free from delusions.

All the beams of sunlight mix together to dispel all the darkness in the
world but this is just outer darkness. Here, all the numberless buddhas mix
together to become one in the dharmakaya to carry out the one action
of dispelling the inner darkness of the two obscurations, the disturbing-
thought obscurations and the subtle obscurations to knowing. In other
words, through various means the buddhas perform the highest action of
revealing the teachings, *illuminating with transcendental wisdom*, and thus
dispelling the inner darkness of the obscurations. When sunlight dispels
external darkness, we see objects clearly. When the buddhas dispel our inner
darkness, our minds are completely illuminated and become omniscient,
the transcendental wisdom of the dharmakaya.

It is helpful to remember this quotation from Maitreya Buddha when we
begin each session of guru yoga practice and in our daily life when we meditate on *Six-Session Guru Yoga*.

Referring again to *Ornament of Mahayana Sutras*, Pabongka Dechen
Nyingpo gives the example of rivers entering the ocean and mixing together.
When we then take one tiny drop of water from the ocean, it embodies
every single river that has gone into it; that one drop from the ocean is a
mixture of all the waters that came into it from various places. Before entering the ocean, all the various rivers appear different, but after entering the
ocean, they all become one. Like this, all the buddhas are of one taste in the
dharmakaya.

The dharmakaya, the absolute guru, the holy mind of all the buddhas,

is like the ocean. Just as all the rivers are mixed in the ocean, all the buddhas are mixed in this dharmakaya, this absolute guru. Like drops from the
ocean, all the many different aspects of buddha—the One Thousand Buddhas, the Thirty-five Buddhas, the eight Medicine Buddhas—are manifestations of the absolute guru. Each of the millions of different manifestations
that guide sentient beings, whether in the form of an animal, a human being
or a deity, is a manifestation of all the buddhas. All the different deities we
visualize are actually just one being. No matter how many different forms
we see, one buddha is all the buddhas. As in the example of the ocean, all
buddhas are of one taste in the dharmakaya.

Each of the buddhas is the embodiment of all the buddhas and each of
the buddhas is the embodiment of the guru. If the guru is the embodiment
of one buddha, he has to be the embodiment of all the buddhas. There is no
buddha who is not an embodiment of the guru; there is no guru who is not
an embodiment of buddha. There are different aspects but just one being,
the absolute guru, the dharmakaya, the transcendental wisdom of nondual
bliss and voidness. And when we become enlightened, we become one with
all the buddhas.

No matter how many buddhas we visualize or whether we visualize them
all as one, they are all the guru. Whether we visualize one into many or
many into one, it is the guru, as Pabongka Dechen Nyingpo mentions in
Calling the Lama from Afar.[118]

The guru is the transformation of the transcendental wisdom of all the
buddhas; the guru is the embodiment of all the countless buddhas who
abide in the ten directions. A transformation of Guru Shakyamuni Buddha
or Vajradhara has to be a transformation of all the buddhas. Although they
manifest in different aspects and have different names, all the buddhas are
one in essence. The absolute guru manifests in Vajradhara, the Five Dhyani
Buddhas, Lama Tsongkhapa, and the rest, as well as in the ordinary aspects
that we can see. We should be aware of this.

Even though there are different appearances—Tara, Manjushri, Vajrapani, Guru Shakyamuni Buddha and so forth—in reality each buddha is all
the buddhas. One buddha's action of guiding us is all the buddhas' action of
guiding us. Therefore, even if we practice only the one deity, such as Chenr-

---

[118] The hundred, five and three families, however many elaborated, are the lama. The pervasive master himself in whom they are all included is also the lama. I beseech you, Lama, as
master of all families, please look after me always without separation, in this life, future lives
and the bardo. (V. 8.)

ezig, when we become enlightened in the essence of Chenrezig, at that time we achieve the enlightenment of all the buddhas. When we achieve Chenrezig's enlightenment, there is no such thing as our not having achieved the enlightenment of Manjushri, Vajrapani, Yamantaka or any other buddha. It is not that in order to achieve Yamantaka's enlightenment we have to start all over again from the beginning of the path. When we achieve Chenrezig's enlightenment we achieve all the buddhas' enlightenment. That is the reality.

As mentioned in *Guru Puja* in relation to the virtuous friend,

> You are my guru, you are my deity,
> You are the dakini and Dharma protector....[119]

The virtuous friend is all the various deities. When we say "Shakyamuni Buddha," it is the virtuous friend; there is no separate Shakyamuni Buddha. When we say "Manjushri," again it is the virtuous friend. No matter what name we use—Chakrasamvara, Yamantaka, Guhyasamaja, Maitreya, Tara, Vajrapani—it is the name of one being, the virtuous friend. The dakas and dakinis and all the different Dharma protectors are also one being, the virtuous friend. This is the reality and this is the way to practice guru yoga.

Whether there is one aspect, such as Shakyamuni Buddha, Chenrezig or Tara, or many, it is the guru; it is one in essence. When we think of the guru, we can think of the conventional guru, the ordinary human form of the guru that we see, but that being is the absolute guru, the dharmakaya, the holy mind of all the buddhas, the transcendental wisdom of nondual bliss and voidness. Because it is bound by infinite compassion, it manifests in (or through) these ordinary human forms to guide us to enlightenment.

With this understanding of guru yoga we know that all the buddhas are communicating with us. Shakyamuni Buddha, Tara, Manjushri and all the rest of the numberless buddhas are guiding us through this ordinary human form; they are giving us initiations, vows, oral transmissions and commentaries.

In guru yoga, the essential point to understand is that all the buddhas are of one taste in the dharmakaya. The dharmakaya is the absolute guru, and

[119] V. 53.

this is all the buddhas. This is the very heart of guru yoga practice. Without understanding this there's no way to practice guru yoga comfortably. Even if we do the visualizations it won't be completely satisfactory because we'll be unclear as to how buddha is the embodiment of the guru and the guru is the embodiment of buddha. However, it will be extremely clear if we understand the very heart of guru yoga, that the guru is buddha and buddha is the guru.

We can integrate this understanding into our guru yoga practice by thinking in the following way. When we become enlightened, if there is one sentient being who can be guided by a manifestation of Tara, we will manifest in the aspect of Tara to guide that sentient being. Now, that Tara is the manifestation of all the Taras and all the other buddhas. It is not that there is a separate Tara with a separate mind who guides that particular sentient being and there are billions of other Taras who guide other sentient beings but not that particular one.

When a sentient being is ready to be guided by an aspect of a buddha and be taught Dharma, the buddha who reveals the Dharma to them has to be all the other buddhas. Otherwise that sentient being would not be guided by all the buddhas but by some buddhas and not others. This way of thinking creates problems in the mind. When Manjushri or any other buddha guides us, that guidance is the guidance of all the buddhas and that manifestation is the manifestation of all the buddhas.

In reality, even though there are numberless different aspects of buddhas, the holy mind of all the buddhas is one but appears in different aspects to guide us sentient beings, just as all the rivers that go into the ocean become one.

The dharmakaya is like the ocean in which many waters are mixed and our various gurus are like drops from the ocean. All our gurus are manifestations of the dharmakaya, the absolute guru, the holy mind of all the buddhas; the absolute guru manifests in an ordinary form in accordance with the level of our karma. This ordinary form is the conventional guru, the essence of which is the absolute guru.

When we actually see or visualize a deity or see statues or paintings of deities we should recognize that they are all the guru. There is no deity other than the guru.

The *guru* in guru yoga means our present gurus, who guide us to enlightenment by teaching us the alphabet, giving us commentaries, oral transmissions, tantric initiations, vows and personal advice; they are the embodiments of the dharmakaya, the absolute guru, the transcendental wisdom of nondual bliss and voidness. When we do *Guru Puja*, *Six-Session Guru Yoga* or any other guru yoga practice we shouldn't think that the central figure has nothing to do with our guru. When we are doing *Lama Tsongkhapa Guru Yoga* or *Guru Puja* we have to remember that there is no Tsongkhapa who is not our guru.

When we visualize Lama Tsongkhapa, the aspect we visualize is Tsongkhapa but our main focus should be on *Lama*, the guru. When we say "*Lama* Tsongkhapa" we know that we are talking about the dharmakaya of all the buddhas and that Tsongkhapa is the particular embodiment of this dharmakaya that is of one taste with the holy mind of all the buddhas. This will bring some change in our mind because we will quickly receive blessings. The mind that was previously dry and uninspired will develop great respect, devotion and inspiration to practice. Through effort in our practice, realizations of the lam-rim path will then come. This is how it is possible for us to achieve enlightenment.

Otherwise, if we concentrate just on the aspect of Tsongkhapa and not on the meaning of *Lama* when we practice *Lama Tsongkhapa Guru Yoga* or *Guru Puja*, we leave out the guru yoga practice. Of course we can still accumulate merit by making offerings and so forth simply with the thought that Tsongkhapa is a buddha; after all, we accumulate merit by making offerings to bodhisattvas, Sangha, and even our parents, even though they are not buddhas. But for us to generate all the realizations from perfect human rebirth up to enlightenment, the blessings of the guru have to enter our heart.

It is similar when we meditate on Guru Vajradhara in the practice of *Six-Session Guru Yoga*. Vajradhara is the particular aspect we visualize, but it is more effective to focus on the absolute guru. It makes sense to relate to the absolute guru every time we hear or say "guru" or "lama." It would be strange to simply think of the relative guru, the guru who appears to us in ordinary aspect and gives us teachings and not think of the absolute guru; it would be strange to think of the aspect and not the essence. If when we meditated on Guru Shakyamuni Buddha we saw him in essence as an ordinary person, a sentient being, we wouldn't see any purpose in doing the meditation. If we meditate in this way, we haven't understood guru yoga practice. We have to meditate on the absolute guru.

Otherwise, if we have no feeling of devotion in our heart and see the guru as an ordinary being, we won't see any purpose in making requests to him;

we'll feel that we're trying to get milk from a cow's horn. We'll think, "What is the point of making requests to an ordinary person, somebody who has been born from a mother's womb and has the same flesh-and-blood body as I have? What am I doing praying to somebody who is a human being the same as I am?" Even if we say the prayers, we'll have no feeling for them. Our heart will feel empty, as if there's a hole in it.

Whenever we do guru yoga meditations or think of or physically see our guru we should immediately think, "This is buddha." The instant we see the particular form of our mother, for example, even in a large crowd of people, we are instantly aware that it is our mother. There is the immediate recognition, "This is my mother." It is similar with guru yoga practice. We should immediately be aware that our guru is in essence the absolute guru. At the moment we have to apply effort to think this but later a definite understanding that the guru is buddha will spontaneously arise in our heart, without need for logical reasoning or quotations, just as when we see our mother's form we don't have to exert any effort to think it's our mother. This is the way to develop stable realization of guru devotion.

When we serve our guru with this awareness of the absolute guru, the holy mind of all the buddhas, even if we are offering only a cup of tea, we are spontaneously aware that we are offering the tea to all the buddhas. If we are sitting next to our guru we are aware that we are sitting next to all the buddhas of the ten directions. When our guru gives us advice, teachings or an initiation we are aware that all the buddhas are giving us the advice, teachings or initiation. Even if we don't have realization of this, it is effective to attempt to listen to teachings with this awareness. We will then feel much more connection; we will feel much closer to all the buddhas.

Geshe Senge mentioned one high lama in Tibet who used "Guru" in front of the name of every buddha; he would say "Guru Arya Tara," "Guru Yamantaka" and so on. Many lamas relate to deities in the same way because the guru is the source of all the buddhas and the Triple Gem. From where do all the buddhas come? From the guru. From where do Buddha, Dharma and Sangha come? From the guru. And what is that guru? It is the absolute guru, the dharmakaya, the transcendental wisdom of nondual bliss and voidness.

The real meaning that we should constantly remember when we use the word *guru* and also when we see the guru is *primordial unified savior*, the extremely subtle primordial mind of dharmakaya, the absolute guru. When we think of the guru as the primordial unified savior, the dharmakaya, we see that because this dharmakaya is bound by infinite compassion to us sentient beings, it has to manifest in various forms to guide us. As we don't have the karma to directly see aspects of buddha, it has manifested in the ordinary aspects of the gurus that we visualize. If we miss the real meaning of guru we will think that a guru is simply someone from whom we have received teachings and won't be able to figure out how all the deities are manifestations of him.

As the great yogi Buddhajñana said,

> Before what is called "guru" there is not even the name "buddha."
> All the buddhas are manifestations of the guru.

If we don't relate this quotation to the absolute guru it doesn't make sense, and neither will many of the prayers in *Guru Puja*. In other words, buddha doesn't exist before the guru. All the buddhas, as well as the Dharma and the Sangha, come from the guru.

The essence of all our gurus, even though they appear in ordinary aspects, is one, the absolute guru. Their aspect is called *kun dzob kyi lama* in Tibetan; the translation with which you are familiar is probably "relative guru" or "conventional guru." In guru yoga practice, the relative guru, whose essence is the absolute guru, is visualized in the aspect of Shakyamuni Buddha, Manjushri, Tara, Vajradhara, Lama Tsongkhapa or another enlightened being.

Because we have impure karma, the absolute guru manifests to us in a form with faults. With our present capacity we don't have the pure karma to see the guru in pure form; we can only see the guru in a form with faults. We don't have the pure karma to see the buddhas in the pure aspect of buddha; we have only the impure karma to see buddhas in impure aspects. A buddha's power and sentient beings' karma are equal. Therefore the buddhas manifest to us in ordinary forms with faults, which accord with our own karma, our own level of mind, then guide us through various means that also accord with the level of our minds to the happiness of future lives, liberation and enlightenment.

Every time we say the word "guru" or hear it or think about it, we should remember that it actually means the absolute guru. The absolute guru manifests in various ordinary forms according to our karma. All the buddhas are embodiments of the guru, the absolute guru, and all the gurus are embodiments of the buddhas. Though different names, like "buddha" and "guru," are used, they are talking about one object: the dharmakaya, the absolute guru, just as one object has different names in different languages.

We have to transform our mind into a devotional state that is constantly aware that the guru is a buddha. Using logic and quotations we should transform the mind that doesn't see the gurus as buddhas or, in other words, as the absolute guru, the holy mind of all the buddhas, the transcendental wisdom of nondual bliss and voidness. We have to change the mind that sees our gurus in ordinary aspect as separate from the buddhas. Even though the buddhas manifest in the ordinary forms of these gurus and guide us by revealing teachings and other means, we don't see the gurus in this way but believe them to be separate from the buddhas. We have to transform this state of mind into the devotion that sees the gurus from whom we have received teachings directly as inseparable from the buddhas. We have to see them as manifestations of the absolute guru, the dharmakaya, the holy mind of all the buddhas.

When you spontaneously, constantly, see the guru as a buddha, you have the realization of guru devotion. When you see a buddha, you think it is an embodiment of your guru; when you see, hear or remember your guru, you spontaneously understand in your mind that this is a buddha. Even though the aspect is ordinary, in your heart you understand that this is buddha. It's similar to visualizing yourself as a deity. While you have the appearance of yourself as a deity, at the same time you understand that it is empty of existing from its own side; there is a unification of appearance and emptiness. Like this, whenever you see, hear or remember the guru, you think that this is buddha, without any need to remember the reasons.

At times when you are doing strong guru yoga practice and the guru is also pleased with you, you suddenly feel in your heart, "If this is not Vajrayogini, who else can be Vajrayogini?" or "If this is not Chenrezig, who else can be Chenrezig?" Before when you said "the guru is buddha" you were just repeating the words during meditation, just imitating what the teachings said, but you now feel in your heart the meaning of the quotations and lines of reasoning that you used to think about. Suddenly it all becomes real to you. At the same time you also appreciate the unbelievable kindness of the guru. You can't control the feelings that come.

With this realization, you have the same devotion to your guru as you do to Shakyamuni Buddha, Tara or any other deity. With this devotion, you have complete faith in your guru and follow him. In this way you don't create any obstacles to achieving the path to enlightenment and only create the causes to achieve realizations, and enlightenment.

Unless we understand the importance of the sutra and tantra teachings on guru devotion, unless we have done the analytical meditations on those points, simply thinking that the guru is inseparable from the deity and making requests becomes just words. Guru yoga becomes just words; there's no feeling in our heart. We don't feel that the guru is buddha, that the guru is inseparable from the deity. Unless we know those teachings and do the analytical meditations using the quotations and reasoning, we won't feel that the guru is buddha.

If we don't do any of the meditations on guru devotion as taught in the sutra and tantra teachings but simply recite some short guru yoga prayer or even *Guru Puja* thinking that the guru is inseparable from the deity, results will never come in our mind. Such practice is merely given the name "guru yoga" and will have little benefit. It won't bring quick development. It won't bring the result of having meditated on guru yoga, which is that we feel incredibly joyful to devote ourselves to the virtuous friend with thought and with action. Feeling unbelievably happy to carry out whatever advice or work the guru gives us and finding no difficulty in doing it are the results of having done meditation on guru yoga. Wanting to confess from our heart as quickly as possible any mistakes we have made in the past is also the result of having done effective guru yoga meditation. The wish not to make the same mistakes again also naturally and effortlessly comes.

With devotion, the thought of finding faults doesn't arise. When there is constant devotion, seeing every action the guru does as pure, respect will naturally and effortlessly arise by remembering the kindness of the guru from the depths of our heart. This also means that the guru yoga meditation we have done has been effective.

Trulshik Rinpoche, Portugal, 2001

20. Guru Devotion in *Six-Session Guru Yoga*

─────────── ❧❦ ───────────

T HE LONG VERSION of *Six-Session Guru Yoga*[120] has a section on guru devotion after the mandala offering, with verses that explain what the guru is and the kindness of the guru. It is very effective to meditate on guru devotion with these verses, which contain all the important points of correctly devoting to the virtuous friend. You can use the quotations and logical reasoning from the lam-rim to meditate on seeing the guru as a buddha, then also meditate on remembering the kindness of the guru.

When you meditate on *Six-Session Guru Yoga*, think that Vajradhara is the embodiment of all your gurus; do the guru yoga meditation by simply visualizing Vajradhara—the essence of all your gurus embodied in one aspect. From the syllable HUM at the heart of Vajradhara, your gurus in their ordinary aspects are transformed on the tips of beams, then surround Vajradhara. That one being, Vajradhara, manifests in the different aspects of your gurus.

In this way you see that the essence of all your gurus is Vajradhara. Looking at all of them as one in essence helps you to generate devotion and also to generate more devotion for the gurus toward whom you have difficulty generating devotion. By looking at your gurus as one in essence you can generate the same strong devotion for other gurus as you feel for the guru for whom you feel the greatest devotion. They are simply different manifestations, but otherwise the same.

Don't think only of your gurus of this life. Your present gurus are one in essence with all your past gurus during beginningless samsaric lifetimes

───────────────────────

[120] See *Six-Session Guru Yoga* for a commentary on this text.

and with all your future gurus until you achieve enlightenment. Remember each of your gurus and think that he is one in essence with all your past and future gurus.

The first verse in this section says,

> All Those Gone to Bliss of the three times and ten directions, manifesting in the aspect wearing monk's robes to subdue beings, perform the actions of the Victorious Ones in numberless realms. To you, precious guru, I make requests.

Those Gone to Bliss [Skt: *sugatas*] means the buddhas. The verse mentions the guru manifesting in the aspect of a monk but this is just an example; it doesn't mean that the guru manifests only in this aspect. An ordained aspect is referred to because it is generally easier for us to generate faith in this aspect and take it as an example to follow in order to achieve liberation and enlightenment. We can think of this aspect but we can also relate the words to other gurus who are not ordained.

To subdue beings means that the buddhas manifest various forms in accord with the karma of different sentient beings in order to subdue them.

This verse contains the essence of guru yoga meditation. It's useful to remember the outlines of the eight benefits of correct guru devotion and the eight shortcomings of incorrect devotion then recite and meditate on the meaning of this verse.

Devoting to the guru with thought means regarding the guru as a buddha—or here, in *Six-Session Guru Yoga*, as all the buddhas *of the three times and ten directions*. All the buddhas of the three times and ten directions have taken an aspect wearing robes or whatever other aspect is needed to subdue sentient beings. To subdue our mind, all the buddhas manifest in this aspect that accords with the level of our fortune. At this time, even though we can't see the guru as a buddha, we're fortunate to be able to see the guru in the form of a monk rather than in the form of a dog or a monkey.

Each of our gurus has been performing the actions of the buddhas in numberless realms. During beginningless lifetimes they have been guiding us from happiness to happiness to enlightenment. Among all the deeds of a buddha, the supreme deed is that of the holy speech, giving teachings. Unless we are given teachings on the path to enlightenment, there is no way we can follow the path and achieve enlightenment. Our virtuous teachers giving us commentaries, oral transmissions, initiations and advice are all the actions of the buddhas of the three times. Even from their giving us teachings on the path to enlightenment, we can understand that the actions our gurus are performing for us are the deeds of the buddhas. There are no other actions of the buddhas to point out that are separate from what our gurus do for us. From these lines we can understand that all the buddhas are working for us, guiding us.

In the past Guru Shakyamuni Buddha generated bodhicitta to achieve enlightenment for the benefit of sentient beings. Solely for the sake of sentient beings, he then entered the Mahayana path and accumulated merit for three countless great eons. He worked very hard and experienced much hardship in following the path to enlightenment. Buddha achieved enlightenment solely for the sake of us sentient beings, to guide us out of the suffering of samsara and lead us to enlightenment. And it is the same with the numberless other buddhas.

If Guru Shakyamuni Buddha himself and all the other buddhas, after achieving the state of omniscient mind with that motivation, abided in that blissful state without working for sentient beings, they would be cheating all sentient beings. That is impossible. Even when they were bodhisattvas they worked for sentient beings. Even from the time they first generated bodhicitta and entered the Mahayana path, they completely renounced the self-cherishing thought and had only the thought of cherishing others. If they worked solely for sentient beings even when they were bodhisattvas, why wouldn't they do so after they had achieved enlightenment? The buddhas are definitely working for sentient beings, including us.

How do the buddhas work for sentient beings? There is nothing other than the work that our gurus are doing for us to point out as the buddhas' work to save us from the suffering of samsara and gradually lead us to enlightenment.

With respect to remembering the kindness of the guru, only this manifestation, which accords with our own karma, can guide us to enlightenment; otherwise, there is no one to guide us. In relation to this verse, think about what the guru is and how the guru is performing the actions of all the countless buddhas in numberless realms. This is remembering the guru's kindness. Remembering this kindness doesn't mean simply thinking of the guru giving us the complete teachings of sutra and tantra, ordinations and initiations but thinking of the guru doing whatever actions benefit us and other sentient beings.

What is being requested with *To you, precious guru, I make requests*? It is the same as what we request in *Guru Puja*:

> In this life, the bardo and all future lives,
> Hold me with your hook of compassion;
> Free me from samsara's and nirvana's fears,
> Grant all attainments,
> Be my constant friend and guard me from interferences.[121]

We are requesting the guru to liberate us from samsara, grant all realizations and protect us from all interferences, including all wrong conceptions, from those toward the guru up to the subtle dual view, the very last of the wrong conceptions.

Six-Session Guru Yoga then continues,

> You are praised by Vajradhara for sentient beings of lower mind
> as a field of merit more precious than the mandalas of infinite
> buddhas. To you, precious guru, I make requests.

The phrase *mandalas of infinite buddhas* refers to the principal and surrounding deities of mandalas such as those of Thirteen-deity Yamantaka, Guhyasamaja, Heruka Chakrasamvara and so forth. Even though there are infinite such merit fields, transformations of the deity's bliss and voidness, the guru is more precious than all of them.

Also, the guru is a more precious field because the guru is the highest among all holy objects, including the buddhas. Remember the guru's kindness in being this object with which we can accumulate the most extensive merit. It is the guru who provides the quickest means of finishing the work of accumulating merit and thus of achieving enlightenment. Our gurus are so much more precious and kind than all the buddhas.

You can't plant crops in an ordinary field all the time but have to work according to the seasons; you can plant and harvest crops only at certain times. But in the holy field of the guru you can plant merit, the seed of all happiness up to enlightenment, all the time, twenty-four hours a day. The only problem is if, from your own side, you don't attempt to do it because

---

[121] V. 53.

you are careless or lazy, don't have faith or don't realize what an incredibly precious opportunity you have. You don't have to plant this field only in the right season; you can plant it every moment of every day. If you have faith and understanding and aren't lazy, you have an unbelievable opportunity with the merit field of the guru to create the cause of all this happiness in every second.

This verse is mainly about remembering the kindness of the guru; here we should remember his kindness in the past, present and future. In terms of qualities, the guru and the buddhas are equal, but in terms of kindness, the guru is kinder.

We don't have the karma to see Yamantaka, Guhyasamaja, Heruka or any other deity and receive initiation from them but we do receive initiation from our gurus. We don't receive teachings on sutra and tantra from Guru Shakyamuni Buddha as we have no karma to see Guru Shakyamuni Buddha. None of the infinite nirmanakaya and sambhogakaya aspects of deities can give us teachings because we don't have the karma to see them, but our gurus do give us teachings.

Vajradhara manifested in the aspect of our gurus, whether ordained or lay, to us, ordinary sentient beings with little merit. Vajradhara also manifested in all the nirmanakaya and sambhogakaya aspects of deities and as the dakinis, protectors and even all the lineage lamas as well. Since we didn't have the karma to see or receive teachings from them, we have been left out, unable to be directly subdued by them. These manifestations of Vajradhara, our gurus, have much greater kindness than all the buddhas of the three times and all the beings in the merit field.

If our guru had not manifested in his present human body but in a lower form such as that of an animal, we couldn't recognize him. It would be impossible for us to recognize an animal as an embodiment of Vajradhara and communicate with or receive teachings from him. As Chengawa Lodrö Gyaltsen said, we are extremely fortunate not to see our gurus in the aspect of dogs and donkeys but to see them in human aspect.

If the aspect of our guru were higher or purer than his present one— if he were to manifest in the nirmanakaya or sambhogakaya aspect, for example—again we wouldn't have the karma to see him and receive teachings. The only aspect that accords with our level of mind—one that we can see and receive teachings and guidance from—is the one we now see. This aspect exactly suits our present karma. Therefore our guru is extremely kind.

Without even thinking of all the complete teachings we have received many times, we can see that our guru is unbelievably kind in showing the aspect that suits our present level of mind.

If we think of the meaning of this second verse in this way and meditate on it, it has great taste, great meaning. It helps us feel the guru's kindness from the bottom of our heart.

We can also think of what His Holiness the Dalai Lama sometimes says to the Tibetan people: "If the Tibetan people don't follow my advice well, the Dalai Lama might become sick and unable to do any activity."

We may have found a guru but if he is always sick or unable to teach, we won't receive teachings. In their present manifestations, our gurus are able to give whatever teachings we wish. If we meditate more specifically in this way we will feel the kindness of our guru more deeply.

Only our present gurus are actually revealing to us the methods to achieve liberation from samsara and enlightenment. Only our gurus are granting us ordinations, the bodhisattva and tantric vows, and commentaries on sutra and tantra. Therefore they are more precious than all the infinite buddhas.

Without our gurus, we would be barbarians; if our present gurus were not revealing the teachings to us, we would be barbarians with no understanding of karma. Being reborn as a human being is imperfect if we don't meet gurus and the teachings. Just think of the Indian villagers in Dharamsala. Without any understanding of karma, they don't have the opportunity or the freedom to stop creating negative karma. Without the kindness of our present gurus in manifesting exactly according to our karma, we'd be barbarians, completely without guidance. Even if we weren't born in the lower realms, we would still be barbarians.

Without our gurus, we couldn't even receive a human body. To receive a human body we have to create good karma and without a virtuous teacher we can't create it. We need to receive teachings in order to practice virtue and obtain a human body.

As *The Essence of Nectar* says,[122] it is through the kindness of our gurus

---

[122] Therefore, when our gurus have revealed to us
The methods of escaping from the three evil-gone realms,
Kindly giving us the chance to enjoy for a while
The perfections of gods and humans;
And they then show us well the highest method
For pacifying all the degenerations of samsara and nirvana,
And lead us to the exalted state of the three kayas—
Why is this kindness not supreme? (Vv. 126–127.)

that we are guided from the lower realms, placed in the state of a human and given teachings and temporal enjoyments, and from this we gradually achieve enlightenment. *Guided from the lower realms* doesn't mean taken by the hand but given teachings so that we can create merit.

There are two ways to think about how the guru is kinder and more precious than the buddhas. One is to think that our present virtuous teacher, who appears in an ordinary aspect, is a manifestation of the absolute guru and everything—including Buddha, Dharma and Sangha—comes from the absolute guru.

The other way is to think that the numberless buddhas can't guide us in the aspect of buddhas because we don't have the karma to see them; only our present gurus can guide us. Without them we'd be without a guide, like a child without parents. We would be like a crawling baby, who doesn't know anything, not even what to eat.

After the verse about the kindness of the guru, devoting to the guru with action comes in this verse of request:

> Seeing that all general and sublime realizations depend upon correctly devoting myself to you, my savior, I give up my body and even my life. Please grant me blessings to practice only what pleases you.

This is an extremely important prayer. It's important to always please the guru and never displease him for even a moment. We should say this prayer and dedicate merits in this way as many times as possible every day. If we dedicate merit in this way, in this life and future lives we will be able to do more Dharma practice and practice more correctly. It gives us the opportunity to be a successful Dharma practitioner.

Devoting ourselves to the guru doesn't mean that we feel devotion and respect only at the times when our guru smiles at us, gives us things or does something that we like, then give up the guru at other times when he is angry at us, tells us our faults or does something we don't like.

A text says,

> By receiving Dharma, we should have good reliance. We should correctly devote ourselves to the virtuous friend until we achieve enlightenment.

In relation to *give up my body and even my life*, even if it endangers our life to follow a piece of advice from our guru, we should be willing to give up our body and life to do that, as in the stories of Naropa and Milarepa. Remember the twelve great hardships that Naropa experienced in following the advice of Tilopa.

What if somebody tells us that they will kill us if we follow our guru's advice? In *Liberation in the Palm of Your Hand*, Pabongka Dechen Nyingpo tells the story of somebody who said to a monk, "If you don't give up refuge in Buddha, Dharma and Sangha, I will kill you." Rather than give up his refuge, the monk chose to be killed and was then reborn in a pure realm.

Giving up our body and life to accomplish our guru's holy wishes has incredible advantages. The alternative, protecting our life and going against our guru's advice, has many shortcomings, even in this life. Even if we live a few years longer by protecting our life, our mind won't be happy.

The next line, *Please grant me blessings to practice only what pleases you*, also has great meaning. When we recite this request, we should think, "From this moment until I achieve enlightenment, may my body, speech and mind be *only* pleasing to my guru. May I never displease him for even a moment." If our virtuous friend is happy and pleased with us, that is the best purification. Even if billions of other sentient beings criticize and are unhappy with us, it doesn't matter as long as our guru is pleased with us.

We purify even heavy negative karmas accumulated in the past with sentient beings or with our gurus by doing actions that please our guru's holy mind. It is explained in the teachings that even the heaviest negative karmas, those accumulated in relation to the guru, are purified by following the guru's advice and pleasing him. Even if billions of other sentient beings are unhappy with us, we will still have happiness in our life. In this life and in the future, we will succeed in our practice.

These three verses in *Six-Session Guru Yoga* have unbelievable meaning. It's a waste if we just race through the words and don't think of their meaning. We lose the richness of the prayers.

21. Guru Devotion in *Calling the Lama from Afar*

❧ ❧

CALLING THE LAMA FROM AFAR, written by Pabongka Dechen Nyingpo, is very effective for the mind as it combines guru yoga practice and lam-rim. It is a very effective way to do direct meditation on the three principal paths and the two stages of Highest Yoga Tantra because this prayer came from Pabongka Dechen Nyingpo's own experiences. Everything in this prayer has deep meaning.

I liked this prayer so much that I especially requested the oral transmission of it from my root guru, His Holiness Trijang Rinpoche. I received the oral transmission on my own in His Holiness's room in Dharamsala, two or three years before Kyabje Rinpoche passed away. I think this must have been the last teaching I received from His Holiness.

The full title of this prayer is *Calling the Lama from Afar: A Tormented Wail Quickly Drawing Forth the Blessing of the Lama, the Inseparable Three Kayas*. Tormented by samsaric sufferings, one is expressing unsurpassable devotion to the guru through seeing what the guru is and understanding his kindness. Unbearable devotion is expressed in this prayer and this devotion quickly brings the blessings of the guru, who is the inseparable three kayas.

When you recite *Calling the Lama from Afar*, visualize your root guru on your crown or in front of you as the embodiment of all gurus, Buddha, Dharma and Sangha, and then do the meditations as described in the verses of the prayer. The very essence of the meditation is to concentrate on the guru as the absolute guru, the dharmakaya, the holy mind of all the buddhas, the transcendental wisdom of nondual bliss and voidness. The absolute guru manifests in all the numberless different aspects of buddha to guide us sentient beings and also takes ordinary forms to reveal the teachings. Each of our gurus is all the buddhas and all the buddhas are each of our gurus.

> Lama, think of me.
> Lama, think of me.
> Lama, think of me.

When we recite this—*lama khyen, lama khyen, lama khyen* in Tibetan—we are appealing to the guru for help. We are asking the guru to pay attention to us, to think of us. The word *lama* can be used in various ways, but here it means our own personal lama, with whom we have had Dharma contact with the recognition of a guru-disciple relationship.

With your root guru visualized on your crown, be aware of the real meaning of guru. Remember in your heart that the guru is the absolute guru, the dharmakaya, the holy mind of all the buddhas. The absolute guru, or all the buddhas, is working through the ordinary aspect of the conventional guru, just as the sun must shine through a magnifying glass to burn dry grass. All the buddhas work through this ordinary manifestation, whose appearance accords with the quality of your own mind. Through giving oral transmissions, initiations, commentaries, vows, teaching the alphabet and so forth, the guru completely burns all your delusions, all the faults of your mind; then, by actualizing the path, you are guided to enlightenment.

> The wisdom of great bliss of all buddhas, one taste with the dharmakaya, is itself the ultimate nature of all kind lamas. I beseech you, Lama, dharmakaya, please look after me always without separation, in this life, future lives and the bardo.

While this is the translation that you might be accustomed to, I prefer to translate this verse in the following way:

> The transcendental wisdom of all the buddhas, one taste in the great bliss dharmakaya, is only the kind guru, the ultimate nature of all. To the Lama, dharmakaya, from my heart I request: please guide me in this life, future lives and the intermediate state, without separation.

Instead of linking bliss to wisdom, I have joined it to dharmakaya, because it is describing what the dharmakaya is. However, I'm not saying that wisdom is not great bliss. Here *ultimate nature of all* means of all the buddhas; the kind guru is the ultimate nature of all the buddhas. This is the way to meditate to realize that the holy mind of the guru is dharmakaya. Generally, *guide* means to take someone to the place they wish to be for their happiness, so here it refers to bringing us to enlightenment.

When we can recognize the object to be refuted as false and empty, we can develop complete faith that ignorance and the wrong conceptions arising from ignorance can be eliminated. This is how we develop definite faith that it is possible for us to achieve enlightenment. In a similar way, by understanding the four kayas as explained in the Highest Yoga Tantra path, we gain faith that enlightenment is possible. By understanding clearly the two stages of the Highest Yoga Tantra path, especially the second one, the completion stage, we understand much more clearly and have much more faith in how it is possible to achieve the result of the four kayas. We then have much more faith when we recite *Calling the Lama from Afar*.

This first verse holds the key to guru devotion. It is the essence, the very heart of the teaching on guru devotion, and all the rest of the prayer is an elaboration of this. Without understanding this verse, there is no way to understand such quotations as Buddhajñana's, "Before what is called 'guru,' there is not even the name 'buddha.'" When we understand this verse we will also understand why *Namo gurubhya* rather than *Namo buddhaya* comes first when we recite the refuge section in *Guru Puja*. We will also understand why we say *guru-buddha* and not *buddha-guru*. When we understand this verse we'll understand why the guru comes first. It's not just because the guru is kinder than buddha, which is true but only part of the reason.

In the early times at Kopan, Lama Yeshe used to do examinations of the Western Sangha. One monk or nun, with no prior knowledge of the day's subject, would be singled out to sit below the throne. All the students, including the thirty or forty Kopan monks, sat in the gompa as that Sangha member was questioned by Lama. Once, when Lama and I stayed a long time in Tushita Retreat Centre in Dharamsala, Jhampa Zangpo was questioned. I think I put the question, "Why does the guru come first?" One geshe helped Jhampa answer by saying, "Because the guru is kinder than the buddhas." There is a much deeper reason and I'm sure the geshe understood that but didn't get to complete the answer. This verse gives the reason.

The point expressed in the first verse of *Calling the Lama from Afar*, that the transcendental wisdom of all the buddhas is of one taste in the great bliss of dharmakaya, is the ultimate secret of tantra. To hear the explanation of what the dharmakaya is you really need to have received a Highest Yoga Tantra initiation. By introducing the ultimate guru, this verse talks about the very essence, the very meaning, of guru, and what we ultimately have to realize.

During teachings he gave in Mongolia, Kyabje Denma Lochö Rinpoche mentioned that Pabongka Rinpoche gives the clearest explanation of how all the buddhas are one in essence. No other lama has explained it so clearly. Pabongka Dechen Nyingpo said, "All sentient beings become one in essence when they become enlightened."

As I've already explained, in *Ornament of Mahayana Sutras* Maitreya Buddha uses the example of how the innumerable beams of the sun mix together and always engage in the one activity of illuminating the world to show how the innumerable buddhas mix in the dharmakaya to perform the one activity of illuminating the minds of sentient beings.

All the buddhas are one in the dharmakaya and from the dharmakaya, like innumerable beams emitting from a single sun to engage in one activity, numberless forms of buddhas, all the different nirmanakaya and sambhogakaya aspects, manifest to guide sentient beings. Since at the moment, with our obscured minds, we can't see the nirmanakaya and sambhogakaya aspects and receive direct guidance from them, the buddhas also manifest in ordinary forms to work for our benefit. With various methods, but especially by revealing Dharma, these manifestations cause us to engage in virtue and thus enjoy happiness.

The other example that Maitreya Buddha uses in *Ornament of Mahayana Sutras* is water from various different sources flowing into an ocean, where it mixes to become one. Before entering the ocean, different bodies of water are in different places and perform different functions. Some of the water is in springs, rivers, waterfalls, ponds, under the ground and even in swimming pools. This is like sentient beings, who before enlightenment had separate minds but when they become enlightened, they become one, like all the water flowing into the ocean. This means all the water is in one place, the water itself becomes one, and its function also becomes one. In the dharmakaya, which is like an ocean, the holy minds of all the buddhas mix to become one in essence—and that is the absolute guru.

Before we enter enlightenment we have a separate body and a separate mind and our individual activities are also separate. Because we are separate beings in separate bodies, our activities are different. Also, before we enter enlightenment, the work that we do for sentient beings is limited.

We should apply this example to understand *the transcendental wisdom of all the buddhas, one taste in the great bliss dharmakaya*. After sentient beings enter enlightenment, there is no separate body and no separate mind, just as there are no separate streams once they have entered an ocean.

When you put one drop of water into an ocean, it becomes one with all the rest of the water. After the drop has gone into the ocean, there is no way that you can discriminate the drop from the ocean. In a similar way, after sentient beings have entered enlightenment, there are no separate bodies, no separate minds and no separate activities.

The mind has three levels: gross, subtle and extremely subtle. It is in terms of the extremely subtle mind and wind that the point of the example of the drop of water and of this verse becomes clear. This extremely subtle wind-mind doesn't have any resistance, and because of that it pervades all existence. If there were resistance, there could be separation. Since the drop of water in the ocean doesn't have any resistance to keep it separate from the ocean, it becomes one with all that large ocean. In a similar way, the transcendental wisdom of all the buddhas is of one taste in the dharmakaya.

After the drop of water goes into the ocean, does the drop exist or not? All the water becomes one after it goes into the ocean. It's not that the water—whether you call it a stream, waterfall or drop—doesn't exist. It does exist, the continuation of that water does exist, but as a whole ocean. Like this, the transcendental wisdom of all the buddhas is of one taste in the great bliss of dharmakaya.

When a sentient being becomes enlightened, it's not that the continuation of its consciousness is stopped; the continuity of its consciousness is still there. The separate, or individual, identity is not there but the continuation of consciousness is there, but as a whole. Just as the drop becomes of one taste with the ocean, the transcendental wisdom of all the buddhas becomes of one taste with the dharmakaya. *This* is what is called "guru." When we think of the guru, when we hear or say the word "guru," when we see the guru, when we meditate on the guru, it should be this one, the transcendental wisdom of all the buddhas of one taste in the dharmakaya. This is the understanding that should immediately come in our mind when we recite prayers about the guru or think about, see or meditate on the guru. This is how the realization comes that all the buddhas are the guru and that all the gurus are buddha.

The verse concludes, *please guide me in this life, future lives and the intermediate state, without separation*. How does the guru look after, or guide, us? At the moment we ourselves cannot mentally see the guru in the dharmakaya. We also can't see the guru in sambhogakaya and nirmanakaya aspects. We don't have the karma to see the guru in the aspect of a buddha. We have the karma to meet and receive teachings and guidance from an ordinary person with samsaric aggregates, with delusions and with the sufferings of rebirth, old age, sickness and death. We are being guided by that aspect, by that ordinary form.

The water in the ocean evaporates from the ocean to again become springs, waterfalls and ponds, to go into fields to grow crops, and to perform many other activities. In a similar way, the absolute guru—the wisdom of all the buddhas that is of one taste with the great bliss of dharmakaya—manifests in the conventional guru and through that form then guides sentient beings. It also manifests in various other forms, including the numberless aspects of buddhas; it immediately appears in whatever form is necessary to guide each sentient being. As a sentient being's karma ripens, the absolute guru spontaneously manifests without even a second's delay, then guides that sentient being.

Now, with this recognition of what the guru is, with this understanding of the absolute guru, it is easy to relate to all the buddhas of the ten directions. No matter how many different external aspects there are—male, female, two arms or a thousand—they are all manifestations of the guru, and the guru is all those buddhas. This is the very essence of the following verses in *Calling the Lama from Afar*, which relate to how the guru is various deities, the Triple Gem and so forth:

> Wisdom's own illusory appearance, the conqueror with seven branches[123], is itself the ultimate basis of emanation of all kind lamas. I beseech you, Lama, sambhogakaya, please look after me always without separation, in this life, future lives and the bardo.

This verse relates to the sambhogakaya, or the holy body of complete enjoyment. Why is it called *complete enjoyment*? Because the transcendental wis-

---

[123] The seven branches are complete enjoyment, union, great bliss, non-inherent existence, great compassion, uninterrupted continuity and non-cessation.

dom of nondual bliss and voidness has nothing more to develop in terms of enjoyment. Great bliss is ultimate enjoyment.

The term translated here as *seven branches* is sometimes translated as "seven kisses," but that looks as if it refers to kissing seven times, which is wrong. The sambhogakaya manifests a goddess with a similar aspect and they abide in the manner of facing each other in sexual union. It is actually one being, not two separate beings. It shows that the mind is always experiencing great bliss, that method and wisdom are unified.

Experiencing great bliss through union with the goddess is the second branch, or characteristic. The third is that this great bliss is unceasing; there is no way it can be exhausted. The being is perfect and complete, which means it has no delusions. It exists in this form as long as samsara exists. The holy body of the sambhogakaya doesn't exist by nature; it doesn't have a truly existent nature. This sambhogakaya is dependent on causes and conditions. It always has non-objectifying great compassion. Then, while it is impermanent, the sambhogakaya, the holy body of complete enjoyment, effortlessly grants all wishes. It works unceasingly for sentient beings. It is not that this sambhogakaya sometimes has energy to work for sentient beings and sometimes is lazy about working for them. The sambhogakaya works unceasingly for sentient beings, immediately appearing wherever there is a fortunate sentient being who is an object to be subdued.

The sambhogakaya doesn't have cessation; it always abides, without passing into the sorrowless state. When we request the guru to have stable life until samsara ends, we make that request to the nirmanakaya, because it is the one that shows the action of passing into the sorrowless state.

> The play of various emanations, suiting the dispositions of the many to be subdued, is itself the behavior of the sambhogakaya of the kind lamas. I beseech you, Lama, nirmanakaya, please look after me always without separation, in this life, future lives and the bardo.

This ultimate transcendental wisdom of nondual bliss and voidness manifests in the holy body adorned with the thirty-two signs and the eighty exemplifications. That one is the holy body of nirmanakaya.

A later verse says,

> Thinking of how you show the excellent unmistaken path to me,
> an unfortunate wretched being, abandoned by all the buddhas—
> reminds me of you, Lama.

Here *abandoned by all the buddhas* refers to the buddhas before Shakyamuni Buddha. We didn't have the merit, or fortune, to be subdued by the
three buddhas who descended in this world before Shakyamuni Buddha.
And with Guru Shakyamuni Buddha, Manjushri, Maitreya, Asanga, Nagarjuna and the other pandits and yogis in India and Tibet, we still didn't have
the merit to be their direct disciples and be guided by them. Numberless
buddhas, bodhisattvas and holy beings have appeared in this world in the
past but we didn't have the merit to be directly guided by them.

What is *the excellent unmistaken path* that reminds us of the guru? Here,
it specifically refers to Lama Tsongkhapa's teachings, not just the general
teachings of Buddhadharma. The excellent unmistaken pure path of Lama
Tsongkhapa's teachings, which unify sutra and tantra, have the clearest
explanation of what Buddha taught. Without talking about liberating
other sentient beings, even liberating yourself from the oceans of samsaric
suffering depends on cutting the root of samsara, ignorance, and this can
happen only by realizing the Prasangika Madhyamaka view of emptiness,
which leads to the understanding of subtle dependent arising, that things
exist in mere name, merely imputed by mind. Lama Tsongkhapa put special effort into presenting the Prasangika school's view very clearly; it is
the clearest explanation. That is a main aspect of *the excellent unmistaken
path*.

Another aspect is Lama Tsongkhapa's clear teachings on calm abiding,
especially on subtle sinking thought, which it seems is not always clearly
explained in other traditions. Such a clear explanation makes it easy to
achieve calm abiding. Guided by Lama Tsongkhapa's clear explanation, you
first gain a correct intellectual understanding of the practice; then you put
it into practice and achieve correct realization. It doesn't take very long and
isn't very difficult because the teaching is very clear.

Lama Tsongkhapa also clearly explained all the special techniques to
achieve bodhicitta. With respect to tantra, Lama Tsongkhapa gives the
clearest explanation on how to achieve the illusory body, the direct cause
of the rupakaya.

Though there are many others, these are the main examples of Lama
Tsongkhapa showing the pure unmistaken path in the clearest way, so that

there is no danger of being misled, of being led to suffering rather than to liberation and thus wasting one's life.

It is important to relate this verse to Lama Tsongkhapa's excellent unmistaken path, because you will then feel how fortunate you are in this life. First of all, the number of Buddhists in this world is small when compared to the number of non-Buddhists; among Buddhists, the number of Mahayanists is very small; and among Mahayanists, those who meet Lama Tsongkhapa's teachings, which contain pure conduct and pure view, are even fewer.

Then, *reminds me of you, Lama* means that thinking of how you have received all this reminds you of your guru. It means not just remembering your guru but remembering his kindness and practicing and actualizing the teachings he has given you as well.

The word *Lama* is related more to your root guru, the aspect that you are meditating on. You can relate the verse to your other gurus, but keep your mind one-pointedly on the aspect of your root guru. Otherwise, you could say *Lamas*.

> Thinking of this excellent body, highly meaningful and difficult
> to obtain, and wishing to take its essence with unerring choice
> between gain and loss, happiness and suffering—reminds me of
> you, Lama.

We receive a perfect human rebirth, which is difficult to find and has great meaning, by the kindness of the guru. All the eight freedoms and ten richnesses, each of which is extremely rare, are received by the kindness of the guru. Such a body, which will be extremely difficult to find again, has been found this time by the kindness of the guru; and with this perfect human body, we can achieve the three great meanings, also by the kindness of the guru.

This rebirth gives us the freedom in this life to choose between profit and loss, between happiness and suffering. In every moment, we can choose enlightenment or hell. We have the freedom to choose now, during this life, this year, this month, this week, this day, this hour, this minute, even this second. We can choose to achieve hell or enlightenment, samsara or liberation, the realm of a suffering migratory being or the realm of a happy migratory being. Even in each moment we have the freedom to choose to take the unmistaken essence.

How do we take the unmistaken essence? By meditating that our own mind, the guru's mind and the deity's mind are one. Our own mind is one with our own special deity's mind, the transcendental wisdom of nondual bliss and voidness, which is the absolute guru. Seeing all these three as one should be our meditation in daily life. Twenty-four hours a day we should see ourselves, the deity and the guru as one.

With this guru yoga practice, from morning until night, all our enjoyments become the means of accumulating the most extensive merit. With this meditation, every single sense pleasure—eating, drinking, washing—rather than becoming negative karma naturally becomes a method of accumulating the most extensive merit. Since we are seeing all three as one, every sense pleasure becomes an offering and develops bliss and voidness, the essence of the Highest Yoga Tantra path, within us. In this way, drinking a mouthful of tea or eating a mouthful of food collects much more merit than making offerings to all the buddhas. Eating and drinking then make our life extremely rich and meaningful. And it is the same with all our other enjoyments; washing, wearing clothes, and everything else become only the means to accumulate the most extensive merit.

If we make offerings in this way, everything helps us to develop the transcendental wisdom of nondual bliss and voidness, and meditation on emptiness naturally has to come with every enjoyment. Every enjoyment experienced with awareness of emptiness becomes a remedy to cut the root of samsara. All the sense objects we enjoy are also manifestations of the dharmakaya, the absolute guru, the transcendental wisdom of nondual bliss and voidness. Everything we do becomes guru yoga practice. Living our life in this way is the way to become enlightened in one brief lifetime of a degenerate time. Those yogis who became enlightened in one life did so because they practiced guru yoga in this way, seeing all three—their own mind, the deity's holy mind and the guru's holy mind—as one. This is what enabled them to achieve enlightenment within one life, or within even a few years.

Since these actions are also done with bodhicitta, they are again causes of enlightenment. First of all, by the power of the guru-deity, everything becomes a cause of enlightenment. Second, since the practice is done with bodhicitta, it again becomes a cause of enlightenment. It makes our life beneficial for all sentient beings.

Our own mind is dharmakaya, the deity's holy mind and the guru's holy mind. How is that experienced? We see everything as empty, oneness with bliss. There is this pure appearance. No ordinary things appear to this dharmakaya, only pure things, and everything appears as empty of existing from its own side.

What obliges us to do all these practices of guru yoga, bliss and voidness and bodhicitta and thus make our life most meaningful is awareness of impermanence and death, awareness that we are going to die and that our death could happen at any time, even today. This stops the concept of permanence. It cuts distractions and gives us the energy and perseverance to continue the other practices. It enables us not to be born in hell and to achieve enlightenment. It enables us to be free from samsara, to achieve liberation from true suffering and true cause of suffering. Even if we don't become enlightened in this life, it helps us not to be born in the lower realms and to be born as a deva or a human in our next life. This is the very essence of the lam-rim, the three principal paths.

> Thinking of the experience of not knowing what to do when the
> great fear of death suddenly descends upon me—reminds me of
> you, Lama.

I think it's very good to meditate on this verse. If death suddenly happens upon you, what are you going to do? Of course, how much success you have at the time of death, which means being able to meditate well, depends on how much merit you have collected. In other words, it really depends on how well you have devoted yourself to your virtuous friend. If death were to happen right now, what would you do? Here Pabongka Dechen Nyingpo is reminding you to prepare for death. Even if you have done extensive study of the five root philosophical texts and the Indian and Tibetan commentaries as well, even if you are a famous *lharampa* geshe, if you didn't practice Dharma, if you didn't practice the lam-rim, and suddenly death comes, you won't know what to do. You will suddenly be lost and overwhelmed by fear. You will have no time to practice as there is no way to postpone death.

> Thinking of the experience of just now suddenly separating from
> the perfections of this life and going on alone—reminds me of
> you, Lama.

When this happens, there is nothing to rely upon except the guru. That's why it reminds you of the guru.

> Thinking of the experience of my naked body falling into the
> terrifying fires of hell and being unable to bear it—reminds me
> of you, Lama.

Here, when it comes to the suffering of the lower realms, it's good to make this request: "Please, guru, protect me right now from the unbearable suffering of the hell realms." Since there is no other object of refuge for you, you take refuge in your guru. Even though there are numberless buddhas and bodhisattvas, the best, most powerful refuge is the guru. As I mentioned before, the guru is the origin of all the other objects of refuge, of all the buddhas, Dharma and Sangha.

It's also very good to relate to this suffering by thinking, "When I fall into the hell realms, may I experience the sufferings of hell of all sentient beings." You remember your guru and request to be able to use the suffering of rebirth in the lower realms to practice bodhicitta. You can think this at the end of the verse. By praying like this now, when you are born in hell, you will be able to remember bodhicitta and take on yourself all the hell beings' sufferings at that time. You also allow other sentient beings to take all your happiness up to enlightenment.

To think in either of these two ways is good.

> Thinking of how the suffering of hunger and thirst, without a
> drop of water, is directly experienced in the unfortunate preta
> realm—reminds me of you, Lama.

Pretas are unable to find even a drop of water or a spoonful of food for thousands of years and experience only suffering. On top of that, they create negative karma. It is a most unbearable life. Thinking, "I have no other method except to take refuge in my guru," you remember your guru and again ask him to protect you.

You can also generate bodhicitta, thinking that when you are reborn there in the preta realm you will experience the preta sufferings of all sentient beings.

> Thinking of how very repulsive and wretched it is to become a
> foolish stupid animal and what it would be like to experience it
> myself—reminds me of you, Lama.

Here it is talking about animals in general, but it is more effective to relate this verse to specific animals that you have seen because, as ordinary people, we don't have clairvoyance; we don't see how much animals suffer. Some people, whose minds are very obscured, don't even think animals have a mind; they think of them as plants. Relate this verse to specific animals whose suffering you can remember. Not only are animals suffering but they are also continuously creating negative karma because it is very difficult for an animal to generate a virtuous thought.

As a hell being, preta or animal, no matter how much unbearable suffering you are experiencing, it doesn't stop; you don't die. Because of your heavy karma, obstacles have gathered, and no matter how difficult your life is, you don't die until that karma is exhausted.

> Thinking of a refuge to protect me from this, since I am now about to fall into the wretched states of bad migration—reminds me of you, Lama.

This is also a very powerful meditation. Think, "Anything could have happened to me by this afternoon or tonight. I could be in a terrifying hell realm or reborn as a millipede, a worm or some other creature. In an hour, or even a minute, I could be in the lower realms." Reflect on the sufferings of the lower realms. They are unbearable but you have to experience them until the karma finishes. You have no choice. That experience of the sufferings of the lower realms could appear even in the next minute.

This is a powerful meditation on impermanence, on how nothing is definite. Thinking to look for refuge, for protection from being born in the lower realms, you see that there is none other than your guru. Relying upon your guru, taking refuge in your guru, is the best protection.

> Thinking of how white and black actions are experienced and of how to practice thorough and precise engagement and restraint—reminds me of you, Lama.

Reflect on karma and delusions, the causes of suffering, particularly the suffering of the lower realms. Think of the negative karma you have collected during beginningless rebirths and which you continue to collect every day with motivations of anger and attachment clinging to this life.

All the results of unbearable suffering from the numberless causes you have created are waiting to be experienced. You could fall down into the lower realms and experience that suffering right now—not just today but even in an hour, a minute or a few seconds from now. You could breathe out and not breathe in again and suddenly a hell realm could appear to your mind.

There is no object of refuge other than the guru, the ultimate object of refuge. As described in the first verse, the holy minds of all the buddhas become one in the dharmakaya, like all the different rivers flowing into the ocean. Think of that meaning of the guru as the ultimate object of refuge, origin of all the numberless past, present and future buddhas, the Dharma and the Sangha.

> Thinking of a method to escape this prison of endless existences,
> the source of all suffering—reminds me of you, Lama.

Thinking of the guru immediately protects you from having to experience rebirth in the lower realms. Remembering the guru liberates you from that suffering. Remembering the ultimate object of refuge, the guru, you don't need to be afraid.

The way not to be born in the lower realms is to protect karma: to abandon both gross and subtle negative karmas and to practice gross and even subtle good karmas. Being able to do this depends on the guru giving teachings to you and your then practicing those teachings. You then purify the causes of the lower realms already collected and don't create any more. The way to get out of samsara is to follow the guru's teachings and advice. This is also related to the kindness of the guru.

This samsaric prison is the origin of all suffering, which has no beginning because the continuity of mind has no beginning and delusion, the cause of samsara, has no beginning. Not only does delusion have no beginning but it is also difficult to see its end. Again, when you think of ending the oceans of samsaric suffering, the continuity of which has no beginning, there is no better means than by relying upon the guru, taking refuge in the guru. The guru protects and guides you, liberating you from samsara by revealing the teachings to you and enabling you to practice them and thus accomplish his advice. This is what is contained in the words *reminds me of you, Lama*. Thinking of a means of protection and liberation, *reminds me of you, Lama*.

Thinking of the plight of my pitiful old mothers, pervasive as space, fallen amidst the fearful ocean of samsara and tormented there—reminds me of you, Lama.

Remember how each sentient being has been your mother numberless times and kind in the four ways. Your present mother was kind in giving you life, enabling you to practice Dharma and attain not only temporary but ultimate happiness. She protected you from hundreds of dangers to your life each day and underwent many physical and mental hardships for your well-being, often creating much negative karma in doing so, thereby creating the causes of much more suffering for herself in samsara. She provided you with all temporal needs, not only in this life but in beginningless lives in samsara. And she educated you in the ways of the world.

All sentient beings have been kind to you in these four ways number-less times and they are now suffering as hell beings, hungry ghosts, animals, humans, asuras, suras and intermediate state beings. It is not just one mother sentient being that is suffering. In each of the six realms numberless of them are experiencing sufferings, one after another. Not only are they dying and being reborn in the six realms and experiencing unbearable suffering but because of their ignorance and other hallucinated minds, they are creating further negative karma. This is unbearable. Without choice, they are suffering unbearably but can't do anything until their karma finishes. No matter how many eons it takes, they have to go through that suffering.

This is a source of inspiration for you to quickly achieve enlightenment by developing compassion, the special attitude[124] and bodhicitta. You need to actualize the three principal paths and the two stages of tantra as a means to help liberate sentient beings from the ocean of samsaric sufferings and bring them to enlightenment.

In the following nine verses, you request very strongly to be granted all the realizations of the path to enlightenment without even a second's delay. The final verse is then:

In short, please abide inseparably in the center of my heart until the great enlightenment and mercifully bless me, the child, to follow after you, the father.

---

[124] This is the special intention that assumes personal responsibility for leading all sentient beings to enlightenment.

You are requesting to be able to achieve enlightenment as Guru Shakyamuni Buddha did, by developing renunciation and entering the path. You, the spiritual child, wish to follow the father, the guru, with recognition of what the guru really is as expressed in the very first verse of *Calling the Lama from Afar*. The meditation is done with understanding of that state.

At this point you do the meditation of the guru entering your heart, with your own body, speech and mind becoming one with the guru's holy body, holy speech and holy mind.

> Lama, think of me.
> Lama, think of me.
> Lama, think of me.

You can then conclude by reciting the following prayers.

> In whatever way you appear, glorious guru,
> With whatever retinue, lifespan and pure land,
> Whatever noble and holy name you take,
> May I and others attain only these.

> May I never arise heresy even for a second
> In the actions of the glorious guru.
> May I regard whatever actions are done as pure.
> [With this devotion] may I receive the blessings of the guru
>   in my heart.

> Magnificent and precious root guru,
> Please abide on the lotus and moon seat at my heart.
> Guide me with your great kindness,
> And grant me the realizations of your holy body, speech and mind

22. Teaching and Studying Guru Devotion

Teaching guru devotion

I HAVE ELABORATED quite a bit on the various ways of practicing guru devotion, the root of the whole path to enlightenment. I have also explained the four lam-rim outlines of guru devotion, based on Pabongka Rinpoche's *Liberation in the Palm of Your Hand*, which has many details on these outlines, with extensive quotations and logical reasoning. Hearing and understanding them will deepen your guru devotion.

I think that even for a new student who hasn't heard about guru devotion before, I have explained enough reasons as to why this practice is important. Even if you don't use all these different techniques in your daily life, you can choose whichever meditations you find most effective in generating guru devotion within your mind. Some of the techniques might also be useful when you explain guru devotion to others.

In meditation courses, since there is usually a mixture of people, with always some new people, the subject of guru devotion is hardly ever mentioned. Usually just the outlines or essence of the practice is covered, without any real details about its benefits. Since you don't generally hear much on this subject, I thought it extremely important to amplify a little, because it is the root of all realizations. If you are able to practice guru devotion well, success in all the rest of the realizations of the path, up to enlightenment, will come very easily.

It is the teacher's responsibility to explain the advantages of guru devotion. The subject of guru devotion is extremely important and it is also extremely important to explain it with compassion. There needs to be a motivation of compassion, a wish to guide other sentient beings properly and to guard them from the heaviest negative karma and the heaviest suffering. I find it an uncomfortable subject to talk about because of the lack of compassion within my mind, but it is dangerous to leave it out.

In the past, during the early courses at Kopan, I found it quite easy and comfortable to talk on the subject of guru devotion, but now I find it more difficult. It might be a sign that my mind has degenerated, because now it makes me uncomfortable. I feel more self-conscious at the thought that it might appear as if I'm saying that I'm a buddha.

You might also feel uneasy talking about guru devotion if you yourself are engaged in teaching Dharma. However, the correct way to do it is with compassion for others. If you leave others in complete ignorance of this subject, they will make many mistakes all the way through their Dharma practice. No matter how much they learn about other Dharma teachings and no matter how much they try to meditate, because they don't know about guru devotion they will constantly make mistakes in their practice. From the very beginning of their Dharma practice they will make many mistakes and collect many heavy negative karmas because of their lack of understanding of guru devotion.

For university studies, where someone is learning about a religion or culture to obtain a degree or get a job teaching others, it isn't necessary to teach guru devotion because the student's aim isn't to practice Dharma. If the subject involves study of a lam-rim text, you can just go over the text so that your students learn it. But the situation is different if a student's motivation is to develop her mind because to do that she has to take care of her mind, which means clearing away obstacles and not creating further causes for obstacles.

Of course, you can't talk about guru devotion at the very beginning. It has to be taught at the right time. Generally speaking, Lama Tsongkhapa was very wise when he set up the lam-rim—he was, of course, following Lama Atisha—to put the subject of guru devotion at the very beginning. Before beginning any Dharma practice, people are then fully aware of the teachings on guru devotion; they are then careful from the very beginning. They know why they have to pay the most attention to and put the most effort into guru devotion; they also know what is their biggest obstacle to success. It is good to start your spiritual life with a pure practice rather than one full of mistakes. So with compassion, concern for others, you should explain guru devotion practice to guide your students, to make them fully aware, so that they don't make mistakes from the very beginning.

If someone doesn't have enough merit and has thick obscurations, there is no way you can prove reincarnation to him no matter what intelligent philosophical reasoning you use. Even if you are an expert in logic, like the ancient Indian pandits, even if you use the most intelligent reasoning, there is no way you will be able to prove reincarnation to that person. If the person has thick obscurations, he won't understand or develop faith in reincarnation. Even though the reasons you give are correct and brilliant, they won't work for that particular person. However, when someone has a lot of merit and has purified his negative karma, just from a very simple reason or a few simple words, nothing brilliant or profound, that person can understand and have faith in karma and reincarnation.

It is the same with guru devotion. If someone's mind is not purified, no matter how many quotations and lines of reasoning you use, it will be like talking to a rock. It won't go into his heart; it won't affect him at all. But when his heavy negative karma becomes less and he has more merit, a few simple words, nothing deep, can click in his mind. Before, I mentioned the importance of purifying obscurations but here I also want to emphasize the importance of collecting merit. Developing such devotion depends on having collected extensive merit.

Basically it depends on the good heart. People who have a good heart, who are generous and sincere, do better with the subject of guru devotion than those who are selfish and have strong worldly concern. It seems that people who are less sincere generally find guru devotion more difficult to practice.

Of course, guru devotion shouldn't be taught with the motivation to receive respect or some other advantage for yourself. It can be misused in that way. You should explain it out of your concern for the people who are relying on you, out of your concern to guide them to successfully attain realizations of the path. In short, you teach guru devotion so that disciples can be successful in achieving liberation and enlightenment, so that they can then achieve their goal of working perfectly for sentient beings. There will be no problem if you explain guru devotion with compassion, but without that motivation there can be difficulties.

Unlike before, nowadays there are many books available on the subject of guru devotion, which you can research for yourselves; many lam-rim and tantric teachings that explain guru devotion practice according to sutra and tantra have been translated into English.[125] However, one key way to teach

---

[125] See Suggested Further Reading, p. 461 ff.

guru devotion without many words is by you yourself being an inspiring example.

Studying guru devotion

Some Westerners who are trying to practice Dharma generate wrong views of guru devotion practice because they don't really understand the philosophical points. And if you miss the point of guru devotion because you don't have the root understanding, then no matter how many quotations or outlines you can talk about, guru devotion won't mean much to you.

When we study the subject of guru devotion in *Liberation in the Palm of Your Hand* and other texts, we have to follow the outlines, read the commentary slowly and really think about the points. Just as fog has to be cleared away before the sun can be seen, we have to clear away our obscurations. It's a question of clarifying our mind. If we just skim through the whole text quickly, we'll see nothing logical in it, even though many logical reasons are explained and many quotations given.

When we study lam-rim texts, especially the section on guru devotion, we have to understand that any block we encounter is not in the text but in our own mental continuum. These are valid teachings written from the experiences of numberless beings, including Guru Shakyamuni Buddha himself. They describe the realizations of numberless past yogis and pandits from various countries and present living meditators, who have practiced as Buddha taught, as Lama Tsongkhapa taught, as Marpa taught, as Milarepa taught. The problem is not from the side of the texts but from our own.

We have to gather all the necessary conditions together: intensive purification, accumulation of extensive merit, and especially training in guru devotion. Strong purification especially clears away our karmic obscurations, the fogginess of our mind. And when our obscurations are cleared away, the quotations and logical reasons that didn't make much sense before or didn't give us much feeling suddenly make a lot of sense. Suddenly we are able to see the truth of what is being said. Before receiving teachings on guru devotion we may find the idea uncomfortable and difficult to relate to but as we come to understand the teachings and practice guru devotion, our way of thinking completely changes.

On top of that, I think that if you develop strong guru devotion, your mind will naturally become more compassionate and less egotistic, less selfish. Your motivation will naturally become more compassionate and more renounced.

When teachers talk about the advantages of guru devotion, the thought could arise, especially for beginners who haven't heard anything about the subject of guru devotion, that the gurus are praising themselves or inflating their own importance, asking disciples to look at them as a buddha and make offerings to them. To the ear of somebody with a certain type of mind, somebody who hasn't accumulated much merit or planted many seeds of the teachings, it can sound a little strange to say that you need guru devotion to achieve realizations of the path to enlightenment; it can look like Dharma politics, like the guru is taking advantage of you by telling you this. It looks as if the guru is talking about these advantages in order to get more followers or receive more offerings.

However, the practice of guru devotion is not something that Tibetan lamas made up for their own benefit. There is a whole sutra taught by Buddha on this subject, *Laying Out of Stalks*, and you find many references to it when you read lam-rim teachings on guru devotion. In these teachings, there are many quotations from Guru Shakyamuni Buddha's teachings, especially from the sutras *Laying Out of Stalks* and *Essence of the Earth,* as well as from many Indian and Tibetan pandits and yogis. It may appear as if guru devotion is some kind of Tibetan lamas' trip, something they made up for their own benefit, but it's not like that. There are pure references to Buddha's teachings.

Those who have heard guru devotion teachings many times and have been practicing guru devotion understand how the guru really is the root of their own happiness and perfections, as mentioned in *Guru Puja,*

> Through the power of having made offerings and respectful requests
>   to you,
> Holy and perfect, pure gurus—supreme field of merit,
> I seek your blessings, saviors and root of well-being and bliss,
> That I may come under your joyful care.[126]

No matter how much someone who practices guru devotion hears the guru speak about the advantages of guru devotion, the thought that the guru is praising himself won't arise at all; that person knows that the guru is speaking purely for the disciples' benefit, for their happiness and profit. The thought that the guru is praising himself can arise, however, if we don't understand how to listen to the teachings.

Another factor is karma. If you don't have much understanding of or faith in Buddha's teachings on karma, the subject of guru devotion won't make much sense to you. If your understanding of karma is weak—and I don't mean your intellectual understanding but the understanding that comes with feeling, with faith—you will find the subject of guru devotion difficult and your faith in it will be weak. If your understanding of karma isn't very deep, your faith in the guru will also be superficial, like *tsampa* thrown on water. Understanding karma and having faith in it from the depths of your heart will also help your guru devotion practice a great deal. The more care you take of karma, the more care you will take of your practice of guru devotion.

The guru devotion outlines are presented in accordance with the experiences of great yogis who achieved enlightenment by perfectly following their gurus, by cherishing their gurus more than their own body and life. They themselves practiced guru yoga in this way and accomplished every goal that they had. As you have heard in the life stories of the lineage lamas, starting with Guru Shakyamuni Buddha and including all the great Indian pandits and Tibetan yogis, guru yoga practice was presented to them by their gurus in this way and they then practiced it exactly as they were advised. They tried to understand the meaning of what they had heard, reflected and meditated on the correct meaning that they had understood, and then achieved infallible realizations. From their own experiences of how to practice and find realization they then presented the teachings on guru devotion in the same way, according to the outlines of the graduated practice. Their becoming enlightened is the proof of their practice. If we follow their example, we will have the same result.

From the biographies of the lineage lamas you can understand how they practiced Dharma and had realizations. By hearing and reading about the life of Milarepa, for example, you can understand that his incredible practice of guru devotion enabled him, in that brief life, to achieve realizations equal to space, including enlightenment. If you read the life stories of the past pandits and yogis and even those of the present high lamas from all four traditions, you will understand that there hasn't been anyone who achieved enlightenment without practicing guru devotion.

What happens in this life is the result of past lives. Whether we are able to meet a virtuous friend, what kind of virtuous friend we find and how well we are able to practice guru devotion are the results of our practice of guru devotion in past lives. And how much success we will have in future lives depends on how well we practice guru devotion in this life. This present life holds the responsibility for the success of all our future lives, for the development of our mind in the path to enlightenment.

Even if we find the most qualified virtuous friend in the world, our success depends on how much we, as disciples, are able to correctly devote ourselves to that virtuous friend. If we are able to practice correctly with a pure mind of devotion we will continuously receive blessings and continuously develop our mind in the path to enlightenment. From the biographies of the lineage lamas we can understand the importance of guru devotion, but the actual proof comes from our own experiences of meditating on the path.

Serkong Rinpoche, Dharamsala, India, ca 1976

23. The Realization of Guru Devotion

THE ACTUAL PROOF of how experiences and realizations of the path to enlightenment depend on the root of strong guru devotion comes when we practice. Our own experiences answer any questions we might have about the importance of guru devotion. We can clearly see the difference in our everyday life between times when we're correctly devoting ourselves to the guru with thought and action and times when we're not.

Realizing guru devotion doesn't depend so much on intellectual understanding or logical reasoning. It mainly depends on constantly working hard at purifying negative karma and accumulating merit. Even if you have memorized all the texts and can recite them by heart, your mind will still be like a rock if you have no actual experience of guru devotion. Nothing will be happening, even though you know all the words; experiences come only when you perform powerful purification and accumulate extensive merit. This applies not just to the experience of guru devotion but to any other experience of the path to enlightenment.

What the teachings say becomes real to you when strong guru devotion arises because you are doing Vajrasattva practice, prostrations to the Thirty-five Buddhas, mandala offerings or other practices or because you are experiencing powerful purification through working hard on the advice of your guru. At such times you feel that your mind has been transformed into what the texts describe. Even though before you might have felt a big gap between what the texts say and your own mind, there is now a connection. Your mind actually becomes what the texts describe.

When your guru devotion is strong you also have strong experience of whatever you are meditating on: impermanence and death, renunciation of samsara, bodhicitta, emptiness. You find it very easy to feel the meditations. Because you are continuously receiving blessings, any meditation you do is effective and any prayer you do moves your mind and brings understanding. Even though you might have been saying the same prayer for many years, each word now affects you because you discover its meaning. This is a sign that your mind has been ripened through strong practice of purification and accumulation of merit in dependence upon the holy object of the guru.

With strong devotion, you also have complete trust in your guru and no difficulty in following whatever advice he gives you; you find it very easy and enjoyable to follow it. When your mind is filled with devotion you also experience great inner peace. Your heart is full of incredible joy and you see yourself as unbelievably fortunate. Even though there might be other difficulties in your life, such as no money, no visa or no job, your strong guru devotion overwhelms your problems and external things don't bother you much. Your life becomes very enjoyable and very meaningful.

When there is no devotion in your heart, however, your mind is dry and empty, like a hot desert where nothing grows. At that time, there's not the happiness and richness that you feel when you have devotion. When you have no devotion or your devotion is weak, like a thin cloud about to disappear in the sky, you have no feeling for any of the rest of the path. It is difficult for you to have any feeling for impermanence and death, renunciation, bodhicitta or emptiness. No matter how many times you repeat the words, no matter what lam-rim teachings you read, no matter what you meditate on, you feel nothing from your heart. Everything becomes just words. Your mind is like a rock.

When guru devotion decreases, everything degenerates, even pure practice. If you don't correctly devote yourself to the virtuous friend, your life becomes messy. There is no development in any of your practices. You continuously make mistakes and find it difficult to follow the guru's advice and it is then very difficult for you to develop your mind. Your mind creates many obstacles to being able to follow the guru's advice, which means many obstacles to practicing the path to enlightenment. Besides being unable to practice Dharma, many other problems arise, such as depression and *lung*.

Since negative thoughts toward the guru disturb your mind, you have no peace or happiness. During such times it is very difficult to feel anything in your meditations and even prayers don't affect your mind. Even if you read the lam-rim, which is especially set up to tame the mind, it doesn't affect you. When your mental state is like that, it is difficult for even the lam-rim to move your mind.

If you're not making progress in developing your mind, there's something wrong with your practice of guru devotion. You have to examine what is missing or what mistakes you have made in your guru devotion practice. When changing your mind by doing the basic lam-rim meditations is difficult, something is wrong in your practice there at the root of the path. You have to examine your guru devotion practice and then, by recognizing your mistakes, correct your practice. You then need to do strong practice of purification.

This is a scientific explanation, not by scientists but by meditators, inner scientists. For something to be a scientific explanation, it doesn't have to come from a scientist. You can see from your own experiences that the teachings on guru devotion are true.

You have generated the realization of guru devotion, of seeing the guru as buddha, when you spontaneously recognize that there is no buddha other than the guru and that there is no guru other than the buddha. Whenever you see or think of a guru, you immediately recognize that that guru is an actual buddha. Whenever you see or think of a buddha, you immediately recognize that it is the guru. The understanding that the guru and buddha are one arises naturally, effortlessly, from your heart. In the beginning you see the guru and buddha as separate, but when you have the realization of guru devotion you see them as inseparably mixed, like water poured into water.

We should understand and remember during guru devotion meditation and at all other times, that guru means buddha and buddha means guru. We should think that they're just different names for the same person. When someone acting in a play comes out dressed as a king, he's called a king; when the same person comes out dressed as a general, he's called a general. It's the one person but because there are different costumes, different labels are given.

It's important to understand even from the names that there aren't two separate beings. Someone who has ceased all faults of the mind and completed all realizations is called a guru and is also called a buddha. *Guru* and *buddha* are just different names given to one being. There's no separation between them; it's just that each receives a different label.

When you have the experience that all the buddhas are the guru and all the gurus are the buddha, you have the realization of guru devotion. At that time you don't need to use much reasoning or many quotations to feel that what the teachings describe is real, but you still need to stabilize the realization. To preserve the experience you need to continue the guru devotion practice every day; otherwise the experience will degenerate. The feeling should be stable, not just last a few minutes or one or two hours and then disappear.

However, a sudden experience of seeing the guru as buddha is also a good sign. While we are meditating on guru devotion, doing strong Dharma practice or offering service to the guru, the thought can suddenly come, "If this guru is not buddha, who else can be buddha? There is no other buddha." Even though the experience mightn't last long, it's a sign of having received the blessing of the guru. We have to try to hold this experience without losing it, then develop it, so that it leads to the actual realization of guru devotion.

Unless we clearly establish the reasons that we have to practice guru devotion, our guru devotion will be dependent on external factors and not stable, or fully established, as explained in the lam-rim teachings. It can then disappear at any time. Whenever we perceive some mistake in the actions of the guru's holy body, speech or mind, guru devotion that is not well established through reasoning will disappear. If our devotion is established through wisdom, however, even if in our view there appear to be faults in the actions of the guru, we won't believe it is the reality. Because of our stable devotion, any appearance of faults won't affect our mind or cause us to lose our devotion. It also depends on how much merit, or good karma, a disciple has. It's not easy to shake the devotion of those with a lot of merit and those who understand how to practice guru devotion. Their devotion is very strong.

In the first verse of *The Foundation of All Good Qualities*, Lama Tsongkhapa says,

> The foundation of all good qualities is the kind and perfect, pure
>   guru;
> Correct devotion to him is the root of the path.
> By clearly seeing this and applying great effort,
> Please bless me to rely upon him with great respect.

The reason that Lama Tsongkhapa stresses great effort is that seeing the guru as a buddha doesn't come from the side of the guru; it has to come from our own mind, with great effort. It's not easy to practice guru devotion. We have to put effort into achieving the realization of seeing the guru as a buddha.

Lama Tsongkhapa's saying *great effort* has much meaning. Because guru devotion is the most difficult realization to achieve, we need to put a lot of effort into it. Just doing the meditations a few times can't transform our mind into the realization of seeing the guru as a buddha. We won't feel this after doing the meditations for just a few months—or even a few years. Since we can't easily stop the faults of our mind and generate this devotional thought, we need to apply great effort. Since guru devotion is the root of the path, we absolutely must have this realization; therefore, no matter how long it takes, no matter how many years or even lifetimes it takes, we have got to face the hardships involved in generating this realization.

From the very beginning of our guru devotion practice we should do much analytical meditation as explained in the sutra and tantra teachings. We shouldn't be satisfied by thinking about a few of the points just once or twice. That won't help us to generate the realization. We must reflect on the points over and over again, using quotations and reasoning, until we generate the realization. As the Indian master Chandragomin said in the text *Confession and Praise,*

> The mind, which has been ignorant for such an incredible length of time, will need to have treatment for a long time. For example, if a person has lost his hands and feet to leprosy, taking medicine just a few times won't do anything for him.

These days we could say that if a person has cancer or AIDS, taking medicine just a few times won't do anything for him; he has to take the medicine for many years. In a similar way, we should continue to constantly train our mind in guru devotion until we have the stable realization.

If our guru devotion is well established through logical reasoning and analytical meditation, we'll be able to transform our mind into the devotion that sees the guru as a buddha. We then stabilize our devotion by doing fixed, or single-pointed, meditation on our feeling that the guru is a buddha. In this way, we preserve that experience of devotion. We train again and again with analytical and then fixed meditation. After we have transformed our mind into the devotion that sees the guru as a buddha, we keep our mind in that state of devotion for as long as possible. If possible, we should do guru devotion meditation every morning when we meditate on lam-rim, then try to continue the experience during the rest of the day. This is the best way to ensure quick and stable development of the guru devotion realization.

Apart from calm abiding, all the lam-rim meditations are analytical. First we transform our mind into the experience of the meditation subject through quotations and valid logical reasoning, then we do fixed meditation on that experience.

As we train our mind more and more in this way, the feeling of devotion becomes very stable. According to those who have the realization of guru devotion, at that time you feel that each buddha is all the gurus and each guru is all of the numberless buddhas. Whenever you think of a buddha or say the word "buddha," in your heart you understand that it's the guru. Whenever you see, hear or think of a guru or say the word "guru," in your heart you understand that it's buddha. Even when you visualize yourself as a deity or visualize a deity in front of you, it's the guru. For those with the realization of guru devotion, there is no separation between the two.

We should attempt to meditate continuously until we have stable realization of guru devotion, spontaneously seeing the guru as buddha. When our understanding faith[127] that the guru's holy mind is dharmakaya becomes definitive, it will arise spontaneously, just as we spontaneously think "That is my mother" when we see our mother, even among many other people. We don't need to go through a process of reasoning, thinking of how we were born from her body, of how she acted as our mother and so forth. Whenever we see our mother's body, no matter what she is wearing or what she is doing, the thought that she is our mother instantaneously and effortlessly comes to us. It is exactly the same when we have the understanding faith that the guru's holy mind is dharmakaya. No matter what wrong action we see our guru doing, it can't disturb our mind because we have the definitive understanding that our guru's holy mind is the dharmakaya. The thought that the faults we see are the faults of our guru doesn't come. At that time, seeing faults can't disturb our mind or change our devotion.

The more we are able to look at the guru with devotion, and especially if we have the realization of guru devotion, we will be able to see the guru as a buddha without the slightest doubt. We will have very stable faith. No

[127] See note 57, p. 169.

matter how the guru appears to us, if we have the realization of guru devotion, nothing will disturb us. No matter what appears to us, it won't affect our mind; it won't affect our devotion. We will always see the guru as a buddha. Any fault that appears to us will appear to be an act. We will relate to any appearance of faults as a projection of our own impure mind. Or we will think that since buddhas appear in all kinds of forms and perform all kinds of actions to benefit sentient beings, this action must definitely have some purpose.

Whether or not we visualize the guru in the pure form of a deity, we must constantly think that the guru is in essence Guru Shakyamuni Buddha or our own special deity. We have to think that the guru has ceased all faults and possesses all good qualities; that the guru is in essence the dharmakaya, the absolute guru, Guru Shakyamuni Buddha or our own special deity. Even if we don't have the actual realization of guru devotion, once we start to train our mind in the devotion that sees the guru as in essence dharmakaya, if our guru says or does something that is contradictory to Dharma, we will see it as an act, like someone acting in a play or a movie. We won't cling strongly to the wrong conception that what we are seeing is true and negative thoughts won't arise. With this practice of guru devotion, seeing the guru as a buddha, nothing causes us to lose our realizations and degenerate our mind.

No matter what appears in our view, we have to completely decide that the guru's mind is the dharmakaya, the holy mind of all the buddhas, with cessation of all faults and completion of all good qualities. That is the main point to remember. It is especially important when we see mistakes in the actions of the guru, when the guru scolds or beats us or when we see the guru showing faults of anger, pride, jealousy, attachment or ignorance. Even if we see the guru as ordinary and not in the aspect of a buddha, we should have this understanding in our mind, just as when somebody tells us that a particular woman is a transformation of Vajrayogini or Tara and convinces us of it with amazing stories—even though we still see the woman as an ordinary person, we understand that she is a completely pure being.

Seeing the guru as buddha stops the arising of the thought of faults and the negative actions we create in relation to the guru. Once we have generated and stabilized the realization that sees the guru as buddha, since no thought of faults can arise, we don't create the heaviest obstacle to realization, negative karma in relation to the guru. Any fault that we see in the guru's actions appears to us as an act, not as real. Even if the guru kills hundreds, thousands or millions of people, steals, tells lies or commits sexual misconduct, it all appears to us as an act. Even if faults appear to us, we don't believe in this appearance.

It is similar to the way that you see everything as illusory after you have realized emptiness. Even though everything still appears to you as if it exists from its own side, since in your heart you know that it is empty, you don't cling to the way things appear to you as true and you don't create obstacles to your achievement of liberation and enlightenment. In a similar way, even though faults in the guru might still appear to us, because we have the realization that the guru is buddha, we don't believe what appears to us to be the reality. This is a great protection as it doesn't allow us to generate anger, heresy or the thought of faults. In this way, we don't create the greatest obstacle to the development of our mind.

Seeing the guru as buddha stops wrong views and mistakes in our practice. Even though we still see an ordinary impure aspect, we have no belief that the guru's faults are real faults, just as when we see a mirage, we have no belief that there is real water. There's an ordinary aspect, an appearance of faults, but we don't believe that there are faults in reality. Because of our faith, even if we see a fault, we have no belief that it is a fault in reality. This gives space in our mind to develop the path to enlightenment.

The purpose of meditating on guru devotion is to stop wrong conceptions and avoid the eight shortcomings of incorrect devotion to the guru, each one of which is a heavy result. If we train our mind to have stable devotion that the guru is buddha, the thought of finding faults in the guru never arises and we are also able to rely completely upon the path shown by the guru and to practice it without doubts. Even if we don't have the realization of guru devotion, seeing the guru as a buddha, at least we should stop generating anger, heresy and other wrong thoughts toward the guru so that we don't create obstacles. If there are no obstacles, there is then space for the development of our mind. That is the whole point. We can see that the practice of guru devotion is for our own sake.

The thought of finding faults in the guru, which is the opposite to devotion, is the greatest obstacle to the development of our mind and to all our happiness, now and in the future; it is the greatest obstacle to the happiness of future lives, liberation and enlightenment. Without guru devotion, the thought of faults arises and this then blocks the development of our mind. Nothing happens in our mind; no realizations grow. And instead of experiencing more happiness, we experience only more problems. We can see very clearly how important it is to develop guru devotion and how it comes to be the root of the path to enlightenment.

Once you have the realization of guru devotion, it is very easy to meditate on any subject. Your mind, like dough, can be made into any shape. You can make dough into bread, noodles and many other shapes. With realization of guru devotion, you easily feel any subject you meditate on. Normally when you recite a prayer, the words you recite and your heart are totally separate but when you have realized guru devotion, your heart is living in the meaning of the words you are reciting. When you are reciting words about compassion, your mind feels compassion. When you recite or think of words about impermanence and death, bodhicitta or emptiness, your mind is easily transformed into that. Your mind becomes easy to tame, like a dog. It is very easy for you to have the realization of whatever you meditate on. Because of the realization of guru devotion, it is also more difficult for delusions to arise in your daily life, and even if they do, they are weak and easy to overcome. It is then very easy to practice Dharma.

It doesn't matter whether we can intellectually understand our experience of guru devotion or explain it in words, as long as we feel the way it is explained in the teachings. The main thing is to have the experience. If we feel that the guru is buddha, we have achieved what needed to be achieved. However, having the intellectual understanding helps to stabilize the experience. Then, even if we lose the experience, because we know all the logical reasoning, by meditating we can again generate the experience of guru devotion.

How quickly and easily we can actualize the path and achieve enlightenment depend on how strong our realization of guru devotion is. The skillful way to meditate on lam-rim and complete the lam-rim realizations is to realize guru devotion. Once we have realized guru devotion, realizations of the rest of the path then come without difficulties, like falling rain. However, to generate bodhicitta and the rest of the realizations of the path, it's not necessary to wait until we can see the guru as a buddha, which might take several lifetimes. If we are going to wait for that, no realizations will be generated for that many lifetimes.

Seeing the guru as buddha and seeing all sentient beings as mother are generally regarded as the most difficult lam-rim realizations for most people to achieve, though it still depends on the individual. That's why it's emphasized that we should train our mind in these meditations at least once every day. Every day, first thing in the morning, we should meditate on guru devotion. As Shantideva and Geshe Chekawa mention, there's nothing that we can't train our mind to become; whichever way we train our mind, it becomes that. If we do the meditations on guru devotion every morning and remember them throughout the day, this practice will become easier and easier. When the wrong conception seeing faults comes, because we have meditated and trained our mind, we will immediately be able to recognize it as a mistake that is creating obstacles to our enlightenment and to our performing extensive works for all sentient beings.

While we should try to generate the realization of guru devotion in this life, the skillful way to train our mind in lam-rim and quickly accomplish the path is not to spend our whole life solely on trying to generate the realization of seeing the guru as buddha. We would then not get the chance to generate renunciation, bodhicitta, emptiness or any other realization. When we died, we then wouldn't have any lam-rim realizations in our mind. Since it is the superstitious thoughts toward the guru that disturb our generating the rest of the realizations of the path, when we are capable of not allowing such thoughts to arise we can start to train our mind in the rest of the path to enlightenment.

As we develop our guru devotion more deeply and strongly, we purify more of our obscurations, and any lam-rim meditation we do makes great sense to us. Our mind is no longer hard like a rock, but extremely soft. With any meditation we do, we feel confident that if we really tried for some weeks or months, we could generate the realization of that meditation. What were mere words in the beginning, we now feel strongly from our heart.

By developing this realization of guru devotion, we then generate the realizations of the graduated path to enlightenment. With the generation of bodhicitta, we enter the Mahayana path, which has five divisions. The first, the path of merit, has three divisions. When we achieve the great path of merit, we see the guru in nirmanakaya aspect. When we achieve the Mahayana path of seeing and become an arya bodhisattva, we see the guru in sambhogakaya aspect. When we then achieve the path of no more learning, we cease even our subtle obscurations and our mental continuum is complete in realizations. When the continuation of our present consciousness becomes omniscient mind, our own mind becomes dharmakaya, which is the absolute guru. We achieve the absolute guru. When we achieve the absolute guru, we achieve the guru; we meet the guru mentally, becoming one.

24. Dedications

Dedication prayers related to the guru are very important in our everyday life because they create the cause for us to be successful in this life and all future ones until we achieve enlightenment. Without obstacles and without taking much time, we can achieve the path to enlightenment. I often dedicate merit with various dedication prayers related to the guru. Since guru devotion is the most important practice, we should always pray and dedicate merit to be able to correctly devote ourselves to the virtuous friend. Dedicating merit to be able to fulfill the guru's holy wishes creates the cause to be able to carry out whatever advice we are given. We should also dedicate our merit for the long life of our gurus.

"Due to all the merits of the three times accumulated by me and by all the buddhas, bodhisattvas and all other beings, may I, my family and all other sentient beings be able to meet perfectly qualified Mahayana virtuous friends in all our future lifetimes. From our side may we always see them only as enlightened beings and do actions of body, speech and mind that only please their holy minds. May I be able to fulfill all their holy wishes by myself alone.

"Due to all the merits of the three times accumulated by me and by all other beings, in all our lifetimes may we never give rise for even a second to anger or heresy toward the virtuous friend; may we see all their actions as pure. Through this devotion, may we receive the guru's blessings in our hearts.

"Please grant blessings for me and all other sentient beings to realize that attaining the common and sublime realizations depends on correctly devoting ourselves to the virtuous friend. From now until enlightenment, giving up our own bodies and lives, may we do actions only pleasing to the virtuous friend.

"May my body, speech and mind be only pleasing to my gurus. May I never displease them for even a second.

"May the lives of the glorious gurus be long and stable and may all their holy wishes be accomplished immediately.

"Due to all the merits of the three times collected by me and by others, in all lifetimes may I belong to a good family, have clear wisdom, be free of pride, have great compassion, have respect for my gurus and live in the samaya of the guru.[128]

"From this moment until my enlightenment, please grant me blessings to follow with devotion, in thought and action, the spiritual friend, who is the source of all goodness. By acquainting my mind with the path that pleases the buddhas, may I attain the peerless state of enlightenment.

"Please grant blessings for my body to be inseparable from you the father's holy body, my speech to be inseparable from you the father's holy speech and my mind to be inseparable from you the father's holy mind.

"May I become just like you."

---

[128] This means to correctly devote to the guru with thought and action.

Appendix 1. Guru Devotion Outline

The purpose of a meditation outline is to enable us to integrate all the various meditations and important points of the practice and transform our mind into the path without confusion. With an outline the meditations do not become confused. If we follow the outlines, the subject becomes much clearer, and no matter how extensive the subject, we can meditate in an elaborate or in a condensed way, with a few words that are enough for meditation. The numbering in outlines also makes it easy to meditate, like adding up the total cost of a big bill. If we follow the outline of the guru devotion meditation, we cover all the important points necessary to transform our mind into the realization of seeing the guru as a buddha.

The fourth major lam-rim outline, as found in extensive lam-rim commentaries such as *The Great Treatise on the Stages of the Path to Enlightenment* and *Liberation in the Palm of Your Hand*, "How to lead the disciple by showing the actual body of the advice," which means the teachings of the steps of the path to enlightenment, has two divisions: "The root of the path: how to devote to the guru" and "By devoting to the guru, how to train the mind in the steps of the path to enlightenment." Kyabje Chöden Rinpoche explained during a commentary on *The Great Treatise* that these two outlines are equal in importance. I think that Rinpoche's observation has a rich taste.

All the important points in the sutra teachings about the first of these two outlines, "The root of the path: how to devote to the guru," can be condensed into four main outlines:

1. The benefits of correctly devoting to a guru
2. The shortcomings of not devoting to a guru or of devoting incorrectly
3. How to devote to a guru with thought
4. How to devote to a guru with action

The detailed outline is as follows:

1. The benefits of correctly devoting to a guru (p. 80)
    (1) We become closer to enlightenment (p. 80)
        (a) We become closer to enlightenment by practicing the advice given by our guru (p. 81)
        (b) We become closer to enlightenment by making offerings to and serving our guru (p. 89)
    (2) We please all the buddhas (p. 100)
    (3) We are not harmed by maras or evil friends (p. 102)
    (4) Our delusions and negative actions naturally cease (p. 105)
    (5) All our realizations of the paths and bhumis increase (p. 106)
    (6) We will never lack virtuous friends in all our future lives (p. 117)
    (7) We will not fall into the lower realms (p. 120)
    (8) We will effortlessly accomplish all our temporary and ultimate wishes (p. 122)

2. The shortcomings of not devoting to a guru or of devoting incorrectly (p. 129)
    (1) If we criticize our guru we criticize all the buddhas (p. 131)
    (2) Each moment of anger toward our guru destroys merit for eons equal in number to the moments of our anger and will cause us to be reborn in the hells and suffer for the same number of eons (p. 135)
    (3) Even though we practice tantra, we will not achieve the sublime realization (p. 140)
    (4) Even if we practice tantra with much hardship, it will be like attaining hell and the like (p. 143)
    (5) We will not generate any fresh knowledge or realizations and our previous knowledge and realizations will degenerate (p. 145)
    (6) We will be afflicted even in this life by illness and other undesirable things (p. 151)

---

[129] Traditionally, these four outlines are presented in the opposite order, starting with "Vajradhara asserted..." and finishing with "There is nothing to trust..." but Lama Zopa Rinpoche feels it is more suitable to think about and meditate on them as shown.

Lama Zopa Rinpoche and Lama Yeshe, New Delhi, India, 1975

Appendix 2. Abbreviated
Calling the Lama from Afar[130]

Lama, think of me.
Lama, think of me.
Lama, think of me.

Magnificently glorious guru, dispelling the darkness of ignorance;
Magnificently glorious guru, revealing the path of liberation;
Magnificently glorious guru, liberating from the waters of samsara;
Magnificently glorious guru, eliminating the diseases of the five
   poisons;
Magnificently glorious guru, who is the wish-granting jewel;
I beseech you, please bless me.

Magnificently glorious guru, please bless me to remember impermanence and death from my heart.
Magnificently glorious guru, please bless me to generate the thought
   of no-need in my mind.
Magnificently glorious guru, please bless me to abide one-pointedly
   in practice in isolated places.
Magnificently glorious guru, please bless to not have any hindrances
   to my practice.
Magnificently glorious guru, please bless me so that all bad condi-

---

[130] See *Essential Buddhist Prayers, Volume 1*, pp. 135–37 for the Tibetan phonetics of this prayer.

tions appear as a support.

Magnificently glorious guru, please bless me to accomplish effortlessly the two works of self and others.

Magnificently glorious guru, please bless me soon, very soon.
Please grant me blessings on this very cushion.
Please grant be blessings in this very session.

*After reciting these verses, recite any requesting prayer to your own guru that
you wish.*

May I not arise heresy even for a second
In the actions of the glorious guru.
May I regard whatever actions are done as pure.
[With this devotion] may I receive the blessings of the guru in my
    heart.

Then recite the following verse and meditate on the guru entering your heart.

Magnificent and precious root guru,
Please abide on the lotus and moon seat at my heart.
Guide me with your great kindness,
And grant me the realizations of your holy body, speech and mind.

Colophon

His Eminence Shyalpa Rinpoche informed us that the original text for *Calling the Lama
from Afar* was composed by Zarongfu Sangyä Ngawang Tenzin Rinpoche, who His Eminence thinks "must have been very close to the previous incarnation of Lama Zopa Rinpoche." Translated by Lama Zopa Rinpoche in 1985. Transcribed and edited by Ven. Thubten
Döndrub. The two final verses following the main prayer were also translated by Lama Zopa
Rinpoche. Lightly edited by Ven. Constance Miller. Revised January 2003 by Kendall Mag-
nussen, FPMT Education Department. Colophon updated December 2003.

APPENDIX 3. PURIFYING MISTAKES
IN GURU DEVOTION

This is Lama Zopa Rinpoche's reply to a letter from a student asking about how to correctly meditate on guru devotion and what to do when samaya with the guru has been broken.[131]

My very dear (name withheld),

Sorry I took so long to reply to you. Actually, I meant to call you from Milarepa Center[132] or send an email. I thought about it but it didn't happen. I heard that you think and have told some of your friends that I said your negative karma can't be purified.

According to Buddhism, no matter how much negative karma one has created, it can be purified. According to the teachings on karma (cause and result), non-virtue has one good quality and that is that it can be purified. Therefore, Buddhism teaches that even the heaviest negative karma can be purified. Otherwise, there would be many sentient beings who could never ever achieve enlightenment and it would then become a little bit like Christianity, which says that when one is born in hell, one will be there forever. So, it would mean that having buddha-nature does not function and does not benefit, which would mean that you couldn't purify delusion and negative karma or actualize liberation from samara and enlightenment. You

---

[131] For more advice from Rinpoche on guru devotion and many other topics, see his online advice book at www.LamaYeshe.com.

[132] An FPMT center in Vermont, USA.

would then have a dead buddha-nature. But your buddha-nature is alive, not dead—and should be a smiling one, of course!

From your side, training your mind in guru devotion means looking at the guru as a buddha. By using quotations and logical reasoning, you transform your mind into guru devotion. By developing guru devotion, you are then able to see one guru as all the buddhas and all the buddhas as all your gurus. You shouldn't have this realization for just a few hours or a few days; it should be stable. You should feel this from the bottom of your heart, without the slightest doubt, all the time.

No matter how many years it takes, you should do guru devotion meditation until you have the realization. Guru devotion is the root of the path to enlightenment, so you have no choice. You have to realize it correctly to achieve realizations and complete the path to enlightenment.

Especially, use the mistakes that you see in the guru to develop devotion and not lose your faith or destroy your enlightenment, liberation, realizations and merit.

In the outline of the disadvantages of incorrect guru devotion, it says that if anger arises toward the guru it destroys the merits you have accumulated for lifetimes—not just in this life but in an uncountable number of past lifetimes. Therefore, eons of merit are lost. You are also reborn in the hell realms and have to suffer there for eons equal in number to the moments of your anger. Not only are eons of merit equal to the number of moments of your anger destroyed but your realizations and enlightenment are delayed for the same number of eons.

That is why the sutra and tantra teachings place so much emphasis on having pure samaya with the guru. Correctly devoting to the virtuous friend and pure samaya are essential.

In order to purify, first you should confess directly to the guru. This is the most urgent thing. You should do it without even a second's delay because now you can see how dangerous and harmful every single negative karma in relation to the guru is. You can confess by actually meeting your guru and confessing directly or you can confess in a letter or by telephone. If you haven't already done this, you should do it immediately. Respectfully thinking, "This is a buddha manifesting to me in this form," confess until your guru accepts.

Another powerful practice to purify the negative karma is to do something that most pleases the holy mind of the virtuous friend. In our daily life, whenever we do something that pleases the guru's holy mind, it is a most powerful purification practice and there's no question that it collects the most extensive amount of merit. It means all the buddhas are happy and that means you become so much closer to enlightenment. It is much easier to achieve realizations by fulfilling the guru's holy wishes.

The other thing is to change your mind, your attitude. Even if you have lost faith, you have to generate faith again. Do self-initiation with strong thought of purifying that specific negative karma. Also, you can do prostrations to the Thirty-five Buddhas and Vajrasattva and Samayavajra practice. These are very good practices for purification. You can also do tsog offering with *Guru Puja* or *Lama Tsongkhapa Guru Yoga*. Offer tsog especially to the guru in relation to whom you have created heavy negative karma. Tsog is very good for that as it pleases the guru and this makes a huge difference, an unbelievable difference. There is so much less negative karma. The first and most important thing is to make confession directly to the guru and again establish a good relationship, good samaya.

Here I am going to mention a brief meditation in which you use the mistakes you see in the guru to develop devotion and achieve realizations of the path to enlightenment.

First think that it is all a hallucination. We have so many wrong concepts, such as seeing impermanent things as permanent, and we also have no ability to see what is going to happen tomorrow or even in the next moment. So we are deeply ignorant. We have to recognize the many hallucinations we believe in. We have so many mistaken thoughts, so many wrong concepts.

First establish that the guru is a bodhisattva. Make sure you understand and believe that bodhisattvas have no thought of seeking happiness for themselves, not even for a moment. They think only of others and work only for others with bodhicitta, the wish to benefit all sentient beings.

After you have established this, think of how bodhisattvas collect the two types of merit in order to achieve enlightenment for sentient beings, which includes you. Think, "There are numberless bodhisattvas working for sentient beings and working for me."

Then think, "There are numberless buddhas who have completed the two types of merit and ceased all gross and subtle defilements by actualizing the paths of method and wisdom. These numberless buddhas have omniscient mind. They see all sentient beings, including me. They see all my sufferings, my needs, my karmas, my characteristics, the level of my intelligence—everything. Without the slightest mistake, they can see all the methods that fit me, that can lead me from happiness to happiness to enlightenment, and know as well the methods that fit every single one of the numberless other sentient beings. Not only do they have perfect knowledge of my mind but they can see everything directly; they can see all the past, present and future. They also have the perfect power to reveal these methods according to my karma and the karma of all sentient beings. Not only that, but their mind is trained in great compassion that embraces and hooks me and every single sentient being. And they have even more compassion for those with more negative karma and more suffering. The buddhas have unbearable compassion for them.

"Buddha never gives up on sentient beings for even a moment and Buddha has perfected all the qualities to guide me and all sentient beings. All the buddhas are guiding me even right now. So, who are they? There is no one to find except my gurus, especially this one guru toward whom I feel anger or heresy, this one that I see as having faults, this guru that I see as having delusions and suffering aggregates and making mistakes in his actions.

"If the guru manifested lower than this, as an animal, it would be difficult for me to recognize him and difficult to receive his guidance. If the guru manifested more purely than this, I wouldn't have the pure karma, the pure mind, to see him. Therefore, I have the impure karma to see only a guru in this aspect and acting in this way: having delusions, suffering aggregates and making mistakes in his actions, such as acting in an immoral way.

"Therefore, to guide me, the guru-buddha manifests in this ordinary aspect, which means one having faults, exactly according to my karma. How unbelievably kind it is!" Repeat this over and over again—twenty-one times or for even half a mala or a mala.

After that think, "This ordinary aspect with faults is the only one that can guide me." Repeat this over and over again, then do fixed meditation on it. Then think, "How precious it is!" Also repeat this over and over again. "This is the most precious, most important one in my life. This ordinary aspect liberates me from the lower realms, from samara and from even the lower nirvana and brings me to enlightenment by revealing the holy Dharma and by various other methods. How unbelievably kind the guru is!" Repeat this over and over again, then do fixed meditation.

"Shakyamuni Buddha, Manjushri, Chenrezig, Vajrayogini, Tara, Guhyasamaja, Heruka, Yamantaka, Machig Labdron and all the rest of the numberless buddhas guide me though this ordinary aspect (or in this manifestation)." Think, "How precious this ordinary aspect is, how precious it is...." Repeat this over and over again. "This is the most precious, most important one in my life." Repeat this over and over again, then do fixed meditation.

After that think, "Any action any of my gurus does for me is definitely leading me to enlightenment. Doing the action of giving even the oral transmission of a few syllables of a mantra or a verse of sutra or tantra leaves a positive imprint on my mental continuum that enables me to be closer to again receiving a precious human body in my next life, to meeting the Buddhadharma and understanding the words and meaning of the teachings, to accumulating merit and purifying, which ceases all the gross and subtle delusions. In this way, it leads me to enlightenment. So there is no doubt about the result of my guru giving me refuge and other vows, initiations, oral transmissions and instructions. Other actions such as praising me, speaking sweetly to me, giving me food, drink and gifts and even scolding me with wrathful words are helping me, inspiring me to practice Dharma and bringing me to enlightenment.

"Even though my ordinary mind believes that my gurus are ordinary, they are actually doing the work of guiding me and bringing me to full enlightenment by teaching me these methods. In my ordinary view it seems that the numberless buddhas are doing nothing for me. That is absolutely impossible. The buddhas have skies of qualities. Therefore, these gurus who are guiding me and taking care of me right now are buddhas.

"My normal concepts are totally wrong. I constantly project wrong views. My normal concept is to see faults in the guru, to see the guru as not being pure, not having discipline and so forth. My mind sees all this and believes it to be true even though it is invalid. This is the most harmful thing in my life."

Bhikshu Sunakshatra, who was together with and served the Buddha for twenty-two years, saw the Buddha as only a liar. He didn't see any good qualities in the Buddha, who had been enlightened for an incredible number of eons, while numberless others saw the Buddha as a fully enlightened being. This is similar to how we see the guru.

Even if you see your guru as ordinary, others can see him as a real buddha and generate the happy, healthy mind of pure devotion toward him. Therefore, there is not a single doubt that he is a buddha. Do fixed meditation on this.

"How we see something, whether as pure or impure, depends on how we look at it, on whether we look at it with a pure mind or an impure mind. Good, bad, happy, unhappy—my view of something comes from the label that I apply, from the pure or impure thought that I create." Using this example, think, "Therefore, my guru is definitely a buddha." Again do fixed meditation on this.

There is a story from Tibet about a teacher who lived very high on a mountain. One day two of his disciples went to visit him. They arrived very tired and the teacher offered them cold tea. One of the disciples thought, "We came so far and are so tired and our teacher didn't even bother to offer us hot tea." The other disciple thought, "How unbelievably kind our teacher is! He purposely gave us cold tea to quench our thirst."

The disciple who was positive became very happy and received much benefit and blessing but the other disciple, who looked at the situation in a negative way, was very unhappy and possibly even got angry, so he received only shortcomings.

You can see things as pure or impure according to the kind of mind you look at them with. It all depends on whether you look at something with a pure mind or with a negative, or impure, mind. So whether you receive great blessings or small blessings doesn't depend on the actual object itself; it depends on how you look at it.

"Even the guru showing faults, which means manifesting in an ordinary aspect, is the most skillful way to guide me to enlightenment. Since my guru does this to bring me to enlightenment, if he is not buddha then who else is? He is definitely buddha." Again do fixed meditation on this.

Here really meditate on how the guru is manifesting in an ordinary aspect, which means having delusion and suffering, making mistakes in his actions, such as acting in an immoral way and so forth. Here this aspect becomes the most urgently needed, most important one in your life, more important than anything else.

"Without this manifestation that shows mistakes, I would be totally without a guide. I would be totally lost in samsara, like a baby left in a desert where there is nothing and nobody to take care of them. Besides that, in this vast desert there is great danger from poisonous rattlesnakes and many other vicious animals. Like this, my life would be in great danger."

Pabongka Rinpoche mentions the example of being lost alone in a forest at night, with no moon or stars. You can't see because it's totally dark and the forest is filled with tigers and other vicious animals. Not only are you without a guide but you are in incredible danger. Being in samsara is like that.

"Apart from these buddhas that are showing ordinary aspects, my gurus, there is nobody to guide me." Make a strong determination that all your gurus, especially this guru in whom you see faults and toward whom you have generated anger and heresy, are definitely Guru Shakyamuni Buddha. After you have made the determination that this guru is the Buddha, do fixed meditation, holding that feeling and recognizing him as Buddha.

This is a brief meditation that you can practice every day. If you can, while doing the meditation also recite your gurus' name mantras,[133] especially the name mantra or requesting prayer (which is usually one stanza in length) of that particular guru. If you are able to, do that while you meditate.

Also, it is always important to do the special request for the three great purposes[134] at the end of mandala offerings.

Any time you see a mistake you should immediately think, "This is Buddha manifesting in an ordinary aspect, showing an immoral aspect, giving wrong explanations or teachings, or saying 'I don't know.'" Immediately thinking this will stop the thought of faults from arising; thinking "this is what *manifesting in ordinary aspect* means" will stop the thought of faults.

With much love and prayers,
Lama Zopa Rinpoche

Colophon

This letter was dictated to Ven. Holly Ansett at Kachö Dechen Ling, Aptos, California, in November 2002.

---

[133] A guru's name mantra consists of his name in Sanskrit inserted between OM AH GURU VAJRADHARA and SARVA SIDDHI HUM HUM. Lama Zopa Rinpoche's name mantra, for example is OM AH GURU VAJRADHARA MUNI SHASANA KSHANTI SARVA SIDDHI HUM HUM.

[134] I prostrate and go for refuge to the guru and the Three Precious Gems:
Please bless my mind.

I am requesting you to immediately pacify all the wrong conceptions, from incorrect devotion to the guru up to the subtle dual view of the white, red and dark visions, that exist in my mind and in the minds of all mother sentient beings.

I am requesting you to immediately generate all the right realizations from guru devotion up to enlightenment in my mind and in the minds of all mother sentient beings.

I am requesting you to pacify all outer and inner obstacles to actualizing the entire graduated path to enlightenment in my mind and in the minds of all mother sentient beings. See *Lama Chöpa*, p. 47.

Lama Zopa Rinpoche and Lama Yeshe, Lake Arrowhead, California, 1975

Appendix 4. *Calling the Lama from Afar: A Tormented Wail Quickly Drawing Forth the Blessing of the Lama, the Inseparable Three Kayas*[135]

Lama, think of me.
Lama, think of me.
Lama, think of me.

The wisdom of great bliss of all buddhas, one taste with the dharma-kaya, is itself the ultimate nature of all kind lamas. I beseech you, Lama, dharmakaya, please look after me always without separation, in this life, future lives and the bardo.

Wisdom's own illusory appearance, the conqueror with seven branches, is itself the ultimate basis of emanation of all kind lamas. I beseech you, Lama, sambhogakaya, please look after me always without separation, in this life, future lives and the bardo.

The play of various emanations, suiting the dispositions of the many to be subdued, is itself the behavior of the sambhogakaya of the kind lamas. I beseech you, Lama, nirmanakaya, please look after me always without separation, in this life, future lives and the bardo.

---

[135] See *Essential Buddhist Prayers, Volume 1*, pp. 127–33 for the Tibetan phonetics of this prayer.

The play of the inseparable three kayas, appearing in the form of the lama, is itself one with the very essence of all kind lamas. I beseech you, Lama, the inseparable three kayas, please look after me always without separation, in this life, future lives and the bardo.

All the infinite peaceful and wrathful yidams are also the lama's nature, and since no yidams exist apart from the kind lama himself, I beseech you, Lama, who comprises all yidams, please look after me always without separation, in this life, future lives and the bardo.

The ordinary form of all buddhas arises in the aspect of the lama, therefore no buddhas are observed apart from the kind lama himself. I beseech you, Lama, who comprises all buddhas, please look after me always without separation, in this life, future lives and the bardo.

The very form of all conquerors' wisdom, compassion and power arises as the lama, therefore the supreme arya lords of the three families are also the kind lama himself. I beseech you, Lama, who combines three families in one, please look after me always without separation, in this life, future lives and the bardo.

The hundred, five and three families, however many elaborated, are the lama. The pervasive master himself in whom they are all included is also the lama. I beseech you, Lama, as master of all families, please look after me always without separation, in this life, future lives and the bardo.

The creator of all buddhas, Dharma and Sangha is the lama. The one who combines all three refuges is the kind lama himself. I beseech you, Lama, whose presence combines all refuges, please look after me always without separation, in this life, future lives and the bardo.

Thinking of how the actual form of all the buddhas arises in the aspect of the lama and mercifully looks after me—reminds me of you, Lama.

Thinking of how you show the excellent unmistaken path to me, an unfortunate wretched being, abandoned by all the buddhas—reminds me of you, Lama.

Thinking of this excellent body, highly meaningful and difficult to obtain, and wishing to take its essence with unerring choice between gain and loss, happiness and suffering—reminds me of you, Lama.

Thinking of the experience of not knowing what to do when the great fear of death suddenly descends upon me—reminds me of you, Lama.

Thinking of the experience of just now suddenly separating from the perfections of this life and going on alone—reminds me of you, Lama.

Thinking of the experience of my naked body falling into the terrifying fires of hell and being unable to bear it—reminds me of you, Lama.

Thinking of how the suffering of hunger and thirst, without a drop of water, is directly experienced in the unfortunate preta realm—reminds me of you, Lama.

Thinking of how very repulsive and wretched it is to become a foolish stupid animal and what it would be like to experience it myself—reminds me of you, Lama.

Thinking of a refuge to protect me from this, since I am now about to fall into the wretched states of bad migration—reminds me of you, Lama.

Thinking of how white and black actions are experienced and of how to practice thorough and precise engagement and restraint —reminds me of you, Lama.

Thinking of a method to escape this prison of endless existences, the source of all suffering—reminds me of you, Lama.

Thinking of the plight of my pitiful old mothers, pervasive as space, fallen amidst the fearful ocean of samsara and tormented there—reminds me of you, Lama.

Therefore, Lama, please bless me to generate in my mental continuum effortless experience of the profound three principles of the path and the two stages.

Please bless me to strive in one-pointed practice of the three trainings with the intense thought of renunciation, in order to reach the secure state of liberation.

Please bless me to train in the precious supreme bodhicitta with the special attitude taking responsibility to liberate all migrators by myself alone.

Please bless me to follow after the ocean of conquerors with the will to cross to the very end of the great waves of deeds of the conqueror's children.

Please bless me to realize the supreme view, free of extremes, in which emptiness and dependent arising, appearance and emptiness, complement each other.

Please bless me quickly to generate the experience of taking the three kayas into the path, ripening the bases of birth, death and bardo.

Please bless me to arise as the illusory divine body itself, the play of the four joys and four emptinesses when the wind and mind absorb in the central channel.

Please bless me to meet the ultimate lama—the bare face of my innate mind with the covering of perception (of true existence) and perceiving (it as true) removed.

Please bless me to be one with your three secrets, Lama, in the vast dharmakaya of great bliss, which has exhausted the elaborations of the two obscurations.

In short, please reside inseparably in the center of my heart until the great enlightenment, and mercifully bless me, the child, to follow after you, the father.

Lama, think of me.
Lama, think of me.
Lama, think of me.

Colophon

Calling the Lama from Afar: A Tormented Wail Quickly Drawing Forth the Blessing of the Lama, the Inseparable Three Kayas was composed by Pabongka Tulku at the great insistent request with the offering of three hundred silver coins of Gelong Losang Rabgye of Bompa in the faraway area of Tsawa. The scribing was done by the monk Losang Dorje from the area of Den. Translated by Dawa Dondrup at Kopan in June, 1985, based on commentary given by his guru, Geshe Dawa, and on an earlier translation by Gelongma Wendy Finster and Gelong Thubten Samphel. Edited and retranslated by Gelong Thubten Tsultrim at Istituto Lama Tzong Khapa, Italy, September 1989. Lightly edited for publication in the FPMT Prayer Book by Ven. Constance Miller, January 1999.

Lama Yeshe and Lama Zopa Rinpoche, Kopan, Nepal, 1980

Appendix 5. Guru Devotion in *The Essence of Nectar*[136]

The Essence of Nectar is a good book to use as a pocket lam-rim as the words and the arrangement of this text are very tasty and effective for the mind. The author, Yeshe Tsöndrü (1761–1861), was himself a lineage lama of the lam-rim and these teachings came from his experiences. While *The Essence of Nectar* doesn't have elaborate explanations of every lam-rim topic with all the stories and logical reasoning, it is direct, clear and easy to read. You can open *The Essence of Nectar* and do direct meditation on any subject by reading the text. For those who want to understand the guru devotion meditations, *The Essence of Nectar* gives quite a detailed explanation of how to do them.

> The compassion of all the numberless Victorious Ones
> Manifested in the holy body of the supreme virtuous friend who reveals the path.
> To the kind root guru, I request,
> Please bless my mental continuum.[137]

---

[136] There are two English translations of the entire text available. *The Essence of Nectar* contains just the root text; *The Essential Nectar* also contains a commentary by Geshe Rabten. See Suggested Further Reading, pp. 463 & 464. The verses here were translated by Lama Zopa Rinpoche.

[137] V. 78. This verse comes at the end of the requesting prayer to the lineage lamas.

The benefits of devoting to a guru

Devoting with thought and action
To the holy virtuous friend, who reveals
The perfect, unmistaken, supreme path to enlightenment,
Has inconceivable benefits.

The great unification is difficult to achieve
Even with hundreds of efforts for oceans of countless eons;
But it can be attained in one brief life of a degenerate time
If we rely upon the power of the guru.

When a disciple correctly follows the holy virtuous friend,
The thought that this practitioner will quickly be liberated from
    samsara
Profoundly pleases the holy minds of all the Victorious Ones,
Like a mother who sees that her son has been benefited.

It is said that when a disciple correctly follows the guru,
Even if not invoked, the buddhas will happily enter
The guru's holy body, accept all the offerings,
And also bless the mindstream of the disciple.

At that time, because the blessings of all the buddhas
Enter the opening of the devotional mind,
One isn't harmed by multitudes of maras and delusions and
Realizations of the paths and bhumis are generated and increase.

If one always devotes to the virtuous friend,
All delusions and wrong conduct spontaneously cease.
The white dharmas spontaneously develop,
So one achieves extensive happiness in this and future lives.

If we please the guru properly in this life,
Experiencing the result similar to the cause
Will be that we will meet supreme virtuous friends in all future lives
And hear the perfect, unmistaken holy Dharma.

In short, by devoting to the virtuous friend one temporarily
Finds the body of a god or human, free of non-freedoms;
Ultimately, one finishes all the sufferings of samsara
And achieves the holy state of definite goodness.

The shortcomings of devoting incorrectly

Just as there are inconceivable advantages
In correctly devoting to a virtuous friend,
There are also inconceivable shortcomings
In not devoting or incorrectly devoting to a virtuous friend.

It is said that the actions of all the Victorious Ones
Appear in one's own guru.
Disrespecting him is thus disrespecting all the Victorious Ones.
What could have a heavier ripened aspect result than that?

However many moments one is angry at the guru
Destroys merit accumulated for eons equaling that number
And one will be born in hell for the same number of eons,
It is said in the *Kalachakra Tantra*.

Even one who has done heavy negative karmas,
Such as the five uninterrupted actions and so on,
Through tantra, can achieve sublime realization in this very life.
But those who abuse their guru from the heart,
Even though they practice for eons, will achieve no realization at all.

The person who intentionally abuses and despises
The virtuous friend who reveals the path,
Even if he puts effort into trying to realize the meaning of tantra,
Giving up sleep, dullness and distractions,
It is, a tantra explains, like working for hell and so on.

If one is devoid of devotion for the sublime object, the guru,
Qualities are not generated and those generated degenerate.
In this life disease, demon harms, untimely death and so on happen.
In future lives, one will wander endlessly in the evil-gone realms.

If, by chance, one finds the body of a happy migratory being,
Because of experiencing the result similar to the cause
Of not having respected the guru,
One will be born in unfortunate states without freedom
And one won't even hear the words "holy Dharma" or "virtuous
    friend."

In short, if the way one devotes to the guru is wrong,
One won't have the opportunity to achieve higher states or
    liberation,
But will wander forever in samsara, in general,
And the lower realms, in particular.

Since the benefits and shortcomings are beyond conception,
And even the roots of the multitudes of goodness appear here,
From now on, without running to the object of superstition,
Why don't I devote to and respect the virtuous friend?

The root, training our mind in devotion

The virtuous friends who reveal the path
Are like the one moon in the sky reflected,
Without effort and at the same time,
In all the waters of this world.

A sutra says, The transcendental wisdom of the buddhas
Appears without effort in the holy bodies of
Sambhogakaya, nirmanakaya and ordinary virtuous friends,
To the pure and impure objects who are to be subdued.

Many tantras, in particular, teach
That at the end of the age, omnipresent Lord Vajradhara
Will appear in the form of ordinary gurus
And guide degenerate beings.[138]

---

[138] Verse 116 was omitted from the original translation. This verse is Martin Willson's translation, as found in *The Essential Nectar*.

Whatever holy body and actions are shown,
In fact there is no doubt
That all the Victorious Ones of the ten directions
Are showing the holy bodies that subdue us,
In order to guide us in the path to liberation.

As for the appearance of faults:
Devadatta, Sunakshatra and the *tirthikas,*
Saw the Founder, with all stains gone and qualities complete,
As full of faults.

Like a person with jaundice sees a white conch as yellow,
Because the veils of my evil karma and obscurations are so thick,
I see the faultless as having only faults.
How is it possible that in fact they have faults and vices?

For sentient beings, it is said, the Victorious Ones
Show themselves in any form, such as maras and so on.
How do I know that these actions, which appear purely as mistakes,
Are not purposely shown?

Until we are free from our obscuring negative karma,
Even if all the buddhas without exception descended directly in
     front of us,
We have no fortune to see the sublime holy body adorned with the
     holy signs and exemplifications—
Only this present appearance.

Therefore, all the aspects of faults
In my teacher's actions are
Either the hallucinated appearance of my evil karma
Or they are purposely shown.

Therefore, whatever appears to me,
In fact their essence is that they encompass in one
Each and every one of the infinite Victorious Ones of the
     infinite fields,
Having ceased all faults and perfected all qualities.

Remembering the guru's kindness

Not only are these, my saviors,
Of the essence of all the Victorious Ones;
In constantly guiding me with the nectar of holy Dharma,
Their kindness is much greater than that of all the
    Victorious Ones.

If a man is suffering in prison
And someone frees him from that prison,
Then has him taken to a place of perfect enjoyments,
We definitely recognize that as great kindness.

Therefore, when our gurus have revealed to us
The methods of escaping from the three evil-gone realms,
Kindly giving us the chance to enjoy for a while
The perfections of gods and humans,

And they then show us well the highest method
For pacifying all the degenerations of samsara and nirvana,
And lead us to the exalted state of the three kayas—
Why is this kindness not supreme?

If it's said that the kindness of teaching a single verse
Cannot be repaid by making offerings for eons
Equal in number to its letters,
How can one measure the kindness
Of having shown the complete pure path?

It is by the kindness of our precious gurus
That we renounce family life, which is like being in the center
    of a fire,
Then, living in a sage's righteous conduct in a solitary place,
We experience the sublime taste of the nectar of holy
    Dharma.

It is by the kindness of our holy instructors
That we have met the teaching of the Jamgön Lama,

Which is difficult to find even on searching for many thousands
   of eons,
And that we have confidence in the methods of his teaching.

Therefore, my virtuous friends are:
Rescuers, rescuing me from the lower realms,
Captains, taking me across the ocean of samsara,
Guides, leading me to upper realms and liberation,

Doctors, curing the chronic disease of delusion,
Streams of water, extinguishing the great fire of suffering,
Lamps, dispelling the darkness of ignorance,
Suns, illuminating the path to liberation,

Liberators, releasing me from the bonds of the samsaric
   prison,
Rain clouds, showering a rain of holy Dharma,
Relatives and friends, bringing benefit and dispelling harm,
Parents, always caring for me with love.

Devoting with action

Every single benefit of samsara and beyond
Comes through the kindness of the guru.
Although I can never completely repay this kindness,
In order to try to repay it, I will try to please him.

Just as one plants seeds in a fertile field,
Even though the guru doesn't depend on offerings and respect,
To quickly complete my own great accumulation of merit,
Why don't I attempt to plant seeds in this supreme field
By making offerings and showing respect?

It is said that making offering to one pore of the guru
Who has revealed to us the unmistaken path
Collects greater merit than honoring and making offering
   to the multitudes of aryas:
Hearers, self-conquerors, bodhisattvas and buddhas.

Many holy beings, such as Naropa, Milarepa,
Dromtönpa, Sakya Pandita and Chayulwa,
Gave up without a thought their body, life and wealth
For their gurus and achieved many realizations.

Therefore, I shall strive to respect and serve with my body and
   speech,
Such as by offering all my cherished possessions,
Prostrating, rising, giving massages and baths,
And speaking respectfully, praising and so on.

Especially, I will attempt day and night without distraction
To practice the complete, unmistaken graduated path:
The best way to please my guru with my three doors.
I will please my guru with the offering of practicing in accord with
   his advice.
Please grant me blessings to be able to do this.[139]

Colophon

These verses, translated by Lama Zopa Rinpoche with additional commentary, were dictated to Nick Ribush from August to October 1982 and to Kyogan O'Neil from December 1982 to February 1983 at Kopan Monastery, Nepal. They have been further edited for inclusion in this book.

[139] Vv. 97–139.

Appendix 6. Protecting the Mind

This is Lama Zopa Rinpoche's advice to a female student who was very disturbed by an experience with her guru and felt that something should be done about it.

You are asking about a very urgent and very important practice—in other words, a protection for the development of your mind in the path to enlightenment.

I'm not sure whether you have heard what His Holiness the Dalai Lama has said in regard to this matter—at the Western Teachers' Conference, for example. That advice was given according to the Western world. If it is not given that way, this topic is dangerous and becomes a problem for the Western mind.

In monasteries, of course, there are generally an abbot, a disciplinarian and many others who can punish whatever mistakes are made in monastic rules or personal vows. They can even kick a person out. But up to now I have never heard that a disciple kicked a guru out of a monastery or sued a guru. In the East, I have never heard of this.

According to the texts, the teachings of the Buddha and the lam-rim, one should look only at the good qualities of the guru and speak only praise of the guru. Acting contrary to that, generating anger or heresy and criticizing the guru in speech, creates the heaviest negative karma.

It is said in many tantric teachings, such as the Kalachakra and Guhyasamaja root texts, that even if one has accumulated the five uninterrupted negative karmas, one can still achieve the sublime vehicle in this life, in particular the Highest Yoga Tantra path, which has the most skillful means to grant enlightenment in the brief lifetime of degenerate times. But those who criticize the guru from their heart will not achieve this, even if they practice the sublime vehicle.

Lama Tsongkhapa's lam-rim clearly mentions that even giving rise to the thought that the virtuous friend is an ordinary being becomes a cause of losing realizations. This also means that it becomes an obstacle to developing the mind in the path.

The very important thing is to analyze and check as much as possible before making Dharma contact. Once the Dharma contact is established with recognition of a guru-disciple relationship, there is no going back. One has to have a new relationship. It is another world, in which you look at that person with a new mind, a pure mind.

Pabongka Dechen Nyingpo, the great enlightened being, the actual Heruka, said that if one is able to stop all thought of faults and look only at the good qualities, seeing the guru as only a buddha, one can achieve enlightenment in this life.

This is not only for this life. Generally, one cannot get enlightened while seeing mistakes in the virtuous friend. But, with the realization that sees all buddhas as the guru and all gurus as buddha, one can. This is said in both sutra and tantra and in all four Tibetan Mahayana traditions.

Making mistakes by allowing anger or heresy to arise or by criticizing or giving up the virtuous friend becomes the cause not to find a guru in future lives. It is said in *The Essence of Nectar*[140] that it causes one to be unable to hear the sound of the holy Dharma, not to mention being unable to find a virtuous friend, and that one becomes impoverished in terms of a virtuous friend in all one's lifetimes (the last of the eight shortcomings of incorrectly devoting to a virtuous friend).

And I often mention this quotation from the Fifth Dalai Lama: "One's own mistakes appear to one's own hallucinated mind in the actions of the guru. One must realize that this is one's own mistake and abandon it like poison."

This means that, with this guru devotion meditation, one must abandon

---

[140] If, by chance, one finds the body of a happy migratory being,
  Because of experiencing the result similar to the cause
  Of not having respected the guru,
  One will be born in unfortunate states without freedom
  And one won't even hear the words "holy Dharma" or "virtuous friend." (V. 111.)

the belief that there is a mistake in the actions of the virtuous friend. With this mindfulness, you look at that person as a buddha, one who has ceased all faults and has all good qualities.

If your guru asks you to do something that you don't have the capacity to do because your mind hasn't reached that level, with mindfulness of the pure thought that I mentioned before, you respectfully explain to your guru that you are incapable of doing it. In this way you try to get the guru to excuse you from doing it.

This is what is mentioned in *Fifty Verses of Guru Devotion* and in the *Vinaya*. If the guru says to do something that is not Dharma, you can ask permission not to do it.[141] It doesn't say to have negative thoughts toward, criticize or sue him.

This last part is the way to practice guru devotion, the way to deal with this problem without its becoming an obstacle to developing your own mind in the path.

Of course, as His Holiness the Dalai Lama mentions all the time, when a special guru and special disciple meet together, the disciple does every single thing the guru says to do, like Naropa and Tilopa or Milarepa and Marpa.

The main thing here is to be skillful, to try not to hurt the holy mind of the guru. Hurting the mind of the guru is the greatest obstacle to developing your own mind in the path to enlightenment.

Many tantric teachings, especially, say that one should understand the path by hearing it from the holy mouth and realize it by pleasing the holy mind of the virtuous friend. Many secret things like that are mentioned.

Once a guru-disciple connection is made, even if the guru kills many thousands of people, it is the responsibility of the disciple to look at this as a positive action. It is said in the teachings by the past realized practitioners of the Tibetan Mahayana traditions that even if the guru kills someone, one should look at it as a positive action, as a quick way of enlightening an evil being by sending his consciousness to a pure land. The conclusion is that this particular action of the guru is guidance for the benefit of that person.

---

[141] (Disciples) having great sense should obey the words of their guru joyfully and with enthusiasm. If you lack the knowledge or ability (to do what he says), explain in (polite) words why you cannot (comply). (V. 24.)

There are a few quotations like this, describing how the past and present practitioners of the Tibetan Mahayana traditions practiced guru devotion. It is also mentioned that even the action of having sex should be looked at as the guru enjoying the wisdom of great bliss and so forth.

You should ask Istituto Lama Tzong Khapa for a copy in English of a small pamphlet in which I translated these quotations during a short talk on guru devotion. The teaching was given there because many other people had experienced similar problems.

If a mistake has already been made, you must confess if from your heart. In this way, you will get the profit of lightening and purifying the negative karma. Of course, you can do Samayavajra, self-initiations and many other practices, but one very good thing to do is to offer some service or some practice that pleases the holy mind of the virtuous friend.

I know you mentioned sincerity, but in my view this sincerity is without wisdom. Sincerity is beneficial to others when it is combined with wisdom and compassion. If there is wisdom there is usually also compassion, which means the wisdom is vast.

For example, what if a man who wants to kill someone comes along and asks you where that person went? If you think you should be sincere, without wisdom—which should also include compassion—you would tell him where the person went instead of saying you don't know, which would save the person's life.

Another point is that in the West people have many extra concepts that were not in the East, especially among Tibetans—for example, looking at a child's mental or physical problems as being the fault of the parents. Now, even in America, people are finding out that this is not true. In *Time* there have been reports that what was thought to be the fault of the parents now turns out not to be so. Even parents who loved their children very much can later experience many problems because of this concept.

There are many other additional concepts that I had never heard about until I met Western people, even though I've traveled and lived in different parts of the East. Now, of course, people in the East are trying to get their education from the Western world, so some people who follow Western culture in India, for example, talk like this now.

So, I am just making conversation with you about what I think, from my experience; just trying to give you more background.

The other thing is that when we look at the guru, we will see mistakes; we will always find mistakes. It's just a question of whether the mistake is big or small. Even if it's not sex, there will be something else—too much anger, too much miserliness, too much pride, too partial a mind.

If you look from the side of mistakes, you will see mistakes.

Colophon

Rinpoche dictated this advice at Kopan Monastery, Nepal, 20 April 1994. Edited by Ven. Lhundrup Damchö.

Gomchen Khampala, Solu Khumbu, Nepal, 1977

Appendix 7. Gomchen Khampala's
Advice on Guru Practice

Lama Thubten Zopa Rinpoche's introduction: Gomchen-la is a great medita-
tor from the mountains of Solu Khumbu not far from where I was born. He's
originally from Tibet. He rejoices greatly that Western people are saying prayers
and meditating on the Buddhadharma, because it's unusual, not normal. It's
as if the impossible has happened. Therefore, he rejoices. I have asked him to
give the Western students some instruction, and it seems he has much energy to
do so. He's also saying that I should translate everything he says and not hold
anything back!

I HAVE SPENT only one night at Kopan, but the feeling here is very good.
I think it's because everybody is living in refuge; it's the power of people's
minds living in refuge and their becoming inner beings, or Buddhists.

In Lama Zopa Rinpoche's previous life he lived in Solu Khumbu as the
Lawudo Lama, and at that time, you were also probably born around that
area and made karmic contact with him. Because of that and your good fortune as well, even though in this life you were born in far-distant foreign
countries, you have found a teacher who can explain Dharma in your own
language, which other lamas can't do. Therefore, you are greatly fortunate.
You should take this opportunity and, in particular, take great care with
your guru practice.

There are many lamas from the different schools—Nyingma, Kagyü,
Gelug and Sakya—who can explain the Dharma very well, but the problem
is language.

In Buddhadharma, guru practice is the most important thing. In fact, the only object to whom we need pray is the guru, because the guru encompasses the entire Triple Gem—Buddha, Dharma and Sangha. Therefore, first of all, it is necessary to find a perfect guru, but I'm not going to talk about that here.

In the sutra teachings, we take refuge in Buddha, Dharma and Sangha, but in tantra, we take refuge in the guru. As it says in the *Guru Puja*,

> You are my guru, you are my yidam,
> You are the dakinis and Dharma protectors.
> From now until enlightenment,
> I shall seek no refuge other than you.

This is the tantric way of taking refuge. You should try to actualize this; gain experience of it. Lama Zopa Rinpoche should explain this practice to you and from your side you should make heartfelt requests to receive teachings on the practice of guru yoga.

When I was in Tibet, I asked my guru to explain it to me, but he said, "If I talk about guru practice it will look as if I'm praising myself; as if I'm saying, 'I am good; I am the best,'" and would not explain it to me. He told me, "You can study the details of guru practice in books to understand what it entails. If the lama explains it the disciples might think he's just aggrandizing himself or boasting that he's the best."

I rejoice that you are not only reciting prayers but analyzing the meaning of the teachings as well; thinking of the meaning and concentrating on the fundamental path. Say that there were many millions of billions of galaxies full of stupas full of Buddha's relics and every day you made offerings to all of them, there would be enormous benefit in that. But as it says in the mahamudra teachings, "Meditating on the fundamental path for just a short time has more benefit than every day making offerings to millions of billions of galaxies full of stupas containing relics of the Buddha." Therefore, I thank Lama Zopa Rinpoche and all of you.

There are many people who can recite the words and give clear intellectual explanations of the teachings but don't practice or analyze the meaning. Here, you are doing both: not only are you thinking about what the words mean but at the same time you are trying to put that meaning into practice. Study combined with meditation—meditating while receiving the teaching—is called "experiencing the commentary"—while the teacher is giving the commentary the disciples try to gain experience of it. That's a wise and excellent way to practice.

There's a prayer of request to the guru that goes,

> Magnificent and precious root guru,
> Please abide on the lotus and moon seat at the crown of my head.
> Guide me with your great kindness,
> And grant me the realizations of your holy body, speech and mind.

What is the kindness to which this prayer refers? It's what's happening here at Kopan Monastery—being guided by the guru, who out of his great kindness gives commentaries on the teachings and confers initiations, which ripen the mind.

With respect to the last line of this prayer, the essence of whatever deity you're meditating on—for example, Avalokiteshvara—is the guru. Meditational deities are manifestations of the guru. When we request the realizations of our guru's holy body, speech and mind, we receive the blessings of the guru's holy body, speech and mind. These blessings purify the negativities of our own body, speech and mind, which then become one with our guru's holy body, speech and mind.

Once, the great pandit and yogi Naropa was reading texts in the extensive library of a great temple when a dakini suddenly appeared out of a dark cloud in the space in front of him and said, "You know the words but you don't know the meaning."

"Where can I learn the meaning?" Naropa asked.

She replied, "There's a great yogi called Tilopa. You can receive the commentaries from him."

Consequently, as directed by the dakini, the great pandit Naropa went to West Bengal, in the north-eastern part of India, in search of his guru, Tilopa. When he got there, he asked the local people if they knew Tilopa. They said, "There are two Tilopas: a rich one and a poor one, a beggar. There are two." Naropa said, "Tilopa, the guru I have to find, doesn't necessarily have to be rich or poor."

Later, as he went around, he found Tilopa by the river, pulling fish from the water, cooking them over a fire and eating them. Seeing this, instead of criticizing Tilopa or being shocked by his behavior, he remained silent; not a hair of his body moved. He just stood there quietly, without a single negative or disparaging thought, and simply reflected, "Since sentient beings are so ignorant, in order to release them from ignorance and lead them to enlightenment, Tilopa has manifested in this form, catching fish and eating them."

Thinking like this is one way of practicing guru yoga. In previous lifetimes, Naropa had created the incredible merit and karma necessary to meet a guru such as Tilopa and never generate a single negative thought toward him. Therefore, when he finally did meet this great guru, he realized he was a true saint and saw him in only a positive light. Similarly, you people have also created good karma in previous lives. In fact, your karma might be even better than Naropa's was because you see your guru in a better aspect—as a monk in robes.

Anyway, when Naropa saw Tilopa, he said, "Please guide me," meaning, "Please lead me to enlightenment."

At first, Tilopa replied, "I'm just a simple beggar, I can't do it; I can't accept your request. I can't help you." But finally he did accept, after which Naropa followed his guru impeccably.

One day while they were walking along the edge of a high cliff, Tilopa said, "Is there anybody here who can fulfill the guru's command?" which is the way to become enlightened in the one lifetime. The command was to leap off the cliff.

Naropa replied, "None other than me can do it, so I will," and he threw himself over the cliff.

He lay there at the foot of the cliff, badly injured, for three days, during which time Tilopa completely ignored him. Finally Tilopa asked Naropa, "What happened. What's wrong with you?"

"This is the result of following the guru's orders," Naropa said. Then, just by Tilopa's laying his hand on Naropa, all his injuries were completely healed.

Naropa underwent twelve such life-threatening experiences following his guru's orders. It would take too long to recount them here and anyway, I'm quite old and don't remember them very well.

Another time, Tilopa told Naropa to go get some soup from farmers working in a field. They wouldn't give him any so he tried to steal some, but they caught him and beat him very badly. Again, Tilopa just left him lying there for three days, after which time he asked, "What's up with you?"

The whole point is that without a single exception, Naropa did exactly what his guru told him to do. Like the time they came across a royal wedding, where a king was getting married. There was a magnificent procession with the bride on horseback. Tilopa said, "The disciple who wants enlightenment in this life should go grab that bride." Naropa thought, "That's me," and without any hesitation or doubt went straight up to the wedding party, pulled the woman off the horse and tried to drag her away. All the people immediately jumped on Naropa, bashed him up and even cut off some of his limbs.

Again, Tilopa left him for three days and finally returned to ask, "What's the matter with you?"

"This happened because I followed my guru's orders." Once more Tilopa healed Naropa just by touching him and his severed limbs were miraculously restored.

There's another story about the day that Tilopa hit Naropa on the head with his shoe so strongly that he passed out. When Naropa came to, his mind and his guru's holy mind had become one; whatever knowledge Tilopa had, so did Naropa. This was the result of his impeccable guru devotion and doing exactly what Tilopa told him to do.

As the teachings explain, you have to decide completely that the guru is definitely buddha. If you don't come to that conclusion, then no matter what Dharma practices you do, they won't be of much benefit; they won't become a quick path to enlightenment.

Another teaching says, "Meditating on the guru's holy body is hundreds of thousands of times more powerful than meditating on trillions of deities in all their various aspects." However, whatever deity you meditate on, you have to remember, "This is my guru's holy body." You should not think, "This is the deity; the guru is something else."

Also, following your guru's instructions is far more beneficial than reciting the deity's mantra trillions of times.

There are two stages of the Highest Yoga Tantra path to enlightenment: generation and completion. While there is great benefit in meditating on the completion stage, doing it for even many eons pales in comparison to invoking the guru's holy mind just once.

I don't have that much more to say. I just wanted to say a few words about guru practice, so I'm simply emphasizing a few of the important points.

As I mentioned, you should request Lama Zopa Rinpoche for teachings on guru devotion and from your side pray to the guru as one with the deity. But remember what my guru told me when I asked for teachings on guru practice: "You can understand the practice of guru devotion by reading the texts; if I explain it to you, it will appear as if I'm extolling my own virtues; boasting that I'm the best of all."

These days, people can't practice like the great pandits of old. It's very difficult. Instead of following our gurus' orders like those fortunate beings did we have a bad attitude toward our teachers; instead of generating devotion we criticize them; instead of doing what they suggest we do the opposite.

However, even though we can't practice like those great pandits did—purifying their negativities by following their guru's orders—we can purify in other ways. For example, we can do prostrations, make mandala offerings, recite Vajrasattva mantras and so forth.

There are many different tantric deities but in essence all of them are the guru. Therefore, when we make offerings to the various deities, we are actually making offerings to the guru.

The way to receive blessings is not to think that Avalokiteshvara is separate from your guru but that they are one. The really quick way to receive blessings is to concentrate on the guru and make your mind one with his holy mind, like mixing water with milk.

Don't think that Avalokiteshvara is somewhere else, is more beautiful than your guru, or has no relationship to the guru from whom you receive teachings. It is not like that. Avalokiteshvara, or any other deity, *is* the guru. This is what I really want to emphasize.

There was once a yogi called Tsang-nyön-pa. Tsang is the name of a place; *nyön* means crazy. This yogi led an ascetic life and wandered around a lot. Before eating, he would always offer his food to his guru. One day he was in a forest and met a shepherd, who gave him some tsampa. He hadn't eaten for a long time and was very hungry, so he started eating it immediately. But the moment he put the food into his mouth, he thought, "Oh, I forgot to offer it." So he took the tsampa out of his mouth and, with incredible devotion, offered it to his guru.

At that moment his guru was giving teachings many miles away. All of a sudden, the food that Tsang-nyön-pa offered appeared in his guru's mouth and he had to stop speaking. He said, "Today my disciple Tsang-nyön-pa, who hadn't eaten for a long time, got some tsampa and offered it to me with such great devotion and single-pointed concentration that it actually came into my mouth."

The amount of Dharma you know, the number of realizations you gain, depends on how much devotion you have for your guru—the greater your devotion, the greater your Dharma understanding and realizations. It all depends on guru devotion.

Colophon

Ngawang Norbu Gomchen Khampala gave this talk, translated into English by Lama Zopa Rinpoche, to Western students at Kopan Monastery on 10 January 1975. It was edited by Nick Ribush and published in Teachings from Tibet: Guidance from Great Lamas.

Lama Zopa Rinpoche and Lama Yeshe, Bangkok, Thailand, 1974

Appendix 8. *Practicing Guru Devotion with the Nine Attitudes*

In *The Great Treatise on the Stages of the Path to Enlightenment* Lama Tsong-khapa explains nine attitudes in relation to practicing correct devotion to the virtuous friend; he condenses the real practice of guru yoga into nine points. There is no elaborate, detailed explanation of guru devotion, but the nine points are very clear and to the point. It is very effective to read and remember them.

When you have some problem with your guru, something that you find difficult or confusing (of course, the difficulty is created by your own concept), remembering these nine attitudes immediately solves the difficulty. The difficulty or confusion suddenly disappears after you read this prayer. It's like an atomic bomb in destroying negative thoughts toward your guru. It makes everything very simple.

> I am requesting the kind lord root guru,
> Who is more extraordinary than all the buddhas:
> Please bless me to be able to devote myself to the qualified lord guru
> with great respect in all my future lifetimes.

> By realizing that correctly devoting myself to the kind lord guru—
> who is the foundation of all good qualities—is the root of happiness
> and goodness, I shall devote myself to him with great respect, not
> forsaking him even at the cost of my life.

Thinking of the importance of the qualified guru,
May I allow myself to enter under his control.

May I be like an obedient son,[142]
Acting exactly in accordance with the guru's advice.

Even when maras, evil friends and the like
Try to split me from the guru,
May I be like a vajra, inseparable forever.

When the guru gives me work, whatever the burden,
May I be like the earth, carrying all.

When I devote myself to the guru,
Whatever suffering occurs (*hardships or problems*),[143]
May I be like a mountain, immovable.
(*The mind should not be upset or discouraged.*)

Even if I have to perform all the unpleasant tasks,
May I be like a servant of the king,
With a mind undisturbed.

May I abandon pride.
Holding myself lower than the guru,
May I be like a sweeper.

May I be like a rope,
Joyfully holding the guru's work,
No matter how difficult or heavy a burden.

---

[142] It has been suggested to change "son" to "child," however, according to Lama Zopa Rinpoche, "The term 'son' is not used in dependence upon the characteristics of the body but of the mind. The term is used because it is normally the son who becomes king. The daughter becomes the queen but not the king. Because this example is applied here, the disciple is called 'the son of the vajra master,' but it has nothing to do with the body."

[143] The words in parentheses are added to clarify the text and should be kept in mind but not recite.

Even when the guru criticizes, provokes or ignores me,
May I be like a dog without anger;
Never responding with anger.

May I be like a (ferry) boat,
Never upset at any time to come and go for the guru.

O glorious and precious root guru,
Please bless me to be able to practice in this way.
From now on, in all my future lifetimes,
May I be able to devote myself to the guru in this way.

By reciting these words aloud and reflecting on their meaning in your mind, you will have the good fortune to be able to devote yourself correctly to the precious guru, from life to life in all your future lifetimes.

If you offer service and respect and make offerings to the precious guru with these nine attitudes, even if you do not practice intentionally, you will develop many good qualities, collect extensive merit and quickly achieve full enlightenment.

Colophon

This prayer was written by the highly attained lama, Shabkar Tsokdrug Rangdrol, translated by Lama Zopa Rinpoche at Kachoe Dechen Ling, Aptos, California, in February 1999, written down by Lillian Too and Ven Thubten Dekyong (Tsenla) and edited by Nick Ribush and Ven. Connie Miller.

Lama Zopa Rinpoche and Lama Yeshe, Dharamsala, ca 1972

Glossary

(Skt = Sanskrit; Tib = Tibetan; Eng = English)

abhidharma. One of the three baskets (*Tripitaka*) of the Buddhist canon, the others being the *vinaya* and the *sutra*; the systematized philosophical and psychological analysis of existence that is the basis of the Buddhist systems of tenets and mind training.

Action Tantra (Skt: Kriya Tantra). The first of the four classes of tantra, which mainly emphasizes external activities.

aggregates (Skt: skandha). The association of body and mind; a person comprises five aggregates: form, feeling, recognition, compositional factors and consciousness.

Amdo. The northeastern region of Tibet that borders on China.

Amoghadarshi (Skt; Eng: Meaningful to Behold). One of the bodhisattvas who accompanied Shakyamuni Buddha.

anger. A disturbing thought that exaggerates the negative qualities of an object and wishes to harm it; one of the six root delusions.

arhat (Skt). Literally, foe destroyer. A being who, having ceased their karma and delusions, is completely free from all suffering and its causes and has achieved liberation from cyclic existence.

arya (Skt). A being who has directly realized emptiness.

Asanga. The fourth-century Indian master who received directly from Maitreya Buddha the extensive, or method, lineage of Shakyamuni Buddha's teachings; guru and brother of Vasubandhu.

attachment. A disturbing thought that exaggerates the positive qualities of an object and wishes to possess it; one of the six root delusions.

Ashvaghosha (or *Aryasura*). The third-century Indian master, renowned for his scholarship and poetry, who is the author of *Fifty Verses of Guru Devotion*.

Avalokiteshvara (Skt). See *Chenrezig*.

Bakula Rinpoche (1917–2003). A Ladakhi lama, the reincarnation of one of the sixteen arhats, who served for many years in the Indian parliament and as Indian ambassador to Mongolia.

bardo (Tib). The intermediate state; the state between death and rebirth, lasting anywhere from a moment to forty-nine days.

Bhagavan (Skt). Epithet of a buddha.

bhikshu (Skt). See *gelong*.

bhumi (Skt). Literally, stage, or ground. Bodhisattvas must traverse ten bhumis on their journey to enlightenment, the first being reached with the direct perception of emptiness.

Bodhgaya. The small town in the state of Bihar in north India where Shakyamuni Buddha became enlightened.

bodhicitta (Skt). The altruistic determination to achieve full enlightenment in order to free all sentient beings from suffering and bring them to enlightenment.

bodhisattva (Skt). One who possesses bodhicitta.

Boudhanath. A village just outside Kathmandu that is built around the Boudhanath stupa, a famous Buddhist pilgrimage site.

Brahma. A powerful Hindu deity in the god realm.

Buddha (Skt). A fully enlightened being. One who has purified all obscurations of the mind and perfected all good qualities. See also *enlightenment, Shakyamuni Buddha*.

Buddhadharma (Skt). See *Dharma*.

Buddhajñana (Tib: Sangye Yeshe). The eighth century Indian teacher who founded one of the Guhyasamaja systems; studied the *Perfection of Wisdom* teachings with Haribhadra.

buddha-nature. Refers to the emptiness, or ultimate nature, of the mind. Because of this nature, every sentient being possesses the potential to become fully enlightened.

Buxa Duar. A small town in West Bengal in eastern India, where most of the Tibetan monks who escaped to India in 1959 were accommodated.

calm abiding. See *shamatha.*

causative phenomena. Things that come about in dependence upon causes and conditions; includes all objects experienced by the senses, as well as the mind itself; impermanent phenomena.

chakras (Skt). Literally, wheels. Formed by the branching of channels at various points along the central channel, the six main chakras are at the brow, crown, throat, heart, navel and sex organ.

Chakrasamvara (Skt). Heruka Chakrasamvara. A male meditational deity of Highest Yoga Tantra, whose tantra especially emphasizes clear light.

chang (Tib). Beer made from fermented grain, often barley.

Chengawa Lodrö Gyaltsen (1390–1448). A disciple of Khedrub Je, one of Lama Tsongkhapa's heart disciples.

Chenrezig (Tib; Skt: Avalokiteshvara). The Buddha of Compassion. The male meditational deity that embodies the compassion of all the buddhas. The Dalai Lamas are said to be emanations of this deity.

chöd (Tib). A tantric practice aimed at destroying self-grasping, often performed in frightening surroundings, such as charnel grounds.

Chöden Rinpoche (b. 1933). An ascetic, learned Gelugpa lama who meditated in a small room in Lhasa for nineteen years after the Chinese occupation; a guru of Lama Zopa Rinpoche.

Chökyi Dorje. The great fifteenth century siddha whose chief disciple was Gyalwa Ensapa.

chu-len (Tib). Or taking the essence, in which food is replaced by pills made from minerals or flowers as an aid to concentration.

circumambulation. A practice of purifying negative karma and accumulating merit in which a person walks clockwise around a holy object such as a stupa or statue.

clear light. Very subtle mind. This subtlest state of mind occurs naturally at death and through successful tantric practice and is used by practitioners to realize emptiness.

compassion. The sincere wish that others be free from suffering and its causes.

completion stage. The more advanced of the two stages of Highest Yoga Tantra.

daka (Skt). The male equivalent of a dakini.

dakini (Skt). Literally, sky-goer; a female being with tantric realizations of the generation or completion stages.

Dalai Lama, His Holiness the Fourteenth (b. 1935). Gyalwa Tenzin Gyatso. Revered spiritual leader of the Tibetan people and tireless worker for world peace; winner of the Nobel Peace Prize in 1989; a guru of Lama Zopa Rinpoche.

degenerate time, or *age (Skt: kaliyuga).* See *five degenerations.*

deity (Tib: yidam). The form of a deity used as the object of meditation in tantric practices.

delusions. The disturbing, negative thoughts, or minds, that are the cause of suffering. The three root delusions are ignorance, anger and attachment.

Denma Lochö Rinpoche (b. 1928). A learned Gelugpa lama, a former abbot of Namgyal Monastery, who is one of Lama Zopa Rinpoche's gurus.

dependent arising. The way that the self and phenomena exist conventionally as relative and interdependent. They come into existence in dependence upon (1) causes and conditions, (2) their parts and, most subtly, (3) the mind imputing, or labeling, them.

desire realm. One of the three realms of samsara, comprising the hell beings, hungry ghosts, animals, humans, asuras and the six lower classes of suras; beings in this realm are preoccupied with desire for objects of the six senses.

deva (Skt). A god dwelling in a state with much comfort and pleasure in the desire, form or formless realms.

Devadatta (Tib: Lhä-jin). Shakyamuni Buddha's cousin, who was jealous of Buddha and constantly tried to harm him.

Deva's Son (Skt: devaputramara). One of the four types of maras; interferes with meditation by increasing desire for sensual pleasures. See *four maras.*

Dharma (Skt). In general, spiritual practice; specifically, the teachings of Buddha, which protect from suffering and lead to liberation and full enlightenment.

dharmakaya (Skt). Truth body; the blissful omniscient mind of a buddha.

Dharma protectors. Beings, some worldly and others enlightened, who protect Dharma teachings and practitioners.

Dharmarakshita. The guru with whom Lama Atisha studied the *abhidharma* for twelve years.

disturbing thoughts. See *delusions.*

dob-dob (Tib). A monk not involved in the monastic study program but more with physical activities within the monastery.

Domo Geshe Rinpoche (d. 1936). A famous ascetic meditator in his early life who later established monastic communities in the Tibet-Nepal border area and in Darjeeling; the guru of Lama Govinda, who wrote *The Way of the White Clouds*.

dongka (Tib). The maroon or maroon and gold upper garment worn by Tibetan Buddhist monks and nuns.

Dorje Khadro (Tib; Skt: Vajradaka). A male deity who acts to purify negativities through a specific fire puja practice.

Dragpa Gyaltsen (1147–1216). A great scholar and early teacher of the Sakya school; uncle and guru of Sakya Pandita.

Drepung Monastery. The largest of the three major Gelugpa monasteries; founded near Lhasa by one of Lama Tsongkhapa's disciples. Now reestablished in exile in south India.

Dromtönpa (1005–64). Lama Atisha's heart disciple and chief translator in Tibet; propagator of the Kadampa tradition.

drops (Skt: kundalini). Blissful liquid energy that exists throughout the channels of the body.

du-ra (Tib). The subject, preliminary to debating, in which basic terms and definitions are explained.

eight freedoms. The eight states from which a perfect human rebirth is free: being born as a hell-being, hungry ghost, animal, long-life god or barbarian or in a dark age when no buddha has descended; holding wrong views; being born with defective mental or physical faculties.

Eight Mahayana Precepts. One-day vows to abandon killing; stealing; lying; sexual contact; intoxicants; high seats; eating at the wrong time; and singing, dancing and wearing perfumes and jewelry.

eight worldly dharmas. The worldly concerns that generally motivate the actions of ordinary beings: being happy when given gifts and unhappy when not given them; wanting to be happy and not wanting to be unhappy; wanting praise and not wanting criticism; wanting a good reputation and not wanting a bad reputation.

emptiness (Skt: shunyata). The absence, or lack, of true existence. Ultimately, every phenomenon is empty of existing truly, or from its own side, or independently. (See *merely labeled*.)

enlightenment. Full awakening; buddhahood; omniscience. The ultimate goal of Mahayana Buddhist practice, attained when all faults have been removed from the mind and all realizations completed; a state characterized by the perfection of compassion, wisdom and power.

evil-gone realms. See *lower realms.*

faith. There are three kinds: believing, or pure-hearted, faith; lucid, or understanding, faith—faith based on logical conviction; and yearning, or aspirational, faith.

Fifth Dalai Lama (1617–82). Gyalwa Ngawang Losang Gyatso; "The Great Fifth"; unified Tibet as its spiritual and temporal leader.

fire puja. (Tib: jin-sek). A ceremony that concludes certain retreats and that can also be used for peaceful, increasing, controlling and wrathful activities.

five degenerations. The degenerations of mind, lifespan, sentient beings, times and view.

five Dhyani buddhas. The buddhas of the five families: Vairochana, Amitabha, Akshobhya, Ratnasambhava and Amoghasiddhi.

five Mahayana paths. The five paths leading to buddhahood: merit, preparation, seeing, meditation and no more learning.

five precepts. The vows against killing, stealing, lying, sexual misconduct and taking intoxicants taken by lay Buddhist practitioners.

five Sakya Lords. Sachen Kunga Nyingpo, Sönam Tsemo, Drakpa Gyaltsen, Kunga Gyaltsen (Sakya Pandita) and Lodro Gyaltsen (Chögyal Pakpa).

five uninterrupted negative karmas. Killing one's father, mother or an arhat; maliciously drawing blood from Buddha; causing a schism within the Sangha.

form realm. The second of samsara's three realms, with seventeen classes of gods.

formless realm. The highest of samsara's three realms, with four classes of gods involved in formless meditations.

Four Guardians (Tib: gyalchen zhi). The four kings of the four cardinal directions, who offer protection against harmful influences. Drawings of them are usually found at the entrances of Tibetan temples and monasteries.

four kayas. Nirmanakaya, sambhogakaya, dharmakaya and svabhavikakaya.

four maras. Skandhas, delusions, death and Deva's Son.

four noble truths. The subject of Shakyamuni Buddha's first teaching, or first turning of the wheel of Dharma: true suffering, true cause of suffering, true cessation of suffering and true path.

Gampopa (1074–1153). The "sun-like" disciple of Milarepa and author of *The Jewel Ornament of Liberation*; also known as "The Physician from Dakpo"; guru of the first Karmapa.

Ganden Monastery. The first of the three great Gelugpa monastic universities near Lhasa, founded in 1409 by Lama Tsongkhapa. It was badly damaged in the 1960s and has now been reestablished in exile in south India.

Ganden Tripa (Tib). The representative of Lama Tsongkhapa; head of the Gelug tradition.

Gelek Rinpoche (b. 1939). A lay lama, resident in the U.S., founder of Jewel Heart, an organization that aims to preserve Tibetan culture and Buddhism.

gelong (Tib). A fully ordained Buddhist monk. Female: *gelongma.*

Gelug (Tib). One of the four traditions of Tibetan Buddhism, it was founded by Lama Tsongkhapa in the early fifteenth century and has been propagated by such illustrious masters as the successive Dalai Lamas and Panchen Lamas.

Gelugpa (Tib). A follower of the Gelug tradition.

gen (Tib). Literally, elder. A title of respect.

generation stage. The first of the two stages of Highest Yoga Tantra.

Gen Jampa Wangdu (d. 1984). An ascetic meditator who was a close friend of Lama Yeshe and a guru of Lama Zopa Rinpoche.

geshe (Tib). Literally, spiritual friend. The title conferred on those who have completed extensive studies and examinations at Gelugpa monastic universities.

Geshe Chayulwa (1075–1138). Also known as Zhonnu Ö; a Kadampa geshe renowned for his impeccable devotion to Geshe Tölungpa and Geshe Chengawa.

Geshe Chekawa (1101–75). The Kadampa geshe who composed the famous thought transformation text *Seven-Point Mind Training.*

Geshe Chengawa (1038–1103). Also known as Chengawa Tsultrim Bar; patriarch of the Kadam Instruction lineage and one of Dromtönpa's three main disciples.

Geshe Lekden. A former abbot of Sera Je College and former resident geshe at Chenrezig Institute, an FPMT center near Eudlo, Australia.

Geshe Neusurpa (1042–1118). Also known as Yeshe Bar. A disciple of Geshe Potowa and a guru of Langri Tangpa.

Geshe Ngawang Dhargyey (1921–95). A tutor to many Gelug *tulkus* and resident teacher at the Library of Tibetan Works and Archives in Dharamsala, India, before leaving to establish his own centers in New Zealand, where he passed away.

Geshe Potowa (1031–1105). Also known as Potowa Rinchen Sel. Entered Reting Monastery in 1058 and became its abbot for a short time; one of the three great disciples of Dromtönpa, patriarch of the Kadampa Treatise lineage.

Geshe Rabten (1920–86). The learned Gelugpa lama who was a religious assistant to His Holiness the Dalai Lama before moving to Switzerland in 1975; a guru of Lama Yeshe and Lama Zopa Rinpoche.

Geshe Senge. The Mongolian lama who was abbot of both Sera Je and Sera Me Colleges in Tibet under the Chinese; a guru of Lama Zopa Rinpoche.

Geshe Sharawa (1070–1141). Ordained by Geshe Potowa and guru of Geshe Chekawa.

Geshe Tölungpa (1032–1116). Ordination name was Rinchen Nyingpo; disciple of Geshe Chengawa and guru of Geshe Chayulwa.

getsul (Tib). A novice Buddhist monk. Female: *getsulma.*

god. See *deva.*

Gomo Rinpoche (1921–85). A lay lama, guru of both Lama Yeshe and Lama Zopa Rinpoche, who taught at many FPMT centers, especially in Italy; passed away and reincarnated in Canada.

gompa (Tib). Usually refers to the main meditation hall, or temple, within a monastery.

Gönpawa (1016–82). Gönpawa Wangchuk Gyaltsen; a direct disciple of Lama Atisha and patriarch of the Kadam Lam-rim lineage.

graduated path to enlightenment. See *lam-rim.*

great compassion. Taking personal responsibility for freeing all sentient beings from suffering and its causes.

great insight. The meditative understanding of impermanence and emptiness that overcomes ignorance and leads to liberation.

Guhyasamaja (Skt). A male meditational deity of Highest Yoga Tantra, whose tantra especially emphasizes the illusory body.

Gungtang Tenpai Drönme (1762–1823). A disciple of the first incarnation of the great Jamyang Shepa; known for his eloquent spiritual poetry and philosophical works.

guru (Skt; Tib: lama). Literally, heavy, as in heavy with Dharma knowledge. A spiritual teacher, master.

guru devotion. The sutra or tantra practice of seeing the guru as a buddha then devoting to him with thought and with action.

Guru Puja (Tib: *Lama Chöpa*). A special Highest Yoga Tantra guru yoga practice composed by Panchen Losang Chökyi Gyaltsen.

guru yoga (Skt). The tantric practice of meditating on the guru and deity as inseparably one, then merging this guru-deity with one's own mind; the various sadhanas that incorporate these meditations.

Gyalwa Ensapa (1505–66). A disciple of Chökyi Dorje; achieved enlightenment within a few years without bearing much hardship; predecessor of the Panchen Lamas; a guru of Khedrup Sangye Yeshe.

Gyalwa Götsangpa or *Gönpo Dorje* (1189–1258). A Kagyü master who was a disciple of Tsangpa Gyare.

hearer (Skt: shravaka). Followers of the Hinayana, who strive for nirvana on the basis of listening to teachings from a teacher.

hell. The samsaric realm with the greatest suffering. There are eight hot hells, eight cold hells and four surrounding hells.

heresy. A general term for negative thoughts toward the guru; the opposite of devotion.

Heruka (Skt). See *Chakrasamvara*.

Hevajra (Skt). A male meditational deity of Highest Yoga Tantra, belonging to mother tantra.

Highest Yoga Tantra (Skt: maha-anuttara yoga tantra). The fourth and supreme of the four classes of tantra, which mainly emphasizes internal activities.

Hinayana (Skt). Literally, the Lesser Vehicle. The path of the arhats, the goal of which is nirvana, or personal liberation from samsara.

hungry ghost. See *preta*.

ignorance. A mental factor that obscures the mind from seeing the way in which things exist in reality. There are basically two types of ignorance, ignorance of karma and the ignorance that holds the concept of true existence, the fundamental delusion from which all other delusions arise.

illusory body. A subtle body generated through practice of the completion stage of Highest Yoga Tantra; the cause of the rupakaya.

impermanence. The gross and subtle levels of the transience of phenomena.

imprints. The seeds, or potentials, left on the mind by positive or negative actions of body, speech and mind.

Indra. A powerful Hindu deity in the god realm.

inherent existence. See *true existence*.

initiation. Or empowerment. The transmission of the practice of a particular deity from a tantric master to a disciple, which permits the disciple to engage in that practice.

inner fire. See *tummo.*

Jampel Lhundrup. Dagpo Rinpoche. Pabongka Rinpoche's root guru for lam-rim teachings; author of the *Jor-chö* text *A Necklace for the Fortunate*; his reincarnation has lived in France for many years.

Jamyang Shepa (1648–1721). Renowned Gelugpa master and scholar; author of textbooks used in Drepung Monastery.

Je Drubkhangpa Gelek Gyatso (1641–1712). A renowned lam-rim master who meditated in a cave above Sera Monastery.

Kachen Yeshe Gyaltsen (1713–93). Tsechok Ling Rinpoche. A recent lineage lama of mahamudra; tutor of the Eighth Dalai Lama; founded Tsechok Ling Monastery in Lhasa.

Kadampa geshe. A practitioner of the Buddhist tradition that originated in Tibet in the eleventh century with the teachings of Lama Atisha. Kadampa geshes are renowned for their practice of thought transformation

Kagyü (Tib). One of the four traditions of Tibetan Buddhism, having its source in such illustrious lamas as Marpa, Milarepa, Gampopa and Gyalwa Karmapa.

kaka. Slang for feces.

Kalachakra (Skt). Literally, Cycle of Time. A male meditational deity of Highest Yoga Tantra. The Kalachakra Tantra contains instructions in medicine, astronomy and so forth.

karma (Skt). Literally, action. The working of cause and effect, whereby positive actions produce happiness and negative actions produce suffering.

Keutsang Jamyang Mönlam. Eighteenth century Gelugpa lama and author of lam-rim texts.

khatag (Tib). A white cotton scarf used by Tibetans for greetings and for offering to holy objects.

Khedrup Sangye Yeshe. A disciple of Gyalwa Ensapa and a guru of the first Panchen Lama, Losang Chökyi Gyaltsen.

King Indrabhuti. One of the eighty-four *mahasiddhas*; renounced his huge kingdom to practice Dharma.

Kirti Tsenshab Rinpoche (1926–2006). A highly attained and learned ascetic yogi who lived in Dharamsala, India, and who is one of Lama Zopa Rinpoche's gurus.

Kopan Monastery. The monastery near Boudhanath in the Kathmandu valley, Nepal, founded by Lama Yeshe and Lama Zopa Rinpoche.

Krishnacharya (Tib: Nagpo Chöpa). Also known as Krishnachari and Kanhapa; one of the eighty-four mahasiddhas.

Khunu Lama Tenzin Gyaltsen (1894–1977). A renowned bodhisattva born in northern India; a scholar of Sanskrit who studied in Tibet with many teachers from different schools; gave His Holiness the Dalai Lama an extensive commentary on *A Guide to the Bodhisattva's Way of Life*; a guru of Lama Zopa Rinpoche.

Kyabje (Tib). Literally, lord of refuge. A title of respect.

lama (Tib). See *guru*.

Lama Atisha (982–1054). The renowned Indian master who went to Tibet in 1042 to help in the revival of Buddhism and established the Kadam tradition. His text *Light of the Path* was the first lam-rim text.

Lama Chöpa. See *Guru Puja*.

Lama Lhundrup Rigsel (b. 1941). Abbot of Kopan Monastery.

Lama Ösel (b. 1985). The Spanish reincarnation of Lama Yeshe.

Lama Suvarnadvipi (Tib: Lama Serlingpa). Also known as Dharmamati. The renowned bodhisattva who instructed Lama Atisha in the practice of bodhicitta in Sumatra for twelve years.

Lama Tsongkhapa (1357–1419). The revered teacher and accomplished practitioner who founded the Gelug order of Tibetan Buddhism. An emanation of Manjushri, the Buddha of Wisdom.

Lama Tsongkhapa Guru Yoga. A guru yoga practice related to Lama Tsongkhapa that is performed daily in Gelugpa monasteries.

Lama Yeshe (1935–1984). Born and educated in Tibet, he fled to India, where he met his chief disciple, Lama Zopa Rinpoche. They began teaching Westerners at Kopan Monastery in 1969 and founded the Foundation for the Preservation of the Mahayana Tradition (FPMT) in 1975.

lam-rim (Tib). The graduated path to enlightenment. A presentation of Shakyamuni Buddha's teachings as step-by-step training for a disciple to achieve enlightenment.

Langri Tangpa (1054–1123). Dorje Senge. Author of the famous *Eight Verses of Thought Transformation*.

Lawudo. The cave in the Solu Khumbu region of Nepal where the Lawudo Lama meditated for more than twenty years. Lama Zopa Rinpoche is recognized as the reincarnation of the Lawudo Lama.

Lhasowa. An accomplished sculptor and a disciple of Geshe Tölungpa.

liberation (Skt: nirvana; Tib: thar-pa). The state of complete freedom from samsara; the goal of a practitioner seeking their own freedom from suffering.

lineage lama. A spiritual teacher who is in the line of direct guru-disciple transmission of teachings, from Buddha to the teachers of the present day.

Lingrepa (1128–88). A lay practitioner and important Kagyü teacher; the Drukpa Kagyü line originated from Lingrepa.

Ling Rinpoche (1903–83). The late Senior Tutor to His Holiness the Fourteenth Dalai Lama; the Ninety-seventh Ganden Tripa; a guru of Lama Zopa Rinpoche.

loving kindness. The wish for others to have happiness and its causes.

lower realms. The three realms of cyclic existence with the most suffering: the hell, hungry ghost and animals realms.

Luipa. One of the eighty-four mahasiddhas and founder of one of the three main lineages of Heruka Chakrasamvara practice.

lung (Tib). Literally, wind. The state in which the winds within the body are unbalanced or blocked, thus causing various illnesses. Can also refer to an oral transmission.

Machig Labdron (1031–1126). Disciple and consort of Padampa Sangye; established a chöd lineage in Tibet.

Madhyamaka (Skt). The Middle Way School, a philosophical system founded by Nagarjuna, based on the *Perfection of Wisdom Sutras* of Shakyamuni Buddha, and considered to be the supreme presentation of Buddha's teachings on emptiness. One of the two main Mahayana schools of Buddhist tenets.

Mahakala (Skt). A wrathful male tantric deity.

mahamudra (Skt). Literally, great seal. In sutra, it refers to the emptiness of the mind; in tantra, it refers to the union of simultaneously born wisdom and emptiness. Mahamudra also refers to the meditations for developing these realizations.

mahasiddha (Skt). An accomplished tantric yogi; a saint.

Mahayana (Skt). Literally, Great Vehicle. The path of the bodhisattvas, those seeking enlightenment in order to enlighten all other beings.

Maitreya Buddha (Skt; Tib: Jampa). The Loving One. The next buddha, after Shakyamuni, and fifth of the thousand buddhas of this present world age.

Maitripa. An eleventh century Indian mahasiddha, famous for his mastery of mahamudra, who was a disciple of Naropa and one of Marpa's main gurus.

mala (Skt; Tib: threng-wa). A rosary of beads for counting mantras.

mandala (Skt). The purified environment of a tantric deity; the diagram or painting representing this.

mandala offering. The symbolic offering of the entire purified universe.

Manjushri (Skt; Tib: Jamyang). A male meditational deity that embodies the wisdom of all the buddhas.

mantra (Skt). Literally, mind protection. Sanskrit syllables usually recited in conjunction with the practice of a particular meditational deity and embodying the qualities of that deity.

maras (Skt). Internal interferences, such as those from karma and delusions, or external interferences, such as those from spirits or devas. See also *four maras.*

Marpa (1012–1096). A great Tibetan Buddhist translator; a founding figure of the Kagyü tradition and root guru of Milarepa.

meditation. Familiarization of the mind with a virtuous object. There are two main types of meditation: analytical and concentration, or fixed.

merely labeled. The subtlest meaning of dependent arising; every phenomenon exists relatively, or conventionally, as a mere label, merely imputed by the mind.

merit. The positive energy accumulated in the mind as a result of virtuous actions of body, speech and mind. The principal cause of happiness.

merit field. Or field of accumulation. The visualized holy beings in relation to which one accumulates merit by going for refuge, making offerings and so forth and to which one prays or makes requests for special purposes.

method. All aspects of the path to enlightenment other than those related to emptiness, principally associated with the development of loving kindness, compassion and bodhicitta.

Middle Way. See *Madhyamaka.*

migtsema (Tib). A verse of praise recited during the practice of *Lama Tsongkhapa Guru Yoga.*

Milarepa (1040–1123). A great Tibetan yogi and poet famed for his impeccable relationship with his guru, Marpa, his asceticism and his songs of realization. A founding figure of the Kagyü tradition.

mind. Synonymous with consciousness. Defined as "that which is clear and knowing"; a formless entity that has the ability to perceive objects.

Mind Only (Skt: Chittamatra). One of the two main Mahayana schools of Buddhist tenets, for whom subtle selflessness is the non-difference in entity between mind and external phenomena, subject and object.

momo (Tib). A fried or steamed dumpling, usually filled with meat; a favorite food of Tibetans.

Mount Kailash. The sacred mountain in south-western Tibet that is a holy place of Heruka Chakrasamvara.

Mount Meru. The center of the universe in Buddhist cosmology.

mudra (Skt). Literally, seal. Symbolic hand gestures used in images of Buddha or in tantric rituals.

naga (Skt). Snake-like beings of the animal realm who live in or near bodies of water; commonly associated with fertility of the land, but can also function as protectors of religion.

Nagarjuna. The great second-century Indian philosopher and tantric adept who propounded the Madhyamaka philosophy of emptiness.

Nalanda. A Mahayana Buddhist monastic university founded in the fifth century in north India, not far from Bodhgaya, which served as a major source of the Buddhist teachings that spread to Tibet.

Naropa (1016–1100). The Indian mahasiddha, a disciple of Tilopa and guru of Marpa and Maitripa, who transmitted many tantric lineages, including that of the renowned Six Yogas of Naropa.

negative karma. See *non-virtue.*

ngakpa (Tib). A lay tantric practitioner.

nirmanakaya (Skt). Emanation body; the form in which a buddha appears to ordinary beings.

nirvana (Skt). See *liberation.*

non-virtue. Negative karma; that which results in suffering.

Nyingma (Tib). The oldest of the four traditions of Tibetan Buddhism, it traces its teachings back to Padmasambhava, or Guru Rinpoche.

nyung-nä (Tib). A two-day Thousand-Arm Chenrezig retreat that involves fasting, prostrations and silence.

object to be refuted. The true, or inherent, existence of the self and other phenomena.

obscurations. The negative imprints left on the mind by negative karma and delusions, which obscure the mind. The disturbing-thought obscurations (Tib: *nyön-*

drib) obstruct attainment of liberation and the more subtle obscurations to omniscience (*she-drib*) obstruct attainment of enlightenment.

OM MANI PADME HUM *(Skt)*. The *mani*; the mantra of Chenrezig, Buddha of Compassion.

omniscient mind. See *enlightenment.*

oral transmission (Tib: lung). The verbal transmission of a teaching, meditation practice or mantra from guru to disciple, the guru having received the transmission in an unbroken lineage from the original source.

Pabongka Dechen Nyingpo (1871–1941). An influential and charismatic lama of the Gelug order, Pabongka Rinpoche was the root guru of His Holiness the Dalai Lama's Senior and Junior Tutors. He also gave the teachings compiled in *Liberation in the Palm of Your Hand.*

Padampa Sangye (d. 1117). A great Indian yogi who lived at the same time as Milarepa and spread the teachings, especially chöd, in India, China and Tibet.

Padmasambhava. The eighth-century Indian tantric master mainly responsible for the establishment of Buddhism in Tibet, revered by all Tibetan Buddhists, but especially by the Nyingmapas.

Panchen Losang Chökyi Gyaltsen (1570–1662). The first Panchen Lama, who composed *Guru Puja* and *Path to Bliss Leading to Omniscience*, a famous lam-rim text; a tutor of the Fifth Dalai Lama.

pandit (Skt). A great scholar and philosopher.

paramitas (Skt). See *perfections.*

Paramitayana (Skt). Literally, Perfection Vehicle. The bodhisattva vehicle; a section of the Mahayana sutra teachings; one of the two forms of Mahayana, the other being Tantrayana.

perfect human rebirth. The rare human state, qualified by eight freedoms and ten richnesses, which is the ideal condition for practicing Dharma and attaining enlightenment.

perfections (Skt: paramitas). The practices of a bodhisattva. On the basis of bodhicitta, a bodhisattva practices the six paramitas: generosity, morality, patience, enthusiastic perseverance, concentration and wisdom.

Performance Tantra (Skt: Charya Tantra). The second of the four classes of tantra.

pervasive compounding suffering. The most subtle of the three types of suffering, it refers to the nature of the five aggregates, which are contaminated by karma and delusions.

Prajnaparamita (Skt; Eng: Perfection of Wisdom). The second teaching, or turning of the wheel, of Shakyamuni Buddha, in which the wisdom of emptiness and the path of the bodhisattva are explained. See also *Rajghir*.

Prasangika Madhyamaka (Skt). The Middle Way Consequence School; considered to be the highest of all Buddhist philosophical tenets.

pratimoksha (Skt). The vows of individual liberation taken by monks, nuns and lay people.

preliminaries. The practices that prepare the mind for successful tantric meditation by removing hindrances and accumulating merit.

preta (Skt; Eng: hungry ghost). One of the six classes of samsaric beings, pretas experience the greatest sufferings of hunger and thirst.

prostrations. Paying respect with body, speech and mind to gurus, buddhas, deities and other holy objects; one of the tantric preliminaries.

protector. A worldly or enlightened being who protects Buddhism and its practitioners.

phurba (Tib). A tantric ritual dagger.

Phurchog Ngawang Jampa (1682–1762). A disciple of Je Drubkhangpa and also in the lineage of the Ganden Oral Transmission.

puja (Skt). Literally, offering; a religious ceremony.

pure realm. A pure land of a buddha where there is no suffering; after birth in a pure land, the practitioner receives teachings directly from the buddha of that pure land, actualizes the rest of the path and then becomes enlightened.

purification. The removal, or cleansing, of negative karma and its imprints from the mind.

quarrelling time. See *five degenerations*.

Rachevsky, Zina (1931–1973). Lama Yeshe's and Lama Zopa Rinpoche's first Western student, she helped them establish Kopan Monastery and died in retreat at Thubten Chöling, Trulshik Rinpoche's monastery in Solu Khumbu.

Rajghir. A small town in the north Indian state of Bihar; the site of Vulture's Peak, where Shakyamuni Buddha taught the *Heart Sutra*, or *Essence of Wisdom*, in the second turning of the wheel.

Ra Lotsawa. This eleventh century translator from Ra introduced into Tibet a lineage of the Yamantaka tantra.

Realm of Thirty-three. A god realm in the desire realm; the abode of Indra.

Rechungpa (1083–1161). Also known as Dorje Drakpa; the "moon-like" disciple of Milarepa.

refuge. The heartfelt reliance upon Buddha, Dharma and Sangha for guidance on the path to enlightenment.

relics. Small, pearl-like pills that manifest spontaneously from holy objects such as statues, stupas or the cremated bodies of great practitioners.

renunciation. The state of mind not having the slightest attraction to samsaric pleasures for even a second and having the strong wish for liberation.

Ribur Rinpoche (1923–2006). Recognized as a reincarnation by the Thirteenth Dalai Lama; a geshe of Sera Me; suffered under Chinese oppression for twenty-one years; a guru of Lama Zopa Rinpoche; lived in the USA and taught in many Western countries.

Rinpoche (Tib). Literally, precious one. Generally, a title given to a lama who has intentionally taken rebirth in a human body to continue helping others. A respectful title used for one's own lama.

Rongtha Rinpoches. Brothers recognized as incarnate lamas; lived at the Ladakh Budh Vihar in Delhi for many years.

rupakaya (Skt). Form body; the pure body of an enlightened being, of which there are two aspects: sambhogakaya and nirmanakaya.

Sadaprarudita (Tib: Taktu-ngu; Eng: Always Crying). A bodhisattva, renowned for his unwavering perseverance in guru devotion practice, who appears in the *Prajnaparamita* literature.

sadhana (Skt). Literally, method of accomplishment. Meditational and mantra practices associated with a particular deity, often performed as a daily practice.

sadhu (Skt). A wandering Hindu yogi.

Sakya (Tib). One of the four principal traditions of Tibetan Buddhism, it was founded in the eleventh century by Drokmi Shakya Yeshe (933–1047).

Sakya Pandita (1182–1251). The title of Kunga Gyaltsen, a master of the Sakya tradition, who spread Tibetan Buddhism in Mongolia and China.

samaya (Skt). A practitioner's pledged vows and commitments.

Samayavajra (Skt; Tib: Damtsig Dorje). A Highest Yoga Tantra deity practiced to specifically purify negativities created in relation to the guru.

sambhogakaya (Skt). Complete enjoyment body; the subtle body in which a buddha appears to arya bodhisattvas.

samsara (Skt; Tib: khor-wa). Cyclic existence; the six realms: the lower realms of the hell beings, hungry ghosts and animals, and the upper realms of the humans, demigods and gods; the recurring cycle of death and rebirth within one or other of the six realms. It also refers to the contaminated aggregates of a sentient being.

Sangha (Skt). The third object of refuge; absolute Sangha are those who have directly realized emptiness; relative Sangha are ordained monks and nuns.

Saraha. One of the eighty-four mahasiddhas; an arrow smith famous for his songs of spiritual realization.

self-cherishing. The self-centered attitude of considering one's own happiness to be more important that that of others; the main obstacle to the realization of bodhicitta.

self-conqueror (Skt: pratyekabuddha). Or solitary realizer. Followers of the Hinayana, who strive for nirvana in solitude, without relying on a teacher.

self-initiation. Or self-entry; the practice in which a practitioner, after completing a deity retreat and fire-puja, can enter the deity's mandala and receive initiation.

sentient being. Any unenlightened being; any being whose mind is not completely free of ignorance.

Sera Monastery. One of the three great Gelugpa monasteries near Lhasa; founded in the early fifteenth century by Jamchen Chöje, a disciple of Lama Tsongkhapa; now also established in exile in south India. It has two colleges, Sera Je, with which Lama Zopa Rinpoche is connected, and Sera Me.

Serkong Dorje Chang (1920–79). The great twentieth century yogi who lived for many years at the holy place of Swayambhunath in Nepal; a guru of Lama Zopa Rinpoche.

Serkong Tsenshab Rinpoche (1914–83). A guru and master debate partner of His Holiness the Dalai Lama and also a guru of Lama Zopa Rinpoche; reborn in Spiti, India, in 1984.

seven-limb practice. The seven limbs are prostrating, making offerings, confession, rejoicing, requesting to turn the Dharma wheel, requesting the teachers to remain in the world and dedicating.

Seventh Dalai Lama (1708–57). Gyalwa Kelsang Gyatso; built Norbulinka, the magnificent summer palace; famous for his spiritual poetry.

Shakyamuni Buddha (563–483 BCE). The founder of the present Buddhadharma. Fourth of the one thousand founding buddhas of this present world age, he was born a prince of the Shakya clan in North India and taught the sutra and tantra paths to liberation and full enlightenment.

shamatha (Skt; Tib: shi-nä). Calm abiding; a state of concentration in which the mind is able to abide steadily, without effort and for as long as desired, on an object of meditation.

Shambhala (Skt). The pure land of Kalachakra.

Shantideva (685–763). The great Indian bodhisattva who wrote *A Guide to the Bodhisattva's Way of Life*, one of the essential Mahayana texts.

Shantipa. One of the eighty-four mahasiddhas; a disciple of Naropa; a great scholar who taught in Sri Lanka as well as India.

Shavaripa. One of the eighty-four mahasiddhas, a hunter and hermit; a lineage lama of mahamudra; disciple of Nagarjuna and guru of Maitripa.

shemthab (Tib). The maroon lower, skirt-like garment worn by Tibetan monks and nuns.

single-pointed concentration. The ability to focus effortlessly and for as long as one wishes on an object of meditation.

Six-Session Guru Yoga. A guru yoga practice performed in six sessions each day as a life-long commitment after taking a Highest Yoga Tantra initiation.

Sixth Dalai Lama (1683–1706). Gyalwa Tsangyang Gyatso; the only Dalai Lama who gave back his monk vows; famous for frequenting the taverns around the Potala and for his songs of tantric attainment.

Six Yogas of Naropa. A set of completion stage tantric practices: inner fire meditation, the yoga of the illusory body, the yoga of clear light, transference of consciousness, transference into another body and the yoga of the intermediate state.

Solu Khumbu. The area in north-eastern Nepal, bordering Tibet, where Lama Zopa Rinpoche was born; populated by the Sherpas.

sojong (Tib). The fortnightly confession ceremony for monks and nuns.

Song Rinpoche (1905–84). A powerful Gelugpa lama renowned for his wrathful aspect, who had impeccable knowledge of Tibetan Buddhist rituals, art and science. He was reborn in India in 1985.

spirits. Beings not usually visible to ordinary people; can belong to the hungry ghost or god realms; can be beneficent as well as harmful.

stupa (Skt). A reliquary symbolic of the Buddha's mind.

subtle obscurations. See *obscurations*.

Sunakshatra (Tib: Legpa'i Karma). Shakyamuni Buddha's attendant for more than twenty years, who knew the Tripitaka by heart but never had proper devotion to Buddha.

sutra (Skt). The open discourses of Shakyamuni Buddha; a scriptural text and the teachings and practices it contains.

svabhavikakaya (Skt). The buddha-body of nature; the emptiness of the dharmakaya.

thangka (Tib). Painted or appliquéd depictions of deities, usually set in a framework of colorful brocade.

Tangtong Gyalpo (1385–1509). A renowned Tibetan mahasiddha, considered a manifestation of Chenrezig, who traveled extensively in Tibet and China; famous as a great engineer, building many temples and iron bridges, and also as a great doctor.

tantra (Skt). The secret teachings of the Buddha; a scriptural text and the teachings and practices it contains. Tantric practices generally involve identification of oneself with a fully enlightened deity in order to transform one's own impure states of body, speech and mind into the pure states of that enlightened being.

Tara (Skt; Tib: Drolma). A female meditational deity who embodies the enlightened activity of all the buddhas; often referred to as the mother of the buddhas of the past, present and future.

ta-rig (Tib). Or signs and reasoning; the study of logic.

Tashilhunpo. The Panchen Lamas' monastery in Shigatse in Tibet; built by the First Dalai Lama, Gyalwa Gendun Drubpa; now reestablished in exile in south India.

tathagata (Skt). Literally, Thus Gone; an epithet of a buddha.

ten non-virtues. The three non-virtues of body are killing, stealing and sexual misconduct; the four non-virtues of speech are lying, slander, harsh speech and gossip; the three non-virtues of mind are covetousness, ill will and wrong views.

ten richnesses. The ten qualities that characterize a perfect human rebirth: being born as a human being, in a Dharma country and with perfect mental and physical faculties; being free for the five uninterrupted negative karmas; having faith in Buddha's teachings; being born when a buddha has descended, when the teachings are still alive, when there are still followers of the teachings and having the necessary conditions to practice Dharma.

Thirteenth Dalai Lama (1876–1933). Gyalwa Thubten Gyatso; "The Great Thirteenth"; the great mystic and statesman who tried to protect Tibet's independence from China.

Thirty-five Buddhas. Used in the practice of confessing and purifying negative karmas, the group of thirty-five buddhas visualized while reciting *The Sutra of the Three Heaps* and performing prostrations.

Thogme Zangpo (1295–1369). Also known as Gyalsä Rinpoche. A great master of the Nyingma and Sakya traditions and author of *Thirty-seven Practices of a Bodhisattva.*

thought training (Tib: lo-jong). A powerful approach to the development of bodhicitta, in which the mind is trained to use all situations, both happy and unhappy, as a means to destroy self-cherishing and self-grasping.

thought transformation. See *thought training.*

three doors. Body, speech and mind.

three great meanings. The happiness of future lives, liberation and enlightenment.

three higher trainings. The higher trainings in morality, concentration and wisdom.

three kayas. Dharmakaya, sambhogakaya and nirmanakaya.

three principal paths. The essential points of the lam-rim: renunciation of samsara, bodhicitta and right view, or emptiness.

Tilopa (988–1069). Indian mahasiddha and guru of Naropa; source of many lineages of tantric teachings.

tirthika (Skt; Eng: Forder). A proponent of non-Buddhist tenets, especially ancient Indian philosophical traditions other than Buddhist ones.

torma (Tib). A ritual cake, traditionally made from roasted barley, flour, butter and sugar, that is offered to the buddhas and other holy beings during religious ceremonies.

Trehor Kyörpen Rinpoche. A geshe from Drepung who, after exile from Tibet, led a group of ascetic meditators in strict retreat in the hills around Dalhousie.

Trichen Tenpa Rabgye. The eighteenth-century lama who was the second Reting Rinpoche and one of the Ganden Tripas.

Trijang Rinpoche (1901–81). The late Junior Tutor of His Holiness the Fourteenth Dalai Lama and root guru of Lama Yeshe and Lama Zopa Rinpoche; also editor of *Liberation in the Palm of Your Hand.*

Tripitaka (Skt). The three divisions of the Dharma into vinaya, sutra and abhidharma.

Triple Gem. The objects of Buddhist refuge: Buddha, Dharma and Sangha.

true existence. The type of concrete, real existence from its own side that everything appears to possess; in fact, everything is empty of true existence.

Trulshik Rinpoche (b. 1924). A Nyingma lama, revered in Nepal, who is one of Lama Zopa Rinpoche's gurus.

tsampa (Tib). Roasted barley flour, a Tibetan staple food.

Tsang-nyön-pa. Also known as Tsang-nyön Heruka; the crazy Kagyü yogi who collected Milarepa's 100,000 songs and wrote biographies of Marpa and Milarepa.

Tsangpa Gyare (1161–1211). The Kagyü lama, a disciple of Lingrepa, who was the founder of a branch of the Drukpa Kagyü and of many monasteries, including in Bhutan.

tsa-tsa (Tib). A print of a buddha's image made in clay or plaster from a carved mold.

Tsechok Ling Rinpoche. See *Kachen Yeshe Gyaltsen*.

tsog offering. The offering of blessed food to the merit field; usually performed on the 10th and 25th days of the Tibetan month.

tummo (Tib). A completion stage tantric meditation technique, the first of the Six Yogas of Naropa, in which all the winds are brought into the central channel to generate the clear light.

Tushita (Skt). The Joyous Land. The pure land of the thousand buddhas of this eon, where the future Maitreya Buddha and Lama Tsongkhapa reside.

two stages. The generation and completion stages of Highest Yoga Tantra.

unification. Enlightenment; the final union of the actual clear light and pure illusory body.

Vaibhashika (Skt). The Great Exposition School, one of the two principal Hinayana schools of Buddhist tenets.

vajra and bell. Implements used during tantric rituals: the vajra, held in the right hand, symbolizes bliss and the bell, held in the left, emptiness.

Vajradhara (Skt; Tib: Dorje Chang). Male meditational deity; the form in which Shakyamuni Buddha revealed the tantric teachings.

vajra guru (Skt). A guru from whom one has received tantric initiation.

Vajrapani (Skt; Tib: Chana Dorje). An extremely wrathful male meditational deity that embodies the power of all the buddhas.

Vajrasattva (Skt; Tib: Dorje Sempa). A male tantric deity used especially for purification.

Vajravarahi (Skt; Tib: Dorje Phagmo). An aspect of Vajrayogini.

Vajrayana (Skt). Also known as Tantrayana, Mantrayana or Secret Mantra. The quickest vehicle of Buddhism, capable of leading to the attainment of full enlightenment within one lifetime.

Vajrayogini (Skt; Tib: Dorje Näljorma). A semi-wrathful female deity in the Chakrasamvara cycle.

Vasubandhu. The fifth-century Indian master who wrote the *Treasury of Knowledge* (Skt: *Abhidharmakosha*); disciple and brother of Asanga.

vinaya (Skt). The Buddha's teachings on morality, monastic conduct and so forth.

virtue. Positive karma; that which results in happiness.

virtuous friend (Tib: ge-wai she-nyen). See *guru*.

voidness. See emptiness.

wheel-turning king. Or universal monarch; a powerful king who propagates the Dharma.

wind disease. See *lung*.

winds. Energy-winds. Subtle energies that flow in the channels in the body, which enable the body to function and which are associated with different levels of mind.

wisdom. All aspects of the path to enlightenment associated with the development of the realization of emptiness.

wish-granting jewel. A jewel that brings its possessor everything that they desire.

yaksha (Skt). A terrifying cannibal spirit.

Yamantaka, or Vajrabhairava (Skt). The wrathful male deity that is the Highest Yoga Tantra aspect of Manjushri.

Yeshe Tsöndrü (1761–1861). Also known as Kongpo Lama. The eighteenth-century lama who was the author of *The Essence of Nectar*.

yidam. See *deity*.

yoga (Skt). Literally, to yoke. The spiritual discipline to which one yokes oneself in order to achieve enlightenment.

Yoga Tantra (Skt). The third of the four classes of Buddhist tantra.

yogi (Skt). A highly realized meditator. Female: *yogini*.

Zimey Rinpoche (1927–1996). The twentieth century lama who was a close disciple of His Holiness Trijang Rinpoche and a guru of Lama Zopa Rinpoche.

BIBLIOGRAPHY

SŪTRAS AND TANTRAS (LISTED BY ENGLISH TITLE)

Diamond-Cutter Sutra. Āryavajra-cchedikanāmaprajñāpāramitāmahāyānasūtra, 'phags pa shes rab kyi pha rol tu phyin pa rdo rje gcod pa shes bya theg pa chen po'i mdo.

Essence of the Earth Sutra. Daśacakrakṣitigarbhanāmamahāyānasūtra, 'dus pa chen po las sa'i snying pa'i 'khor lo bcu po'i mdo.

Extensively Manifesting. Āryalalitavistaranāmamahāyānasūtra, 'phags pa rgya cher rol pa shes bya be theg pa chen po'i mdo.

Guhyasamaja Root Tantra. Sarvatathāgatakāyavaccittarahasyaguhyasamājanāma mahākalparāja, De bzhin gshegs pa thams cad kyi sku gsung thugs kyi gsang chen gsang ba 'dus pa zhes bya ba brtag pa'i gyal po chen po.

Heaped Flowers Sutra. Buddhāvataṃsakanāmamahāvaipulyasūtra, Sangs rgyas phal po che shes bya ba shin tu rgyas pa chen po'i mdo.

Kalachakra Tantra. Paramādibuddhoddhṛitaśrīkālacakranāmatantrarāja, Mchog gi dang po'i sang rgyas las byung ba rgyud kyi rgyal po dpal dus kyi 'khor lo shes bys ba.

The Lamp of the Three Jewels Sutra. Dkon mchog sgron me'i mdo.

Laying Out of Stalks Sutra. Gaṇḍavyūhasūtra, Ldong po mkod pa'i mdo.

Meeting of Father and Son Sutra. Āryapitraputrasamāgamanāmamahāyānasūtra, 'phag pa yab dang sras mjal ba shes bya ba theg pa chen po'i mdo.

Net of Illusion Tantra. Māyājālamahātantrarāja, Rgyud kyi rgyal po chen po sgyu 'phrul dra ba.

One Hundred Thousand Lines Perfection of Wisdom Sutra. Śatasāhasrikārajñā-pāramitā, She rab kyi pha rol tu phyin pa stong phrag brgya pa.

Ornament of the Vajra Essence Tantra. Vajrahṛidayālaṃkāratantra, Dpal rdo rje sny-ing po rgyan gyi rgyud.

Perfection of Wisdom Sutras. Prajñāapāramitāsūtra, Shes rab kyi pha rol tu phyin pa'i mdo.

Samputa Tantra. Saṃpuṭanāmamahātantra, Yang dag par sbyor ba shes bya ba'i rgyud chen po.

The Ten Dharmas. Āryadaśadharmakanāmamahāyānasūtra, 'phags pa chos bcu pa shes bya ba theg pa chen po'i mdo.

Two Investigations. Dvikalpa, Brtags pa gnis.

Vajrapani Empowerment Tantra. Āryavajrapaṇyabhiṣekamahātantra, 'phags pa lag na rdo rje dbang bskur ba'i rgyud chen mo.

White Lotus Sutra. Saddharmapuṇḍḍarīkanāmamahāyānasūtra, Dam pa'i chos padma dkar po shes bya ba theg pa chen po'i mdo.

INDIAN WORKS (LISTED BY ENGLISH TITLE
FOLLOWED BY AUTHORS NAME)

Buddha's Lions (Abhayadatta). *Caturaśītisiddhapravṛtti, Grub thob brgyad bcu rtsa bzhi chos skor*

Commentary on the Difficult Points of the Krishnayamari Tantra (Ratnākaraśānti). *Kṛṣṇayamārimahātantrarājapañjikāratnapradīpa, Dpal gzhin rje dgra nag po'i rgyud kyi rgyal po chen po'i dka' 'grel rin po che'i sgron ma.*

Compendium of Valid Cognitions (Dharmakīrti). *Pramāṇavārttikakārikā, Tshad ma rnam 'grel gyi tshig le'ur.*

Confession and Praise (Candragomin). *Deśanastava, Bshags pa'i bstod pa.*

Fifty Verses of Guru Devotion (Aśvaghoṣa). *Gurupañcāśika, Bla ma lnga bcu pa.*

Five Stages (Nāgārjuna). *Pañcakrama, Rim pa lnga pa.*

Guide to the Bodhisattva's Way of Life (Śāntideva). *Bodhisattvacāryāvatāra, Byang chub sems dpa'i spyod pa la 'jug pa.*

Light of the Path to Enlightenment (Atiśa). *Bodhipaṭhapradīpa, Byang chub lam gyi sgron ma.*

Ornament of Mahayana Sutras (Maitreya). *Mahyānasātrālaṃkārakārikā, Theg pa chen po'i mdo sde'i sgyan gyi tshig le'ur byas pa.*

Ornament of Clear Realizations (Maitreya). *Abhisamayālaṃkārakārikā, Mngon par rtogs pa'i rgyan gyi tshig le'ur byas pa.*

Treasury of Knowledge (Vasubandhu). *Abhidharmakośa, Chos mngon pa'i mdzod.*

TIBETAN WORKS (LISTED BY ENGLISH TITLE FOLLOWED
BY AUTHOR'S NAME IN PHONETIC LETTERS)

Abbreviated Notes from Explanatory Discourses Given on [the First Panchen Lama's] Six-Session Guru Yoga, [*Candragomin's*] Twenty [Stanzas on the Bodhisattva Vows, [*Aśvaghoṣa's*] Fifty Stanzas on the Guru, *and the Root and Secondary Tantric Vows* (Pabongka Dechen Nyingpo). *Thun drug bla ma'i rnal 'byor dang dom pa nyi shu pa bla ma lnga bcu pa sngags kyi rtsa ltung sbom po bcas kyi bshad khri gnang ba'i zin tho mdor bsdus.*

Calling the Guru from Afar: A Tormented Wail, Quickly Drawing Forth the Blessing of the Lama, the Inseparable Three Kayas (Pabongka Dechen Nyingpo). *Bla ma rgyang 'bod sku gsum dbyer med bla ma'i byin rlabs myur 'dren gdung dbyangs zhes bya ba zhugs so.*

Collection of Advice from Here and There (Tsunba Jegom). *Bka' gdams gsung thor bu.*

Commentary to the Blue Manual (Geshe Dolpa). *Be'u bum sngon po'i 'grel pa.*

Foundation of All Good Qualities (Tsongkhapa). *Yon tan bzhi gyur ma.*

Guru Puja (Panchen Losang Chökyi Gyaltsen). *Zab lam bla ma mchod pa'i cho ga bde stong dbyer med ma dang tshogs mchod bcas.*

The Great Treatise on the Stages of the Path to Enlightenment (Tsongkhapa). *Skyes bu gsum gyi rnyams su blang ba'i rim pa thams cad tshang bar stong pa'i byang chub lam gyi rim pa.*

Hundred Stanzas to the People of Tingri (Padampa Sangye). *Pha dam pa sangs rgyas kyi zhal gdams ding ri brgya rtsa ma.*

In Praise of Dependent Arising (Tsongkhapa). *Rten 'brel bstod pa.*

Lama Chöpa. See Guru Puja.

Lam rim chen mo. See The Great Treatise.

Liberation in the Palm of Your Hand (Pabongka Dechen Nyingpo). *Rnam sgrol lag bcangs su gtod pa'i man ngag zab mo tshang la ma nor ba mtshungs med chos kyi rgyal po'i thugs bcud byang chub lam gyi rim pa'i nyams khrid kyi zin bris gsung rab kun gyi bcud bsdud gdams ngag bdud rtsi'i snying po.*

Lines of Experience of the Graduated Path to Enlightenment (Tsongkhapa). *Byang chub lam gyi rim pa'i nyams len gyi rnam gzhag mdor bsdus te brjed byang du bya ba.*

Lam rim bsdus don. See Lines of Experience.

Ornament for the Throats of Fortunate Ones (Jampel Lhundrup). *Byang chub lam gyi rim pa'i dmar khrid myur lam gyi sngon 'gro'i ngag 'don gyi rim pa khyer bde bklag chog bskal bzang mgrin rgyan.*

Six-Session Guru Yoga (Pabongka Dechen Nyingpo). *Thun drug gi rnal 'byor.*

The Essence of Nectar (Yeshe Tsöndru). *Byang chub lam gyi rim pa'i gdams pa zab mo rnams tshigs su bcad pa'i sgo nas nyams su len tshul dam chos bdud rtsi'i snying po.*

Thirty-Seven Practices of a Bodhisattva (Thogme Zangpo). *Rgyal sras lag len so bdun ma.*

SUGGESTED FURTHER READING

Abhayadatta. *Buddha's Lions: The Lives of the Eighty-Four Siddhas.* Translated by James B. Robinson. Berkeley: Dharma Publishing, 1979.

Asvaghosa. *Fifty Verses of Guru Devotion.* Translated by Translation Bureau of the Library of Tibetan Works and Archives. Dharamsala: Library of Tibetan Works and Archives, 1975.

Berzin, Alexander. *Relating to a Spiritual Teacher: Building a Healthy Relationship.* Ithaca, New York: Snow Lion Publications, 2000.

Chang, Garma C. C. (trans). *The Hundred Thousand Songs of Milarepa.* Boston & London: Shambhala Publications, 1962, 1999.

Cleary, Thomas (trans). *The Flower Ornament Scripture: A Translation of the Avatamsaka Sutra.* Boston & London: Shambhala Publications, 1993.

Conze, Edward (trans). *The Perfection of Wisdom in Eight Thousand Lines & its Verse Summary.* San Francisco: Four Season Foundation, 1973, 1995.

Dhargyey, Geshe Ngawang. *An Anthology of Well-Spoken Advice on the Graded Paths of the Mind.* Translated by Sharpa Tulku. Edited by Alexander Berzin. Dharamsala, India: Library of Tibetan Works and Archives, 2001.

———. *Tibetan Tradition of Mental Development: Oral Teachings of Tibetan Lama Geshe Ngawang Dhargyey.* Dharamsala: Library of Tibetan Works and Archives, 1992.

Dilgo Khyentse Rinpoche. *Guru Yoga: According to the Preliminary Practice of Longchen Nyingtik.* Translated by Matthieu Ricard. Edited by Rigpa. Ithaca, New York: Snow Lion Publications, 1999.

———. & Padampa Sangye. *The Hundred Verses of Advice: Tibetan Buddhist Teachings on What Matters Most.* Translated by the Padmakara Translation group. Boston & London: Shambhala Publications, 2005.

Dorje, Rig'dzin. *Dangerous Friend: The Teacher-Student Relationship in Vajrayana Buddhism.* Boston & London: Shambhala Publications, 2001.

Dorje, Wang-chug, the Ninth Karmapa. *The Mahamudra Eliminating the Darkness of Ignorance*, with commentary by Beru Khyentze Rinpoche, and *Fifty Stanzas of Guru-Devotion*, by Asvaghosa, with commentary by Geshe Ngawang Dhargyey. Translated and edited by Alex Berzin. Dharamsala: Library of Tibetan Works and Archives, 1978.

FPMT. *Essential Buddhist Prayers: An FPMT Prayer Book, Volume 1, Basic Prayers and Practices*. Portland: FPMT, Inc., 2006.

Gampopa. *The Jewel Ornament of Liberation*. Translated and annotated by Herbert V. Guenther. Boulder: Shambhala Publications, 1971.

———. *The Jewel Ornament of Liberation: The Wish-fulfilling Gem of the Noble Teachings*. Translated by Khenpo Könchog Gyaltsen. Edited by Ani K. Trinlay Chödron. Ithaca, New York: Snow Lion Publications, 1998.

Guenther, Herbert V. *The Life and Teaching of Naropa*. Boston & London: Shambhala Publications, 1963, 1986.

Gyältsän, Losang Chökyi, the First Panchen Lama. *Lama Chöpa: Expanded Edition in Accordance with the Advice of Lama Zopa Rinpoche*. Portland: FPMT, Inc., 2004.

———. *Guru Puja*. Translated by Alexander Berzin, Jampa Gendun et al. Dharamsala: Library of Tibetan Works and Archives, 1979, 2000.

Gyaltsen, Khenpo Könchog (trans). *The Great Kagyu Masters: The Golden Lineage Treasury*. Edited by Victoria Huckenpahler. Ithaca: Snow Lion Publications. 1990, 2006.

Gyatso, Tenzin, the Fourteenth Dalai Lama. *Illuminating the Path to Enlightenment: A Commentary on Atisha Dipamkara Shrijnana's* A Lamp for the Path to Enlightenment *and Lama Je Tsong Khapa's* Lines of Experience. Translated by Geshe Thupten Jinpa. Edited by Rebecca McClen Novick, Thupten Jinpa and Nicholas Ribush. Boston: Lama Yeshe Wisdom Archive, 2002.

———. *The Meaning of Life: Buddhist Perspectives on Cause and Effect*. Translated by Jeffrey Hopkins. Boston: Wisdom Publications, 1992, 2000.

———. *Opening the Eye of New Awareness*. Translated and Introduced by Donald S. Lopez, Jr. Boston: Wisdom Publications, 1984, 1999.

———. *Path to Bliss: A Practical Guide to Stages of Meditation*. Translated by Geshe Thubten Jinpa. Edited by Christine Cox. Ithaca, New York: Snow Lion Publications, 1991.

———. *The Path to Enlightenment*. Edited and translated by Glenn H. Mullin. Ithaca, New York: Snow Lion Publications, 1995.

———. *The Union of Bliss and Emptiness: A Commentary on the Lama Choepa Guru Yoga Practice*. Translated by Thupten Jinpa. Ithaca, New York: Snow Lion Publications, 1988.

Heruka, Tsang Nyön. *The Life of Marpa the Translator: Seeing Accomplishes All*. Translated by the Nalanda Translation Committee. Boston & London: Shambhala Publications, 1982, 1995.

———. *The Life of Milarepa*. Translated by Lhalungpa, Lobsang P. London: Penguin Books (Arkana), 1977, 1992.

Jinpa, Thupten (trans). *The Book of Kadam: The Core Texts*. Boston: Wisdom Publications, 2008.

Kongtrul, Jamgön. *The Teacher-Student Relationship*. Translated and introduced by Ron Garry. Ithaca, New York: Snow Lion Publications, 1999.

Kunga Rinpoche, Lama and Brian Cutillo (trans). *Drinking the Mountain Stream: Songs of Tibet's Beloved Saint, Milarepa*. Boston: Wisdom Publications, 1995.

Loden, Geshe Acharya Thubten. *Path to Enlightenment in Tibetan Buddhism*. Melbourne: Tushita Publications, 1993.

———. *Meditations on the Path to Enlightenment*. Melbourne: Tushita Publications, 1996.

Mullin, Glenn H. *The Fourteen Dalai Lamas: A Sacred Legacy of Reincarnation*. Edited by Valerie Shepherd. Santa Fe, New Mexico: Clear Light Publishers, 2001.

Pabongka Rinpoche. *Liberation in the Palm of Your Hand: A Concise Discourse on the Path to Enlightenment*. Edited by Trijang Rinpoche. Translated by Michael Richards. Boston: Wisdom Publications, 1991, 2006.

———. *Liberation in Our Hands, Part Two: The Fundamentals*. Transcribed and edited by Trijang Rinpoche. Translated by Geshe Lobsang Tharchin with Artemus B. Engle. Howell, New Jersey: Mahayana Sutra and Tantra Press, 1994.

Patrul Rinpoche. *The Words of My Perfect Teacher*. Translated by the Padmakara Translation Group. Boston: Shambhala Publications, 1998.

Rabten, Geshe. *The Essential Nectar: Meditations on the Buddhist Path*. Editing and verse translation by Martin Willson. Boston: Wisdom Publications, 1984, 1992.

——— and Geshe Ngawang Dhargyey. *Advice from a Spiritual Friend*. Translated by Brian Beresford. Boston: Wisdom Publications, 1977, 1996.

Ribush, Nicholas (ed). *Teachings from Tibet: Guidance from Great Lamas*. Boston: Lama Yeshe Wisdom Archive, 2005.

Rinchen, Geshe Sonam. *Atisha's Lamp for the Path to Enlightenment*. Translated and edited by Ruth Sonam. Ithaca, New York: Snow Lion Publications, 1997.

———. *The Three Principal Aspects of the Path*. Translated and edited by Ruth Sonam. Ithaca, New York: Snow Lion Publications, 1999.

Shantideva. *A Guide to the Bodhisattva's Way of Life*. Translated by Stephen Batchelor. Dharamsala: Library of Tibetan Works and Archives, 1979, 1992.

———. *A Guide to the Bodhisattva Way of Life*. Translated by Vesna A. Wallace and B. Alan Wallace. Ithaca, New York: Snow Lion Publications, 1997.

———. *The Way of the Bodhisattva: A Translation of the* Bodhicharyavatara. Translated by the Padmakara Translation Group. Boston: Shambhala Publications, 1997.

Sherbourne, Richard. S.J. *A Lamp for the Path and Commentary*. London: George Allen & Unwin, 1983.

Sopa, Geshe Lhundub, with David Patt. *Steps on the Path to Enlightenment: A Commentary on Tsongkhapa's* Lamrim Chenmo. *Volume I: The Foundation Practices.* Boston: Wisdom Publications, 2004.

Tegchok, Geshe Jampa. *Transforming the Heart: The Buddhist Way to Joy and Courage.* Edited by Thubten Chodron. Ithaca, New York: Snow Lion Publications, 1999.

Tharchin, Geshe Lobsang. *Six-Session Guru Yoga: An Oral Commentary with a Detailed Explanation of the Bodhisattva and Tantric Vows.* Howell, New Jersey: Mahayana Sutra and Tantra Press, 1999.

Thurman, Robert A. F. *Essential Tibetan Buddhism.* New York: HarperSanFrancisco, 1995.

——— (ed). *Life and Teachings of Tsong Khapa.* Dharamsala: Library of Tibetan Works and Archives, 1982.

Trungpa, Chögyam. *Cutting through Spiritual Materialism.* Edited by John Baker and Marvin Casper. Berkeley: Shambhala Publications, 1973.

———. *Illusion's Game: The Life and Teaching of Naropa.* Edited by Sherab Chödzin. Boston & London: Shambhala Publications, 1994.

Tsöndru, Yeshe. *The Essence of Nectar.* Translated by Geshe Lobsang Tharchin. Dharamsala: Library of Tibetan Works and Archive, 1979.

Tsong-kha-pa. *The Great Treatise on the Stages of the Path to Enlightenment: Volume One.* Translated by the Lamrim Chenmo Translation Committee. Ithaca, New York: Snow Lion Publications, 2000.

———. *The Fulfillment of All Hopes: Guru Devotion in Tibetan Buddhism.* Translated and edited by Gareth Sparham. Boston: Wisdom Publications, 1999.

———. *Preparing for Tantra: The Mountain of Blessings.* Translated by Geshe Lobsang Tharchin with Michael Roach. Howell, New Jersey: Mahayana Sutra and Tantra Press, 1995.

———. *The Principal Teachings of Buddhism.* Translated by Geshe Lobsang Tharchin with Michael Roach. Howell, New Jersey: Mahayana Sutra and Tantra Press, 1988.

Wangmo, Jamyang. *The Lawudo Lama: Stories of Reincarnation from the Mount Everest Region.* Boston: Wisdom Publications, 2005.

Wangyal, Geshe (trans). *The Door of Liberation: Essential Teachings of the Tibetan Buddhist Tradition.* Boston: Wisdom Publications, 1995.

Willis, Janice D. *Enlightened Beings: Life Stories from the Ganden Oral Tradition.* Boston: Wisdom Publications, 1995.

Yangsi Rinpoche. *Practicing the Path: A Commentary on the* Lam-rim Chenmo. Edited by Miranda Adams. Boston: Wisdom Publications, 2003.

Yeshe, Lama Thubten. *The Bliss of Inner Fire: Heart Practice of the Six Yogas of Naropa.* Edited by Robina Courtin and Ailsa Cameron. Boston: Wisdom Publications, 1998.

———. *Introduction to Tantra: The Transformation of Desire.* Edited by Jonathan Landaw. Boston: Wisdom Publications, 1987, 2001.

Index

LAMA YESHE WISDOM ARCHIVE

The LAMA YESHE WISDOM ARCHIVE (LYWA) is the collected works of Lama Thubten Yeshe and Lama Thubten Zopa Rinpoche. Lama Zopa Rinpoche, its spiritual director, founded the ARCHIVE 1996.

Lama Yeshe and Lama Zopa Rinpoche began teaching at Kopan Monastery, Nepal, in 1970. Since then, their teachings have been recorded and transcribed. At present we have well over 10,000 hours of digital audio and some 70,000 pages of raw transcript. Many recordings, mostly teachings by Lama Zopa Rinpoche, remain to be transcribed, and as Rinpoche continues to teach, the number of recordings in the ARCHIVE increases accordingly. Most of our transcripts have been neither checked nor edited.

Here at the LYWA we are making every effort to organize the transcription of that which has not yet been transcribed, edit that which has not yet been edited, and generally do the many other tasks detailed below.

The work of the LAMA YESHE WISDOM ARCHIVE falls into two categories: archiving and dissemination.

Archiving requires managing the recordings of teachings by Lama Yeshe and Lama Zopa Rinpoche that have already been collected, collecting recordings of teachings given but not yet sent to the ARCHIVE, and collecting recordings of Lama Zopa's on-going teachings, talks, advice and so forth as he travels the world for the benefit of all. Incoming media are then catalogued and stored safely while being kept accessible for further work.

We organize the transcription of audio, add the transcripts to the already existent database of teachings, manage this database, have transcripts checked, and make transcripts available to editors or others doing research on or practicing these teachings.

Other archiving activities include working with video and photographs of the Lamas and digitizing ARCHIVE materials.

Dissemination involves making the Lamas' teachings available through various avenues including books for free distribution and sale, lightly edited transcripts, a monthly e-letter (see below), DVDs, articles in *Mandala* and other magazines and on our Web site. Irrespective of the medium we choose, the teachings require a significant amount of work to prepare them for distribution.

This is just a summary of what we do. The ARCHIVE was established with virtually no seed funding and has developed solely through the kindness of many people, some of whom we have mentioned at the front of this book and most of the others on our Web site. We sincerely thank them all.

Our further development similarly depends upon the generosity of those who see the benefit and necessity of this work, and we would be extremely grateful for your help. Thus we hereby appeal to you for your kind support. If you would like to make a contribution to help us with any of the above tasks or to sponsor books for free distribution, please contact us:

LAMA YESHE WISDOM ARCHIVE
PO Box 356, Weston, MA 02493, USA
Telephone (781) 259-4466; Fax (678) 868-4806
info@LamaYeshe.com
www.LamaYeshe.com

The LAMA YESHE WISDOM ARCHIVE is a 501(c)(3) tax-deductible, non-profit corporation dedicated to the welfare of all sentient beings and totally dependent upon your donations for its continued existence. Thank you so much for your support. You may contribute by mailing a check, bank draft or money order to our Weston address; by making a donation on our secure Web site; by mailing us your credit card number or phoning it in; or by transferring funds directly to our bank—ask us for details.

LAMA YESHE WISDOM ARCHIVE MEMBERSHIP

In order to raise the money we need to employ editors to make available the thousands of hours of teachings mentioned above, we have established a membership plan. Membership costs US$1,000 and its main benefit is that you will be helping make the Lamas' incredible teachings available to a worldwide audience. More direct and tangible benefits to you personally include free Lama Yeshe and Lama Zopa Rinpoche books from the ARCHIVE and Wisdom Publications, a year's subscription to *Mandala*, a year of monthly pujas by the monks and nuns at Kopan Monastery with your personal dedication, and access to an exclusive members-only section of our Web site containing special, unpublished teachings currently unavailable to others. Please see www.LamaYeshe.com for more information.

MONTHLY E-LETTER

Each month we send out a free e-letter containing our latest news and a previously unpublished teaching by Lama Yeshe or Lama Zopa Rinpoche. To see more than seventy back-issues or to subscribe with your email address, please go to our Web site.

THE FOUNDATION FOR THE PRESERVATION OF THE MAHAYANA TRADITION

The Foundation for the Preservation of the Mahayana Tradition (FPMT) is an international organization of Buddhist meditation study and retreat centers, both urban and rural, monasteries, publishing houses, healing centers and other related activities founded in 1975 by Lama Thubten Yeshe and Lama Thubten Zopa Rinpoche. At present, there are more than 160 FPMT activities in over thirty countries worldwide.

The FPMT has been established to facilitate the study and practice of Mahayana Buddhism in general and the Tibetan Gelug tradition, founded in the fifteenth century by the great scholar, yogi and saint, Lama Je Tsongkhapa, in particular.

Every quarter, the Foundation publishes a wonderful news journal, *Mandala*, from its International Office in the United States of America. To subscribe or view back issues, please go to the *Mandala* Web site, www.mandalamagazine.org, or contact:

FPMT
1632 SE 11th Avenue, Portland, OR 97214
Telephone (503) 808-1588; Fax (503) 808-1589
info@fpmt.org
www.fpmt.org

The FPMT Web site also offers teachings by His Holiness the Dalai Lama, Lama Yeshe, Lama Zopa Rinpoche and many other highly respected teachers in the tradition, details about the FPMT's educational programs, audio through FPMT radio, a complete listing of FPMT centers all over the world and in your area, a link to the excellent FPMT Store, and links to FPMT centers on the Web, where you will find details of their programs, and to other interesting Buddhist and Tibetan home pages.

DISCOVERING BUDDHISM AT HOME
*Awakening the limitless potential of your mind,
achieving all peace and happiness*

Over 2500 years ago, Shakyamuni Buddha gained direct insight into the nature of reality, perfected the qualities of wisdom, compassion, and power, and revealed the path to his disciples. In the 11th Century, Atisha brought these teachings to Tibet in the form of the lam-rim—the stages on the path to enlightenment. The lam-rim tradition found its pinnacle in the teachings of the great Tibetan saint Je Tsong-khapa in the 14th Century, and these teachings continued to pass from teacher to student up to this present day.

When Lama Thubten Yeshe and Lama Zopa Rinpoche transmitted these teachings to their disciples, they imparted a deeply experiential tradition of study and practice, leading thousands of seekers to discover the truth of what the Buddha taught. This tradition is the core of *Discovering Buddhism*—a two-year, fourteen-module series that provides a solid foundation in the teachings and practice of Tibetan Mahayana Buddhism.

HOW IT WORKS: Each *Discovering Buddhism* module consists of teachings, meditations and practices, readings, assessment questions, and a short retreat. Students who complete all the components of each course receive a completion card. When all fourteen modules have been completed, students receive a certificate of completion, a symbol of commitment to spiritual awakening!

This program is offered in FPMT centers around the world, as a home study program, and beginning in 2009, as an interactive online program.

HOME STUDY PROGRAM: Each *Discovering Buddhism at Home* module contains audio recordings of teachings and meditations given by qualified Western teachers, a text CD containing the course materials and transcripts of the audio teachings, and an online discussion board overseen by senior FPMT teachers. FAQ pages help the student navigate the program and provide the best of the discussion board's questions and answers. Upon completion of a module, students may have their assessment questions evaluated by senior FPMT teachers and receive personal feedback.

Discovering Buddhism at Home is available from the FPMT Foundation Store, www.fpmt.org/shop.

For more information on *Discovering Buddhism* and the other educational programs and services of the FPMT, please visit us at www.fpmt.org/education/.

Other teachings of Lama Yeshe and Lama Zopa Rinpoche currently available

Books published by Wisdom Publications

Wisdom Energy, by Lama Yeshe and Lama Zopa Rinpoche
Introduction to Tantra, by Lama Yeshe
Transforming Problems, by Lama Zopa Rinpoche
The Door to Satisfaction, by Lama Zopa Rinpoche
Becoming Vajrasattva: The Tantric Path of Purification, by Lama Yeshe
The Bliss of Inner Fire, by Lama Yeshe
Becoming the Compassion Buddha, by Lama Yeshe
Ultimate Healing, by Lama Zopa Rinpoche
Dear Lama Zopa, by Lama Zopa Rinpoche
How to Be Happy, by Lama Zopa Rinpoche

About Lama Yeshe:
Reincarnation: The Boy Lama, by Vicki Mackenzie

About Lama Zopa Rinpoche:
The Lawudo Lama, by Jamyang Wangmo

You can get more information about and order the above titles at www.wisdom-pubs.org or call toll free in the USA on 1-800-272-4050.

Transcripts, practices and other materials

See the LYWA and FPMT Web sites for transcripts of teachings by Lama Yeshe and Lama Zopa Rinpoche and other practices written or compiled by Lama Zopa Rinpoche.

DVDs of Lama Yeshe

We are in the process of converting our VHS videos of Lama Yeshe's teachings to DVD. *The Three Principal Aspects of the Path*, *Introduction to Tantra*, *Offering Tsok to Heruka Vajrasattva*, *Anxiety in the Nuclear Age* and *Bringing Dharma to the West* are currently available. More coming all the time—see our Web site for details.

DVDs of Lama Zopa Rinpoche

There are many available: see the Store on the FPMT Web site for more information.

What to do with Dharma teachings

The Buddhadharma is the true source of happiness for all sentient beings. Books like the one in your hand show you how to put the teachings into practice and integrate them into your life, whereby you get the happiness you seek. Therefore, anything containing Dharma teachings, the names of your teachers or holy images is more precious than other material objects and should be treated with respect. To avoid creating the karma of not meeting the Dharma again in future lives, please do not put books (or other holy objects) on the floor or underneath other stuff, step over or sit upon them, or use them for mundane purposes such as propping up wobbly tables. They should be kept in a clean, high place, separate from worldly writings, and wrapped in cloth when being carried around. These are but a few considerations.

Should you need to get rid of Dharma materials, they should not be thrown in the rubbish but burned in a special way. Briefly: do not incinerate such materials with other trash, but alone, and as they burn, recite the mantra OM AH HUM. As the smoke rises, visualize that it pervades all of space, carrying the essence of the Dharma to all sentient beings in the six samsaric realms, purifying their minds, alleviating their suffering, and bringing them all happiness, up to and including enlightenment. Some people might find this practice a bit unusual, but it is given according to tradition. Thank you very much.

Dedication

Through the merit created by preparing, reading, thinking about and sharing this book with others, may all teachers of the Dharma live long and healthy lives, may the Dharma spread throughout the infinite reaches of space, and may all sentient beings quickly attain enlightenment.

In whichever realm, country, area or place this book may be, may there be no war, drought, famine, disease, injury, disharmony or unhappiness, may there be only great prosperity, may everything needed be easily obtained, and may all be guided by only perfectly qualified Dharma teachers, enjoy the happiness of Dharma, have love and compassion for all sentient beings, and only benefit and never harm each other.

LAMA THUBTEN ZOPA RINPOCHE was born in Thami, Nepal, in 1945. At the age of three he was recognized as the reincarnation of the Lawudo Lama, who had lived nearby at Lawudo, within sight of Rinpoche's Thami home. Rinpoche's own description of his early years may be found in his book, *The Door to Satisfaction*. At the age of ten, Rinpoche went to Tibet and studied and meditated at Domo Geshe Rinpoche's monastery near Pagri, until the Chinese occupation of Tibet in 1959 forced him to forsake Tibet for the safety of Bhutan. Rinpoche then went to the Tibetan refugee camp at Buxa Duar, West Bengal, India, where he met Lama Yeshe, who became his closest teacher. The Lamas went to Nepal in 1967, and over the next few years built Kopan and Lawudo Monasteries. In 1971 Lama Zopa Rinpoche gave the first of his famous annual lam-rim retreat courses, which continue at Kopan to this day. In 1974, with Lama Yeshe, Rinpoche began traveling the world to teach and establish centers of Dharma. When Lama Yeshe passed away in 1984, Rinpoche took over as spiritual head of the FPMT, which has continued to flourish under his peerless leadership. More details of Rinpoche's life and work may be found in *The Lawudo Lama* and on the LYWA and FPMT Web sites. In addition to several LYWA and FPMT books, Rinpoche's other published teachings include *Wisdom Energy* (with Lama Yeshe), *Transforming Problems, Ultimate Healing, Dear Lama Zopa, How to Be Happy* and many transcripts and practice booklets.

AILSA CAMERON first met Buddhism at Tushita Retreat Centre in India in 1983 and has since been involved in various activities within the FPMT, primarily in relation to the archiving, transcribing and editing of the teachings of Lama Zopa Rinpoche and Lama Yeshe. With Ven. Robina Courtin, she edited *Transforming Problems* and *The Door to Satisfaction*, by Lama Zopa Rinpoche, and *The Bliss of Inner Fire*, by Lama Yeshe, for Wisdom Publications. She also edited Rinpoche's *Ultimate Healing* and *How to Be Happy* for Wisdom. After working originally in India and Nepal, she went to Hong Kong in 1989 to help organize the electronic version of the LAMA YESHE WISDOM ARCHIVE. Ordained as a nun by His Holiness the Dalai Lama in 1987, she has been a member of the Chenrezig Nuns' Community in Australia since 1990. She is currently a full time editor with the LAMA YESHE WISDOM ARCHIVE, for whom she has edited many teachings, including *Teachings from the Mani Retreat, Teachings from the Vajrasattva Retreat, How Things Exist* and *Teachings from the Medicine Buddha Retreat*.